COMMUNICATION IN AN ERA
OF GLOBAL CONFLICTS

Principles and Strategies for 21st Century Africa

Edited by

Ritchard T. M'Bayo
Chuka Onwumechili
Bala A. Musa

Foreword by Ali A. Mazrui

University Press of America,® Inc.
Lanham · Boulder · New York · Toronto · Plymouth, UK

Dedication

This book is dedicated to

Yema, Rita, Dandibor, Sedia, and Faith Fatima

Adora, Chiamaka, Kamso, and Kaodinna

Daniel Rimanyang, David Irarimam, and Sharon Termam

CONTENT

Foreword

Silence and Communication as Agents of Conflict

The relationship between conflict and communication is multifaceted. There are occasions when certain methods of communication have been a major trigger for the outbreak of violence. The Rwandan genocide of 1994 was partly promoted by vitriolic radio broadcasts against the Tutsi and their sympathizers. We may therefore say that Rwanda was a case in which the genocidal impulse used communication as an ally. Rwanda became the fastest genocide in recorded history. Eight hundred thousand people were killed within three months.

On the other hand, the Nazi holocausts against the Jews adopted for its ally not open communication domestically or internationally, but a conspiracy of silence at both levels. Most of Europe knew that Jews were captured and sent to concentration camps. But far fewer people were aware that the camps were not prisons but killing fields. The camps were not detention-enclosures or military prisons, but gas chambers.

Of course many German citizens at home and international observers abroad, preferred not to know what the Nazis were doing to Jews, Gypsies and homosexuals. "If ignorance be bliss, it is folly to be wise"! This ancient dictum was meticulously used as a guide by those who were in denial about what was going on in the Third Reich. The Nazi genocide prospered under the umbrella of conspiratorial silence – while the Rwanda genocide half a century later was fuelled by the loud blare of incitement to collective violence.

The Nazis had used *silence* as a deadly weapon of secrecy in their execution of the Holocaust. The Rwandan militants had used *communication* as an ally to slaughter.

Africa has posed other paradoxes of its own. Why is it that the conflict in Darfur in Sudan has generated so much publicity, while the more deadly conflicts in the Democratic Republic of the Congo and the 20-year old conflict in Yoweri Museveni's Uganda were barely on the international radar screen?

A major trigger of international attentiveness in this twenty-first century is the word "Islam" or "Arab" when identified in a conflict. Neither the horrendous civil conflicts in the Congo nor the prolonged blood letting in Northern Uganda involved a clash with Muslims or Arabs. Although the casualties in the Congo ran into millions, and the Lord's Resistance Army in Northern Uganda perpetrated the most brutal atrocities and amputations against children as well as adults, few governments abroad paid much attention. Black people killing Black people was not an interesting phenomenon unless an Arab or Islamic factor could be identified – or unless black violence reached the rapidity of the Rwandan genocide.

Cartoons have been used in different versions as a distinct form of parodying human behavior, or humanizing the behavior of animals. The most famous of all humanized cartoon creatures is Walt Disney's Mickey Mouse.

The use of cartoons to "tell truth to power" and satirize the mighty has partly depended upon how open a society is. Western democracies have carried satirical political caricature further than anybody else.

The paradox of Egyptians is that they are descended from people who once worshipped their ancient rulers [Pharaohs like Ramses II] but have now become the Arab world's greatest satirist of their modern rulers [life-presidents like Hosni Mubarak].

But fewer cartoons in world history have had a more provocative international impact than the Danish newspaper cartoons of 2005, satirizing the Prophet Muhammad. Muslim boycott of Danish goods cost Denmark millions of dollars worth of foreign trade. The Danish cartoons might also have won a few more recruits for Al-Qaeda, the militant movement of radicalized Islam. The cartoons certainly incensed hundreds of thousands of Muslims across the world.

About a quarter of century before the Danish cartoons the British novelist, Salman Rushdie, published his explosive book *The Satanic Verses*. It was a measure of the new communications revelation that a novel published in London rapidly triggered riots from Karachi to Kano, from Liverpool to the Cape of Good Hope. Dozens of people died in the demonstrations in India and Pakistan. In Nigeria friends of Wole Soyinka, the distinguished playwright, were concerned about his safety in Nigeria when he appeared to defend his fellow writer, Salman Rushdie.

During the Nigerian Civil War more than a decade before the publication of *The Satanic Verses*, Wole Soyinka had captured a radio station by force of arms in order to protest what he regarded as a war against the Igbo. Long before the Hutu militants in Rwanda had used the radio to inflame a civil war, Wole Soyinka had captured a radio station in an attempt to stop a civil war. Wole Soyinka ended up in prison, his detention culminated in his prison book entitled *The Man Died.*

But communication and silence do not always trigger or facilitate conflicts. They can at other times serve the interests of peace and stability. African governments have often tried to prevent some ethnic incidents in one part of the country from being over-publicized in another part of the country. Muslim-Christian conflicts locally could all too easily result in widespread sectarian conflagration in Nigeria. Nigerian leaders have often tried to contain a localized dispute from setting nationalized, special appeals to editors of newspapers and radio stations have sometimes been necessary.

On a longer term scale nations need to learn that the secret of nation-building is partly to know what to forget. Painful grievances of the past should find a burial in the collective silence of the present. One might go further and echo the French philosopher who said that each nation needed to get its own history *wrong*. A nation needs to communicate what is positive about its history, or even deceptive about what went wrong in the past. Once again the paradox of calculated communication versus purposeful silence is at the center of the collective human condition.

This volume focuses on Africa's own experience of violence, communication and the quest for loss of memory. When does Africa need to silence the impulse to communicate? When does Africa – like Mao Tse Tung's China – need to let a hundred flowers bloom?

Behold the rose, the lily, the violet;
Behold the peacock beside a baobab tree;
Behold the crested crane, the palm tree
and the flowers of the Savannah;
Behold the open spaces of Africa.

Ali A. Mazrui, Ph.D.
State University of New York at Binghamton, New York, USA
2008

Acknowledgments

Special thanks and appreciation are due to many people for the support that made this project possible. We wish to express profound appreciation to our families for their understanding and sacrifices without which we could not have accomplished this project. We thank our institutions and departmental colleagues at the American University of Nigeria, Bowie State University and Azusa Pacific University for the supportive and enabling environment for teaching and conducting research, and for the exchange of ideas. We are grateful to Professor Muhammadou Kah, Dean of the School of Information Technology and Communication at the American University of Nigeria for his encouragement at a particularly stressful moment of this project. Special thanks to Dr. Kehbuma Langmia of the Department of Communications at Bowie State University and Oloruntola Sunday of the University of Lagos, Department of Mass Communication, who were frequently used throughout this project as sounding boards for coherence and readability of many of the chapters in this book. We also appreciate the encouragement to pursue this project and the feedback on early drafts of some of the articles from professional colleagues in the African Studies Association, Third World Studies Conference, and the National Communication Association.

Support from the Council of International Exchange of Scholars (CIES), through the Fulbright Fellowship program, was invaluable from the inception to the present stage of the book.

Thanks to the contributors to this volume for their enthusiasm, commitment and tolerance in working through the multiple revisions. We are also grateful to Professor 'Lai Olurode, former Dean of the Faculty of Social Sciences at the University of Lagos for his support and encouragement throughout this project. Our students have also helped sharpened our thinking by their insightful and thought provoking questions and inputs. Many of them read and reacted to the chapters in this book, and we are particularly grateful to Natalie Cole, Christine Grant, Deanna Walls, Kellee Poindexter, and Makeda Knott.

At a very short notice Professor Ali A. Mazrui gracefully granted our request for a foreword, and contributed two chapters to the book. We found this world renowned scholar to be most amiable, and we thank him also for his support of this project.

Part 1: Theories of Conflicts

Chapter 1

Attribution, Psychodynamics and Communication Behaviors of Conflict Actors

Ritchard T. M'Bayo, Ph.D.
American University of Nigeria, NIGERIA

Introduction

In 2007, George Tenet, former director of the Central Intelligence Agency (CIA), published his book with the title: *At the center of the Storm: My years at the CIA,* a blistering testimony of the agency's role in the events leading to the U.S. war against Iraq. When Bob Woodward reviewed the book for the *Washington Post* he summarized Tenet's exposition of the complex web of events prior to the war in a most parsimonious statement by saying: "What we have here is a failure to communicate" (Woodward, 2007).

Woodward's assessment of Tenet's book underscores a recurring theme in this work–the pivotal role of communication in conflict situations. Conflict, whether at the micro or macro level, almost always involves some element of a failure of communication; and without *effective* communication conflict resolution can remain illusive.

In the last 50 years or so, the world has witnessed unprecedented innovations in communication systems and technologies. The implications of these innovations now undergird nearly every significant trend and social interactions among people everywhere. Because of these innovations, communication among people in the global community as a whole is now more efficient, more instantaneous, more dependable, and more globally oriented than ever before. During the first half of the 20th century such megatrends in communication as the satellite were left only to the imagination; the Internet and the World Wide Web were even beyond the creative minds of the science fiction writers. But as the second half of that century began, there were inevitable signs of an epoch of communication that would engender peace and harmony in the global community. Today the communication satellite, computers that are capable of just about everything, and the Internet and World Wide Web are here, connecting people and creating unbelievable opportunities for dialogue among people everywhere. Though current trends in communication have had significantly positive impact on the global community, peace and harmony continue to elude the world, with explosive events and internecine conflicts dominating the daily news. Sometimes one wonders whether too much communication has been good or bad for the health of the global community.

On the one hand technology has without doubt enhanced communicative interactions at all levels–interpersonal, group, intercultural, organizational, international, etc. leading to increased prospects for global peace and harmony. On the other hand there is plenty of evidence of the culpability of the traditional forms of mass communication, the new media (Internet and the World Wide Web), and other advanced communication systems in processes used to instigate or fuel conflicts in the global community. The world, it appears, is now more chaotic and more conflict prone than ever before.

This chapter focuses on the conflict in Sierra Leone (1991-2001), a small country in the West African subregion, which shook the moral conscience of the global community. With what happened in Sierra Leone, Rwanda, the Democratic Republic of the Congo (DRC), Somalia, Ethiopia, Eritrea, Sudan, South Africa, etc., the fireworks that heralded the 21st century brought nothing but cautious optimism about the new era. The chapter draws on two basic theoretical propositions–*attribution* and *psychodynamics*–and discusses conflict and communication using the Sierra Leone civil war and other crises as backdrops to explicate the theories. It then identifies selected key players and peripheral actors, their communication behaviors in the Sierra Leone conflict, and the implications for the outcome of the conflict as it progressed.

Perspectives from Attribution and Psychodynamics

Attribution and psychodynamic theories focus on the actors, the people involved in a conflict situation. The theories presuppose that understanding the human relations aspects of a conflict as well as the inherently peculiar attributes and traits associated with the actors provide important clues for understanding conflicts. According to Folger, Poole, and Stutman (2007, p. 46), psychodynamic theory proposes ideas that are fundamental to an understanding of conflict. Cahn and Abigail (2007) add that when diagnosing conflict situations, an understanding of the foundations of psychodynamic theory reminds us that the first task is to determine who are the conflict actors.

Attribution Theory

Conflicts, especially wars, are complex and they are the products of a complex web of factors both human and natural. Who or what caused a particular conflict is a question at the core of attribution theory and the implications and prospects for resolution. The *blame game* or attribution is a manifestation of all conflicts. One party deflects the fault and blames the other as the cause of the conflict. Attribution, inevitably influences the course of the conflict and the behavior of the parties involved. The basic premises of the theory include: (1) people act as they do in conflict situations because of the conclusions they draw about each other, and (2) attributions may be internal, related to the person's general personality, or external, related to the other person's circumstances (Cahn and Abigail, 2007, p. 138). In a much earlier study, Rosenberg and Wolsfeld (1977) observed that:

> The process of making attributions about the other may discourage the selection of integrative or collaborative conflict strategies because the process of attribution may shift the blame from oneself to the other. This reciprocal relation between making attributions and the escalation of a conflict also can affect international conflict: The tendency to maintain attributional consistency (i.e., to generate an explanation of the other's behavior and stick to it) and consequent misinterpretation of information increases the likelihood of escalating conflict and prolonged hostilities in international conflict.

According to Folger, Poole, and Stutman (2005, p. 52):

> When trying to make sense of others' behavior, we scrutinize environments, settings, and people's actions in search of reasons behind their actions. After discovering a plausible reason or cause, the other's behavior is attributed to one of two categories: (1) dispositional factors or (2) situational factors.

Dispositional factors are inherent and may include the psychological traits that influence our reactions to external conditions, whereas situational factors may include external environmental conditions such as the ascribed causes of a conflict. A "fundamental attribution error" in conflict situation is the tendency for people to attribute others' behavior to dispositional factors and their own behavior to situational factors (Folger, Poole, and Stutman, 2005, p. 52), and:

> To maintain and enhance self-esteem individuals often defensively attribute actions resulting in negative consequences to external forces and attribute positive

consequences of the action to themselves. This self-serving bias is especially likely to occur in situations involving success and failure" (p. 53).

In general discussions about the outcome of the Sierra Leone conflict, for example, President Tejan Kabbah is sometimes accused of taking more credit for the ultimate peaceful resolution to the conflict than he deserves. Corp. Foday Sankoh, before his death and despite the numerous golden opportunities for sustainable peace that he shunned or abused, such as the dividends from the power sharing agreement for him and his rebel group, used to proclaim that peace would not have been achieved in Sierra Leone without a change of heart and attitude of the RUF.

Psychodynamic Theory

Psychodynamic theory assumes that some people are more likely to engage in conflict or act in peculiar ways once they are involved in conflict compared to other people? For example, are there personality traits associated with Libyan Leader Muammar al-Qadaffi, former Nigerian President Olusegun Obasanjo, the late Kwame Nkrumah of Ghana, the late Julius Nyerere of Tanzania, late Jean Bokassa of Central African Republic, Charles Taylor of Liberia, and Tejan Kabbah of Sierra Leone and the late Idi Amin of Uganda that will make them more conflict-prone or behave in peculiar ways in conflict situations? Are there personality traits that are predictive of conflict behavior?

According to the theory, people's behavior in conflict situations is due primarily to their individual dispositions, ways of thinking, and their intrapersonal states (Cahn and Abigail, 2007, p. 135). Furthermore, it posits that individuals respond to conflict situations in light of their aggressive impulses and anxieties. This then brings up the discussion of psychodynamics and conflict actors.

Psychodynamics and Conflict Actors

When the war in Sierra Leone started in 1991, the two protagonists in the conflict were Corp. Foday Sankoh on the rebel side, and President Joseph Momoh on the government side. Regime changes (violent as well as nonviolent) brought new players into the picture, including Capt. Valentine Strasser (1992), Brigadier Mada Bio (1995), Mr. Tejan Kabbah (1997), and Maj. Johnny Paul Koroma (1997). All these players, except Mr. Kabbah, had military background, with only secondary school education and minimal or no mainstream political experience. Mr. Kabbah, on the other hand, a former civil servant, lawyer by profession, and a retired UN personnel with nearly 20 years of experience, stood apart from all the other key players. None of this is meant to cast aspersion on anyone. However, according to psychodynamics, it is important to understand these and other motivating factors that predispose people toward certain kinds of behavior in conflict situations and, therefore, are considered as significant variables in conflict analysis. Although there is no definitive formula to predict such behavior, an important question is whether personality traits are significant variables in conflict analysis. Are conflict actors with military background more likely to seek military style approaches to conflict than actors with a different background. Personality traits, psychological as well as sociological, have been key variables in studies dealing with Adolf Hitler of Germany, Idi Amin of Uganda, Jean Bokassa of Central African Republic, etc. Over the years, the line-up of players in the Sierra Leone crisis was as follows:

1991-1992:	Foday Sankoh (quasi-military) vs Joseph S. Momoh (military/civilian).
1992-1995:	Foday Sankoh (quasi-military) vs Valentine Strasser (military).
1995-1997:	Foday Sankoh (quasi-military) vs Mada Bio (military)
1997-1999:	Foday Sankoh (quasi-military) vs Tejan Kabbah (civilian).
1999-2000:	Foday Sankoh (quasi-military) and Johnny Paul Koroma (military) vs Tejan Kabbah (civilian).
2000-2002:	Foday Sankoh (quasi-military vs Tejan Kabbah (civilian).

Sierra Leone Conflict: A Synopsis

As the curtain came down on the 20th century, Sierra Leone was also closing the chapter on its 10-year civil war, probably one of the most brutal and horrendous of Africa's conflicts in the last half of that century.

War came to Sierra Leone in 1991, the same year that the country joined the global debate on the need to open up its political processes to all its citizens after nearly 30 years of a one-party system. While constitutional reforms were being made to prepare the country for the democratic project, Sierra Leoneans were unwary of the fact that a neighboring country would become their nemesis, and that a breakdown of law and order in that country would eventually culminate into events that would frustrate their own aspirations for a new society.

On Christmas Eve, 1989, Charles Taylor, in his bid to unseat then President Samuel K. Doe, led an invading force that attacked Liberia from Côte d'Ivoire. Within months, the Liberia crisis escalated so fast that three warring factions emerged: Samuel K. Doe and his Liberian Army, Charles Taylor and his National Patriotic Force of Liberia (NPFL), and a break-away group from the NPFL led by Prince Yommie Johnson.

To contain the crisis the Economic Community of West African States (ECOWAS) formulated a peace plan and put in force what became known as the ECOWAS Monitoring Group (ECOMOG). Sierra Leone played a key role in putting that peace plan together, and several of the initial peace talks were held in Freetown, the capital of Sierra Leone. Not only that, as part of the efforts to deploy ECOMOG forces in Liberia, Sierra Leone provided a base to coordinate the initial activities.

As negotiations continued between the Liberian warring factions, President Samuel Doe was captured and tortured to death by forces loyal to Prince Yommie Johnson. As a result, the peace efforts stalled. While ECOWAS was finding ways to jump start the peace process, Charles Taylor was fomenting his own plan to complicate matters. On March 23, 1991, his NPFL forces backed a dissident group of Sierra Leoneans, who announced themselves as the Revolutionary United Front (RUF), and invaded Sierra Leone which share borders with Liberia and Guinea. The invasion triggered a crisis that would escalate into a 10-year civil war (1991-2001).

By the time the war officially ended in 2001 following several aborted peace agreements, the country held an array of unflattering records: (1) Some 500,000 Sierra Leoneans had died, had been displaced or become refugees; amputations and other horrendous crimes against humanity had been committed in Sierra Leone, (2) The largest United Nations Peacekeeping force of over 17,000 military personnel was deployed in the country, and later (3) a United Nations Special Court, the second such institution in Africa, was set up in Sierra Leone to prosecute those responsible for crimes against humanity during the war years. (See Figure 1 for the Factions and Peripheral Actors in the conflict; Table 1, Factions, Peripheral Actors, Communication Behaviors, and Implications for Conflict Outcomes).

Communication Options and Strategies

Contemporary societies and peoples of the world are now able to have shared experiences wherever they may be, in real or delayed time, through global media and communication infrastructures or through national communication systems. International communication is also at the crossroads of global conflicts and peace initiatives, environmental crises as well as diplomacy and international commerce. As Robert S. Fortner once noted:

> International communication is part and parcel of our everyday lives, often functioning in the background of our experience, unacknowledged and largely unknown. Yet it touches us profoundly, affecting the supply of goods in our stores, the nature of our political and cultural life, and the dimensions of our religion (1993, p. xix).

Main Factions
Government of Sierra Leone (GOSL)
Revolutionary United Front (RUF)

Peripheral Actors

Libya ▪ Burkina Faso ▪ Cote d'Ivoire
Nigeria ▪ Liberia ▪ Guinea

Peacekeepers/Mediators

United Nations
United Kingdom
United Nations Mission in Sierra Leone (UNAMSIL)
Economic Community of West African States (ECOWAS)
ECOMOG

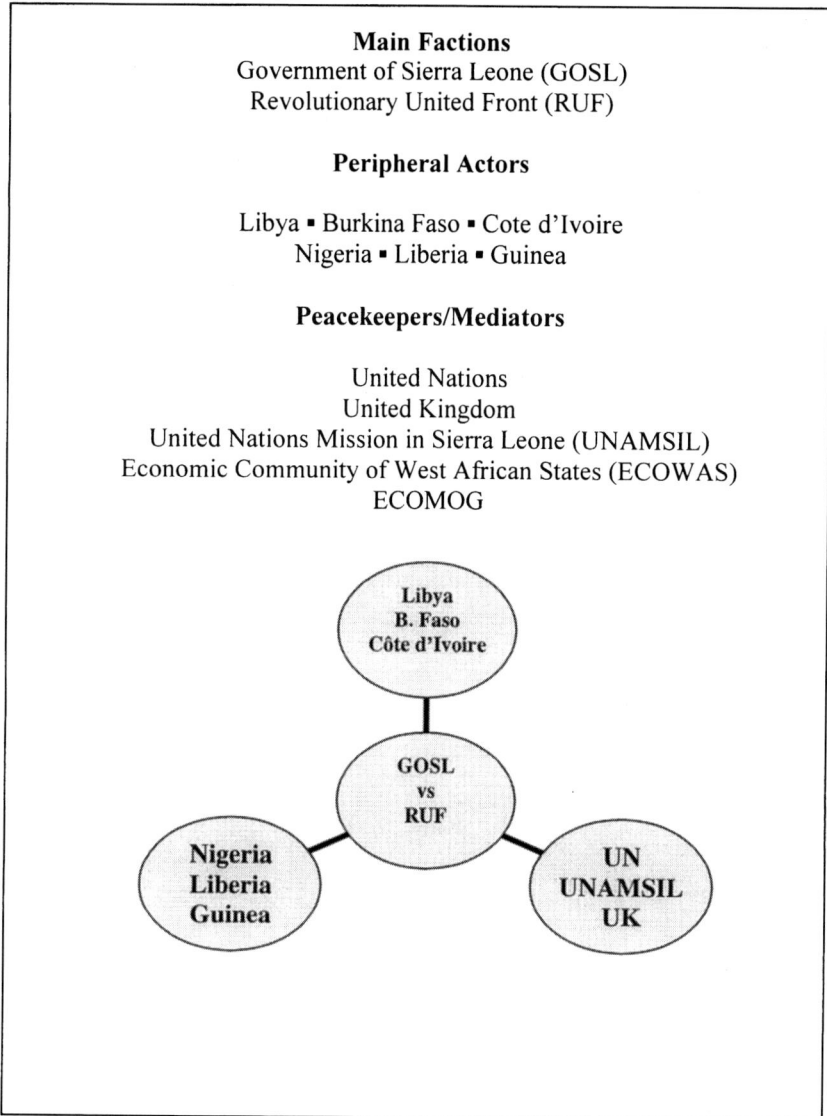

Figure 1: Key Players and Peripheral Actors in the Sierra Leone Conflict

ACTOR	COMMUNICATION BEHAVIOR	IMPLICATION
Key Players		
Government of Sierra Leone (GOSL)	Verbal Aggression	Conflict Escalation
Revolutionary United Front (RUF)	Verbal Aggression	Conflict Escalation
Peripheral Actors		
Libya	Non-Assertive Communication	Conflict Escalation
Guinea	Non-Assertive Communication	Conflict Escalation
Liberia	Non-Assertive Communication	Conflict Escalation
Peacemakers/Mediators		
ECOMOG	Non-Assertive Communication	Conflict Escalation
ECOWAS	Assertive Communication	Conflict De-escalation
UNITED NATIONS	Assertive Communication	Conflict De-escalation
UNAMSIL	Assertive Communication	Conflict De-escalation
UNITED KINGDOM	Assertive Communication	Conflict De-escalation

Table 1: Factions, Peripheral Actors, Communication Behaviors and Implications for Conflict Outcomes. As the table shows, assertiveness is the only form of communication that leads to conflict de-escalation. Aggressiveness and non-assertiveness lead to conflict escalation.

In today's world, however, international communication itself is no longer an unacknowledged phenomenon because it is rife with conflict and controversy, and few things associated with it happen by mere chance. Furthermore, global commerce and the world economic order are firmly couched upon the means of international communication. Those who control international communication exert tremendous leverage in the socio-political and economic relations of the world. And this fact alone is also a source of major concern for the global community, a concern that has spurred the establishment of national communication systems in the last 50 years, including sectarian outfits such as *Al jazeera*, with unabashed ideological and philosophical orientations.

Within national boundaries, national communication systems also have displayed the same contending attributes–particularly the power dynamics and hegemonic control of these systems–that have been associated with the international communication infrastructure. Meanwhile, conflict actors all over the world have seized the opportunity to take advantage of the situation for their own purposes – to instigate or fuel conflicts or to promote "harmony".

These factors notwithstanding communication systems at all levels, international as well as national are imbued with opportunities for building peace, forestalling conflicts, and promoting societal harmony. Society stands to benefit tremendously if ongoing democratization process are applied also to the democratization of communication systems, a key proposal of the 1980 UNESCO commissioned MacBride Report.

At the interpersonal and group levels, certain communication behaviors were discernible among the key players and peripheral actors in the Sierra Leone conflict. They included: (1) Nonassertive Communication, (2) Aggressive Communication–verbal as well as nonverbal, and (3) Assertive Communication. Our focus in this chapter will be on these three communication behaviors, although there are a myriad of typologies of communication that could also be applied in this regard. These three types may be viewed as a continuum of behaviors, with nonassertiveness at one extreme, and aggressiveness at the other, with assertive communication somewhere in between.

Nonassertive Communication is the ability to avoid a conflict altogether or accommodate to the desires of the other person through the use of verbal or nonverbal acts that conceal one's opinions and feelings (Cahn and Abigail, 2007, p. 60). Nonassertiveness in conflict situations may imply that our communication behavior is at variance with our actions. This was the communication option adopted by the peripheral actors in the Sierra Leone civil war. These peripheral players–Libya, Burkina Faso, and Côte d'Ivoire–positioned themselves as neutral but interested parties to the conflict. Corp. Foday Sankoh, together with Charles Taylor were said to have received training in guerrilla tactics in Libya. Yet, Libyan leader Muammar al-Qadaffi never once assumed responsibility for his role in the conflict, and to this day continues to play the benevolent godfather of Sierra Leone.

Arms shipment for the RUF followed a trail linking the Ukraine to Burkina Faso to Liberia and finally on to the rebel controlled territory in Sierra Leone. Yet the public posture and public communication of Blaise Compaoré of Burkina Faso emphasized that country's neutrality. And even as he faces the War Crimes tribunal at the World Court in the Hague for his role in the Sierra Leone conflict, Charles Taylor continues to deny his involvement in the conflict.

But it was later revealed that all these peripheral actors were actively involved in the conflict and in support of the RUF; their public declarations of neutrality or noninvolvement were merely a disguise of their real positions on the war in Sierra Leone. Before the war ended, a UN Panel of Experts reported that there was conclusive evidence of arms supply lines linking Liberia through Burkina Faso, and eventually to Sierra Leone (UN Report, 2000).

Non-assertiveness, what some might call doublespeak, may lead to the escalation or prolongation of conflict as motives and interests which constitute key elements of the solution are concealed and kept under the table.

While the peripheral actors engaged in nonassertive communication behavior, the key players in the conflict, the Government of Sierra Leone (GOSL) and the Revolutionary United Front (RUF) adopted verbal and nonverbal aggression. Aggressive communication is carried out with the intention of attacking the self-concept of others and inflicting physical and psychological pain, injury, or suffering on one's opponent (Cahn and Abigail, 2007, p. 61)

In Sierra Leone, the RUF public communication and propaganda literature were full of unbridled diatribe and recrimination against real and perceived opponents of the rebel group–the government of Sierra Leone and those who opposed and condemned its trade mark tactic of amputations, which also constituted a form of aggressive communication to the general public.

The government of Sierra Leone, on the other hand, portrayed members of the rebel RUF as somewhat akin to a subhuman group of ruthlessly violent people. In the early years of the war, there was speculation that the RUF rebels were not even Sierra Leoneans because "real" Sierra Leoneans were incapable of committing such horrendous crimes. Even the RUF leader, Corp. Foday Sankoh, who had not given interviews or allowed to be photographed initially, was presumed to be a "fake", a Liberian ruse Charles Taylor was using to get back at Sierra Leone for not supporting his bid to oust Samuel K. Doe.

Both factions, but particularly the RUF, skillfully used the international media, including the BBC and the VOA, as the platform for verbal aggression against each other. This communication behavior then merely served to escalate or prolong the conflict as the actors became more concerned with scoring points, legitimizing their positions, and making "friends" in the international community at the expense of clearly stating their respective agendas for changing the situational factors that might have been the source of the conflict in the first place.

Verbally aggressive communication behaviors have been used by the key players in the Iraqi war as well. Thus, the Americans see "insurgents", "terrorists", and "suicide bombers" or "enemies" in referring to anyone predisposed to opposing the American intervention; to many Iraqis and people of the Arab world, the Americans are "unbelievers", "infidels", and "invaders" representing the continuing hegemony of the western world. These labels, justified or not, certainly do not help matters.

The current impasse and mutually antagonistic attitude between the United States and Iran over the latter's nuclear ambition provide another example of aggressive communication and its potential implication of a looming nuclear crisis. A caption from "The Riddle of Iran," a special report by the *Economist* (2007, July 21-27), describes Iran's communication behavior as "uncompromising," and that of the United States as "uncomprehending." The report suggests that because of these behaviors, both country "may be stumbling to war" (p. 2).

Whether it is at the interpersonal level or at the national or international levels, prejudice against the opponent and stereotyping the enemy are common reactions in conflict situations. These prejudices and stereotypes are perpetuated through our communications behavior and disseminated through prevailing systems of communication infrastructures. The level of prejudice and stereotype we harbor about other people may predicate conflict behavior. That is why dialogue, participation and exchange designed to promote understanding among people is a panacea for our conflict prone global community. These forms of communication promote peaceful if not a conflict free society.

Finally, another mode of communication behavior of relevance to this discussion is assertiveness. Assertive communication encourages parties in a conflict to seek their own interests and assert their rights, but with consideration for the interests and rights of others involved in the conflict. Being assertive means that key players as well as peripheral actors and mediators must adopt an open minded approach, be empathic and willing to accept the strong points of the opponent's arguments and *reasonable* demands. Mediators and peacemakers adopt this method as the most viable approach to conflict resolution, which conflict experts often refer to as dialogue or the diplomatic option.

After years of verbal aggression against each other, ECOWAS, the UN, and the UK prevailed upon the parties involved in the Sierra Leone conflict to be assertive, especially when it had become quite clear that the military option would not bring about a solution to the conflict, let alone a sustainable peace.

Conclusion

Using the Sierra Leone civil war (1991-2001) as a backdrop, this chapter explores the principles of psychodynamic and attribution theories that point to certain variables that are significant in understanding the dispositions of conflict actors. In keeping with the theme of the book, the chapter demonstrates the significance of communication in conflict situations, and draws attention to *non-assertiveness, aggressiveness*, and *assertiveness* as communication behaviors that conflict actors often adopt. As defined in the chapter, non-assertive and aggressive verbal and nonverbal communication behaviors are dysfunctional because they tend to produce undesirable outcomes, such as escalation and prolongation of conflict. On the other hand, assertiveness is functional because it leads to desirable outcomes such as settlement or peaceful negotiations. Unfortunately, conflict actors often resort to assertiveness only as a final option and often with the intervention of outsiders (peacekeepers or mediators) who propose the approach as a viable modality for conflict resolution.

References

Cahn, D. D. and Abigail, R. A. (2007). *Managing conflict through communication, 3rd edition.* New York: Allyn and Bacon.

Economist. (2007, July 21st-27th). The riddle of Iran: A special report, pp. 1-16.

Folger, J. P., Poole, M. S., Stutman, R. K. (2005). *Working through conflicts: Strategies for relationships, groups, and organizations, 5th edition.* New York: Allyn and Bacon.

Rosenberg , S. W. and Wolsfeld, G. (1977). International conflict and the problem of attribution. *Journal of Conflict Resolution*, vol. 21, 75-103.

Tenet, G. (2007). *At the center of the storm: My years at the CIA.* New York: Harper Collins.

UN. (2000). Report of the Panel of Experts appointed pursuant to UN Security Council Resolution 1306.

UNESCO. (1980). *Many voices, one world.* New York: Unipub

Woodward, B. (2007, May 6-7). What we have here is a failure to communicate. *Washington Post Book World*, pp. 1, 3-4

Chapter 2

Media Messages, Sins of Distortion and Signs of Wisdom

Ali A. Mazrui, Ph.D.
State University of New York at Binghamton, USA

This chapter starts from the premise that what Nigerians learn about the rest of Africa comes disproportionately from Western sources of information. Nigerian media (electronic or print) cannot afford to have their own correspondents in major African capitals, or war reporters in Darfur and the Democratic Republic of the Congo. African media cannot send filming or taping crews of their own to meetings of the Pan African Parliament in South Africa or meetings of African foreign ministers in Banjul or Abidjan.

One of my favorite illustrative predicaments concerns my own country, Kenya. Kenya shares borders with five other African countries, each of which has had major convulsive breakdowns – Somalia, Ethiopia, Sudan, Uganda and even Tanzania if we include the convulsions of Zanzibar.

Therefore, Kenya is surrounded by major news stories across five borders. And Kenya has the best African news media for its size outside Southern Africa. And yet most of the big stories that Kenya's media have carried about its neighbors have relied disproportionately on Western sources.

Uganda's worst political breakdowns occurred during the reign of Idi Amin and the second administration of Milton Obote. It was Idi Amin's reign which drove me out of Uganda.

A few years after I left Uganda there was a big story about my old university in Kampala. The World Press reported that Amin's soldiers had invaded the Makerere campus, raped women students, looted the Halls of Residence and offices, and even mutilated the breasts of some of their female victims and some were killed.

Although I was already based in the United States at that time, I happened to be in Nairobi, Kenya, when the news broke. My wife in North America was visiting Canada. She broke down when she heard the story on the radio. She then called me in Nairobi to check how I was taking it.

I told her that although I was devastated, I was also bewildered that all the Kenyan newspapers and broadcasts were quoting British sources, especially the British Sunday paper, *The Observer*.

Why were the Kenya media relying almost exclusively on a British newspaper for an event which had occurred next door in broad daylight, in the capital city of Uganda, on the campus of the country's most distinguished educational institution?

Fortunately, I was scheduled to have lunch with Milton Obote in Dar es Salaam two days later. Obote, who had been overthrown by Idi Amin, was in exile in Tanzania.

At the lunch with Obote was David Martin, the British correspondent responsible for the horrendous story. I asked David Martin if he had been to Idi Amin's Uganda to check out the story. He had not. He said he got the story from students who had escaped across the border.

Then Obote challenged me to telephone my friends in Uganda to verify. I said such a phone call about such a subject might, if overheard, endanger my friends' lives under the Amin regime.

The story continued to be headline news in Britain, Africa and much of the rest of the world for another week or so.

We subsequently discovered that while Amin's troops had invaded the Makerere campus, their worst atrocities were slapping people, kicking people and intimidating everyone in sight. There were no rapes or murders authoritatively reported and certainly no mutilation of female breasts. The enormity of the original blood-chilling story shrunk to one more incident of African soldiers misbehaving themselves.

But the world had been ready to believe any brutal story from Africa. And even neighboring African countries had no sources of confirmation independently of the West.

At that time, African media consisted primarily of print, radio, television and social institutions like churches and mosques.

Today the Internet would facilitate more cross-checking between African neighbors. African citizens can send e-mails to each other, and African governments are not yet sophisticated enough to keep track. Idi Amin would have been none the wiser in the age of the Internet.

But external stories covered in the African media continue to depend disproportionately on the messages and images transmitted between the West and the rest of us. And those messages and images are influenced by seven biases of perception across cultures.

The *racial* bias tends to ensure that a train accident which kills four white folks is a bigger story than an overturned bus which kills twenty Africans. The *gender* bias focuses more on the achievements of men than of women. The *elite* bias rewards the famous with additional fame – and regards the powerful as newsworthy. The *urban* bias attracts reporters to cities and urban centers – and pays far less attention to rural folks. The *generation* bias pays more attention to older folks than to the young – unless the young are at the center of exceptional events. The *exotic* bias is attracted to female circumcision, rather than high school graduation; to African witchcraft rather than African brain surgeons. As for the bias of *negativism*, this almost always ensures that real bad news is bigger news than happy news tends to be.

Let us return to the Makerere saga under Idi Amin. The *racial bias* made most of the world credulous about any story of barbarism coming out of Africa. The *gender bias* in the Makerere story was about women as passive creatures and preeminent victims of the ruthless lust of macho men. The *urban bias* was the setting of the story in the capital city of an African country and in broad daylight. The *elite bias* was the obvious linkage with a university, the premier educational institution of a postcolonial African country. The *exotic bias* was Africa's allegedly ruthless sexual drive – from promiscuity to rape. This time it allegedly involved Idi Amin's lust-activated warriors.

The *generation bias* in the Makerere story included negative and positive elements about young people. The Makerere students symbolized the youth as victims. But Idi Amin's soldiers were themselves disproportionately young. These symbolized the youth as alleged perpetrators. The one or two students who escaped across the border to break the story to David Martin would have been heroes had their story not been so ridiculously exaggerated. They must have been pro-Obote partisan witnesses.

Finally, the overarching *bias of negativism*. Massively cruel stories – true or false – make bigger news than heart-warming stories of human kindness. The Makerere saga encapsulated all the seven biases of messages and images between the West and the rest.

The Media and Seven Functions of Culture

The Internet in Africa operates in the context of thee civilizations – Africa's own indigenous legacy combined with the legacy of Islam, and both under the impact of Western culture. The *triple heritage* consists of Africanity, Islam and the West. The Internet and other media affect those three civilizations by influencing the seven functions of culture.

1.   *Culture as Perception*

Culture is how we view the world and how we are viewed by others. The most objectionable portrayal of Muslim women in the world presents the women of Islam as *over-clothed*, with hijab and sometimes the veil.

The former British Foreign Minister has asked any Muslim visiting woman in his office to unveil: "We cannot meet face to face if one face is veiled." *France* wants Muslim women to abandon the hijab when going to school. *Turkey* does not want women members of Parliament to wear a head scarf in the House.

On the other hand, the most objectionable portrayal of indigenous African women (non-Islamized) is when the women are portrayed as *under-dressed* — targeting such dress codes as that of the Nuba, or of the Maasai or of the traditional Tiv.

There is a big debate now on the campus of Binghamton University concerning an exhibition of photographs of nude African women taken among under-clothed African cultures in the 1950s.

On November 9, 2006 on campus the particular curators of the photographic exhibition confronted their critics. One of the speakers was a Maasai post-doctoral fellow on campus.

The media in the West revels in debates about over-clothed Muslim women and under-clothed indigenous African women. Nakedness is in the eye of the beholder.

2.   *Culture as Standard of Judgment*

What are the criteria of good and evil, beautiful and ugly? Where is the Internet leading us?

3.   *Culture as a Spring of Motivation*

How can we motivate African rulers to be honest, fair-minded, incorruptible and democratically accountable? One answer from the Nile Valley as the cradle of African civilization. The latest civilizing gesture from the Nile Valley comes in 2006 from a Sudanese-Egyptian benefactor — offering billions of dollars to motivate African rulers to be just and incorruptible, in exchange for $5 million in retirement, and more money later.

In the past, we thought we would try to motivate good behavior in our rulers by threatening impeachment and trial. This was motivation by the *stick*. Now the Nile Valley seeks to motivate African rulers by the carrot — a financial reward.

The media's responsibility is to keep track of the performance of our rulers. The Internet's role is to facilitate greater debate.

4. Culture as Means of Communication

Are the media aggravating the marginalization of indigenous African languages by concentrating on the Euro-imperial languages, like English, French and Portuguese?

Is the Internet widening the linguistic gap between users of Euro-international languages and users of African indigenous languages?

The cellular phone as an oral tradition is multi-lingualizing users of telephones across the world; but the Internet as a written tradition is held hostage by the dominant languages of the world.

Even in Africa, the Internet friendly languages tend to be the big indigenous ones, such as Yoruba, Igbo, Hausa, Kiswahili, and, of course, the Arabic language.

5. Culture as a Basis of Identity

The breakdown of culture as a basis of identity is most manifest in Africa's worst cases of instability.

The Somali people share the same language, the same religion, the same political culture based on clans and the same love of poetry.

In the pre-colonial period Somali governance was based on ordered anarchy. Then colonialism imposed on the Somali institutionalized order. Since then, the post-colonial period has eroded the artificial institutions and restored the old anarchy, but without the old order.

Was the absence of the mass media in Somalia one of the causes of the cultural breakdown? The Somali language remained unwritten until long after the colonial period. The Somalis could not make up their minds about the appropriate alphabet. Should it be the *Arabic* alphabet or the *Roman*, or a uniquely *indigenous* Somali alphabet which had already been invented?

A Somali military government subsequently chose the Roman or Latin alphabet in the 1970s. Would the Somali people have been nationally integrated better if they had had an alphabet for a mass media during their yesteryears as a people of ordered anarchy?

Even today, the Somali people are greater users of the *cell phone* (the oral tradition one to one) than of the *Internet* (the written tradition of collective accessibility).

In Somalia shared culture has continued to break down as a foundation of shared empathy.

There are other African examples of cultural breakdowns. Where in Africa has a shared language disastrously failed as a basis of national integration? One colossal example is Rwanda. The Hutu and Tutsi in Rwanda speak the same native language – Kinyarwanda. Yet Rwanda goes down in history as the country which had the fastest rate of genocide in recorded history. Eight hundred thousand (800,000) people died within three months. Did the radio in Uganda serve as a trigger of anti-Tutsi massacres? Indeed, did a radio program trigger the anti-Igbo pogrom in Northern Nigeria in 1966?

Where else in Africa has a *shared language* spectacularly failed to hold a country together? In Rwanda's sister country, Burundi, with the same rival groups, Hutu and Tutsi, Kirundi has failed as a language of national concord. Have the media in Burundi fed into mutual ethnic massacres?

Where in Africa has a *shared religion* failed to cement a sense of nationhood? There is the example of *Darfur* in Sudan, where both sides are Muslims and yet many thousands have died in two or three years. Has the Western media served the positive role this time of being a whistle blower to avert the transition from ethnic cleansing to large-scale genocide in Darfur?

Or is the Western media selective where it blows the whistle? Why has it completely ignored twenty years of similar atrocities in Northern Uganda from 1986 to 2006? Is Northern Uganda a case of shared tribality failing to avert catastrophes? An Acholi civil war has raged, killing adults, imprisoning families, and depriving children of their childhood years.

Where in Africa once again has a shared *religion* failed to avert catastrophes? Examples include the Democratic Republic of the Congo (Christian vs. Christian), Algeria (Muslim vs. Muslim), as well as Rwanda and Burundi (Christian vs. Christian).

In those confrontations, the international media has a mixed record. In Rwanda it had been good in covering the final catastrophe (the genocide) and its aftermath, but not good at covering the events which led to the explosion.

In Darfur the international media started covering the calamity mid-stream. The media hope to avert the ultimate catastrophe.

6.   *Culture as a Ladder of Stratification*

Has the basic stratification changed from who *owns* what to who *knows* what? Are computer skills creating new rank-orders? Is Nigeria's North-South divide being digitized?

Although Northerners were historically the first to be *pen-literate* in Nigeria, are Southerners the first to be *computer-literate*? Are Igbo and Yoruba cultures more calculus friendly (numerophile) than Hausa culture? Are Indians of South Asia and Koreans of East Asia more calculus-friendly (numerophile) than Africans or African Americans? Are the Asians better at mathematics?

Islam gets more blame for gender inequality than it gets credit for racial equality. Of the three Abrahamic religions (Judaism, Christianity and Islam), Islam has the best record in *race relations*.

But in modern history Islam may also have the worst record in gender relations. The U.S. doctrine, "Separate but Equal", lasted until 1954 [Brown vs. the Board of Education ruling]. Islam has an implicit doctrine of "Separate but Equal" for genders, rather than races. Gender segregation was potentially more feasible with the advent of the Internet. Women can surf and work at home and eventually make millions – surfing their way to freedom.

On the other hand, the hijab may gradually become impossible, as dating on the Internet becomes more common among the Muslim youth.

7. *Culture as a Pattern of Consumption and Mode of Production*

Much of Africa has borrowed Western tastes without Western skills. It has borrowed consumption patterns without production techniques. It has promoted urbanization without industrialization and has learned capitalist greed without capitalist discipline.

The media have been major instruments for advertising consumption patterns, but not of stimulating new production techniques. On the other hand, they are instruments for exposing corruption and tracking excessive greed.   In the West the media have become indispensable for implementing democracy.   In Africa the struggle to democratize continues with the help of the media worldwide.

Seven Pillars of Media Wisdom

As we confront the subject of democracy, we are stepping into the domain of modern pillars of wisdom. The first pillar of wisdom in contemporary Africa is the imperative of *liberation*. Kwame Nkrumah captured "liberation" at its most optimistic: "Seek ye first the political kingdom and all else will be added unto you" (Nkrumah, 1957).

In some respects, liberation is the means towards democracy. In other respects, liberation is the whole purpose of democratization. Where do the media fit in? The African quest for liberty should influence the selection of stories to be covered and should be a major guide to editorial policy. But liberation does not really translate into democratization unless it is linked to the second modern pillar of wisdom – *accommodation*. The pursuit of liberty needs to be moderated by the principle of accommodating diverse and competitive interests. This second imperative is indeed *accommodation*. If African politics are ethnic-prone, how can African constitutions be ethnic-proof? The African media need

to address this dilemma in creative ways to ensure that liberation and accommodation are not antithetical.

The role of the media in African election campaigns is growing (especially
the radio and newspapers and, less persuasive, television). Although the mass
media have a long way to go before they become as decisive in African campaigns as they are in, say, U.S. elections, the African media have already become very important in African urban constituencies.

The third modern pillar of wisdom is the imperative of *communication*. Do
the African media need to strike a balance between indigenous languages and
Euro-imperial languages in their choice of story coverage and pictorial images?
Should the media simply follow the priorities of the government in language
policy for the country? Or should the media have their own linguistic priorities
– and act on them?

Many Africans who have learned to read only in an indigenous African language (e.g., Kiswahili in Tanzania) often need regular access to a newspaper in
that language if they are to maintain their literacy at all over a long period. Minimally educated Africans can easily relapse to illiteracy if there is no appropriate and interesting reading material to keep them reading day after day. The
print media help to preserve the hard-earned ability to read.

As for ordinary folks who need to be kept informed about local, national
and international affairs during each week, there is nothing to compare with
news bulletins in the local language on the local radio. All these elements are
vital in promoting a relatively sophisticated electorate among the emerging African democracies.

The fourth pillar of wisdom in the media is *androgynization* in the sense of
the imperative of *gender-balance*. This would require a constant effort to balance stories about men with stories about women and to balance male imagery
with female.

Some years ago I was graciously invited by *The Guardian* newspaper in
Lagos, Nigeria, to give their annual Anniversary Lecture at the Nigerian Institute of International Affairs. The newspaper assigned me a topic. I was to lecture on "The Black Woman" (Mazrui, 1991). I agreed to give the lecture provided it was chaired by a woman. *The Guardian* agreed and also invited Mrs.
Maryam Babangida, the First Lady of Nigeria, to be the Distinguished Guest at
the lecture.

In my opening remarks I thanked *The Guardian* for the gender-balance. I
added these words: "Since this year you have invited a man to speak about 'The
Black Woman', I hope next year *The Guardian* will consider inviting a woman
to speak about 'The Black Man'. Until then no woman had ever been invited by
The Guardian to give the annual Anniversary Distinguished Lecture. I would
like to believe that my 1991 lecture helped to trigger a re-evaluation of the
gender-balance in the editorial and public relations policies of *The Guardian*.

But the changes did not come fast enough to spare either *The Guardian* or myself from such Nigerian feminists as Dr. Molara Ogundipe-Leslie, who had at that time just resigned from the University of Ibadan to depart for a visiting professorship in the United States. She launched an attack in an article entitled "Beyond Hearsay and Academic Journalism: The Black Woman and Ali Mazrui" (Ogundipe-Leslie, 1993).

The fifth modern pillar of wisdom is *ecological balance*. The African media should be more sensitized to issues like desertification, population growth, the green-house effect and global warming, and the relationship between the ecology and the human condition. The electronic media may have already begun to respond to the distinction between the ethics and the aesthetics of environmental concerns. Television documentaries about wild animals, the wonders of the sea-bed, the organisms of the deep, the wonders of the reefs, already abound. They concern the *beauty* of the environment (ecological aesthetics). The African media should close ranks with Al Gore, former U.S. Vice-President, in producing documentaries about global warming, the risks of population growth, deforestation and the depletion of the ozone layer (environmental ethics). Although television as a visual medium is more effective with such documentaries than either radio or the print media, there is already a lot of scope for environmental coverage in all the media.

The sixth modern pillar of wisdom is more purely economic, *balancing production, distribution and consumption*. The African media have begun to be effective in covering economic calamities such as draught, famine, and devastating floods. Progress is also being made in covering the work of economic organizations, such as the Economic Community of West African States (ECOWAS), the New Partnership for Africa's Development (NEPAD) and the emerging East African Community (ECA). But the media also need to play a more active role in stimulating and guiding investment and supporting agricultural festivals and livestock exhibitions.

The seventh and final modern pillar of wisdom is eternal vigilance in pursuit and support of *the truth*. This would also include the verification and clarification of each story and a defense of honest *variant interpretations* of the truth.

Conclusion

The pursuit of the truth includes a readiness to blow the whistle when things are going seriously wrong, either in our own society and among our neighbors. We have mentioned earlier the increased readiness of the press in Africa to expose corruption in high places. But the African press should also be ready to tackle even higher crimes and misdemeanors, both within our countries or elsewhere in Africa. The African press has been much slower than the Western press in blowing the whistle about ethnic cleansing in Darfur, or the atrocities of the Lord Resistance Army in Northern Uganda, or the endless civil wars in the Democratic Republic of the Congo.

NEPAD and the African Union encourage *peer-review* between African states – checking on each other on economic performance and the ethics of governance. But there should be peer-review also at the level of the Fourth Estate. The press in each African country and the press between each country should help to raise the alarm about impending or unfolding calamities in our African region.

The Western press continues to be the main source of most of the big stories carried by the African media. But it is hopefully becoming less and less likely that the Makerere saga of Idi Amin's era would be repeated. Perhaps gone are the days when the media among Uganda's neighbors had to rely almost entirely on a single British source for a momentous story from our own neighborhood.

References

Mazrui, A. A. (1991). The Black woman. The 8th annual anniversary lecture of *The Guardian newspaper*. Delivered at the Nigerian Institute for International Affairs, Lagos, Nigeria.

Nkrumah, K. (1957). *Ghana: The autobiography of Kwame Nkrumah*. New York: International Publishers.

Ogundipe-Leslie, M. (1993). Beyond hearsay and academic journalism: The Black woman and Ali Mazrui. *Research in African Lite*ratures, vol. 24, no. 1, pp. 105-112.

Chapter 3

Agenda-Setting, African Media and Conflict

Eronini R. Megwa, Ph.D.
California State University, Bakersfield, USA

Introduction

Towards the end of the 20th Century, Africa witnessed a series of ruinous conflicts in Liberia, Rwanda, and Sierra Leone. Actors involved in these conflicts employed extremely ruthless violent tactics often targeted at the innocent and helpless civilian population. The media were often used voluntarily or involuntarily to instigate or sustain these conflicts (M'Bayo, 2005; Mamdani, 2001).

African countries and the international community have invested enormous resources at local, regional and continental level to prevent and resolve violent conflicts on the continent. However, these preoccupations have given scant attention to the mass media and their potential for generating, promoting and resolving conflicts. It is only recently that we have begun to see an examination of the role of the media in conflict (Frohardt and Temin, 2003). And rarely have these analyses dealt with the role of the African media in conflict from an agenda-setting perspective.

Accordingly, the focus of this chapter is on the agenda-setting role of the African media in promoting, preventing or resolving violent conflicts in Africa. This approach will be useful in answering the question: Do the mass media play a filter or conduit role in promoting or resolving conflict? It will also be useful in establishing the dynamics of influence in a conflict context—identifying the real sources of influence, stages of influence, the specific actors, their influence strategies and tactics, and the interests they represent in this process. This article builds on the Megwa and Brenner (1988) agenda-setting paradigm and stakes out a new conceptual framework for analyzing the role of the African media in conflict states from an agenda-setting perspective as part of a larger interest in the process of media influence on society. The framework will be useful in identifying when and how issues relating to conflict become salient for the public in a media-poor context as well as who creates or instigates, expands or promotes, and consumes these issues in a system that has limited media availability.

Conflict resolution essentially concerns changing attitudes and perceptions of those involved in the conflict. In other words, it is a communication process that involves, to a large extent, information provision, analysis and consumption or what Onadipe and Lord (2000) describe as 'reviewing or "reframing" of the conflict situation with the use of "controlled" communication' which will engender altered perceptions. The media are powerful social institutions in modern African society. They produce, reproduce and distribute information. In this process, they not only create opportunities for people to "review" and "reframe" issues, they also influence how people evaluate the relative importance of issues. As such, their role, especially their agenda-setting influence, should be given due critical and empirical attention as part of the search for effective and sustainable conflict prevention and resolution mechanisms in Africa.

Media agenda-setting studies conducted in Africa are minimal (Pratt, 1992; Anokwa and Salween, 1986) and none of these studies have investigated this phenomenon in a conflict context. It is therefore important to begin to interrogate, from an agenda-setting perspective, the capacity of the African media to function as effective tools for instigating, promoting, preventing, and resolving conflicts in Africa. It is expected that this type of analysis will yield important data that will be useful in the search for effective mechanisms for conflict prevention and resolution in Africa.

The mass media are generally seen as part of the mechanisms for maintaining social order and cohesion in society (Tichenor, Donohue and Olien, 1980). They can help prevent, defuse, or resolve conflicts. They can also and have been used voluntarily or involuntarily to promote conflict as seen in Sierra Leone, Liberia, Rwanda and elsewhere in Africa (Gadzekpo, 2005; M'Bayo, 2005; Onadipe and Lord, 2000) and in the former Republic of Yugoslavia, and the former Soviet Republic of Georgia (Frohardt and Temin, 2003). However, there appears to be little empirical evidence to show how and why the media become complicit in a conflict context in Africa. It is our expectation that an agenda-setting approach will be useful in addressing this gap and especially in identifying specific actors and the specific roles they play in conflict situations. We also speculate that in social systems with weak media such as Africa's, the media are susceptible to manipulation--they are easy targets for fomenters of violence and those who use them to create divisions, instigate conflicts or conduct military coups in society. A social system with weak mass media is defined in this article as one that has interpersonal and oral communication as the predominant mode of communication, and lacks the necessary frameworks and mechanisms to foster free and plural media, promote a diversity of voices, and encourage media professionalism.

It therefore follows that in a social system with weak media, the agenda-setting influence of the media may be severely limited or mediated as a result of the following structural, symbolic and contextual realities: (1) a lack of an enabling environment for the media to operate freely and independently, (2) a dearth of qualified media personnel, (3) absence of a culture of professionalism on the part of journalists, (4) low quality media content, (5) fractured government-media relations, (6) a lack of the necessary policy and institutional framework for promoting freedom of expression and plural media and for encouraging public access to information and a diversity of voices, (7) repressive laws and hostile policy actions specifically aimed at intimidating journalists, (8) a dualistic media ownership structure that discourages independent media, (9) deteriorating social conditions such as poverty, illiteracy and lack of access to social amenities, and (10) use of interpersonal communication and traditional media more often than the mass media (Ugboajah, 1985; Pratt, 1992).

Post-independence African Media

It is difficult to understand the agenda-setting role of the media in post independence states in Africa in conflict contexts without a brief discussion of how the media came to be where and what they are today. Colonial Africa witnessed not only the birth of newspapers owned and operated by the colonial administration, but also the establishment of private and missionary press, and eventually the emergence of nationalist newspapers (DeBeer, et al, 1995). The publishers and editors of nationalist newspapers used them to fight colonial governments, agitate for political freedom, and in many cases climb to power. This brand of journalism, often adversarial in posture, gave voice to the political campaigns of nationalists. In turn, it created an audience with a media consumption orientation that is comfortable with the "watchdog" or even a "hound-dog" role of the media.

Regrettably, post-independence African news media have lost the boldness, conviction and ferment for which their colonial counterparts were known and respected. This has been replaced with a system that serves the selfish interests of government, the ruling party and the elite (Berger, 2003; Kariithi, 1994). Ironically, some of the nationalists who used their journalistic skills and resources to topple colonial government and who subsequently found themselves in the corridors of power, have turned around and adopted legal and extra judicial measures to discourage independent media, punish watchdog journalism and reward lap-dog journalism. As a result, what emerged after independence in most African states was an apotheosis of obsequious and timid media that abdicated their democratic function, embraced a government-say-so philosophy and metamorphosed into "his master's voice" (Berger, 2003). In many post-independence African countries therefore, what has flourished is an orientation that sees journalists as comrades and a media system that has tended to ineffectually report what government officials and the ruling party elites say they are doing for their uncritical citizenry (Berger, 2003; Kariithi, 1994).

In the 1970s and 1980s, many African countries experienced economic downturns. This situation has persisted and has had a blistering effect on the profit-making ability of the African media. As external pressures, most notably threats of economic sanctions from western donors and internal demands from activists, mounted on African governments to reform their political and economic policies in the 1990s, Africa witnessed unprecedented political changes and liberal economic activities. In a handful of countries, the media benefited immensely from these shifts when genuine collaborative efforts by government, the media industry and organs of civil society resulted in the creation of institutional frameworks and mechanisms for pluralizing and diversifying the media system.

At the same time, however, in a majority of African countries, governments under the guise of constitutional rule were busy devising disingenuous measures designed not only to weaken these newly emerging democratic structures, but also curtail the freedom of the media and stifle small independent media. The same governments also took specific actions in some instances to not only undermine the credibility of the independent media and stunt their growth and development, but also to dissuade them from exposing the actions of inept and corrupt public officials and powerful elites (Gadzekpo, 2005). These repressive media policies and high-handed actions have had a decidedly chilling effect on African journalists. In many instances, those who defied these policies and measures faced constant harassment, abuse, imprisonment and even death.

African media markets, as part of the weak economic systems of most African countries, are vulnerable and susceptible to manipulation. In such a situation, the media tend to depend on government subsidies and external funding from non-governmental organizations and are forced to adopt commercial formats driven essentially by profit-making and survivability. Consequently, what emerges, regrettably, is a system that nurtures unhealthy competition among journalists as they engage in unethical and unprofessional behavior that will help them survive. In this context, and especially in conflict and post conflict states where many journalists are not professionally trained, or lack basic formal education, as is the case in many African countries, journalists become susceptible to extra-media influence.

There is an additional problem in post-independence African states posed by the changing profiles of news people and emerging group of media audiences who do not necessarily identify with particular cultural or ethnic groups (Steyn and De Beer, 2004). In some countries, and because of weak national economy and fragile media market, some media owners and managers are compelled to employ and rely on young and inexperienced journalists to fill senior editorial and reportorial positions or even use off-street recruits, usually not on the organization's payroll, as reporters. This situation invariably and negatively affects the quality of journalistic work. The result: negative public perception of media institutions and further erosion of the credibility of an already fragile media institution.

In some African countries, the media themselves are part of the conflict. It therefore does not make sense to ask them to play a disinterested and objective role in such situations. It is critically important to establish mechanisms to identify such media outlets. In most African countries, journalists do not have formal journalistic training. This lack is even more prominent when it comes to specialist training. In general, there is a dearth of qualified and trained news people--the people who are expected to critically, intelligently and responsibly examine and analyze events and policies of government--in most of Africa's news rooms. What has also contributed in no small measure to the lack of respect the news media in Africa face is that African journalism is not home grown. It is rather rooted in the media systems of Western Europe and North America whose economic essence is premised on the economic logic of profit-making and survivability and whose news culture has an unbridled bias for conflict and disorder.

Africa's traditions and cultures occupy significant space in the thought processes and actions of Africans. And regardless of where they are, Africans have a deep respect for their cultures and values. Regrettably, there is a stark absence of these values and cultures in the design and production of news media content in Africa. Many African news people, because of generational factors, inadequate education or lack of professional training, do not have general knowledge of the cultures, values and norms of their countries or the regions they are reporting on or what Ansell (2003) refers to as "useful, relevant, news-linked knowledge needed for national and international news stories to be properly written and contextualized". This is one of the critical factors that contribute to the vulnerability of journalists to abuse by those who have a stake in conflict.

In Africa, and indeed other parts of the world, where the media system is bereft of a history of freedom and where journalists lack a culture of professionalism, the neutrality of journalists is always in doubt and their credibility low, especially in conflict situations. And it is partly as a result of this that some journalists have lost their lives either because they were targets of violence or victims of inadvertent violence. It is also common knowledge in some countries in Africa that some journalists indulge in "hate journalism" or "insult journalism". This type of unprofessional journalistic behavior has been known to precipitate or escalate potential conflict situations as seen in Rwanda, Liberia, Sierra Leone, and the Democratic Republic of the Congo. Consequently, governments and their appointed agents resort to stiff-arm measures to curb independent journalism. This severely slims down media's capacity to play an agenda-setting role in restoring social order, preventing or resolving conflicts. In many instances, the media systems in African countries have lost touch with their audiences and realities on the ground and thus have been reduced to mere "mouth organs" or "his master's voice" as they pander to the interests of those who own and control them.

In some African countries, those who are parties in the conflict also own media outlets, and in some cases, own the only media channels in the country. This is typical, for example, in countries where the government or the ruling party, as one of the parties in the conflict, has monopoly ownership and control of print and broadcast media outlets. There are also situations on the African continent where the so-called independent media are really owned and operated by opposition parties or politicians who have declared or undeclared interest in the conflict (Onadipe and Lord, 2000).

Conflict, Media and Society

Conflicts are a central part of human organization, and so are attempts at resolving them. Conflict resolution usually involves individuals and institutions that command respect, have power, authority and credibility. Respect for authority, the powerful, the wise and knowledgeable are part of the values of the African society. And where conflict mediators or potential mediators lack such credentials, their conflict mediatory capacity is severely limited. Therefore, for the African media to effectively perform conflict prevention and resolution functions, it is paramount that they have power and influence, and be seen by the public as impartial, credible and reliable. Where these conditions are absent, the influence of the media will be in doubt and even more so in a violent conflict situation such as the ones witnessed in some parts of Africa.

This influence may be significantly reduced where media availability is sparse and media reach is limited. And in most of Africa, this media presence is not only minimal but also narrow and restricted to a small number of people who reside in the urban areas. This is one of the major limitations of the African media: inability to reach rural areas and rural people who not only constitute the majority of the African population but also are the most vulnerable, socially and economically. Most newspapers, television and radio broadcasts in Africa are urban-centered in terms of their market and content. Besides physical reach and availability, there is also the related problem of quality of information and language of delivery of media messages. The use of English, French or Portuguese as the predominant languages of the media in Africa, has further exacerbated the situation, as most Africans are unable to read or write in these languages. These factors are critical when examining media influence and especially the agenda-setting influence of the mass media in conflict situations.

The media can be willing or unwilling participants in conflict. Through one-sided and biased reporting, for example, the media can instigate or inflame conflict. They can also passively incite conflict, for example, when journalists have poor journalistic skills, where there is an absence of a free media culture, or where there is no history of independent and plural media (M'Bayo, 2005; Frohardt and Temin, 2003; Onadipe and Lord, 2000). It is equally true that the media may promote dialogue within and among conflicting groups, and provide fair and balanced reporting. Consequently, and in performing their surveillance function in society, the media can help prevent, defuse, or resolve conflicts in society. However, the media are only able to perform these noble functions effectively if the necessary structural and symbolic frameworks are in place in the social system within which they exist and function.

Interestingly, in spite of the limitations of the media in post-colonial Africa, they are able to not only command significant presence in human affairs, but also seem to have extended their reach to a large segment of the African population. The media increasingly serve as a key source of information, particularly for the urban public and especially influential individuals and powerful institutions. And in some instances, this elite public has grown inextricably dependent on the news media for local, national and international news. These elites, in turn, have become a reliable and willing source of the raw material the media need daily for news production. This has inevitably imbued the media and elites with awesome power to not only influence policy and guide the actions of those in positions of power but also shape the opinions of the general public and stimulate social action. This is what, in part, appears to make the media in Africa an attractive propaganda tool for parties involved in conflict. It is also part of what renders the African media vulnerable to misuse and abuse by those who seek to manipulate them in order to deceive, mislead and misinform the public.

Paradoxically, it is also what makes the media potent tools for maintaining social order and cohesion. There is also another paradox: as the media have grown more powerful and influential in human affairs in Africa, the less accessible they have become to the ordinary and majority citizens; the more vital information is for survival in the 21st century African society, the more ill-equipped African citizens are to process and use information to take meaningful and effective part in public governance and development (Megwa, 2002). It is therefore important that our examination of the potential role of the media in conflict in the African society be informed by these socio-economic conditions.

These realities - structural limitations of the media - are partly responsible for dampened expectations of a majority of Africans about the abilities of the African media to effectively fulfill their surveillance and democratic functions in society. Thus the role of the media as impartial and credible providers of critical and meaningful information in a time of conflict and as reliable promoters of genuine dialogues between and among parties involved in conflicts on the African continent is arguable. Those who have a stake in conflict on the continent are acutely aware of the media's limitations and are willing to exploit, and have exploited, them to either limit and privatize or expand and socialize issues designed to promote or escalate conflict. In the violent conflicts in Liberia, Sierra Leone and Rwanda, for example, parties to the conflicts were acutely aware of the inadequacies of their national media systems, the fleeting and complex nature of information in a conflict situation and the information processing capacity of a majority of the African public. They seized on these vulnerabilities and thus were able to effectively use the media to do their bidding (M'Bayo, 2005; Gadzepko, 2005).

Conflict constitutes one of the biggest areas of journalistic work. For example, journalists have intimate and practical experience with communications involving conflict because of the manner in which news media determine newsworthiness. The media relish the dramatic and the unusual. Thus, it appears that conflict is attractive to the media because of its economic benefits. Those who are critical of the performance of the news media complain most often about the "unhealthy amounts of time" the media spend seeking out conflict (Auletta, 2005 p.14). But conflict is not necessarily a negative factor in communication. What is critical, it seems, is how news people, as professionals, conduct themselves in times of conflict. Conflict may increase or attenuate communication and communication, in turn, may increase or reduce conflict (Marceau, 1972; Dahrendorf, 1959). However, we are aware that communication is one of the primary means for resolving conflict and that conflict resolution constitutes one of the major communication goals of political and religious leaders (Pham, 1983).

The mass media may serve as a tool for generating conflict but it is important to also note that they are not primarily organized to create conflict. Rather, depending on the environment and how they are used, the media may function as a tool for detecting, suppressing and resolving conflicts (Tichenor, Donohue, and Olien, 1980). However, by acting as a vehicle for diffusing or defusing ideas or as a channel for expanding or constricting the necessary public space for different sectors or groups in society to examine and evaluate the importance and salience of issues, the news media may wittingly or unwittingly promote or suppress certain viewpoints. In doing so, they may be creating the "necessary and sufficient conditions" for instigating, preventing and resolving conflicts.

Fundamentally, in a market system, the news media deal with issues and proposals of their sources as part of the news production process (Sigal, 1973; Hess, 1986; Bennett, 1988). And this is where the news media's vulnerability partly lies. In such an interdependent system, the media inextricably rely on news sources for information (Entman, 1989). The use of sources, especially authoritative sources, is universally acknowledged in the journalism profession as a strategy for achieving objectivity or balance in news reporting (Tuchman, 1980; Schudson, 1978). In this respect, the media tend to serve ancillary rather than initiating roles in the development and resolution of conflicts in society (Tichenor, Donohue and Olien, 1980).

Media Influence: Processes and Effects

Modern society has become too complex, too subtle, too varied, too fleeting, and too big for people to make sense of it on their own. To understand our world, we engage in selective reduction of complexity and evaluative definition of relevance (Voltmer and Rommele, 2002) or what Bennett (1981) refers to as 'selection' and 'symbolic transformation'. In this process, we rely on the media and other sources in society to construct and reconstruct "pictures in our heads" (Lippmann, 1922) in order to better understand our environment. Similarly, the news media as part of this environment are confronted with a myriad of information in their daily preoccupations and are limited in their capacity to process all this information and provide complete and objective view of the world. In order to manage and make sense of this barrage of information that constitutes the raw material of news, news people inevitably engage in a sophisticated selective process called gate-keeping. The result: refracted and filtered reality (Parenti, 1986; Tuchman, 1980; Paletz & Entman, 1981). The mass media transmit these reconstructed realities to their publics. It is these frames that partly guide our perceptions, attitudes and behavior in society (Lippmann, 1922).

This active sifting of information is part of the strategy the news media have ostensibly adopted to ward off undue influence of news sources and to keep out information that is not newsworthy from making it into the news net (Tuchman, 1980). At the same time, however, the news media use these selective strategies to influence what we think about (Cohen, 1963; McCombs and Shaw, 1972) and how we think (McCombs, 2005). Consequently, the media define the framework within which collective social reality is perceived, thus shaping the basis for social action (Adoni and Mane, 1984; Entman, 1989). The people who supply the media with the raw materials necessary for producing news share this power with the media (Sigal, 1973; Hess, 1986; Megwa, 1991). They skillfully use the very symbolic strategies adopted by the media in determining and defining news, to influence the determination of news (Megwa and Brenner, 1988). As a result, they are able to effectively convey their messages to the public. The ease with which, for example, rebel forces and vigilantes were able to use the media in Rwanda, Liberia and Sierra Leone to transmit horrendous images and unspeakable stories of atrocities to the national and international public is a chilling reflection of the dynamics of this influence process.

The two-step flow theory of influence advanced by Katz and Lazersfeld (1955) is relevant to our discussion of the influence of news sources on the news media. It posits that: *opinion leaders* and *opinion followers* exist at all levels of society; influence flows from opinion leaders to followers and tends to be horizontal rather than vertical; opinion leaders are more gregarious, use media more, actively seek and process information, and are more socially active but often share the same social status as their followers (Katz &Lazarsfeld, 1955; Lazarsfeld, Berelson, & Gaudet, 1944; Baran & Davis, 2003). It follows, therefore, that these opinion leaders are also "gate-keepers"—they actively seek, screen and send information that would help others share their views, thus influencing them in the process (Boran & Davis, 2003). Those who instigate or promote conflict in Africa as seen, for instance, in Liberia, Sierra Leone and Rwanda, are sophisticated, skillful and effective media users (M'Bayo, 2005). They are influential people. They are opinion leaders--politicians, community leaders, activists, government officials, and even journalists (Gazepko, 2005; M'Bayo, 2005). These are people familiar with and skilled in the rhetorical and symbolic strategies used by the media to determine newsworthiness. This assumption is also informed by the phenomenistic theory of influence which advanced that mass communication does not ordinarily serve as a necessary and sufficient cause of audience effects but, rather, functions among and through a nexus of mediating factors and influences (Klapper, 1960). It is our contention, therefore, that the effectiveness of opinion leaders or those who use the media to instigate conflict in Africa is greatly enhanced by the nature of Africa's social system and its communication patterns and structures.

Media Agenda-Setting and Framing

Media influence research in confirming what those who deal with the media on a regular basis have intuitively known for a long time, has consistently shown that powerful actors, groups and institutions who are familiar with the rhetorical strategies and analytical approaches of the news media, exert significant influence on media content (Weaver and Elliott, 1985; Becker, 1982; Gandy, 1982; Turks, 1986; Megwa and Brenner, 1988; Trumbo, 1995). This body of research has also shown that some news sources, under certain conditions, are more successful and effective than others in getting certain issues in or out of the media agenda and on or off the public agenda (Linsky, 1986; Hess, 1986; Megwa, 1991). Sigal, (1973) and Turks, (1986) found that public relations activities in both the private and public sector influence the media agenda.

Agenda-setting research, in general, has shown that the media help set social and political agendas (McCombs and Shaw, 1972). This body of research has further shown that the media select, define, emphasize and amplify issues and that the public and policy makers learn from the media about the relative importance of issues (McCombs and Shaw, 1972; Shaw and McCombs, 1977; Trumbo, 1995). This ability of the media to focus on particular issues and thereby make them prominent in the audience's cognition is referred to as the agenda-setting role of the press (McCombs and Shaw, 1972; McCombs, 2005). The media also convey perspectives, offer solutions, stereotype groups, create anxiety, and legitimate or justify prevailing systems of social control (Halloran, 1980). The process by which issues become salient involves how issues are framed either by news sources for the media or by the media for the public.

Framing is a discriminatory process. In attempting to systematically and efficiently process the myriad of information that confronts them daily as news materials, reporters and editors tend to frame issues and events. In this process, news people simplify, highlight, and make more salient aspects of reality, while obscuring others (Luther and Miller, 2005; Entman, 1993; Gitlin, 1980; Tuchman, 1978) thus influencing the evaluation and interpretation of the reality or the perceived reality (Entman, 1994). Ryan, Carragee and Meinhofer (2005) in their study of news media framing of collective action argue that social actors sponsor frames and that these frames influence journalistic frames. They further contend that news stories serve as a forum for framing contests and political and economic elites are more effective and successful in getting their frames adopted by the media.

Examined from an agenda-setting perspective, the ability of the media to elevate the importance of issues among the public is largely a consequence of emphasis, for example, repetition of these issues over time in the media or the location of the issues in the news flow. As a result, the public incidentally learns of the relative importance of issues as ranked by the media. The media agenda-setting effect varies from individuals and across issues (McCombs and Shaw, 1972; Zucker, 1981). It may also differ depending on the context (Pratt, 1992). In terms of issue transference under conditions of high personal involvement, issue salience of the media agenda may transfer rapidly to the public agenda (McCombs, 2005; Roberts, Wanta & Dzwo, 2002). Differential agenda-setting effects with respect to individual responses to the media agenda are usually explained in terms of the obtrusiveness of the issue and the need for orientation, the assumption that individuals are naturally curious about their world (McCombs, 2005; Zucker, 1981; Lang and Lang, 1981).

Obtrusive issues are the issues that individuals deal with in their daily lives. Unobtrusive issues are those that are far removed from the individual's immediate or personal experience such as budget deficits or civil conflicts in far away places (Zucker, 1981).

On unobtrusive issues, the media serve as the major information source for the individual and may exert considerable influence on the individual depending on the individual's need for orientation which is conditioned by two factors— relevance and uncertainty (Zucker, 1981). The level of interest a person has in an issue depends on the relevance of that issue to him or her. If an issue has low relevance to a person, then that person's need for orientation is low. If there is high relevance, but low uncertainty, the need for orientation is moderate. However, if both uncertainty and relevance are high, the need for orientation is high. Rising levels of need for orientation result in an individual's media use to keep abreast of public affairs as well as acceptance of the media agenda (McCombs, 2005; Zucker, 1981; Lang & Lang, 1981; Roberts, Wanta & Dzwo, 2002). It is possible that these influence dynamics may not be applicable in a social system with limited media presence and where the predominant patterns of communication are interpersonal and traditional or oral media such as is the case in rural areas of African countries and other developing countries.

Media and Agenda-setting in Africa

Although very little empirical data exists about the agenda-setting function of the media in Africa (Anokwa and Salween, 1986; Pratt, 1992), it is, however, generally assumed that the media create images of the world—real and perceived--and that these pictures serve as road maps when we seek to understand ourselves, the people and events around us and those people and events that are far removed from our immediate environment (Lippmann, 1922).

This media influence, and specifically media agenda-setting phenomenon as conceptualized and empirically tested by agenda-setting researchers, may be limited in its applicability in social systems such as sub-Saharan Africa with limited mass media availability (Pratt, 1992) where individuals primarily depend on face-to-face interaction with opinion leaders and others to keep informed of issues and events occurring within and outside their immediate environment. It therefore follows that in such a situation issues that are prominent on the media agenda may not often become prominent on the public agenda as would be expected in a media-rich environment with a media dependent audience. This is because in a system with limited media availability and in which interpersonal communication and oral communication are predominant forms of human interaction, it is generally expected that opinion leaders and others on whom individuals depend for information in this social system, actively mediate the influence of the media (Baran & Davis, 2003; Klapper, 1960; Lazarsfeld & Katz, 1955). In a study of media agenda-setting effects conducted in Ghana, Anokwa and Salween (1986) found that agenda-setting influence of the media was greater among Ghanaian elites than among non-elites.

This limited agenda-setting influence, in part, could be explained by DeFleur and Ball-Rockeach's (1975) observation that the media in any social system operate in a given way to respond to the needs and wants of audiences in that system. Thus, they argue, mass media influence, their role and audience relationship to the media are defined by the nature of and limited to that system

(DeFleur and Ball-Rockeach, 1975). They further contend that the key variable in understanding media effects on audience beliefs, feelings or behavior is the degree of audience dependence on information from the media. Thus, in any social system, not everyone will be equally influenced by the media; those who have greater needs for and thus, greater dependency on media will be most influenced (Baran & Davis, 2003).

Similarly, it is our contention that in a social system with limited media availability and where a majority of the people live in the rural areas and depend more on interpersonal communication and traditional media for daily human interaction as is the case in most of rural Africa, the public will more likely depend on opinion leaders and others than the mass media for information. It therefore follows that those who have the greatest needs for mass media-based information in this context are opinion leaders. They also have the greatest access to the media. Logically, in this social system, opinion leaders will be expected to play a very active role not only in influencing media content but also in transmitting media's agenda to the public and influencing public opinion and guiding social action.

McCombs (2005) observes that agenda-setting effects have considerable consequences for people's attitudes, opinions, and behaviors, and that there is a fundamental link between the prominence of an issue or object in the media and the existence of an opinion. Although we do not dispute this generalization, we however argue that it may not be valid in a social system such as Africa's where modern mass media are urban-based, their content urban-centered and their audience reach limited to a small segment—cities--of the national population and where the majority of this population lives in the rural areas and relies on face-to-face and traditional communication systems for information. It is therefore our expectation that in such a system, the mechanism of media influence, particularly agenda-setting, could differ from what obtains in a system where mass communication is the predominant mode of communication, the media have a pervasive presence, and the audience is dependent on the media for information.

There is no question that the media exert significant influence on public opinion and on the formation of public policy (Wanta, 1989; Trumbo, 1995; Brewer & McCombs, 1996; Edwards & Wood, 1999). But as DeFleur and Ball-Rockeach (1975) have observed, this influence varies from system to system and depends on the role of the media and the relationship of the audience to the media in that system. In this respect, it is therefore our contention that the agenda-setting influence of the media as espoused by Bernard Cohen in 1963 and empirically tested by McCombs and Shaw in 1972 is certainly arguable with respect to its applicability to social systems that have limited media reach and presence. In a system with weak media such as Africa's, for example, the predominant mode of communication is not mass communication but interpersonal (face-to-face) interaction and traditional media or "oramedia" (Ugboajah, 1985). In such a context, the process and mechanism of media influence in general may markedly differ from what obtains in a media-rich social system (Pratt, 1992). In this context, perhaps, communication sources, other than the mass media, may be setting the agenda of both the media and the public.

Agenda-setting, Conflict and the Media in Africa: A Conceptual Framework

Media agenda-setting essentially has generally been posited as an influence concept with universal application. This generalization disregards the reality in media systems with limited media reach and presence where, as we have noted, media influence is likely to be actively mediated by structural, symbolic and contextual factors including and especially the influence of opinion leaders and other channels of communication. Typically, traditional media agenda-setting studies have been conducted in media-rich developed countries of North America, Europe and Asia (McCombs and Shaw, 1972; Shaw and McCombs, 1977; Siune and Borre, 1975; Weaver, et al, 1981; Black and Snow, 1982; Asp, 1983; Mikami, Takeshita, Nakada, & Kawabata, 1994, Takeshita and Mikami, 1995; Lopez-Escobar, McCombs, Tolsa, Martin and Llamas, 1999). But even in communities with limited media availability in the United States there is also evidence of media agenda setting influence (Williams and Larsen, 1977). However, the situation may be different in Africa where the predominant mode of communication is interpersonal interaction and traditional media. For example, Anokwa and Salwen (1986) studied the agenda-setting phenomenon in Ghana and found qualified support for the agenda-setting hypothesis with elites being influenced more than non-elites.

A review of the agenda-setting literature has revealed a stark absence of empirical examination of media agenda-setting influence in conflict situations either in the developed or developing world or in a media-rich or media-poor context. The theories of influence reviewed thus far in this article, particularly those generalizations advanced by Lazarsfeld et al. (1948), Lazarsfeld and Katz (1955), Klapper (1960), and Defleur and Rockeach (1975) provide us with ample grounds to forcefully argue that those who use the media to instigate and inflame conflicts in Africa have an acute understanding of the African social system, the strengths and weaknesses of its media, especially in conflict contexts, and the nature of its public. Accordingly, in Africa and, perhaps, other developing nations, parties in a conflict, armed with this knowledge, exploit the weaknesses of the media in order to influence the media's agenda, shape public perceptions and guide social action. And as Iyengar & Kinder (1987) remind us, in a typical agenda-setting influence process, public opinion is formed and primed and individual and group action is effected.

In the violent conflicts in Rwanda, Sierra Leone and Liberia, for example, the media's bias for conflict was clearly played out as the structural weaknesses of the media in those national systems were effectively exploited by parties involved in the conflicts to advance their own agendas. These actors, it appears, skillfully adopted the symbolic and rhetorical strategies used by the media in determining newsworthiness and in framing issues to set the media's agenda and get them to wittingly or unwittingly play a notoriously prominent role in supporting those who perpetrated atrocities on innocent civilians. The international media was not exonerated in this complicity as M'Bayo (2005, p. 26) writes:

> At the height of the war (Sierra Leone), the access to the international media that the RUF leadership had was often equal to, if not greater than, what the government forces of Sierra Leone had. They invited the media to witness the ruthlessness of the violence they executed upon the nation. Equipped with satellite telephones, they skillfully used the media by regularly calling upon major international broadcasting organizations, such as the BBC and VOA, to report their valor and carnage as they ravaged communities and set whole towns on fire.

Information subsidy: Agenda-setting, African Media, and Conflict

In violent conflict situations all over the world, the mass media's ability to engage in effective and clear communication is severely constrained. As a result, reliable information becomes a rare commodity because interested parties in conflicts engage in what Gandy (1982) refers to as "Information Subsidy"—the strategic withholding or releasing of information to increase or decrease its value to the recipient, to manipulate information to confuse opponents, secure support and create warped and blurred images in the heads of the public. In a conflict situation, and particularly in a country with a weak national economy and vulnerable media system, it is easy for the media to be recruited, co-opted, coerced or intimidated by parties--government and freedom fighters or rebels--involved in conflicts. In this situation, it is expected that parties involved in conflicts employ various framing techniques and agenda-setting strategies to influence the media and the general public.

More than five decades after Lazarsfeld and Merton (1948) raised the question of what or who shapes media content and its implications for public opinion, communication scholars have continued to empirically explore the question of news sources and how effective they are in influencing media content (Sigal, 1973; Tuchman, 1978; Gans, 1979; Fishman, 1980; Strentz, 1989). In this respect research identified people in positions of authority, "high profile" news sources, and those who have power and understand how the news media operate (Weaver and Elliott, 1985; Hess, 1986; Turk, 1986; Rogers and Dearing,

1988; Lasorsa and Reese, 1990; Megwa, 1991). This body of research assumes that media presence is pervasive in a social system and that the public in this system depends on the mass media to make sense of their environment and the world outside their immediate reach.

Source influence studies have typically been conducted in media systems with free-market orientations. Little, if any such explorations have dealt with source influence mechanism in social systems where media reach is not extensive and the public does not depend on the mass media for information. Our assumption, therefore, is that the processes, dynamics and effects of media influence in a media-poor social system will differ from that in which media presence is pervasive, where the media have extensive reach, and the public largely depends on the media for information. However, in a social system with a weak media and where interpersonal communication and oral media are the predominant modes of human communication, it is expected that opinion leaders will have extensive and significant influence on both media content and public opinion.

Schenk and Dobler (2002) have observed that the role of opinion leaders "lies in assessing and evaluating information seen, heard, or read in the mass media; in this way, opinion leaders are an aid to orientation in a confusing, information-overloaded world" (Schenk and Dobler, 2002, p. 49). We concur with and extend this assessment and submit that in a media-poor social system where media availability is limited and social interaction is primarily face-to-face, both the media and the public depend on opinion leaders for information to meet their respective needs. We further contend that this dependence will be heightened in a conflict situation where opinion leaders assume even more important role as major suppliers of the essential and scarce commodity used by the media to produce news. In this context, opinion leaders engage in "information subsidy", deciding which media gets what kind of information, when and how much.

Opinion Leaders and Media Agenda-setting

It is our contention that in a system with limited media reach, such as Africa's, opinion leaders may be setting the agenda of the media. The media then transmit this agenda to another influential but small segment of the public— elites--that has access to and depend on the news media for information to meet their needs. This group in turn transfers this agenda to the general public that has relatively little access to and need for the media. This influence dynamic seems to be consistent with what occurred in the violent conflicts in Liberia, Sierra Leone and Rwanda where parties (opinion leaders and their interest groups) to the conflicts used resources over which they had monopoly control in those contexts to influence media content. The media then transmitted this agenda to those with access to the media who then passed this agenda on to the general public--those with little or no access to and need for the media. It is, therefore, logical that under these circumstances, media agenda-setting influence will be minimal and isolated. And were the media to set the agenda of the public in this circumstance, this influence may be greatly mediated by opinion leaders, communication structures and other social factors.

This influence mechanism is explained, in part, by the assumption that in a conflict situation, information needed by the media to produce news is scarce, those who supply them with this scarce commodity are well sought after by the media, and these suppliers are keenly aware of this reality. These, in large part, account for the relative effectiveness of actors in influencing media content in a conflict situation as was the case in Rwanda, Sierra Leone, and Liberia. The interaction between the news media and opinion leaders in these contexts was structural and mutual in nature or what Rogers and Dearing (1988, p.558) describe as "structural dependency". The news media, in performing their informational function, rely on the expertise of news sources, and news sources in turn depend on the news media for cheap publicity (Entman, 1989; Megwa, 1991). This dependency relationship, the personality, position, knowledge, power, and status of news sources account for the relative success and effectiveness of news sources in shaping news media content (Noelle-Neumann, 1983; Parenti, 1986; Megwa and Brenner, 1988; Entman, 1989, Reese, 1991; Shoemaker and Reese, 1991; Megwa, 1991; Weimann, 1992). This inextricable dependence on news sources (Entman, 1989) is likely to increase in a conflict situation and in a system with weak media and especially where interpersonal communication is the predominant mode of human interaction. In this context, the news media are more likely to depend on opinion leaders for information.

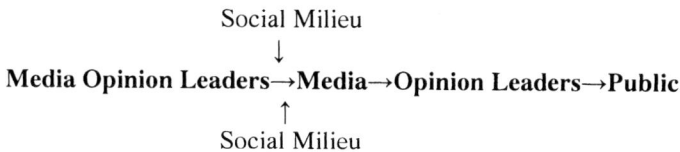

Social Milieu
↓
Media Opinion Leaders→Media→Opinion Leaders→Public
↑
Social Milieu

Thus, in a weak system in a conflict context, the flow of influence is from media opinion leaders to the media to other opinion leaders and to the general public. In this social milieu, for reasons advanced earlier regarding the structural dependency relationship that exists between the media and news sources, media opinion leaders may set the agenda of the news media. The media in turn set the agenda of other opinion leaders/interest groups who then set the agenda of the general public. In this context, and especially in a system with weak media, the news media become susceptible to manipulation by and vulnerable to the influence of media opinion leaders who relish and exploit their virtual monopoly information position to either hoard information or flood the system with information. In this context, the media play more of a conduit (passive) rather than a filter (active) role, uncritically transmitting information from the source to their audience. And given limited media availability in a media-poor context, the media are likely to reach only a small segment of the national population. This audience in all likelihood will be the elites and opinion leaders, who in turn will pass this information on to the general public. This, in part, explains M'Bayo's (2005) lament that during the violent conflict in Sierra Leone, the access RUF had to the international media was equal if not more than that of the government forces. RUF was able to attract media coverage by exploiting the weaknesses of the Sierra Leonean and international media--their penchant for conflict and desire to inform the outside world of what was "actually happening".

Another example of this flow of influence in a conflict situation is demonstrated in the appeal made by Wole Soyinka, the Nobel Peace laureate, to the Nigerian government to defuse the stand-off between militants in the oil rich Niger Delta of Nigeria and the government. In his appeal, Soyinka implored the Nigerian government to exercise restraint in dealing with those holding foreign oil company workers. He suggested that the government go through respected community leaders who will then communicate with interest group leaders and eventually members of interest groups in the Niger Delta area. Soyinka's suggestion acknowledges the supreme influence and importance of opinion leaders in Africa in "making individual decisions or legitimizing a special behavior" (Schenk and Dobler, 2002). Schenk and Dobler (2002) argue that in an interpersonal environment, interpersonal communication has the advantage of permitting new ideas or practices to be evaluated, however, "co-orientation and exchange of opinions determine the real meaning of information and messages from the mass media" (Schenk and Dobler, 2002).

To analyze the agenda-setting influence of the media in a conflict situation in a system with limited media availability and reach, it is important to examine structural, contextual, and symbolic factors that play a central role in this influence process. These factors determine the real media meaning and messages. In the proposed framework for analyzing media agenda-setting influence in a conflict context in a system with limited media reach and presence, structural factors, for example, are those that relate to the training of journalists, efforts to professionalize journalism practice, physical reach of the media, media density, media pluralism, diversity of access, networking, human resources, and equipment. Contextual factors concern the cultural environment in which the media exist and function, the social milieu–poverty and illiteracy, values and norms that influence cultural patterns of journalists, news sources and news media audience–the dominant communication patterns (interpersonal and oral media) of a given community or society that are likely to mediate media influence. These are the factors that affect, for example, how news media people and news sources conduct themselves in their respective communities and organizations, how reporters and editors determine newsworthiness of an event or determine issue importance, select, manage and retain news sources; how news media audience relate to the news media as an institution--their perceptions of news people as members of a powerful social institution, and how audience members process information from the media. Symbolic factors are content-based and are related to the manner and quality of reporting of issues and events.

In this context, and building on Megwa and Brenner's (1988) agenda-setting paradigm, the proposed framework conceptualizes the mechanism of agenda-setting influence in a conflict context in a system with limited media reach and presence as follows: there are four stages in the agenda-setting process in a conflict situation. These stages are (1) *Creation or Instigation*, (2) *Expansion or Promotion*, (3) *Consumption*, and (4) *Participation*. There are also four categories of actors involved in this process–(a) *Opinion Leaders*, (b) *Media*, (c) *Elites*, and (d) *Public*.

Central to this framework is the concept of *Issue Analysis*. Each of the four actor-categories engages in issue analysis. For example, at the Conflict Creation or Instigation stage, opinion leaders are the most involved in analyzing issues. They are also the most involved in terms of issue analysis at the Conflict Expansion stage. Megwa and Brenner (1988, p. 51) define *Issue Analysis* as "a strategy used by the media and interest groups to organize an issue in or out of public awareness". In the framework proposed in this article, *Issue Analysis* is a framing technique adopted by media opinion leaders and the media to elevate the importance of issues so as to attract media attention, influence media content and public perception, and ultimately shape social action. The importance of these issues as conveyed by opinion leaders are then transferred to the elites and subsequently to the public. This framework assumes that in a conflict context in a system with limited media presence and reach, (1) communication is a purposeful and conscious human action, (2) opinion leaders or actors who create or instigate conflict are knowledgeable and skillful consumers of media, and (3) these actors have access to and control information necessary for news production, and (4) the power, position, knowledge and skills of opinion leaders boost their framing capacity. These characteristics, to a large extent, determine the relative framing effectiveness or success of opinion leaders. In a conflict situation in a media-poor context, the media are highly susceptible to the framing influence of opinion leaders. This is because in such a context, the raw materials needed by the media to produce news are in short supply, hoarded by suppliers, in this case, opinion leaders, and released in a strategic manner to obtain the maximum benefits or the highest price for their supplies.

Conclusion

It is reasonable to expect the media to play various roles in conflict situations in different social systems. In general, media influence in any society is mediated by the nature of the social system, the actors including the media and opinion leaders, the nature of the issue, and the relationship between the audience and the media (DeFleur and Ball-Rockeach, 1975; Zucker, 1978; Lazersfeld and Katz, 1955; Klapper, 1960). The proposed framework, by adopting an agenda-setting approach in exploring the role of the media in conflict situations in social systems with weak media, has identified relevant stages and actors in the agenda-setting influence process. The media can be perceived as either fair or parochial; they can stoke the embers of conflict through one-sided, partial and sensational reporting thus fanning hatred and inciting one group against another or calling for violence as was the case in the former Yugoslavia, Rwanda, and the Democratic Republic of the Congo, Sierra Leone, and Liberia (M'Bayo, 2005; Onapide and Lord, 2000).

In general, if used professionally and constructively, the media can serve as a vehicle for gathering and reporting positive alternatives to conflict (Onapide & Lord, 2000; Tichenor, Donohue and Olien, 1980). The media's surveillance capacity and their potential as vehicles for providing balanced and accurate information needed in promoting genuine dialogue between and among parties involved in conflicts can help in making available early warning signals necessary for preventing conflicts from erupting. However, this capacity could be impaired as a result of the activities of opinion leaders and other elites in conflict situations in national systems with weak media and where the predominant means of human interaction is face-to-face communication and traditional or oral media. In such a system, media's agenda-setting influence is greatly mediated by opinion leaders who have monopoly access to and strategically release information needed by the media in such a situation to advance their parochial interests—manipulate the media to instigate violence.

The agenda-setting role of the media in conflict prevention and resolution is greatly boosted when media reach is extended to a majority of the African population, media people are perceived by the public as reliable and trustworthy, and professionally trained journalists report the news in a fair and balanced manner. When a media system lacks credibility and cannot be trusted by the public, such a system would have lost its public essence, its democratic mandate, and its homeostatic function. And as long as the African public perceives its media as unprofessional, unethical, unreliable, untrustworthy, and unable to ward off the influence of people who would want to manipulate the media to promote their selfish interests, so long will the media remain ineffectual tools for detecting, preventing and resolving conflicts on the African continent.

The conceptual framework sketched in this article will be useful in addressing the question of whether the mass media, for example, play passive or active role in a conflict context. Furthermore, it will be useful to researchers and policy makers who are interested in identifying the real sources of influence, the specific actors, their influence strategies, and the interests they represent in conflict states. It will also provide communication practitioners with useful information for planning and designing conflict resolution campaigns.

It is important to extend explorations of the agenda-setting concept to media-poor social systems and investigate the dynamics of this influence in a conflict situation in poor media contexts so as to test the universal applicability of the agenda-setting phenomenon. It is our expectation that the framework proposed in this article will move us closer to these objectives and provide more and useful insight into agenda-setting as an influence phenomenon and, perhaps, yield a more complete explanation of this intriguing concept.

References

Adoni and Mane (1984) "Media and the Social Construction of Reality: Toward an Integration of Theory and Research". *Communication Research*, vol. 2, no.3, pp.323-340.

Anokwa, K. and Salween M.B. (1986). Newspaper agenda-setting among elites and non-elites in Ghana. Presented to the International Communication Division, Association for Education in Journalism and Mass Communication.

Baran, S.J. and D.K. Davis (2003). *Mass communication theory: Foundations, ferment, and future. 2nd edition*. Wadsworth, Belmont, California.

Ansell G. (2003) "What Bias?", *Rhodes Journalism Review* 22, p. 63.

Asp, K. (1983). "The Struggle for the Agenda: Party Agenda, Media Agenda, and Voter Agenda in the 1979 Swedish Election Campaign." *Communication Research*, 10 (July).

Auletta, K. (2005). *Whom Do Journalists Work for?* Kansas City: University of Notre Dame, Universal Press Syndicate.

Becker, L. E. (1982) "The Citizen Assessment of Issue Importance: A Reflection on Agenda-setting Research." In D.C. Whitney, E Wartella and S. Windahl (eds.) *Mass Communication Review Year Book*, Vol. 2, pp.521-36.

Bennett, W. L. (1981). Perception and cognition: An information-processing framework for politics. In Long, S.L (ed.), *The handbook of political behavior*, Vol.1, pp. 69-193. New York: London-Plenum.

Berger, G. (2003). The journalism of poverty and the poverty of journalism. Paper presented to the International Communications Forum, Cape Town, South Africa, 2003-04-5.

Black and Snow (1982). The political agendas of three newspapers and city governments. *Canadian Journal of Communication* 8.

Brewer, M. and McCombs, M. (1996). Setting the community agenda. *Journalism & mass Communication Quarterly*, 73:7-16.

Cohen, B.C. (1963). *The press and foreign policy*. Princeton, New Jersey: Princeton University Press.

Coser, L.A.(1956). *The functions of social conflict*. New York: MacMillian.

Dahrendorf, R. (1959). *Class and class conflict in industrial society*. Palo Alto, Calif.: Stanford University Press.

DeBeer, A.S., Kasoma, F., Megwa, E.R., and Steyn, E. (1995). "Sub-Sahara Africa" In Merril, J. (ed.). *Global journalism: Survey of international communication, 3rd edition*, pp. 209-268. New York: Longman.

DeFleur, M. and Ball-Rockeach, S. (1975). *Theories of mass communication, 3rd edition*. New York: David McKay.

Entman, R. M.(1989). *Democracy without citizens: Media and the decay of American politics*. New York: Oxford Press.

Entman, R. M. (1993). "Framing: Toward clarification of a fractured paradigm. *Journal of Communication*, 43(4):51-58.

____ (1994). "African Americans According T.V. News," *Media Studies Journal* 8:3. pp.29-38.

Fishman, M. (1980). *Manufacturing the News*. Austin: University of Texas Press.

Forhardt, M. and Temin, J. (2003). Use and Abuse of Media in Vulnerable Societies. United States Institute of Peace, Special report #110, pp.1-16.

Gandy, O.H (1982) *Beyond Agenda-setting: Information Subsidies and Public Policy*. Norwood, N.J.: Ablex.

____ (1987). The political economy of communications competence. In V. Mosco and J. Wasko. (eds.) *The political economy of information*. University of Wisconsin Press.

Gans, H. (1979). *Deciding what's news*. New York: Pantheon.

Gitlin, 1T. (1980). *The whole world is watching: Mass media in the making of the New Left*. Berkeley: University of California Press.

Gadzekpo, A. (2005). Ghana: Media complicity in human rights violations. *Ecquid Novi*, vol. 26(1) 21-32.

Halloran, J. D. (1980). Mass communication: Symptom or cause of violence? In Wilhoit, G.C and de Bock, H. (eds.) *Mass communication yearbook*, vol.1 pp 432-449

Hess, S. (1986). *The Ultimate insiders: U.S. Senators in the national media*. Washington, D.C.: Brookings Institution.

Iyengar, S. and Kinder, D.R. (1987). *News that matters: Television and American opinion*. Chicago: University of Chicago Press.

Kariithi, N. (1994). The crisis facing development journalism in Africa. *Media Development Journal*. 4.

Katz, E. and Lazarsfeld, P. F. (1955). *Personal influence: The part played by people in the flow of mass communications*. New York: The Free Press.

Klapper, J. T. (1960). *The effects of mass communication*. New York: Free Press.

Lang, K., and Lang, G. E. (1983). *The battle for public opinion: The president, the press, and the polls during watergate*. New York: Columbia University Press.

Lasorsa, D. L. and Reese, S. D. (1990). News sources use in the crash of 1987: A study of four national media. *Journalism Quarterly*, 67, no.1. pp.60-71.

Lazarsfeld, P. F., Berelson, B. and Gaudet, H. (1944). *The people's choice: How the voter makes up his mind in a presidential campaign*. New York: Duell, Sloan & Pearce.

Linsky, M. (1986). *Impact: How the press affects federal policymaking*. New York: W.W. Norton.

Lippmann, W. (1922). *Public opinion*. New York: Harcourt Brace.

Lopez-Escobar, E., McCombs, M., Tolsa, A., Martin, M., and Llamas, J.P. (1999). Measuring the public images of political leaders: A methodological contribution of agenda-settingtTheory. Paper presented at the World Association for Public Opinion research Conference, Sydney, Australia.

Luther, C.A. and Miller, M.M. (2005). Framing of the 2003 U.S.-Iraqi war demonstrations: An analysis of news and partisan texts. *Journalism and Mass Communication Quarterly*, vol. 82:1, pp. 78-96

M'Bayo, R. T. (2005). Liberia, Rwanda & Sierra Leone: The public face of public violence. *Ecquid Novi*, Vol.26(1) 21-32.

Mamdani, M. (2001). *When victms become killers: Colonialism, nativism, and the genocide in Rwanda*. Princeton, NJ.: Princeton University Press.

Marceau, F.J. (1972). Communication and development: A reconsideration. *Public Opinion Quarterly*, 26, pp. 215-245

McCombs, M. E. (2005). The Agenda-setting function of the press. In Overholster, G. and Jamieson, (eds.) *The press*, pp. 156-168. London: Oxford University Press.

McCombs, M. E. and Shaw, D.L. (1972). The Agenda-setting function of the mass media. *Public opinion Quarterly*, 36:176-87.

Megwa, E. R. (2002). *Democracy without citizens: African media and the challenges of an open global society*. Inaugural Professorial Lecture, Peninsula Technikon, Bellville: South Africa.

Megwa, E. R. (1991). Source Agenda in the Media Agenda-setting Process. Paper presented to the Theory and Methodology Division of the Association for Education in Journalism and Mass Communication (AEJMC), Boston, Massachusetts, 7-10 August.

Megwa, E. R. and Brenner, D.J. (1988). Toward a paradigm of media agenda-setting effects: Agenda-setting as process. *Howard Journal of Communications*. vol. 1, no.1, pp 39-55.

Mikami, S., Takeshita, T., Nakada, M., & Kawabata, M. (1994). The Media Coverage and Public Awareness of Environmental Issues in Japan. Paper presented to the Internacional Association for Mass Communication Research, Seoul, Korea.

Noelle-Neumann, E. (1984). *The spiral of silence*. Chicago: University of Chicago Press.

Onadipe, A. and Lord, D. (2000). African media and conflict.

Paletz, D. L. and Entman, R.M. (1981). *Media power politics*. New York: Free Press.

Parenti, M. (1986). *Inventing reality: The politics of the mass media*. New York: St. Martin's Press.

Pham, R. T. (1983). A two-paradigm science exploration of science issues, *Journalism, and Q Methodology*. Unpublished Dissertation, University of Missouri, Columbia.

Pratt, C. B. (1992). Communication research for development in Sub-Saharan Africa. In Boafo, S. T. and George, N.A. (eds.) *Communication research in Africa: Issues and perspectives*. Nairobi, Kenya: ACCE pp.135-151.

Roberts, M., Wanta, W., & Dzwo, H. (2002), Agenda-setting and issue Salience online. *Communication Research*, 29:452-65.

Rogers, E. M. and Dearing, J. (1988). Agenda-setting research: Where has it been, where it is Going. In J. Andersons (ed.) *Communication yearbook*, vol. 11, pp.555-594.

Ryan, C. Carragee, K.M. and Meinhofer, W. (2005). Framing, the news media, and Collective action. *Journal of Broadcasting & Electronic Media*, 45(winter): 175-82.

Schenk, M. and Dobler, T. (2002). Towards a theory of campaigns: The role of opinion leaders. In Klingemann, H. and Rommele, A. (eds.) *Public information campaigns & opinion research: A Handbook for student & practitioner.* Sage: London. Pp.36-51.

Schudson, M. (1978). *Discovering the news: A social history of American newspapers.* New York: Basic.

Sigal, L.V. (1973). *Reporters and officials.* Lexington, MA: D.C. Heath.

Siune, K. and Borre, O. (1975). Setting the agenda for a Danish election. *Journal of Communication,* 25.

Steyn, E. and DeBeer, A. S. (2004). The level of journalism skills in South African media: A reason for concern within a developing democracy?"*Journalism Studies.*

Strentz, H. (1989). *Reporters and their News Sources: Accomplices in Shaping the News.* 2nd edition. Ames: Iowa State University Press.

Takeshita, T. and Mikami, S. (1995). How did mass media influence voters' choice in the 1993 general elections in Japan?: A study of agenda-setting," *Keio Communication Review,* 17:27-41.

Tichenor, P.J., Donohue, G.A. and Olien, C. N. (1980). *Community conflict and the press.* Beverly Hills, CA: Sage.

Trumbo, C. (1995). Longitudinal modeling of public issues: An application of the agenda-setting process to issues of global warming. In Skovmand, Michael and Schroeder, Kim Christian (eds.) *Reappraising transitional media.* London: Routledge.

Tuchman, G. (1978). *Making the news: A Study in the construction of reality.* New York: Free Press.

Turks, J.V. (1986). Information subsidies and media content: A study of public relations influence on the news. *Journalism Monograph,* N0. 100.

Ugboaja, F.O. (1985). Oramedia in Africa. In F. O. Ugboajah, (ed.). *Mass communication, culture and society in West Africa.* London: Hans Zell Publishers.

Ugboajah, F. O. (1982). Oramedia or traditional media as effective communication options for rural development in Africa. *Communication Studies,* 15:211-221.

Voltmer, K. and Rommele, A. (2002). Information and communication campaigns: Linking theory to practice. In Klingemann, H and Rommele, A. (eds.). Public information campaigns and opinion research: A handbook for students and practitioners. London: Sage.

Weaver, D. H. and Elliott, S. N. (1985). Who sets the agenda for the media? A study of local agenda-building. Journalism Quarterly, 62, 87-94.

Zucker, H. G. (1978). *The variable nature of news media influence.* In B.D. Ruben (ed.). *Communication yearbook,* 2: New Brunswick, N.J.: Transaction Books.

Chapter 4

Framing Theory and Conflict Transformation in Rwanda and Bosnia

Bala A. Musa, Ph.D.
Azusa Pacific University, USA

Introduction

Ethnic cleansing and genocide have been occurring in Africa and other continents for long periods and on varying scales. From imperial and tribal wars to slave raids; and from colonial invasions to communal and political strives, different communities have experienced mass murder, terrorism, and destruction. Most recently the wars in Liberia and Sierra Leone, the conflicts in the Democratic Republic of the Congo, Southern Sudan, Somalia, Ethiopia, Eritrea, and Burundi, and the genocides in Rwanda and Dafur have received relatively significant media and, therefore, global attention. Among the factors that differentiate the aforementioned crises from others prior to or even current tragedies among the Oromo in Ethiopia and the Kuteb in Nigeria is the amount of media attention (Collins, 2005; Ottaway, 1991; Ahmadu, n.d.; De Waal, 2005; Aning, 2005; Bell-Fialkoff, 1999; Isa, 2001).

This chapter examines the dominant interpretive frames employed by the foreign news media (American press in particular) and policy makers in their response to the genocides in Rwanda, 1994 and Bosnia, 1991-1995. Although the focus of this chapter is on African conflicts, a comparative analysis of other conflicts around the globe and the role of the Western press is pertinent to a proper understanding of the forces that shape conflict transformation in the African continent (Mazrui, 2004). The essence of this approach is underscored not only by the reality of globalization but the post-Cold War unipolar superpower politics.

The Hutu-Tutsi conflict that culminated in the massacre of over 800,000 people in 1994 remains a major tragedy, not only for Africa but for the world at large (Kent, 2006; Musa, 1999; Njoku, 2005). International response to the Rwandan genocide was typical of responses to other conflicts in Africa and elsewhere – apathy, misinformation, rationalization, misguided intervention, buck-passing, and regret. Communication scholars have long studied the relationship between media agenda, policy agenda, and public agenda (Wolfsfed, 1997; Shaw & Carr-Hill, 1992; Musa, in press, 2004). The focus has often been the relationship between these institutions and the larger society. While it is assumed that the media and government do influence public events, the goal of research has been to better understand the nature of this relationship.

From functionalist attempt to measure, predict, and control events, and the culturalists' desire to interpret and transform social trends have emerged theories that seek to explain the causes of conflict and how to manage them. A definition of the key concepts of this chapter may be an appropriate starting point. Those key words include:

Conflict: Arno (1984) defines conflict as "a state or quality of on going relationships among social entities, such as persons, groups, or organizations. It results from a lack of agreement over an issue and is expressed in words and actions" (p. 1). According to Rasmussen (1997), conflict is an escalated competition at any system level between groups whose aim is to gain advantage in the area of power, resources, interests, values, or needs, and at least one of these groups believes that this dimension of the relationship is based on mutually incompatible goals (p. 32).

From the above definitions, we can see that a conflict exists when two or more parties in a relationship pursue goals that are incompatible or seek to achieve them in different ways. Differences of opinions and conflicts of interest are bound to arise in any relationship. A healthy dose of individualism and a positive approach to resolving differences are necessary ingredients for social coexistence. Conflicts become detrimental when they are not properly managed.

Conflict Management: It is "the social process of allowing conflict to run its course and perform its beneficial functions in society without becoming destructive to basic structural relationships" (Arno, 1984, p. 3). Different professional and philosophical groups address conflict from different perspectives. The earliest approach was the "conflict resolution" approach, whose primary emphasis was on eliminating conflict (Chigas, et al., 1996, p. 29). There is the "conflict transformation" school, which believes that conflict is an enduring phenomenon of human reality. It cannot be eliminated but can be transformed into a positive force. Conflict management is concerned with the process of containing conflicts, their outcomes and consequences.

Mediation is a form of intervention where a neutral and credible third party brings the protagonists in a conflict into dialogue with a view to finding a workable solution. Governmental and nongovernmental agencies often appoint negotiators to mediate between parties in dispute.

This research examines potentials for peace and conflict in the unfolding global scenario by analyzing how the mass media and diplomatic institutions framed and responded to the catastrophic genocide that occurred in Rwanda in 1994. In particular, it looks at the framing of this crisis in international media and policy circles–*The New York Times, The Washington Post*, the *UN Security Council Resolutions* and the *US Congressional Reports*. It is hoped that this research will shed light on how and why the international community responded to the conflicts as it did. This will in turn help analysts and policy makers to better manage potentially destructive forces in the emerging global culture and learn how to accentuate its desirable elements.

The end of the Cold War has not delivered the promise of global peace and cooperation. For the emerging democracies of Africa, Asia, Latin America, and Eastern Europe, the transitions have been bumpy and rough. The continual balkanization of the Balkan States and the increasing political and social turmoil in most of the developing world have undermined the hope for peace and progress in the post-Cold War society. Tehranian (1993, p. 193) in describing this trend as the new world dysorder laments that:

> The end of the Cold War, however, has unleashed the centrifugal, ethnic, and tribal forces within nation-states....It has led to the breakup of the former Soviet Union, the world's largest multinational empire, the breakdown of multiethnic patchworks such as Yugoslavia and Iraq, has threatened the breakup of other nation-states such as Canada and India and unleashed racial and ethnic violence in the United States, Israel, South Africa, and other multiracial and multiethnic societies.

According to Tehranian (1993), the fundamental forces that underlie this trend include "globalism, regionalism, nationalism, localism, and spiritualism" (p. 197). The manifestations of these tendencies have varied among countries and regions. Nevertheless, a close observation will show that the sound being heard across the globe represents a cacophony of joy and sorrow. It is a mixture of laughter and wailing. The shout of "peace, peace" among the world's superpowers is being drowned by the cries and sighs of victims of communal wars and ethnic conflicts from Bosnia to Burundi, from Columbia to Cambodia, and from Iraq to Ireland.

Similarly, Chigas, McClintock, and Kamp (1996) opine that "rather than ushering in a new world order of democracy and peace, the end of the Cold War brought new tension and violence throughout Europe and the Soviet Union" (p.

25). With the end of the Cold War, they see a contradictory trend of "escalating tensions in many more countries" on one hand, and the decreasing "importance of and the threat posed by regional conflicts to the major powers' basic security interests." In this era, the roles of the major powers, both in conflict-exacerbation and mediation, have evaporated at once.

Framing Theory

According to Entman (1993), Framing essentially involves selection and salience. To frame is to select some aspects of a perceived reality and make them more salient in a communication text, in such a way as to promote a par-ticular problem definition, causal interpretation, moral evaluation, and treatment recommendation of the item described (p. 52). Frames are sense-making cogni-tive systems that enable observers to simplify, peg, and manage complex reality. Research has shown that journalists, policy-makers and conflict-mediators rely on specific frames in interpreting and responding to conflict (Drake & Donahue, 1996; Iyenger, & Simon, 1993; Musa, 1990; Richards & King, 2000). Frames can derive from previous experience, beliefs, expectations, and even biases. Drake & Donahue (1996) observe that "frames do not exist prior to or apart from talk" (301). It is the language, terminology, and reference used in describ-ing a phenomenon that creates and reflects the frame. That accounts for the ap-proach to this study, the content analysis of newspaper coverage as well as dip-lomatic discourse of the conflicts in Rwanda and Bosnia.

A content-analysis of the coverage of the Rwandan and Bosnian crises in two US prestige newspapers (*The New York Times* and *The Washington Post*), as well as their representations in two policy discourses (*US Congressional Bills* and *UN Security Council Resolutions*), were conducted to discover how these issues were framed. The research provides an analysis of the frames used in defining the nature of the conflicts, the conflict resolution approaches empha-sized, and the portrayals of the roles of the internal and external parties in these conflicts. This analysis is cast against the background of traditional Cold War frames, to see whether or not the same patterns of interpretation persist. The study also identifies the types and functionality of the interpretive frames vis-à-vis their implications for future conflict prevention, mediation, and transforma-tion.

Realizing that the present global village is intricately linked, and that the welfare of the whole is the product of the condition of the parts, the UN General Assembly's Special Session on Africa's Economic Crisis declared that:

> The African development crisis is not an exclusively African problem but one that concerns mankind as a living reality. A stagnant or perpetually backward Africa is not in the interest of the world community. Without durable and sus-

tained economic development in the world's poorest regions, of which Africa is a notable example, there is a real danger to international peace and security and impediment to world economic growth and development. The international community recognizes the importance of international cooperation to African development. (Obasanjo, 1991, p. xiv).

This also applies to other parts of the world that are undergoing economic, social or political turmoil. The rest of the world feels a sense of urgency to assist in resolving the Asia economic crisis situation since not only the direct participants, but everyone else is being impacted in one way or another. Bercovitch (1997) expresses a similar concern. According to him, "In an interdependent and increasing fractious world, conflicts affect us all; their proper management is everyone's business" (p. 131).

Methodology

Records of diplomatic policies (the UN Security Council Resolutions (N=26) and US Congressional Bills (N=18) and the news and feature stories on *The New York Times* and *The Washington Post* index from within five-year periods surrounding the two conflicts. The starting point for each data set was the year immediately preceding the outbreaks of the Rwandan genocide to some years after (1993-1997).

A systematic sample of eight weeks' coverage of Rwanda was taken from the two newspapers for the years selected. Only news stories reported within those weeks were included in the samples. Editorials, features, cartoons, and other items were not included as units for analysis. Hard news stories thus became the units of analysis. They were chosen because they constituted the "objective" facts of the events as perceived by the reporters.

For purposes of comparing the similarities and differences in the perceptions of the events by journalists and policy makers, *US Congressional Bills* and *UN Security Council Resolutions* on both conflicts were also analyzed. All the Congressional Bills and Security Council Resolutions on the two conflicts were coded for analysis. The wordings of the Congressional Bills and resolutions also reflected what the policy makers and diplomats considered as the reality of the events and priorities on how to resolve them.

The Washington Post stories were printed out from microfiche database while *The New York Times* stories for the selected weeks were downloaded and printed out from the Lexis-Nexis Newsbank database. Likewise, full texts of US Congressional Bills were downloaded from the CIS Congressional Universe Website located at http://web.lexis-nexis.com/congcom. UN Security Council Resolutions were retrieved from their gopher site at *gopher.undp.org.*

The themes analyzed included violence, militarization, humanitarian concerns, economy, peace processes, foreign intervention, justice,and peace prospects (high, low, unpredictable), fault lines (ethnicity, tribalism, irredentism, rebellion and nationalism, ideology, religion, and politics), and solutions (military intervention, humanitarian aid, non-intervention, sanctions, negotiation), external and local actors.

The warring factions, Hutu and Tutsi, were coded based on the way they were portrayed in each story. They were either portrayed favorably (peace-seekers, victims and cooperative with peace process) or unfavorably (aggressors, villains, uncivilized, and uncooperative). Each story was coded by dateline as originating from (US, War region, Other country/region). Using The New York Times indexing formula, stories were by length coded as long (stories that ran in up to three columns or more), medium (between one and a half to two columns), and short (one column or less). News treatment was categorized as either Episodic (stories that were event oriented, i.e. focused on the immediate episode or event without much background or perspective on the event), and developmental frame (presented in context, i.e. reporting that sheds light on the background to the event is called in-depth reporting). Stories were also looked at in terms of perceived scope of impact as local, regional, or global. Story placement was also examined. Part of the way the news media frame stories is by sensitizing the audience to the importance of the stories. This is done by the way a story is arranged in relation to other stories. In newspapers, page and type-sizes are used to convey the significance of stories. Front-page stories are generally the most important stories of the day. The newspaper stories were coded as front or inside page.

For the period studied, a total of 241 newspaper reports (New York Times = 139; Washington Post = 102) and 44 diplomatic reports (UN Security Council Resolutions = 26; US Congressional Reports = 18) on both the Bosnian and Rwandan crises were found, yielding a sample of N=285.

To test the reliability of the measures, 10% of the data was recorded by a second coder and an intercoder reliability test of the categories considered significant to analysis was conducted, yielding a pi alpha of 0.89. Seven out of the 11 categories were used in computing the intercoder reliability. These were the themes, peace prospects, solutions, role of major external actors, role of local actors, length of story, and news treatment. Scott's (1955) index of reliability (pi) was used because it "corrects not only for the number of categories in the set, but also for the probable frequency with which each was used" and can be "used with ordinal, interval or ratio scales" (Holsti, 1969, p. 140; see also Krippendorf, 1980).

Tests of the hypotheses and research questions based on the data produced the following results: In reporting the Bosnian and Rwandan crises, it was predicted that the media would rely on the Cold War frames of East-West conflict analysis more than on alternative frames. One test of the Cold War frame would be how often the United States and Russia as superpowers are identified as key players or potential players in a conflict. Data showed that of the 285 items analyzed, there was a conspicuous absence of ideological terms or phrases in the framing of the causes of and solution to the two wars. The decision rule for accepting this hypothesis is that both the US and Russia will be mentioned at least 60% of the time actively involved in ways that affect the equations of the conflicts. US government was mentioned 141 times. Most of the time, 74 (52.5%) it was portrayed as sitting on the fence. It was featured as playing an actively positive role only 59(41.8%) times. Even more wanting was Russia which was mentioned only 26 times, majority of the times 17 (65.4%) as a neutral observer. Therefore, the hypothesis that the media will rely on the Cold War frame in reporting the two conflicts is rejected.

Second hypothesis predicted that the newspapers would rely on the episodic approach more than the developmental approach in their coverage of the Bosnian and the Rwandan crises. The study found that in all, the episodic frame was used 138 (57.3%) more than developmental frame 103 (42.7%). The hypothesis that the media would rely on episodic more than developmental approach is therefore accepted.

A comparative analysis showed a statistically significant difference between episodic and developmental news treatment for both countries in The New York Times and The Washington Post $\chi2(4, \underline{N} = 241) = 3.8, \underline{p} < .5$. The Washington Post had more in-depth stories (50%) than the New York Times (37.4%).

The third hypothesis stated that humanitarian themes will exceed military themes in the presentation of the Rwandan crisis. On a scale of 1 (minor theme) to 3 (main theme), Rwanda had a slightly higher mean score on humanitarian concerns 2.2 ($\underline{SD} = 0.83$) than Bosnia 2.1 ($\underline{SD} = 0.82$). However, there were no statistically significant main effects for military themes in the framing of the two conflicts. Therefore, the hypothesis is rejected.

The fourth hypothesis predicted that militarization and military themes will occur more frequently in the representation of the Bosnian conflict than in the Rwandan conflict. An analysis of the appearance of military factors as either main, secondary or minor themes in the contents studied showed a significant variation between images of the Bosnian and Rwandan wars. On a scale of 1 (minor) to 3 (main), the mean score for Bosnia was 1.8 ($\underline{SD} = 0.72$), while the mean score for Rwanda was 1.5 ($\underline{SD} = 0.54$). There were significant main effects for military themes in the stories $\underline{F}$ (1, 167) = 7.8, $\underline{p} < .006$. Therefore, the hypothesis is accepted.

Hypothesis five stated that the Bosnian crisis would be presented as more feasible to be resolved by negotiation than the Rwandan crisis. This hypothesis is tested by looking at the kinds of solutions mentioned in relation to each country.

Table 1 shows that "negotiation" featured as a solution to the Bosnian conflict 22.3% of the time, whereas it was mentioned only 9.1% of the time in relation to Rwanda's conflict. Based on the frequency of mention, negotiated settlement is seen as the third possible solution to the Bosnian crisis. On the other hand, it is framed as the last option, comparable only to nonintervention. Considering also that the statistical analysis showed a very significant difference ($p <$ .002) between the solutions identified for both countries, the hypothesis is upheld.

The sixth hypothesis predicted that the theme of violence would feature more frequently in news reports and diplomatic discussions on Rwanda's crisis. Analysis of variance on dominance of themes showed that violence was represented significantly higher with respect to Rwanda ($\underline{M} = 2.2$, $\underline{SD} = 0.86$) than with Bosnia ($\underline{M} = 1.8$, $\underline{SD} = 0.85$). The test showed a significant difference on the theme of violence between both countries $\underline{F}$ (1, 197) = 6.8, $\underline{p} < .01$. The hypothesis is therefore upheld.

Table 1: Possible Solutions to the Bosnian and Rwandan Conflicts

	Military Intervention	Humanitarian Aid	Non-Intervention	Sanctions	Negotiation	Row Total
Bosnia	36 (20.1%)	50 (27.9%)	6 (3.4%)	47 26.3%)	40 (22.3%)	179 (100%)
Rwanda	21 (27.3%)	32 (41.6%)	7 (9.1%)	10 (13.0%)	7 (9.1%)	77 (100%)

$\chi2(4, \underline{N} = 256) = 17.3 \underline{p} < 002$.

Hypothesis seven states that Rwanda's crisis will be framed as motivated by tribal dispute more than by any other factor. To test this, a comparison was made between the recurrence of the use of the word "tribal war" or phrases like "ethnic violence," "nationalists," "ethnic cleansing" and "nationalist soldiers" and "tribal militia." As Tables 3 and 4 indicate, Rwanda's war was significantly framed as a tribal war between predominantly Hutu government soldiers and Tutsi rebels; while Bosnian war was represented essentially as an ethnic war between nationalist Serbs and Muslim Bosnians.

Table 2: Framing the Causes of Bosnian and Rwandan Crises as Tribal or Ethnic

	Ethnic Cleansing	Tribal War	Row Total
Bosnia	58 (96%)	2 (3.3%)	60 (100%)
Rwanda	15 (40.5)	22 (59.5)	37 (100%)

$\chi 2(1, \underline{N} = 97) = 39, \underline{p} < .000)$.

Also there was a difference in the framing of the identities of the combatants or fighting troops.

Table 3: Images of Warring Groups

	Nationalist Army vs. Secessionist Soldiers	Tribal Militia vs. Rebel Troops	Row Total
Bos-nia	55 (96.5%)	2 (3.5%)	57 (100%)
Rwan-da	5 (17.2%)	24 (82.8)	29 (100%)

$\chi 2(1, \underline{N} = 86) = 57.2, \underline{p} < .000$

From the two tests above, it is obvious that ethnicity and tribalism were presented as the main causes of the conflicts. However, Rwanda's war was framed more as tribal conflict, while Bosnia's war was presented as driven by a "policy" of ethnic cleansing and executed by goal-oriented nationalists. The sixth hypothesis is also upheld.

The eighth hypothesis predicted that journalists and policy makers would emphasize different solutions to these conflicts. A chi-square analysis was employed to examine whether solutions to the conflicts as mentioned in the newspaper reports differed significantly from the focus in the US Congressional Bills and the UN Security Council Resolutions. Table 10 following reflects the distribution.

Although, the original data had five sets of solutions (see Table 5), the policy documents did not mention nonintervention as an option. Therefore, the entire category was recorded to eliminate the empty cell. This was necessary to control for differentials arising from the skewness of the data.

Findings also showed a statistically significant difference between the solutions emphasized by the journalists and those emphasized by the policy makers $(\chi2(3, \underline{N}=244) = 12.8 \; p < .005)$.

The press gave overwhelming attention to humanitarian efforts while the subject of sanctions and embargo dominated the political arena with respect to the solution of the problems. Therefore, the hypothesis is accepted.

Another finding from the data worth noting is the portrayal of the warring factions. In Bosnia-Hercegovina, the Serbs were portrayed overwhelmingly as the aggressors or villains, while the Bosnians were portrayed essentially as victims. Likewise, in Rwanda, the Hutus were portrayed most of the time as the protagonists of the genocide, while Tutsis were shown as victims.

Table 4: Images of the Warring Factions

	Victims	Aggressors	Neutral	Row Total
Bosnian Muslims	130 (79.8%)	19 (11.7%)	14 (8.6%)	163 (100%)
Croats	30 (47.6%)	21 (33.3%)	12 (19%)	63 (100%)
Serbs	21 (13.3%)	128 (81%)	9 (5.7%)	158 (100%)
Hutus	18 (29%)	41 (66.1%)	3 (4.8%)	62 (100%)
Tutsis	40 (62.5%)	20 (31.3%)	4 (6.3%)	64 (100%)

This is a reflection of the tendency among the media and political analysts who like to find linear and simplified explanations to complex situations. Situations are defined in terms of extreme contrasts between good guys and bad guys, aggressors and victims. However, the view that only one side in a dispute is the villain and the other the victim does not reflect real-life situations. In actual experience, the maxim that "it takes two to tango" is a verity. The Bosnian Muslims and the Tutsis who are portrayed as the victims in Bosnia and Rwanda, respectively, have been known to initiate confrontations also. In either case, the Serbs and the Hutus have at some point faced the aggressions of their compatriots.

The data also showed a trend toward regionalization of conflict resolution. The European Union and the NATO alliance were found to be active in the Bosnian crisis but completely absent in Rwanda. The only exception was France, which sent her military troops to protect the refugees and relief workers in Rwanda. Other Western governments were not portrayed on the scene. The Organization of African Unity tried to intervene in the Rwandan situation, but it lacked the capacity to do so. The United Nations withdrew her peacekeeping force, United Nations Assistance Mission in Rwanda (UNAMIR) that had been previously on the eve of the massacre. And the OAU was absent from the Bosnian scene.

Event-oriented Reporting

Prior to the outbreak of the massacres in Bosnia and Rwanda, the two regions received minimal attention from both *The New York Times* and *The Washington Post*. This implies that the media are event-driven rather than issue-driven in deciding what is newsworthy.

The number of times that Rwanda was featured in *The Washington Post* rose dramatically from none at all in 1993 to 169 times in 1994 and gradually fell to 16 times by 1997. Similarly, *The New York Times* had only 3 items on Rwanda in 1993, but this increased to 339 in 1994 and gradually dwindled to 99 appearances by 1997. Therefore, 1994 was chosen as the period of most intensive coverage of Rwanda from the two newspapers.

The story was very different for the coverage of Bosnia. *The Washington Post* listed Bosnia under Yugoslavia. This however did not affect the observation because even in *The New York Times* where Bosnia was listed independently, the news items generally mentioned the region. And the observations showed similar patterns in the frequency of attention paid to the area. Although, on the whole, Bosnia received more attention in the newspapers than Rwanda, the frequency also fluctuated in response to the war. While the region featured in *The New York Times* 372 times in 1991, the frequency rose to 903 and 1164 times in the two succeeding years. The coverage of Bosnia in *The New York Times* peaked in 1993 while it was slightly higher in 1995 in *The Washington Post*. Having risen steadily in both newspapers from 1991 to 1993, it dipped a little in 1994 and picked up again in 1995.

Reasons why the coverage of Bosnia stayed high in both newspapers for a long time include the duration of the war and the role of the US and NATO. The Bosnian war lasted for four years while the Rwandan war lasted for only months. While the death toll in the Bosnian ethnic cleansing was estimated at about one million in three years, a similar number of people were estimated to have perished in Rwanda in six weeks. The coverage of Bosnia also jumped in

1995 because that was the year that US soldiers became actively involved under the United Nation Protection Force (UNPROFOR) and negotiation activities also increased. In other words, as Chang and Lee (1992) noted, besides the calamity caused by continuation of the war, US interest or the safety of her soldiers could be said to account for the continued attention focused on the region. Given this background and the fact that the combined average of the two newspapers' reports for that region showed a higher activity in 1993, that year was chosen as the period for analysis.

A similar pattern of attention was reflected in the number of times these two countries were mentioned in the deliberations of the United Nation Security Council and the US Congress. Based on the concentration of activity around specific stages in the two conflicts, the samples were drawn to permit the highest representation possible from a random selection.

Furthermore, the data analysis shows that the newspapers relied more on the episodic frame 138 (57.3%) than the developmental frame 103 (42.7%) in their reporting style. Therefore, the second hypothesis that said the media would rely more on episodic frame rather than developmental frame in reporting these conflicts was generally supported.

Event-oriented or episodic reporting is a by-product of organizational procedures and professional norms that have long been the hallmark of the journalism tradition. However, the changing environment of the profession and the new challenges facing the global community require media practitioners to re-examine their tools and techniques in order to detect what elements have become obsolete, inappropriate or dysfunctional. In doing so, the profession will be better equipped to perform the watchdog function that is required of her.

One aspect that stands out against this background is the seeming ethical conflict between the doctrine of objectivity in news reporting and the journalist's social responsibility. The episodic news reporting style has a direct bearing on this subject. This relationship is further explored in the following section.

Objectivity and Responsibility in Conflict Reporting

The philosophy that the journalist is a chronicler and not a critique of events has both positive and negative implications. The audience wants to participate in the event they are watching or reading about, though vicariously. Objective reporting is one way by which members of the audience are made to feel that they are getting the picture of the events as they really occurred. In other words, if journalists conform to the tradition of reporting the facts as they really are, then the news will always be the same irrespective of which reporter or what news medium covers it. Therefore, the straight news approach is the closest encounter with the event that the audience can have, short of observing the event firsthand themselves. The importance of this approach for theme or frame analysis is that news theme represents the reality of the event. Through the words, sentences, paragraphs, and news sequences, the reader or analyst is able to identify the theme(s) of the news.

However, the assumption that straight news reports represent sacred facts has also been criticized as a myth. Critics of the objectivity philosophy argue that it is impossible for the media to present news events in a way that is completely devoid of bias (Hatchen, 1992; Sadkovich, 1997; Gans, 1979). They argue that the news is always shaped by several factors. One of those factors is the organizational routine of the news media. The definition of news automatically sets the stage for what qualifies to be reported and what does not. Since the definition is socially constructed, it means that the reality presented as the news is a function of the socio-cultural environment of the news organization and media practitioners.

Organizational routines that influence news presentation also include the size of the news staff and their newsgathering habits. Organizations with fewer staff members do not have the capacity to deploy a reporter to the spot of every breaking event. They often report little foreign news or rely on news agency reports. All forms of editing do, in some way or another, diminish the transparency of the audiences' perception of the event. Even when the media rely on their own reporters the gate-keeping function is ever present. This process of selecting and organizing the story to fit a news format, medium (electronic, print or multimedia), or slot (space or time) contributes to shaping reality in a particular way.

The medium certainly influences the presentation and perception of the event. Each medium has a structural style or story telling format that best suits it. Sadkovich (1998) notes that "newspapers do more analysis and TV more spot news" (p. 2). Even within that context, there are similarities and differences. While print media reports are generally more in-depth than electronic media reports, the news media generally are given to brevity as means of maximizing the limited time or space available for news reporting. On any typical day, there are more news items than can be reported. Therefore, the editors are constrained to curtail the number of stories reported as well as the length of each story.

Even among the print media, disparities exist in terms of the depth of their news reports. Quality newspapers basically have more depth to their reports than tabloids. On the whole, McLuhan's (1964) dictum that "the medium is the message" (p. 7) is valid even in the case of war reporting.

The electronic media are often drawn to the sensational and dramatic because those appeal to the lights, glitter and action format of the medium. In television, as in photojournalism, a picture is worth a thousand words. Sights and sounds are used to convey immediacy and impact. In radio and in the print media, words are used to paint vivid images of the event being reported. In other words, the medium has its own form of reality that it is capable of perceiving and portraying. This is very much like the language of the medium, print (words and pictures), radio (sound), television (sights and sound) through which the content is framed. The communicator is constrained by the medium. There may be some emphasis or impact they wish to convey, but they can only do so within the technological capabilities of the medium.

Others implicated in the shaping or framing of the reality that is perceived as news include bureaucrats, experts, and primary participants in the news events. These "mediators of reality" (Sadkovich, 1998, p. 3) have their biases, blind spots or hidden agenda which influence the news, even in subtle ways. In other words, even when journalists try to exclude personal opinion from the contents of their reports, they have to contend with constraints that are not deliberate. The so-called experts or authorities who provide the sound-bytes or official viewpoints, more often than not, may provide misleading information. This could be due to lack of accurate information or out of a conscious effort to give a version of the situation that is favorable to their case.

Kahler (1995) makes a succinct point that the combined impact of talk radio and expert opinionating in political discourse has privileged "factoids--created facts" over facts. This, according to Kahler, is "particularly prevalent in discussions of international politics, where anyone can play the expert after a short visit to an airport lounge" (p. 19). Roving journalists and their expert sources in the academics as well as official circles all fit this bill.

Even when the communicators seem to have access to and present the truth or facts of the case, responsible journalism calls for more than just reporting the facts. This is because, objectivity as a journalistic ideal also limits discourse. In the bid to maintain a neutral posture, journalists tend to ignore the qualitative implications of their reports. Complex phenomena are reduced to sound-bytes and simplified digests of multiple realities are presented as facts. Routine news does not provide for qualitative discourse. It "limits political consciousness. Politically and socially sterile, the news replaces a 'coherent view of politics' with 'personal melodramas carefully strained of explicit political and social significance'" (Sadkovich, 1998, p. 10; Bagdikian, 1983, p. 208; Fishman, 1990, p. 138). The focus on high points of drama in every event undermines intelligent discourse and overlooks the qualitative differences at various points of the development of the events.

With respect to conflict reporting, for instance, event orientation accounts for the media's inability to detect and forewarn the society of potentially explosive situations. In both Bosnia and Rwanda, the outbreak of violence in 1991 and 1994 respectively only marked the climax of long simmering discontent and misunderstanding.

Particularly in war reporting, objectivity may not always be an ideal. The practicality and relevance of objectivity in news reporting remains a bone of contention among journalism practitioners and critics. What can be said without controversy is that straight news reporting has its merits and demerits. Impartiality is certainly a virtue, not only in news reporting but in other social situations as well. As a way of protecting the sanctity of the facts of an event, objectivity has served the important purpose of letting the audience come as close as they can to witnessing the events personally. It has also created a threshold of truth-telling to which reporters have been held accountable. Without that, it will be impossible to distinguish between fact and fiction.

For instance in reporting the statistics on casualties in a conflict, "all the truth and nothing but the truth" may amount to a disservice if it provokes another round of retaliatory killing. The journalist should be discrete in the use of information so as not to compound the conflict. In this regard, positive advocacy journalism that decries the consequences of the war should be encouraged. There have been circumstances where the so-called CNN effect (Livingston & Eachus, 1995) has brought the plights of war victims to the limelight, thereby mobilizing humanitarian and political assistance on their behalf. Journalists need to define their responsibilities such that they not only detail the tragedies they observe, but also participate in the search for solutions.

An emphasis on peace advocacy journalism will have implications for the practice as well as the product of journalism. As reflected in the longitudinal analysis of the attention given to Bosnia and Rwanda by *The New York Times* and *The Washington Post* within the five-year periods surrounding the wars, traditional journalistic practice is driven by episodes (events) rather than processes (issues). The "ethnic cleansing" in Bosnia and the "tribal war" in Rwanda were not spontaneous outbreaks of violence as the media and diplomats would have the world believe.

Ethnically motivated violence has plagued these regions since the nineteenth century in the case of Rwanda, and since the turn of the century in the case of Bosnia. Warning signs of these tragedies were manifest for many months during the war-mongering propaganda in both the national media of Bosnia and Rwanda.

If journalists had looked beyond the surface, they would have alerted the world in advance of the impending catastrophe. In a world characterized by increased cases of conflict, it is important for journalists to redefine their approaches to suit the prevailing circumstances. This would call for a departure from parachute journalism and a move toward more in-depth, investigative, interpretive, and participatory reporting (Gilboa, 2005; Richard & King, 2000).

It is interesting to note from the analysis of this data, that while *The New York Times* gave higher coverage to the two conflicts, *The Washington Post* had more interpretive stories. While only 37% of *New York Time's* stories on the two conflicts contained in-depth background information, 50% *of Washington*

Post's stories were in-depth news stories. This again underscores the tension between qualitative developmental reporting and quantitative episodic news.

Local Conflicts in a Global Arena

The United States and Russia as erstwhile superpowers are no more as active on the scenes of domestic conflicts around the world as they were in the Cold War era. Findings indicated that they were reluctant to get involved in the Bosnian and the Rwandan crises. Of significance is the disparity between the US and Russia's involvement. The end of the Cold War, more than anything, explains Russia's near-total absence from the scenes of these conflicts. More conspicuous was her lack of involvement in Bosnia, which is geographically adjacent and a former buffer nation. The relatively high reference to Russia's negative role in the news reports may have stemmed from the sympathy of Russian Serbs toward the Bosnian Serbs.

This means the adaptation of local needs or situations to global reality. Used mostly in business contexts, it has been defined as "the process whereby transnational corporations customize products for local markets" (Mohammadi, 1997, p. 21). Glocalization is applied in the context of this research to describe the trend whereby the media and policy makers are globalizing local issues and localizing global issues. Mohammadi (1997), Robertson (1992) and others describe how the global communication networks have helped to project the ethnic conflicts in Bosnia, Kurdistan, Rwanda and Albania into international policy agenda by highlighting their universal consequences. They also cite how global issues such as the environment and human rights are gaining attention at grassroots level. Nowadays, domestic conflicts between ethnic, religious and social groups are more prevalent than conflicts between nations. At the same time, global and regional organizations are replacing the superpower middle-forces that used to manage the conflicts.

One reason why foreign intervention has become a necessary aspect of domestic conflict resolution is the increase in the failure of states (Zartman, 1995). In the Somalian, Liberian and Bosnian conflicts, the legitimacy of the states had been eroded by the actions of the belligerent factions. There was a vacuum of constitutional authority. External intervention became an inevitable option if order and sanity were to be restored. In such situations, where anarchy had become the order of the day, an external force was required to mediate between the groups.

A disturbing characteristic of the ethnic conflicts is that the combatants are mostly militiamen and children rather than regular soldiers. Likewise, the victims are mostly civilians, women and children (Carnegie Commission, 1997). Therefore, the motive for most foreign interventions in domestic conflicts in recent times has been more humanitarian than political or military.

The experiences of failed states and the need for foreign intervention to protect innocent civilians and restore peace has brought to question the need to re-evaluate the doctrine of sovereignty. The recent military interventions in Somalia, Rwanda, Bosnia and elsewhere have been primarily to provide humanitarian aid or protect unarmed victims of the conflicts.

Speaking of the Bosnian crisis, UN Secretary General, Kofi Annan, who was then the Under-Secretary General for Peacekeeping Operations notes that "The UN is the only world policeman today. When the superpowers were around, they shared it with us. Now the Russians are gone and the Americans have no stomach for playing policeman" (Preston, 1993, A28). He was repeating the words of American President George Bush, who in stating the reluctance of the US to risk any life of her soldiers in Bosnia, stated that the US was not the world's policeman. The inability of the US to browbeat India and Pakistan out of conducting nuclear weapon tests, also speaks of the decreasing capacity of the superpower nations to police the rest of the world.

Tehranian (1992) argues that even if the US has the moral and political will to act as the modern-day leviathan in New World Disorder, it does not have the economic capacity to shoulder such a responsibility. He asserts that while the US may have the military capability to enforce peace in any troubled region of the world, its three trillion dollar foreign debt constitutes a sufficient deterrence against embarking on any costly military venture.

Not only the US, even her allies are weary of bearing the financial burden required in carrying out such costly ventures. Tehranian (1992) believes that the 1990 Gulf War, code-named "Operation Desert Storm" is probably the last of such grandiose military operations that the US and her allies would be able to conduct. Recent experiences have validated this notion. Subsequent attempts by the US to mobilize the Allied Forces to enforce Iraq's compliance with the UN resolutions have received very lethargic response.

This reflects a situation where the dawn of the global village is signaling an increasing apathy toward multilateral and unilateral intervention in distant conflicts. Thanks to the media, wars in any part of the globe are now occurring under the full view of the whole world. However, the political will to intervene has disappeared. Even humanitarian tragedies like the Rwandan and Bosnian genocide do not evoke action from the distant neighbors of the global village. The organic tendons of the new community are held together by communication systems that do not promote empathy or feelings of identification. The mediating role of the press tends to distort the perception of the event. Human tragedies, such as the Rwandan and Bosnian crises appear as media events, rather than real life disasters.

The narrative structure gives the news item a life of its own. The emphasis seems to be on the news and not the event. And if it is perceived more as a media drama rather than the actual experiences of real people, the report is bound to elicit a casual response and not a passionate one. According to Shaw (1996), the media's capacity to becloud the reality of an event is typified by French Writer, Jean Baudrillard, who opined that "The Gulf War did not take place" (p. 46). Shaw notes that for Baudrillard, the Gulf War "was only a war of words and signs, waged in the media." If the Gulf War, which had as high casualties and involved more troops from around the world than the ethnic wars in Bosnia or Rwanda, was perceived simply as a media event by the educated class, that says a lot about the impact of war reports on the society at large.

Also the constant barrage of bad news from the media may account for the audience's indifference toward such stories. Moeller (1999) calls this effect, the *compassion fatigue*. In her view, the incessant portrayals of these events in the press tend to desensitize the public to the plight of the victims. Eventually, such news items are treated as routine rather than exceptional. The fact remains that for the media, bad news is good news. This is compounded by parachute journalism on one hand and the dominance of the episodic news frame on the other.

It is tragic that the international community no longer demonstrates the sense of obligation of being one another's keeper, as it did during the Cold War. Although regional blocs are becoming stronger, few of them have the structures and capacities to respond adequately to modern conflicts. While the Bosnian crisis may be perceived as "Europe's quagmire," and the Rwandan conflict treated as "Africa's nightmare," there are no instruments within these regions that are capable of responding to tragedies on the scales witnessed in these two incidences. Although new bodies are being formed to help contain such situations in the future, the need for global action under the auspices of the UN and, as President Bush puts it, "the beneficent intervention of the United States" (Xudo, 1996, p. 100) is still a necessity. In the light of the huge responsibility that the US has shouldered in advancing world peace, it is only logical that the government and citizens are becoming fatigued with the business of foreign peacekeeping.

Past Frames and Future Outcomes

The findings of this study indicate that some of the previous frames of conflict used by journalists in reporting conflicts have been discarded, but also that many still persist. The images of Bosnia as a military zone, the notion that the Bosnian conflict had a higher chance of being resolved by negotiation, and the impression of the Rwandan crisis as motivated by tribal rather than political or economic disputes, all reflect a *deja vu* mentality in the framing of the issues.

Although the hypothesis that humanitarian themes will feature more commonly in reports of the Rwandan conflict than that of the Bosnian is not supported by the data, other findings suggest that historical frames still persist. The fact that humanitarian themes featured equally as prominently in the discourse of both conflicts may be a function of the degree of suffering associated with the two conflicts. The plight of the victims of both conflicts made the humanitarian theme the greatest concern to the public, the media and diplomats.

This is consistent with Jakobsen's (1996) finding that in distant conflict where other nation's national interests are not affected, humanitarian concerns become the main focus of attraction and intervention. This is true of both countries, since the conflicts were essentially domestic. Foreign countries had limited interests at stake, beyond humanitarian concerns, on the outcomes of both conflicts.

Another reason is that the primary response from the international community, though reluctantly, was in the form of humanitarian aid. It is therefore not surprising that emphasis on humanitarian theme was equally reflected in representations of the two wars. Likewise, humanitarian aid ranked highest in frequency as the solution to both the Bosnian and Rwandan crises. Although humanitarian aid is represented as the top-most solution to both crises, it is indicated way higher as a solution to the Rwandan war than to the Bosnian conflict.

The similarity in framing does not extend far beyond the humanitarian theme. As the results show, Rwanda's crisis was perceived as a form of tribal anarchy and having lesser chance of being resolved by dialogue or negotiation. Moreover, military themes feature more commonly in reports about Bosnia than those regarding Rwanda. This is consistent with the perception of the region as a perennial battlefield dating back to World War I. All these suggest that some old frames of analysis continue to dictate the framing of international events.

The data also showed that violence themes are more prevalent in looking at the crisis in Rwanda than in the case of Bosnia. This way of framing the issues is keeping with the image that "in parts of Asia, Latin America, and Africa, civil wars have been endemic" (Shaw, 1996, p. 159). It also agrees with Wall's (1997a) findings that violence themes featured more than diplomatic negotiations in the coverage of Rwanda in leading US news magazines. This is rather not surprising in view of the finding earlier that the international community gave the Rwandan conflict little possibility of being resolved by negotiation.

The media and diplomatic reports rely on history as a reference point for interpreting these events. The search for familiar and convenient frames of analysis is apparent in the presentation of both conflicts. Although the Cold War ideological frames have disappeared, other routines still persist, or have been invented to account for the Bosnian and Rwandan crises. These include the representation of Bosnia as a highly militarized zone, and its actors as civilized parties that can be appealed to through reason and negotiation.

The implication of this was that the international community did not want to further compound the militarism of the region. Therefore, the best solution to the crisis was to impose an arms embargo on the warring factions, while pursuing a peaceful negotiation. Bosnia's war was seen as an aberration in a civilized Europe, while Rwanda's was seen as phenomenon typical of the African

Region. The theory that two wars explain a third (Sadkovich, 1998) was certainly at work here. To this end, Bosnia was essentially seen in the shadow of World Wars I and II, while images of Somalia clouded the visions of Rwanda, for both those viewing from the press gallery and the diplomatic arena.

Since Africa was considered an endemic disaster zone, Rwanda's war was not perceived as resolvable by negotiation. As it proved to be, history was not the best teacher on both counts. US Senator Daniel Coats stated regarding the Bosnian conflict that "we have staked our credibility on one outcome in the Balkans—peace. But it is the outcome that is least likely" (Congressional Digest, 1996, p. 47).

Similarly, Rosenfield (1993) argued that the view that the Bosnian crisis could be easily resolved by dialogue was a misreading of history. According to him, "Clinton, showing a feeble grasp of history, bet on a certain Serb moderation and readiness to compromise. But Serbs have shown a fierce paranoia and arrogance. They are working single-mindedly to build a greater Serbia housing all of the old Yugoslavia's Serbs, continuing military operations and spitting in Washington's face" (p. A21). Likewise both President Clinton and the UN Secretary General, Kofi Anan, who have just completed separate visits to Rwanda, have apologized to the people of Rwanda for the inaction on the parts of their government and organizations, respectively. They acknowledged the act of viewing Rwanda in the light of Somalia was a gross error in judgment.

This distortion in perception sprang from the reliance on simplified scales of analysis designed to fit each new event into predetermined modes of interpretation. As the data depicted, the Rwandan crisis was framed essentially as a display of irrational "tribal war" instinct. This image was consistent with the image of Africa as primitive and uncivilized. In a paper published by the Africa Policy Information Center (1997), it was asserted that the notion of tribe:

> promotes a myth of primitive African timelessness, obscuring history and change. . . . When the general image of tribal timelessness is applied to situations of social conflict between Africans, a particularly destructive myth is created. Stereotypes of primitiveness and conservative backwardness are also linked to images of irrationality and superstition. The combination leads to portrayal of violence and conflict in Africa as primordial, irrational, and unchanging (pp. 1, 2).

This significantly accounts for the media's fixation with "tribal violence" themes in the coverage of Rwanda. A close examination of the remote and immediate causes of the Rwandan conflict would clearly show that political and economic factors, more than ethnicity or tribalism, account for the enduring antagonism between the Hutus and Tutsis (Prunier, 1995; Wall, 1997a, 1997b; D'Souza, 1996; Kamukama, 1993). Such factors as political dictatorship, poverty and foreign intervention played significant roles in the escalation of the Rwandan conflict. According to Shaw (1996), "Although it was clear that some Hutu had been among the victims of the genocide, and the RPF contained Hutu as well as Tutsi, the media could generally only describe the conflict in ethnic terms" (p. 172). Pasteur Bizimungu, himself a Hutu, was appointed President after the victory of the Tutsi-dominated RPF. To describe the conflict as entirely tribal undermines the complexity of the situation.

Not only does the tribal theme downplay the intricacy of the conflict it also presupposes the kind of solution that might be considered. Since the idea of tribe coincides with perpetual anarchy, it is no surprise that both journalists and diplomats did not conceive of a peaceful solution for the conflict. The endemic nature of conflict in "primitive societies" meant that a search for a peaceful solution to the conflict amounted to an exercise in futility.

Stereotypical frames were also prominent in the presentation of the Bosnian conflict. Observers were confused in their emotional reaction to "viewing Balkan nationalisms as anachronistic atavisms and the region as a peculiarly primitive place" (Sadkovitch, 1997, p. 123). According to Sadkovitch, "By depicting all South Slavs as troublesome tribesmen and the war as Serbian rebellion, the media defined the conflict" (p. 124). The geographical location of Bosnia-Herzegovina within Europe was enough ground to regard the people as civilized. However, their "barbaric" actions of genocide, rape and ethnic cleansing made them oddly primitive.

Conclusion

In view of the collective guilt experienced by the global community as a result of the genocides Bosnia and Rwanda and the sense that the media, politicians, and the public failed the victims of these conflicts, many are calling for new emphasis on social responsibility in journalism that is proactive and not reactive, committed and not indifferent. According to Ignatief (1997):

> A journalism that takes its framing and agenda-setting setting seriously "would have to challenge accepted definitions of newsworthiness to intervene before starvation becomes famine, before torture becomes genocide, before racist persecution becomes mass expulsion, and religious conflict becomes civil war. It would have to get to the scene, in other words, before the ambulances arrive" (p. 32).

This calls for rethinking the ethos of journalism to include definitions of newsworthy, objectivity, and social responsibility such that the universal values of peace, human dignity, sanctity of life, and freedom take precedence over the sensational and the dramatic. News media should respond to violence with the sense of the awesome responsibility that the way a story is reported will go a long way in shaping public perception, contributing to policy agenda, and influencing conflict management strategies.

Reference

Ahmadu, I. M. (n.d.). Takum crisis in miniature. In I. James (Ed.), *The settler phenomenon in the Middle Belt and the problem of national integration in Nigeria.* Jos, Nigeria: Midland Press, Ltd.

Aning, E. K. (2005). The challenge of civil wars to multilateral interventions – UN, ECOWAS, and complex political emergencies in West Africa: A critical analysis. *African and Asian Studies, 4*(1-2), 1-19.

Arno, A. (1984). Communication, conflict, and storylines: The news media as actors in a cultural context. In A. Arno & W. Dissanayake (Eds.), *The news media in national and international conflict* (pp. 1-15). Boulder, CO: Westview Press.

Bagdikian, B. H. (1983). *The media monopoly.* Boston: Beacon Press.

Bell-Fialkoff, A. (1999). *Ethnic cleansing.* New York: St. Martin's Griffin.

Bercovitch, J. (1997). Mediation in international conflict: An overview of theory, a review of practice. In I. W. Zartman & J. L. Rasmussen (Eds.), *Peacemaking in international conflict: Methods and techniques* (pp. 125-153). Washington, D.C.: The United States Institute of Peace.

Carnagie Commission on Preventing Deadly Conflict. (1997). *Preventing deadly conflict.* New York: Carnegie Corporation of New York.

Chang, T. & Lee, J. W. (1992). Factors affecting gatekeepers' selection of foreign news: A national survey of newspaper editors. *Journalism Quarterly, 69,* 554-561.

Chigas, D., McClintock, E., & Kamp, C. (1996). Preventive diplomacy and the Organization for Security and Cooperation in Europe: Creating incentives for dialogue and cooperation. In A. Chayes & A. H. Chayes (Eds.), *Preventing conflict in the postcommunist world* (pp. 25-97). Washington, D.C.: The Brookings Institution.

Collins, R. O. (2005). *Civil wars & revolution in the Sudan.* Hollywood, CA: Tsehai Publishers & Distributors.

De Waal, F. (2005). Briefing: Dafur, Sudan: Prospects for peace. *African Affairs, 104/414,* 127-135.

Drake. L. E. & Donahue, W. A. (1996). Communicative framing theory in conflict resolution. *Communication Research, 23*(3), 297-322.

D'souza, F. (1996). Communicating for peace. *Media Development, 1,* 6-9.

Entman, R. M. (1993). Framing: Toward clarification of a fractured paradigm. *Journal of Communication, 43*(4), 51-58.

Fishman, M. (1990). *Manufacturing the news.* Austin: University of Texas.

Gans, H. J. (1979). *Deciding what's news.* New York: Vintage.

Gilboa, E. (2005). Media-broker diplomacy: When journalists become mediators. *Critical Studies in Media Communication, 22*(2), 99-120.

Hatchen, W. (1992). *The world prism: Changing media of international communication.* Ames, IA: Iowa State University Press.

Ignatief, Michael. (1997). *The Warriors Honor: Ethnic War and the Modern Conscience.* New York: Metropolitan Books.

Isa, M. K. 2001). *The state and institutional responses to ethnic conflict in Nigeria: The case of Jukun/Chamba and Kuteb communcal conflicts of Takum Local Government, Taraba State.* Most Ethno-Net Africa Publications. Africa at Crossroads: Complex political emergencies in the 21st Century, UNESO/ENA. *http://www.ethnonet-africa.org/pubs/crossroadskabir.htm.* Accessed May, 18th, 2006.

Iyenger, S. & Simon, A. (1993). News coverage of the Gulf Crisis and public opinion: A study of agenda-setting, priming, and framing. *Communication Research, 20*(3), 365-383.

Jakobsen, P. V. (1996). National interest, humanitarianism, or CNN: What triggers UN peace enforcement after the Cold War? *Journal of Peace Research, 33,* 205-215.

Kahler, M. (1995). A world of blocs: Facts and factoids. *World Policy Journal, XII*(1), 19-27.

Kamukama, D. (1993). *Rwanda conflict: Its roots and regional implications.* Kampala, Uganda: Fountain Publishers Ltd.

Kent, G. (2006). *Framing war and genocide: British policy and news media reaction to war in Bosnia.* Cresskill, NJ: Hampton Press, Inc.

Livingston, S. & Eachus, T. (1995). Humanitarian crises and U.S. foreign policy: Somalia and the CNN effect reconsidered. *Political Communication, 12,* 413-429.

Lukic, R. & Lynch, A. (1996). U.S. policy towards Yugoslavia: From differentiation to disintegration. In R.G.C. Thomas & H. R. Friman (Eds.), T*he South Slav conflict: History, religion, ethnicity, and nationalism* (pp. 253-286). New York: Garland Publishing, Inc.

Mazrui, A. (2004). *Nkrumah's legacy and Africa's triple heritage: Between globalization and counter terrorism.* Accra, Ghana: Ghana University Press.

McLuhan, M. (1964). *Understanding media: The extensions of man.* New York: McGraw-Hill.

Moeller, S. D. (1999). *Compassion fatigue: How the media sell disease, famine, war, and death.* New York: Routledge.

Mohammadi, A. (Ed.). (1997). *International communication and globalization.* Thousand Oaks: Sage.

Musa, B. A. (1990). The mass media and socio-political crisis in Nigeria. In N. Alkali, J. Domatob, & A. Jika (Eds.), *African media issues* (p. 148-157). Enugu, Nigeria: Delta Publications.

Musa, B. A. (1999). *Retribalization and conflict management in the new world (dis)order: The media, diplomacy and framing of domestic implosions in Bosnia and Rwanda.* Doctoral Dissertation, Regent University, 1999. UMI Dissertation Services, 9921561.

Musa, B. A. (2004). *Journalistic ethics and conflict reporting: A critique of objectivity, advocacy, and social responsibility.* Paper presented at the National Faculty Leadership Conference. Washington, D.C., June 24-27.

Musa, B. A. (in press). *Framing genocide: Media, diplomacy, and conflict transformation.* Bethesda, MD: Academica Press.

Njoku, R. C. (2005). Deadly ethnic conflict and the imperative of power sharing: Could a consociational federalism hold in Rwanda? *Commonwealth & Comparative Politics, 43*(1), 82-101.

Obasanjo, O. (1991). Preface. In F. M. Deng & I. W. Zartman (Eds.), *Conflict resolution in Africa* (pp. xiii-xx). Washington, D.C.: The Brookings Institution.

Ottaway, M. (1991). Mediation in transitional conflict: Eritrea. *Annals of the American Academy, 518,* 69-81.

Preston, A. (1996). Television news and the Bosnian conflict: Distance, proximity, impact: In J. Gow, R. Peterson, & A. Preston (Eds.), *Bosnia by television* (pp. 112-116). London: British Film Institute.

Prunier, G. (1995). *The Rwanda crisis: History of a genocide.* New York: Columbia University Press.

Rasmuseen, J. L. (1997). Peacemaking in the twenty-first century: New rules, new role, new actors. In I. W. Zartman & J. L. Rasmussen (Eds.), *Peacemaking in international conflict: Methods & techniques* (pp. 23-50). Washington, D.C.: United States Institute of Peace.

Richards, T. & King, B. (2000). An alternative to the fighting frame in news reporting. *Canadian Journal of Communication, 25,* 479-496.

Robertson, R. (1992). *Globalization: Social theory and global culture.* London: Sage.

Rosenfield, S. S. (1993, March 3). Mercy flights, merciless results. *Washington Post.*

Sadkovitch, J. J. (1998). *The U.S. media and Yugoslavia, 1991-1995.* Westport, CT: Praeger.

Shaw, M. (1996). *Civil society and media in global crises: Representing distant violence.* New York: Pinter.

Shaw, M. & Carr-Hill, R. (1992). Public opinion and media war coverage in Britain. In H. Mowlana, et al. (Eds.), *Triumph of the image: The media's war in the Persian Gulf – A global perspective* (pp. 144-157). Boulder, CO: Westview Press.

Tehranian, M. (1992). Restructuring for peace: A global perspective. In K. Tehranian & M. Tehranian (Eds.), *Restructuring for world peace: On the threshold of the twenty-first century* (pp. 1-22). Creskill, NJ: Hampton Press, Inc.

Tehranian, M. (1993). Ethnic discourse and the new world disorder: A communitarian perspective. In C . Roach (Ed.), *Communication in war and peace* (pp. 192-192-215). Newbury Park: Sage.

Wall, M. A. (1997a). A "pernicious new strain of the old Nazi virus" and an "orgy of tribal slaughter": A comparison of U.S. news magazine coverage of the crises in Bosnia and Rwanda. *Gazette, 59,* 411-428.

Wall, M. A. (1997b). The Rwanda crisis: An analysis of news magazine coverage. *Gazette, 59,* 121-134.

Wolfsted, G. (1997). *Media and political conflict: News from the Middle East.* Cambridge: Cambrigde University Press.

Xudo, G. (1996). *Diplomacy and crisis management in the Balkans.* New York: St. Martin's Press, Inc.

Zartman, I. W. (Ed.). (1995). *Collapsed states: The disintegration and restoration of legitimate authority.* Boulder: Lynne Rienner.

Part 2: Systems Perspectives on Conflict

Chapter 5

Professional and Organizational Influences on Conflict Reporting

Ritchard T. M'Bayo, Ph.D.
American University of Nigeria, NIGERIA

Introduction

Technological innovations are no doubt the force that is pushing advances in contemporary mass communication systems and defining the production of media content in ways that are truly revolutionary. The speed at which media content is produced and disseminated is a function of technological innovations in communication. So also are the enhanced quality, creativity, and interactivity associated with contemporary mass media messages. Yet, content studies rather than studies focusing on the technology that produces the content, continue to be the primary focus of research in the field. Although media researchers have noted that studying media content alone is not sufficient to understand either the forces that produce that content or the nature and extent of its effects (Shoemaker and Reese, 1996), understanding the nature of media content remains to be the most critical aspect of any attempt to understand the impact of the media on society as a whole or on individuals and groups, as well as on cultures. Guido Stempel (2003), for example, has suggested that communication research itself is useful only if it can relate content to the communicator, audience, and effects of the content.

The preponderance of content studies is justified because by studying content we can make inferences about the other key components of mass communication systems: (1) media practitioners, (2) media organizations, (3) audiences,

(4) communication channels, and (5) media effects on individuals, on groups, cultures, and on society in general. Conversely, by studying each of these component elements, we can make inferences about the central activity of media organizations – the production of media content and the nature of that content. But it is media content and its effects that have attracted more attention and provoked more debates than the other components.

It is not surprising then that the literature in mass communication research disproportionately focuses on effects. What is surprising, however, is that the more than half century of research tradition in the field that has focused primarily on media effects has not brought closure to the debates on effects or provide definitive answers about the forces that shape and influence media content. Rather, we are faced with the onion skin analogy where every layer reveals additional layers, suggesting if not the futility of the exercise but the difficulty of tracking influences on media content in the effort to enhance our understanding of the factors that shape content and its effects. Hence, the plight of researchers in the field is somewhat like the plight of the six blind men attempting to describe the elephant. Although media scholars are not blind, the complexity of the object of inquiry and fascination for them is not different from what the elephant is to the blind men.

Systems Perspective

In broader terms, media content is a product of a society. From this perspective, media organizations are only subsystems of the general society (a social system). As such they derive their raw materials (basic information, perceptions, etc. of events) from the society (the external environment), process these materials and give the finished product back to society through a complex web of factors. As Shockley-Zalabak (2006, p. 83) explains:

> In systems theory, the organization takes in materials and human resources (input), processes materials and resources (throughput), and yields a finished product (output) to the general environment.

Media organizations are "open systems" because of the interdependence among their internal components (e.g. the editorial, production, circulation/business departments) and the mutual influence processes between media organizations and their external environment (the society). In other words, as the media influence society, so also are media organizations influenced by societal factors that ultimately will define the nature of the final product they yield to their external environment, that is, media content.

Within this context, mass communication researchers have produced a preponderance of competing and often perplexing explanations about the nature of media content (including media effects). In broad terms, however, we know that influences on media content come from a variety of sources including: (1) the socialization and attitudes of media practitioners, (2) organizational routines such as deadlines and gate-keeping processes within media organizations, (3) social institutions and forces outside media organizations such as audiences, culture, socio-political factors, advertising, etc., and (5) hegemonic tendencies such as media control through concentration of media ownership in the hands of a few powerful individuals in society (Shoemaker and Reese, 1996; McQuail, 2005). We also know that media messages by themselves may produce little or no impact on audiences. However, combined with certain intervening variables they can be a potent force in behavioral as well as attitudinal changes in audience members and their manifestations in conflict situations.

This chapter focuses on (1) the *Communicator* (media practitioners or journalists), the point of contact between the events that will be reported as news, and (2) the *Media Organization* that will carry that news to the general public. The focus on the *communicator* is designed to help us understand the attitudes, values, behaviors, constraints, loyalties and socialization of media practitioners that have implications for conflict reporting. The focus on the *media organization* is to highlight the gatekeeping processes that define media content especially as they relate to conflict reporting - what is news and what ultimately will be packaged and presented to media audiences.

Methodology

A series of focus group discussions and interviews of media practitioners and academics in Lagos, Nigeria were organized as part of the effort to assess the nature of media content relative to conflict reporting. The chapter draws also from previous research on the status of the media in English-speaking West African states (M'Bayo, 2003), which focused on Sierra Leone, Liberia, and the Gambia. Several key topical areas relative to conflict reporting were discussed under two broad categories: (1) factors relating to media practitioners, and (2) organizational factors, as follows:

Factors Relating to Media Practitioners

1. Journalistic Performance
2. Professional Development
3. Constraints
4. Loyalties – ethnic identities and religious and political loyalties
5. Value Orientations and Ideological dispositions

Organizational Factors

1. Ownership and Control
2. Media as Facilitators of Peace or Instigators of Conflict
3. Syndrome of the Oxygen of Publicity
4. Proactive or Reactive Media

The focus group discussions and interviews focused on key questions about the topical areas identified above. I also visited several media houses in Lagos, Nigeria, including the *Sun*, the *Punch*, the *Nation*, the *Champion*, and the *Guardian*. In March, 2006, I spent time at the Sierra Leone News Agency (SLENA) in Freetown, Sierra Leone. These interactions with journalists in and outside of the newsroom provided extremely useful insights into the professional lives of media practitioners and the product of their work–media content, as well as the organizational processes at play in the production of news.

Factors Relating to Media Practitioners

Journalistic Performance

Media performance is connected with media freedom and, ideally, the freedom of the press should be tied to desirable and productive outcomes of media activities. Scholars such as Denis McQuail (2005) see media freedom as a motivating factor that prepares media practitioners to "confront the powerful, take up controversial issues and even take sides or engage in advocacy."

Although media practitioners in many parts of Africa continue to operate at perilous odds with political authority, dictators and rebel leaders in conflicted societies–Zimbabwe, Sudan, Ivory Coast, etc., there appears to be a decline in the moments of anxiety that journalists experienced in previous decades when strongmen and military dictators dominated the African political or apolitical landscape. This reprieve is brought about partly by the democratization processes across the continent, including the re-emergence of political pluralism, and partly through globalization and the diffusion of technological innovations in communication.

Within this decade alone, for example, Nigerian media have emerged to be perhaps the most vibrant and the most outspoken against tremendous odds and in the face of inflexible political authorities of the past and present. Based on the preponderance of media outlets in Nigeria and the relatively decreasing incidents of harassments of journalists in the country, it is not unreasonable to speculate that the Nigerian media also appear to operate with a degree of freedom that far exceeds many others in the West African sub-region if not in Africa as a whole. This is not to suggest that the media environment in Nigeria particularly, or in Africa in general, is completely devoid of repressive measures or the inherent tendencies of political authority of the kind we were accustomed to in the late 1970s and 1980s. But those decades, the era of military dictatorships and life-time presidencies, pale in comparison to the present climate which seems to offer much hope for the future of media organizations in Nigeria, and in Africa as a whole.

Because of these factors, media practitioners generally are doing their work much better than they did in previous decades. More and more journalists have received and continue to receive professional training; in Nigeria, professional media training is requirement for those who want to enter the field, and this requirement alone appears to have paid a big dividend in the quality of journalistic performance in the country. Computer technology, and its associated capabilities, including portability, the Internet and World Wide Web, is providing opportunities to access and to retrieve information in ways that were beyond imagination only a few decades ago. And the news infrastructure within many nations and around the continent has improved tremendously, allowing a more timely and efficient production and dissemination of information. In many African countries, reporters now stay connected with their newsrooms through mobile phones and cybercafés; reporting for television no longer always requires a crew of personnel of camera persons, sound experts and journalists. Reporters are now equipped with miniature digital cameras with video capabilities which enable them to acquire broadcast quality footage of events they cover. Radio correspondents too have their digital recorders and mobile phones used for instant transmission of reports from the field. All of these are reflected in the kinds of media products we now see around the continent, partly generated from within and partly from external sources. Nigerian Television Authority (NTA) demonstrated Africa's potential capability as a key player in international communication with live broadcasts to other African countries of the inauguration of the newly elected Liberian president, Ellen Johnson-Sirleaf, in January, 2006. NTA is already transmitting quality programs into the homes of viewers in the Western world, a historical event the agency undertook in the same year.

There is still quite a lot to be done to improve the quality of performance by Africa's media practitioners. But there is renewed and invigorated hope about the prospects of the media in the continent. Whether it is print, radio, or television, Africa appears to be on the verge of taking off into the new world of international mass communication. Not only that, the continent is experiencing a media explosion that has led to the conclusion that the media in Africa have won their first freedom – the freedom to publish or establish broadcast outfits, although the second freedom, the right to free expression of ideas and the freedom of the press is yet to be won decisively (M'Bayo, 2000).

However, the report card of the media on conflict reporting is not that flattering. That was the assessment at a professional work sponsored by the African Council for Communication Education (ACCE), as media practitioners have tended "to act in very cowardly ways, refusing to confront dictatorship" and sacrificing professionalism by taking a soft approach (ACCE, 2004, p. 27). Participants at the workshop added that:

> (Media coverage) has not been very inspiring as it has tended to ignore the analysis of issues that surround conflict, the motivations and interests of various actors and a way forward in conflict management. Coverage of conflict has tended to be more sensational than directive.

Media practitioners and academics have acknowledged that "the media tend to take sides in conflict situations, loosing objectivity," and unable to define perspectives and deal with conflicts constructively (ACCE, 2004, p. 28).

Views expressed in our focus group discussions held in Nigeria and Sierra Leone suggested also a level of shallowness and a lack of comprehensiveness of reports on conflicts in the African media. These were attributed to the common refrain on the paucity of resources that hinders quality performance by reporters. Media practitioners also do not have the requisite training and understanding of the conflicts they report to their audiences. In many cases, conflict reports focus primarily on the "trigger events", which are devoid of both substance and context, but considered newsworthy because of their sensational value.

Until the late 1980s, foreign correspondents and foreign media dominated this kind of reporting. Africa's conflicts were reported to the world mainly through international media by foreign correspondents. But African journalists are now in the frontlines and in the line of fire in many crises reporting the continents conflicts to Africa and to the world.

The consensus among our discussants was that in many cases, journalists are totally unprepared, intellectually, professionally, and psychologically. Intellectually, they lack broad general understanding of the socio-psychological factors that are both the sources of happiness as well as the causes of conflicts among individuals and groups in a community. In some cases, many of the reporters assigned to conflicts are relatively young with little or no professional experience in conflict reporting.

For most reporters in Liberia and Sierra Leone, the conflicts in these countries were first time experiences in reporting about civil wars that brought about the collapse of the states with perpetrators of these magnitudes that b that provided some sort of on-the-job training. Quite naturally, mistakes were made and some journalists wittingly or unwittingly were caught in the middle of the conflicts they were reporting. These wars brought about the erosion of journalistic values as journalists became part of the conflicts they were reporting to their audiences (M'Bayo, 2005).

In the aftermath of the Rwanda genocide, for example, three journalists faced a war crimes tribunal and were found guilty for instigating thousands of Rwandans into becoming murderers; in Sierra Leone, five journalists were sentenced to death in 1998 for collaborating with the military junta that overthrew the then democratically elected government and terrorized an already war wary population. The journalists won their freedom when rebels stormed Freetown and broke the gates of the Pademba Road Prisons where they were kept on death row.

At our focus group discussions in Lagos, Nigeria, discussants emphasized the differences among the various forms of mass communication and their approach to conflict reporting. It was noted, for example, that during the struggles for independence, television was pretty much in its infancy while the print media were already part and parcel of those struggles. But even after independence and up to date, the print media have been more active, more partisan, more outspoken, more aggressive, more controversial, and perhaps even more committed than the electronic media. The latter generally have been more conservative and more cautious. Part of the reason for this might be the nature of the ownership of the various media. Until the adoption of liberal economic policies in the late 1990s, including the divestiture of public enterprises and the privatization of the electronic media, radio and television outfits were essentially government monopolies. There is, therefore, no doubt that government ownership of broadcast facilities explains the conservatism associated with radio and television, just as private ownership also partly defines the nature of the work media practitioners generally do. Besides, different media establishments have different motives, different philosophical leanings and ideological orientations beyond their manifest function as watchdogs of society.

Professional Development: Conflict and Conflict Resolution

The Department of Mass Communication at the University of Lagos is the alma mater of Nigeria's topnotch journalists who are found at almost every major news organization in the country serving as reporters, editors and managing editors. Yet, even these top performers in the Nigerian media world passed through the department without the benefit of a course in conflict reporting.

Mass Communications programs in Liberia and Sierra Leone started teaching peace and conflict only recently in the aftermath of the conflicts in these countries. It is now clear that media training should include conflict curriculum if members of the Fourth Estate are to contribute toward peaceful environments and the stability of their societies. Even related courses such as ethnic and religious studies and intercultural communication can go a long way in promoting knowledge and understanding about the potential sources of inter-ethnic clashes.

Conflict reporting is probably one of the most difficult assignments. But the complexity is often not appreciated because newsroom practices appear to focus on the trigger events, the explosive moments that capture everyone's attention for the electronic media and sell newspapers and magazines. But the societal forces, what I call *conflict incubators* which breed such incidents often do not meet the standard definitions of news, because they lack the luster and the sensational elements that make media establishments popular among readers and audiences.

For example, public lynching in many parts of the country, often carried out in broad daylight, is the method of choice by spontaneous vigilante groups who react to rumors that resonate with superstition. And there is little or no justice here for the victims; the perpetrators of these dastardly acts often go unpunished.

Even the most ridiculous and laughable rumor in some major urban centers in the country can ultimately have deadly consequences. For instance, the issuance of a new 1,000 Naira note by the Central Bank of Nigeria caused pandemonium in some parts of Lagos, including the deaths of several Nigerians who were accused of kidnappings for human sacrifice associated with the new currency.

The motivations for such behavior are embedded in certain subaltern values of the Nigerian society where superstition is as much alive in the underworld as mainstream religion is in everyday life. To be accused of any purported act as an agent of the evil spirits of the underworld could mean certain and brutal murder of persons suspected of such acts.

But Nigeria is not alone in this. The clash between fetishism and religion and its ugly manifestations is well documented in the Liberian and Sierra Leone civil wars. Alleged cannibalism and human sacrifices, widely reported in these wars were almost always said to be driven by influences and motivations of the subaltern world. Hence, it may be difficult to understand the manifest elements of conflict in these societies without understanding the latent and subaltern dimensions as incubators of conflict.

The urban centers of Nigeria - because of their unbridled vehicular and pedestrian traffic congestions – are conducive to perpetual chaos. People are fired up and psychologically stressed to the limit and could explode at any time even with the smallest act of provocation. Media practitioners should not focus only on the trigger events or on the conflicts emanating from such environments but insist upon making sure that the authorities understand the need for ameliorating the conditions that encourage tension among big city dwellers.

In other words, whether it is in the urban or rural settings, conflict reporting must focus as well on the *conflict incubators* and not exclusively on the conflicts or the events that trigger the conflicts.

Constraints

At almost every gathering of African media practitioners, the constraint on professional practice is always a hot button issue. Although the Nigerian media are much more equipped than their counterparts in Sierra Leone and the Gambia, Nigerian media practitioners equally complain about constraints on their professional activities as their counterparts in Sierra Leone and Liberia. The degree of professionalism is higher in Nigeria than in many other countries in the West African subregion. Nigeria has pioneer institutions for the training of journalists, and can boast of many prestigious national and international awards recipients, including a Pulitzer laureate. Still, in all of these countries, the inventory of constraints includes poor remunerations low levels of commitment to the codes of ethics of the profession, and low levels of development of the news infrastructure. Poor economic conditions, high illiteracy rates, poor network of highways, unreliable power supply, etc. all have implications for media operations and media content.

Loyalties – Ethnic, Religion, Tribal, Political Consciousness

Ethnicity, religious sentiments, tribalism, and political loyalties are part of the African condition. If that is the case, to what extent are African media professionals objective or fair in reporting inter-ethnic, sectarian, or tribal conflicts? African media practitioners are quick to get on the defensive with claims of neutrality in the day-to-day performance of their profession.

When thousands of rioters burned down 15 churches in Maiduguri in February, 2006 in the wake of the cartoon controversy generated by Danish newspaper *Jyllands-Posten* (published in September, 2005), the incident became a test case for Nigerian journalists. *Tell* magazine, for example, assigned two of its "best" reporters to cover the crisis "comprehensively" in both the Northern and Southern parts of the country following the explosive reactions among Muslims and Christians. And the reports were indeed comprehensive. But the magazine toasted itself not solely on the comprehensiveness of its reports on the conflict, but equally on the fact that the two reporters - one Christian and the other Muslim - filed their reports without any measurable religious biases. And although there are more Christian than Muslim journalists in these countries, African media practitioners generally are said to display a degree of sensitivity to religious matters that far exceeds their counterparts in many parts of the world.

Still, our focus group discussants admit that "spirituality" on the part of some journalists do sometimes color certain media reports. In a recent publication by the International Press Center (IPC), it was noted that religious conflicts in Nigeria pose the most severe threats to the nation, and that media reports of these conflicts betray the bias of journalists (IPC, 2006, p. 44). "The disposition of some journalists in covering religion-related conflicts as reflected in their reports is nothing but a brazing display of bias which is a deviation from the ethics of the profession" (IPC, 2006, p. 44).

The tribal and ethnic alliances among journalist are dismissed off handedly, and many journalists are said to be non-tribalistic in their approach to news. However, in Nigeria cleavages persist to the extent that there are clearly identifiable establishments characterized either as the Western Press, Arewa Press (Northern), or Ndigbo Press (Eastern). And these do not merely suggest the regional bases of these media organizations. The categorization is also based on their orientations relative to some national issues. On certain national controversies, the regional media establishments have taken markedly different positions, and often the positions are defined by the alliances to either the North, South or East.

On an individual level, there is no secret about the multiple ethnic identities within Nigerian society that sometimes pose a threat to the country's nationhood. It appears that a large number of Nigerians place their primary allegiance with their ethnic identity: "I am Ibo first," or "I am Yoruba first." It was quite revealing when a young journalist who reports the Niger Delta conflict for his magazine told me that he would take up arms to join the rebel group in that region if the circumstances permit him. On the other hand, in the smaller countries of Liberia, Sierra Leone, and the Gambia, journalists who participated in our focus group discussions appear to emphasize national identity over ethnic identity.

Value Orientations and Ideological Dispositions

War, insurgency, rebels, militias, etc. Do these words convey different meanings to different people, especially to African media practitioners in performing their professional roles?

In an interview with *Africa Today* magazine, Jewel Howard-Taylor, former wife of Charles Taylor, exiled former president of Liberia, said: "Charles Taylor is no monster. There are other leaders on the African continent that are worse and they are darlings of the West." Yet, Charles Taylor now faces charges of war crimes and on trial in a U.N.-backed war crimes tribunal set up in Sierra Leone. Despite his estrangement, Taylor still has strong support in Liberia, and his former wife, Jewel, won a senatorial seat in the New Liberian government partly on the basis of that support.

The late Chief Hinga Norman, Sierra Leone's Deputy Defense Minister until his death in 2006 was a former Commander of the Civil Defense Force (CDF) during the Sierra Leone war. He died in a Senegalese military hospital in Dakar while awaiting a verdict on charges against him for war crimes during the conflict. To his admirers he died as a "war hero." Yet, to others he was a perpetrator of war crimes. And there is no uniform opinion about the man among media practitioners or among the population at large even after his death. Robert Mugabe of Zimbabwe continues to draw heavily from the badge of a freedom fighter which he acquired during that country's protracted struggle for political independence. And he remains quite popular, as a "redeemer" of sorts among the rural masses. To his detractors, however, he is an unconscionable villain who has brought his country to ruins.

These examples are indicative of an enduring problem in conflict reporting. Almost always, the protagonists in conflicts are either insurgents, rebels, militias or terrorists to some people; to others, they are freedom fighters. The problem of nomenclature is not peculiar to the African media. It is a universal concern that reflects our value orientations or ideological beliefs as human beings. But it poses an even more serious challenge for journalists in their professional capacity. Because of this, parties involved in the Iraqi crisis, for example, do not see Western media reporters as neutral observers. Rather, they are generally perceived at best as "taking sides" and at worst as "agents of the West." To some Iraqis the "insurgents" are freedom fighters; to the media, they are what the name suggests. During the wars in Liberia and Sierra Leone, combatants identified their enemies in the media by the choice of words that media practitioners used to describe them.

Organizational Factors

Ownership & Control

How might ownership and control of media outlets influence the way African media professionals report conflict issues? The focus on ownership and control of media organization as influencing factors on media content attracted quite a bit of attention in the last 15 years or so. The debates over ownership are connected with the advances in communication technology. These innovations have not only spawned a convergence of the various forms of mass communication but have also been highly conducive toward the conglomeration of media organizations. The new forms of ownership now include what has been called vertical integration, in which a media giant can own all forms of mass communication – print, broadcast, publishing, movies, etc. - and can use each of these to help other components of the system in producing media content (Biagi, 1999, p. 21). Rupert Murdoch, for example, owns global satellite systems for the dissemination of television programs; book publishing, magazines, and newspapers, as well as television network systems in countries like the United States. He also has interest in the movie production and distribution systems.

The media barons, owners of giant media corporations, are buying out small as well as large media systems they can lay hands on in a manner that has led industry observers to predict that soon a small group of these media barons would own the major channels of communication around the world. Corporate media consolidation around the world is posing a threat to western democratic traditional values such as the freedom of the press, and the right to free expression of ideas. Having the right free expression of ideas is one thing, but without equal access to the channels of communication for expressing these ideas is quite another thing.

Huge corporate media ownership is gradually emerging in Nigeria, unlike its sister countries in the West African sub-region. Although not of the magnitude described above, the ominous signs are already on the communications horizon. The emerging media barons of Nigeria are displaying banking systems, telecommunications, and media outfits as conglomerate inventories. Even when media outfits are not part of this inventory, the corporate giants exert tremendous influence – both overt and subtle – because of their huge media advertising budgets.

In February, 2006, one of the largest Nigerian banks, Zenith, flooded the media market with its multi-million Naira advertising campaign that provoked heated debates about the ethical implications for the media. The campaign was too tempting to resist, and extremely lucrative for future relations with a banking giant that media establishments perceived as a source of huge future revenues.

Zenith Bank's campaign unfolded in the form of what media experts called "rap-around" advertising. For huge sums of money, nearly all the major newspapers and some magazines were dressed up in Zenith outfits that made them appear to unaccustomed eyes as if these publications belonged to Zenith Bank. The adverts consisted of a ¾ page on the front page, full-page inside cover, full-page inside back cover and full-page outside back cover. What space was left on the front page above the Zenith advert was taken by a so-called front page story on Zenith. The bank is reported to have also paid monthly salaries of employees of the papers that wore the Zenith gown. The giant telecommunications company, GLO, also unveiled similar advertising campaign, and the trend is gradually becoming a modus operandi of the corporate giants.

To the corporate advertiser, these campaigns were just smart business deals. Some media practitioners perceived them as a threat to journalistic integrity. How that will affect the content of these publications in the future is clear to many, and remains speculative to some both inside and outside the media industry. However, according to industry observers, "rarely does the average media consumer think of how commercial forces are shaping the content we see everyday, but these forces affect everything from what types of shows are produced to whether a news report critical of an important advertiser is downplayed or even pulled by the media corporation" (Pavlik and McIntosh, 2004, p. 49).

Public ownership of the media in Nigeria remains to be a major concern. Despite the liberalization and privatization policies of the 1990s that opened up media ownership to individuals and private companies, Federal and State Governments continue to exercise de factor monopoly over the electronic media. About 80% of the electronic media, both radio and television, are Federal or State government-owned and operated systems. During national crises and conflicts, these publicly owned and operated media facilities tend to adopt cautious or muted disposition toward these conflicts. Privately owned media, on the other hand, tend to be more aggressive, more outspoken, and more comprehensive in their coverage, and often at the discomfort of certain public figures and authorities. For example, in the wake of the spate of airline disasters in 2005 and 2006 including the crash of a Bellview plane, the National Broadcasting Commission briefly shut down a private television station based on its coverage of the disaster.

Media as Facilitators of Peace or Instigators of Conflict

Do the media in Africa serve as facilitators of peace and social harmony, or do they serve as instigators of conflict and social disharmony? One of the key roles of the media in society is to monitor the environment with the hope of identifying trouble spots or potential trouble spots and bringing these to the attention of the authorities for appropriate action. This surveillance or watchdog function through which the media provide warnings about imminent threats in a society, contributes to the stability of a nation. It helps forestall danger by promoting dialogue among a community of people over nascent or budding conflicts.

In many cases also, the media may be the only channels of communication and dialogue among and between groups involved in conflict situations. The theme adopted throughout this book is the general belief that conflict almost always involves a failure of communication. Hence, as long as there are opportunities for communication and dialogue among people in conflict situations, there are also prospects for peace and harmony. In this sense, the media do serve, among other things, as facilitators of peace in a society.

But there are also a myriad of factors associated with the media that lead to undesirable outcomes or counter productive media performance. These factors may be manifest, such as intentional and self-serving media biases, or latent factors that arise as a result of the very nature of journalistic performance and core value orientations about definitions of "news". Sometimes journalists take sides or engage in advocacy, and regardless of the motivations for doing so, they undermine expected or perceived journalistic objectivity and fairness in conflict reporting.

Syndrome of the Oxygen of Publicity

Do the media, unwittingly or otherwise, allow their systems to be used as platform for the propagation of the views of *militias, terrorists,* and other such groups in society? The *oxygen of publicity* is former British Prime Minister, Margaret Thatcher's brainchild. Thatcher coined the phrase to address this question in 1985 during a hostage crisis involving a commercial airliner, Trans World Airlines (TWA). Thatcher was referring to the unfettered media obsession with conflict situations coupled with the no-holds-barred coverage given to perpetrators of extreme violence. Such media attention does not only fuel conflicts but also sustains the morale of those who engage in violent confrontations (M'Bayo, 2005) "From this point of view, the media intentionally or unintentionally have become life-sustaining platforms for terrorist groups and those who engage in extreme acts of violence as a form of political communication" (M'Bayo, 2005, p. 23)

Almost a decade before Thatcher's controversial concept of the *oxygen of publicity*, several major media organizations had not only acknowledged this media dysfunction, but were also talking about what they had called the *contagion* effect, implying that the more media attention/coverage given to terrorist groups the more the incidents of terrorism by the same or similar groups of perpetrators of terrorist acts. Responding to these realities, these media organizations formulated proactive policies and guidelines designed to avoid creating platforms for terrorists while reporting newsworthy events involving these groups. The following are samples of newsroom policy guidelines of selected western media organizations:

(1) CBS Network

An essential component of the story is the demand of the terrorist/kidnapper, and we must report those demands. But we should avoid providing an excessive platform for the terrorist/kidnaper. Thus, unless such demands are succinctly stated and free of rhetoric and propaganda, it may be better to paraphrase the demands instead of presenting them directly through the voice or picture of the terrorist/kidnapper.

(2) The Courier-Journal and the Louisville Times

... our approach will be one of care and restraint. We will avoid sensationalism in what we write and how we display it, taking care not to play the story beyond its real significance. We will make every effort not to become participants in the event. We will resist being used by the terrorists to provide a platform for their propaganda.

(3) The Sun-Times and Daily News (Chicago)

Coverage should be thoughtful and restrained and not sensationalized beyond the innate sensation of the story itself. Inflammatory catchwords, phrases and rumors should be avoided. Demands of terrorists and kidnappers should be reported as an essential point of the story but paraphrased when necessary to avoid unbridled propaganda.

Do African media organizations have written policies to guide reporters in the coverage of terrorist acts? No such policy was acknowledged in our various discussion groups in Nigeria and Sierra Leone. However, there are quite a number of valuable publications that provide useful guidance for journalists relative to conflict reporting. One such publication cited earlier in this chapter is the IPC (2006) booklet on *Conflict-sensitive journalism: Reporting religion-related conflict*. The publication is a major contribution to enhancing our understanding about the intricacies and complexities of religion and their implications for journalists who report on religious conflicts.

No matter how big or small a conflict, and regardless of its nature, when conflict erupts, there is always a desire on the part of the factions to communicate something beyond the confines of their circles of control. Reporters need to understand what these factions wish to communicate, how they wish to communicate, and the motivations for what they wish to communicate to external audiences. In war situations such as the Sierra Leone and Liberian experiences, conflict reporting should be couched upon a clear understanding of the tactics and strategies used by combatants; recruitment, funding, arms purchase, membership, leadership, alliances, objectives, demands, and the subaltern factors that drive and sustain these conflicts.

Sometimes the demands and objectives of those involved in such conflicts are firm, self-serving, with little or no room for compromise; at other times such demands may be fluid and mercurial, and confusing to outsiders. During the wars in Liberia and Sierra Leone it took quite some time before people began to realize that the conflicts were as much about diamonds and other natural resources as they were about the quest for good governance. Part of the solutions ultimately then were found by designating these mineral resources as conflict or *blood diamonds* and by mounting a huge international campaign about these resources that fueled of the conflicts.

Proactive or Reactive Media

There are no newsroom policies concerning conflict reporting. This fact alone means that every new conflict will present new challenges to reporters. It also means that news organizations are vulnerable to becoming mouth-pieces for individuals or groups of individuals involved in conflicts. The staying power of news organizations, the ability to remain focused on issues as they pass through the conflict phases, or as they escalate or de-escalate, is weak. Hence, the focus on trigger events, which are merely the explosive moments of the conflict.

Quantitatively, African media coverage of conflicts is commendable. Hardly a day passes without some front page story about one conflict or another. Qualitatively, however, such coverage is often "shallow" and lacks "context". This is attributed partly to resource problems, lack of training, and security concerns for journalists.

Covering the Niger Delta crisis in Nigeria effectively will require tremendous investments of resources for the safety of reporters and the quality of their reports. Traveling around the troubled spots in the area require speed or motorized boats. Kidnappings are routine in the area, and real or perceived enemies in the media organizations pry the area at tremendous risk. Only global media giants like CNN and the BBC, with their huge resources – experienced investigative reporters with sophisticated equipment including satellite capabilities - have been able to penetrate the area and bring the Niger Delta crisis to audiences around the world.

Summary and Conclusion

With a primary focus on conflict reporting, this chapter demonstrates the complex interplay of factors that define the production of media messages. From a systems perspective, all forms of media content are manifestations of the society in which they are produced. As business enterprises, media organizations adopt marketing principles that guide the manufacturing of consumer products, including supply and demand. This is especially so with regard to the privately owned and operated media organizations. This perspective, referred to as *commodification,* or news as a commodity, views media messages as products to be bought or sold in the media market (McQuail, 2005, p. 550). As a commodity, concepts such as product exclusivity, supply and demand, timeliness, etc. explain why this product is the way it is. Unlike other consumer products, however, the socialization of media workers, their value orientations, etc. as we have discussed in this chapter, are part of the myriad of factors at play in the production of news.

But if media organizations are subsystems of the larger society, as we have proposed in this chapter, then media content is equally a product of the sociocultural forces of society. These value orientations and ideological beliefs certainly influence media content. Conversely, media messages also help define or redefine these values. Conflict reporting, therefore, is shaped both by factors peculiar to media organizations and by the values of society.

Note:

1. I am using the concept *conflict incubators* to mean the environments that breed conditions (incubating factors) that ultimately lead to violent conflict(s). Incubating factors include extreme poverty, societal stress, inequalities, injustice, etc. The higher the level of these incubating factors, the more pervasive they are, the more likely that a society (an environment) will explode into violent conflict. A whole nation or parts of it (or even one's home – in a domestic sense) can be conceived as a conflict incubator depending on the prevalence of these factors. My conception of an environment as a conflict incubator is inspired by Dr. Bruce Perry's (1997) article, "Incubated in terror: Neurodevelopmental Factors in the 'Cycle of Violence.'"

References

African Council for Communication Education (ACCE). (2004). *Workshop report on media and conflict.* ACCE: Nairobi, Kenya.

Bagdikian, B. H. (2004). *The new media monopoly.* Boston, MA.: Beacon Press.

Baran, S. J. and Davis, D. K. (2003). *Mass communication theory: Foundations, ferment, and future.* Belmont, CA.: Thompson.

Biagi, S. (1999). *Media impact. An introduction to mass media, 4th edition.* Belmont, CA: Wadsworth.

International Press Centre (IPC). (2006). *Conflict-sensitive journalism: Reporting religion-related conflict.* Lagos, Nigeria: IPC.

McQuail, Denis. (2005). *Mass communication theory, 5th edition.* Thousand Oaks, CA.: Sage.

M'Bayo, R. (2005). Public face of public violence: Media and conflict in Africa. *Ecquid Novi,* 26 (1), pp. 21-32

_____ (2003). Status of the media in English-speaking West African states. In *Encyclopedia of international media and communication,* pp. 523-542. New York: Academic Press.

_____ (2001). The press in Africa: Prospects for the new millennium. In Ritchard M'Bayo, Chuka Onwumechili, and Robert Nwankwo, editors. *Press and politics in Africa,* pp. 25-42. New York: Mellen Press.

Pavlik, J. V. and McIntosh, S. (2005). *Converging media: An introduction to mass communication.* New York: Allyn and Bacon.

Perry, B. D. (1997). Incubated in terror: Neurodevelopmental factors in the cycle of violence. In Joy D. Osofsky, editor, *Children in a violent society.* pp. 124-149. New York: Guuilford Press, pp. 124-149.

Shockley-Zalabak, P. S. (2006). *Fundamentals of organizational communication: Knowledge, sensitivity, skills, values, 6th edition.* New York: Allyn and Bacon.

Shoemaker, P. J. and Reese, S. D. (1996). *Mediating the message: Theories of influences on mass media content, 2nd edition.* New York: Longman.

Stempel, G. H. (2003). Content analysis. In Guido H. Stempel, David H. Weaver, and G. Cleveland Wilhoit. (2003). *Mass communication research and theory.* pp. 209-219. Boston, MA.: Allyn and Bacon.

Chapter 6

Media Messages, the Academy and the Internet

Ali A. Mazrui, Ph.D.
State University of New York at Binghamton, USA

In the transmission of messages and images between the West and the developing world there are three means of communication which are particularly powerful. These means of communication are, firstly, Western-style education in our schools and universities; secondly, the mass and news media, including the international news agencies (like Reuters); and, thirdly, the new phenomenon of the Internet and its role in globalizing information.

Between the West and the *rest*, images are distorted by a number of biases which have become imbedded in the mass media and in Western-style educational institutions worldwide. These biases include *race* (a White tragedy is more newsworthy than a Black one); *gender* (what men do is more newsworthy than what women do); *city* (urban news gets more attention than rural); *exotica* (witchcraft stories are more fascinating than news about modern medicine in Africa); *negativism* (bad news gets more extensive coverage than good news); *elitism* (power and wealth attract publicity).

When comparing the media with higher education we shall pay special attention to these six biases (racial, male, urban, exotic, elitist and negativist). But when we subsequently turn to the phenomenon of the Internet we shall switch to the seven functions of culture–the functions of perception, evaluation (judgment), communication, motivation, identification, stratification and the political economy of production and consumption.

The Western media not only inform the West about the rest of the world; it also inform the rest of the world about the rest of the world. For example, what Africa knows about China comes disproportionately from Western sources. Chinese newspapers have no correspondents near Rwanda and Somalia and have to rely on Western information. What India knows about Latin America comes disproportionately from Western sources.

Indigenous knowledge of India is seldom discovered by Koreans; it is discovered by the West. Indigenous knowledge of Africa is seldom discovered by the Chinese, but is discovered by Westerners. The West continues to be the great go-between, between its own knowledge and the knowledge of others, but it has also been the great go-between between other societies as well.

Unfortunately the West is a flawed go-between - a messenger with its own agenda, subject to its own special biases.

In the treatment of non-Western societies, both Western higher education and the Western media are guilty of sins of commission and sins of omission. Sins of commission involve coverage without balance or accuracy. Sins of omission concern the many big stories which are left out of the press or the syllabus because they do not occur in Europe or North America. Very often racial gradation is at play in determining news value. Sins of omission include Third World stories which are marginalized in the dominant international media because of *where* they occur or because of the international ranking order of which countries matter or which races are important.

Pro-democracy movements in Eastern Europe from the late 1980s where heavily covered in the Western Press. These were the years of the "Velvet Revolution" and the exciting demonstrations in Prague, Budapest, Warsaw and Bucharest. Western television screens and university classes allocated massive time to what were regarded as momentous historical events.

Similar pro-democracy activism occurred in Africa from the late 1980s into the 1990s. Indeed, over 30 countries in Africa have legalized political opposition since 1990. Military regimes have sometimes been forced to go to the polls (as in Ghana); founding-fathers have been defeated at the polls and gracefully bowed out of presidential office (as in Zambia and Malawi); one-party systems have been forced to become multiparty (as in Kenya, Tanzania and Côte d'Ivoire). And yet these developments in Africa, involving Black people, received far less publicity in the Western media and the Western classroom than did either the Tiananmen Square demonstrations of 1989 in Beijing or the anti-communist uprisings in Eastern Europe from 1988 onwards. Knowledge across cultures is hampered by varying degrees of cultural and racial prejudice.

More specifically, international media coverage of the non-Western world is distorted by race and other biases. Is higher education similarly vulnerable? There is first the *exotic bias* which makes reporters look for "tribes", "warlords", and "fundamentalists". The vocabulary of discourse is affected by this quest for the exotic. Knowledge across cultures is *exoticized*.

Secondly, there is paradoxically the *urban* bias in Western reporting about the non-Western world. One would have thought that the search for the "exotic" would make Western reporters more interested in living among African villagers. Unfortunately, that is not the case. Western reporters need to be within easy reach of urban telephones and fax machines. Knowledge across cultures is therefore distorted by comparative access to faxing facilities and e-mail equipment.

Thirdly, there is the *elite bias* in international reporting, partly arising out of the urban bias. Reporters and journalists scramble for interviews with those who are locally powerful and mighty and even dissidents are usually from the elite sector of society–the rebels against the privileges of their own class. Rebellious university and college students in the Third World, for example, are usually members of the elite or of a new presumptive elite. Knowledge across cultures focuses on the views and activities of those elites perhaps disproportionately–often showing a total lack of knowledge about the views of the millions of peasants in the countryside.

Then there is the perennial *male bias* in almost all forms of knowledge across cultures, including scholarly and media-coverage. The views and activities of women are grossly under-reported and very often under-valued. Only a small fraction of the news in major newspapers of the world is about women. Quite often, one has to turn to the entertainment pages or the gossip columns of the more popular press to see any female names at all.

The *generation bias* is perhaps the most culturally obstinate of the distortions in knowledge across cultures. Adults write about adults. In some African societies the majority of the people are under the age of 16 years. And yet this is the unreported majority in much of the international media. Is it also academically under-studied? The views, activities and aspirations of *teenagers* generally are under-represented and barely understood. Teenagers only become a major focus of media attention when they become violent against each other, or become a threat to the wider society. Knowledge across cultures suffers from this primordial generation gap.

And then there is the *negativist bias* in privately owned print-media and electronic media. On balance, over two thirds of the news reported from the Third World is bad news - consisting of military coups, rebellions, drought and famine, violence, repression, and violations of human rights. It is as if the Western media had decided that, except for the miraculous attractiveness of Nelson Mandela as a human being, good news from Africa was no news at all! Has the world of scholarship been more objective than the media?

If privately owned media has a built-in *negative-bias*, state-owned media has a *positivist bias.* A bad harvest in that particular society is minimized in state-owned media–and a good harvest is disproportionately enlarged.

Knowledge across cultures is compromised under both biases.

Is there a middle position between public ownership and private ownership of the media which can reduce bias? The British Broadcasting Corporation (BBC) is a public-owned corporation, but financed from a special separate tax (licensing fee for television and radio). The Corporation is also run by an independent Board of Governors - who were less "independent" during the Thatcher years than they have normally been. On the whole, the BBC has achieved a considerable reputation for fairness and balance - fostering less biased knowledge across cultures than average in the media.

The Academy: Pride and Prejudice

Which of these *biases* in knowledge are shared by university education in the Western world? There are certainly sins of *omission* galore in the curricula and syllabi of higher education in the Western world. The debate about multiculturalism in the United States has arisen because of inadequate attention being paid to cultures other than European ones in American schools. This chapter was written against a background of some of those tensions on multiculturalism - especially with *Eurocentrism* on one side and *Afrocentricity* on the other. Knowledge across cultures is at a stalemate in such situations.

What about *sins of commission* in the higher education curriculum? The *exotic bias* is certainly omnipresent when Islam is associated primarily with terrorism and *jihad,* with camels and veiled women, or when Africa is discussed in relation to female circumcision, polygyny and tribal chiefs. Unfortunately this *exoticization* has sometimes provoked excessive defensiveness from the non-Western world. The UNESCO *General History of Africa* even banned the use of the word "tribe" from all the eight massive volumes of its series. African intellectuals - defending themselves against the West - fell into the Western trap of denying the African continent any association with "*tribality*".

In fact, there may be a stronger case for persuading Europe to re-accept the word "tribe" and "de-primitivize" it. The exotic of the distant "Other" may become part of the European "Self" - from Serbia to Scotland.

The *urban bias* in the study of distant societies can also be as big a hazard in higher education as it has been in the media. But in higher education this particular bias varies from discipline to discipline. The urban bias in the study of non-Western societies is strong in such fields as political science, written literature, philosophy, sociology, and even economics. On the other hand, such fields as anthropology and ethnography, are almost by definition, much more representative of the rural populations. Such disciplines have a natural *rural bias* in their approach to knowledge across cultures.

In higher education, the *elite bias* is inevitable in the *end product.*

University graduates in most societies are either members of an already existing elite or members of a presumptive elite. That is what higher education seeks to produce. But what about the process of higher education? Does it promote understanding of less privileged groups or cultures–or simply greater insensitivity? Educational reformers would need to address those issues and find solutions which promote both less elitist *social* attitudes within societies and less elitist *cultural* attitudes across societies.

The *male bias* in higher education is a little less pronounced than it is in the media, but it is still significant enough to be of concern. In the United States some universities have recently been led primarily by women. This would include the author's Binghamton University, part of the State University of New York, where both the President and the Provost are women, and where several of the Deans have also been. But there is no room for complacency in higher education either. While women are well represented in the administrative class, they are still seriously underprivileged in the professorial and academic posts and activities. How has knowledge across cultures been affected by this gender-gap? Perhaps a world of women Presidents and male professors would disseminate balanced knowledge across cultures less widely than a world of male presidents and female professors. Scholarship has to be *androgynized.*

Unlike in the media, the *generation bias* in higher education is part and parcel of the enterprise. Tertiary education is divided between students (usually much younger) and dons and professors (sometimes much older). The question has also persisted whether the younger generation should have greater say in higher education than they do. They certainly do now have more say than they did before the 1960s. Has the limit been reached?

There are those who believe that the technological decline of the United States has been due to the relaxations of the 1960s. There are those who believe that we must entice the brightest young Americans into the challenging world of new incentives. Should the relaxations of the 1960s be reversed in the universities across Africa also?

As for the *negativist bias* of privately owned newspapers, this does raise questions as to whether dissident students' opinions are expressed independently or in response to organized stimulation in Western institutions. University administrators are normally more conservative than academic faculty, and these faculty in turn have tended to be more conservative than the students. Campus debates are often more clearly demarcated than debates in the mass media.

But what about debates on the Internet? The mass media throughout the world have increasingly established websites and made themselves available on the Internet, as well as in hard copy. More and more African newspapers can now be read or consulted on the web thousands of miles away from their headquarters. Also more and more radio and television stations in the Western world have now made some of their programs available on the Internet internationally.

The Internet Between the West and Islam

Let us begin by relating the Internet to the seven functions of culture which I first expounded in my BBC Reith Lectures, *The African Condition* (broadcasted in 1979 and published as a book in 1980).[1]

1. **Culture as Lenses of Perception:** How do we view the world? How has the Internet affected our perception?[2]

2. **Culture as Standard of Judgment:** What are the criteria of good and evil, beautiful and ugly? Where is the Internet leading us?[3]

3. **Culture as a Means of Communication:** How do we transmit messages to each other? What are the signals? What impact has the Internet on communication?[4]

4. **Culture as a Spring of Motivation:** What constitutes incentives and disincentives as cultural values? What are the inducements? Where does the Internet come into the arts of persuasion?

5. **Culture as a Basis of Identity:** Who are the "we" and who are the "they"? How is this determined by culture? Are the boundaries fudged by the Internet?

6. **Culture as a Ladder of Stratification:** Who is up, who is down in gradation? Class, caste, rank, status and the *digital divide* are all part of this ladder of stratification.

7. **Culture as a Pattern of Consumption and a Mode of Production:** What are our tastes and consuming patterns and our methods of productivity? How are they facilitated, fostered or hampered by culture? Is the Internet a help or a hindrance?

In addition to these seven functions of culture, our paradigm of African media is also based on the concept of Africa's Triple Heritage–a concept which visualizes contemporary Africa as being driven by the dynamic of three civilizations, *Africanity*, *Islam* and the *West*.

How does the Internet relate to these three legacies of *Africanity, Islam* and *Western* culture?

In the context of sub-Saharan Africa, the legacy which in the twentieth century was the most resistant to Western science and technology was perhaps the Islamic legacy. In Nigeria the Northern Muslim resistance to Western technology in the twentieth century helped to create a situation in which the Igbo in the North were too successful in modern jobs for their own good–ranging from Westernized professionalism to motor-car garage mechanics and radio specialists.[5] Was this one of the causes of the Nigerian Civil War of 1967-1970?[6]

The question arises whether in today's Nigeria Northerners are slower to adapt to the computer and the Internet than Southern Nigerians? Will a new digital divide in Nigeria aggravate the old north-south divide?[7]

The Internet as Motivation

The use of the Internet as an instrument of *persuasion* and *inducement* was captured in the 1990s by the American bubble of that decade: the Instant-businesses of *.com*.[8] Trade and commerce flourished on the Internet.

Pornography found new computerized ways of enticing minors to sexual dates with strangers.[9] Has the Internet increased the risk of statutory rapes? On the other hand, it may be easier for lonely people to find on the Internet companions and even potential marriage partners–as in the films *"LETTER BOX"* and *"YOU'VE GOT MAIL"*.[10]

The Internet as Communication

I.   The Internet as Communication

(a)   *speed of Internet communication:* This is faster than anything before the Internet. One example is the Henry Louis Gates debate on the television series, "Wonders of the African World", which escalated rapidly.

(b)   *scale of Internet communication:* The extensive reach is to the outer extremities of human habitation. The sun never sets on the slopes of the Internet. The explosion of the debate on Salman Rushdie's novel, *The Satanic Verses*, published in London, rapidly ignited Muslim demonstrations from Kaduna to Karachi, from New Delhi to New York. There were significant casualties in South Asia.[11]

(c)   *Diversity of Internet communication:*
       (i)   verbal communication
       (ii) pictorial communication
       (iii) sound communication
       (iv) codified and numerical communication

But is the Internet harming older forms of communication? Will the quality of the prose decline because of the imperative of speedy response? Are linguistic style and quality suffering? Will the courtesies of verbal communication decline in the brevity of Internet "lingo" and e-mail prose? Are newspapers on the web a pale shadow of their hardcopies?

Certainly in the debate on the Internet about Gates' TV series, "Wonders of the African World", the urgency of each response destroyed many of the usual courtesies of correspondence.[12]

The quality of politeness in a magazine debate between Wole Soyinka and Ali Mazrui in the carefully premeditated exchange in *Transition* magazine in 1991 was in stark contrast to the scurrilous rudeness of the Internet debate between Soyinka and Mazrui in 1999.[13] Does the Internet promote levels of rudeness much greater than manifests itself in a regular magazine?

The Internet as Stratification

The new computer technology and the Internet may be inaugurating new kinds of stratification and new types of reform. For quite a while now distribution of real power in the world has been based not on "who *owns* what" but on "who *knows* what." It has not been the power of property but the power of skill which has been the ultimate international arbiter. Oil-rich Third World countries have not been able to exploit their own petroleum resources without the skills of Western companies and their engineers.

The latest area of skill concerns computer communication and the Internet. Is there uneven distribution of these skills in the world in a manner which is potentially divisive? One major university in the United States may have more computer literate people than the whole of an African country of nearly ten million people.[14] This is the *digital divide* on the world scene–the divide between the computer-skilled and computer-challenged. Literacy as a source of empowerment has shifted from the print to the computer medium. There is the lingering danger that cyberspace will consolidate the gap between the haves and the have-nots, and the forces of global apartheid between the West and the Rest. African access to newspapers and programs on the Internet is growing, but very slowly

One additional anxiety is whether the digital divide will coincide with the racial and class divide even within societies. This issue is beginning to rear its head in the United States. While access to the computer technology is tied to socio-economic background, there is evidence to suggest that even within the same income brackets, African Americans are being left behind in computer skills at least temporarily.[15] Part of the problem is attitudinal: Many young African Americans at school regard proficiency in computers as a form of "imitation of white kids"–and therefore distasteful.[16] Peer pressure continues to discourage many bright African American young men (more so than young women) that mathematical skills are a white man's lifestyle and therefore to be shunned. It is partly such pressures which run the risk of making the digital divide coincide with the race divide. It is already estimated that African Americans constitute less than five percent of computer programmers in the USA.[17]

If African Americans lag behind whites in computer skills, are Asian Americans ahead of whites in such skills? Is culture an important variable in the cultivation of certain skills? There is evidence of considerable mathematical and computer prowess among South Asians and East Asians, especially Indians and Koreans. The number of Asians qualifying for immigration to the United States on the basis of skills has risen dramatically in recent years. The digital divide is affecting comparative migrations of people.

The Information Superhighway has created new dialectics between cultures: calculus friendly cultures vs. calculus challenged cultures; *cultural numerophobia* vs. *cultural numberophilia*; calculus friendly cultures in Nigeria vs. North Korean Americans vs. Italian Americans; Jewish Americans vs. African Americans.

The Internet between Secular Perception and Religious Judgment

In the twentieth century Westerners have debated whether the Protestant Reformation was the mother of capitalism in Europe or whether the Christian Reformation was itself a child of earlier phases of the capitalist revolution. Max Weber's book, *The Protestant Ethic and the Spirit of Capitalism*, puts forward a powerful case for the Reformation as the mother of capitalism rather than a child of economic change.[18] On the other hand, other thinkers have identified pre-Reformation technological inventions as part of the preparation for both Protestantism and capitalism. Francis Bacon identified the compass, the printing press and gunpowder as three forces which have transformed "the appearance and state of the whole world."[19]

In our own day Francis Robinson, Professor of History at the University of London, has placed the printing press centrally in the Protestant movement and within the Catholic counter-offensive. Professor Robinson has argued:

> Print lay at the heart of that great challenge to religious authority, the Protestant Reformation; Lutheranism was the child of the printed book. Print lay at the heart of the Catholic counter-offensive, whether it meant harnessing the press for the work of Jesuits and the office of Propaganda, or controlling the press through the machinery of the Papal Index and the Papal Imprimatur.[20]

The question which has now arisen is whether what printing and the first Industrial Revolution did to Christianity, the Internet and cyberspace and the third industrial revolution will do to Islam. The printing press shook the foundations of Christian tradition. Will the Internet and World Wide Web shake the foundations of Islamic tradition? How will the flow of new information affect issues of faith?

Christianity under the shock of earlier socio-technological changes produced its own Protestant movement. Will Islam in the course of the twenty-first century give birth to its own Martin Luther and its own John Calvin, if not its own King Henry VIII? It is arguable that in Sunni Islam there has not been a major shake up in theology since the death of Abu Abd Allah Malik, the Muslim jurist and founder of the Maliki *madh'hab*, in 795 C.E. Will the new technology of information re-open more widely the doors of *ijtihad*? Will the technology of World Wide Web allow for the emergence of new *madhahib*? Are the gates of Islamic creative synthesis being reopened?

Henry Louis Gates Jr. of Harvard University founded a few years ago an Internet website, *Africana.com*, which he hoped would unify Black people worldwide "in a way that the Catholic Church defined European culture in the Middle Ages."[21] Will the Internet do for the Muslim *ummah* what Gates hopes it will do for the people of African descent?

In some respects the Christian Reformation was a return to the basics of Christianity. Likewise the information revolution may help Islam realize some of its earliest aims more effectively. The first casualty may be national sovereignty – the *shrinkage of sovereignty* in the wake of the Internet and cyberspace. The printed word may have been playing a major role in the construction of nationhood and in reinforcing national consciousness. Computer communication, on the other hand, is contributing to the breakdown of nationhood and may be playing a role in the construction of other trans-ethnic communities.[22]

While the first industrial revolution of capitalist production and the Christian reformation became allied to the new forces of nationalism in the new Western world, the third industrial revolution and any Islamic reformation will be increasingly hostile to the insularity of the nationalism of the state. The second revolution was in global exploration and imperial trade.

Islam and the information revolution will be allies in breaking down the barriers of competing national sovereignties. The new technology will give Islam a chance to realize its original aim of transnational universalism. The Internet and the World Wide Web could in part become the Islamic superhighway.

Many Muslims have already risen to this challenge of the new information age with Islamic Resource Guides on the Internet, Cyber Muslim Guides, Islamic Information and News Network, and Web Servers with Islamic material.[23] What all this means is that the area of shrinkage of sovereignty and in the area of death of distance Islam and the new information revolution are, on the whole, historical allies. And contrary to some assumptions that "modern communications would engender a new and generally Western-oriented cosmopolitanism, they are predominantly spreading the idea of a freedom that is translated by the receivers as endogenous freedom–including freedom to rejoin one's real kinship (whether larger or smaller) and to re-examine the validity of one's own ancient social values."[24] Civilization is pushing towards new frontiers of creative synthesis.

The Internet and the Gender Question

Black American experience demonstrates women stealing a march in education over men. We bear witness to girls in the classroom and boys in the prison cell.[25] The gender-divide may be deepened by the digital-divide in favor of women.

On the gender question the Muslim world has alternated between two doctrines. One doctrine has been to treat genders as separate but equal. The United States before 1954 attempted to implement the constitutional doctrine of treating Whites and Blacks as separate but equal. However, by 1954 the Supreme Court was ready to conclude that separation of the races resulted in or perpetuated inequality. In the momentous decision of Brown versus the Board of Education in 1954, the U.S. Supreme Court at last rejected the doctrine of "separate but equal" for the races. Racial segregation became unconstitutional.[26]

If "separate but equal" was untenable for races, why should the doctrine work for genders? Because genders live together in homes in a way in which races never used to do in the United States. Every man's mother is a woman. So are men's wives, daughters and granddaughters, aunts and other female relatives. So separation of genders is inevitably moderated by family ties. This is a qualitative difference from the separation of races. The gender doctrine of "separate but equal" could theoretically survive the new information revolution.

Under the new technology the computerized *hijab* is at hand: Women can more easily stay at home and still be equal computer workers. This possibility is amply demonstrated by a woman from the British Asian community in her response to a BBC radio presenter who expressed concern that the computer can, in fact, enhance the isolation of women of that community. In the words of the woman interviewee:

> Well, if they're just stuck at home then why not use the Internet to get connectivity with people across the world...Internet can also provide an access for women to possibly start up providing their own services–maybe hobbies that they're interested in or business that they have a keen eye on. For example, if they have a hobby in maybe cooking, or, you know, they have collected a series of recipes over the years–they could then use those recipes–publish them on the Net and start some sort of business. There have been a number of cases in the past where women actually started a business up using the Internet.[27]

The Internet, in other words, is gradually abolishing the distinction between home and the work-place. This is a whole new depth of creative synthesis.

The Internet as Identity

In spite of these new freedoms and new possibilities afforded by the Internet, however, the technology is not necessarily free of existing systems of inequality–economic, political and social. It is in this regard that Jon Snow has commented:

> The Internet is a male world, a lone male world. It is self-seeking, self-serving and self-fulfilling. Surfing shuts out all other physical and environmental contact and takes the user deeper into a world of 'me', 'my choice', and 'fuck you'. Not for nothing is the Net peppered with porn; not for nothing do statistics show that most surfers are men and that the Internet holds less attraction for women.[28]

This may be coming less and less true in the 21st century. But the Internet continues to raise anxieties and issues about both individual personal lives and relationships and more collective social and cultural experiences.

How is the Third World to relate to these "negative" consequences of the Internet and computer communication? How can we ensure that synthesis is creative and not self-destructive? There is now a growing movement among developing societies which are struggling to decolonize scientific (and other forms of) knowledge–perhaps as part of a bigger project, the decolonization of modernity itself. The decolonization of computer communication is seen as a core component of this quest. As Nasim Butt explains for the Muslim part of the Third World:

> As information technologies are becoming the basic tools of manipulation and control, access to them will become the decisive factor between control and power or manipulation and subservience. In this powerful dilemma, the way forward, surely, is to modify the technology at the point of use to meet the needs and requirements – the goals – of Muslim society. All such modifications must, of course, be done in accordance with the ethical dictates of Islam.[29]

Butt, in fact, devotes a full chapter to elucidate an alternative scientific paradigm that is supposedly more in keeping with the values of Islam and to provide some broad guidelines for the Islamization of science and technology.[30] Can similar things be done to reconcile science and technology to African values? The quest for the decolonization of science must continue.

The Internet and the Brain Drain

As more and more Africans become highly skilled in computer technology and usage, some of them will migrate to developed states. As matters now stand, the costs of this kind of brain drain are for the time being weightier than the benefits for African countries. What should constantly be borne in mind is that the intellectual penetration of the south by northern industrial states must one day be balanced with reverse intellectual penetration by the south to the think tanks of the north. Given the realities of an increasingly interdependent world, decolonization will never be complete unless penetration is reciprocal and more balanced. Part of the cost may well be the loss to Africa of highly skilled African computer experts.

Conclusion

We have attempted in this chapter to place the Internet in the context of the much wider issues raised by it. The equipment is a piece of modernity in the technological sense. Its functions in a society have identifiable modernizing consequences. The computer helps to secularize the science of explanation, to technicalize analytical approaches to data, and to promote a capacity for estimating the future and planning for it. The broader context is the role of culture as *perception, motivation, stratification, judgment, communication, identity*, and patterns of *consumption and production*.

In some of these cultural areas there is a level at which journalists and scholars are in an adversarial relationship, within or outside the Internet. Scholars regard reporters as too shallow and manipulative of facts: journalists regard scholars as too "academic" and lost in the mists of the Ivory Tower. And yet are scholarship and journalism different facets of the truth? When is scholarship a precondition of good journalism? When is journalism a stimulus for new research and an ally in the quest for funding?

In the course of the transmission of Western knowledge, the media and higher education are more often allies than adversaries. But in the mission to promote indigenous and traditional knowledge, the media and higher education are more often adversaries than allies. Electronic media and the Internet from the twentieth century and beyond have tended to be disproportionately carriers of Western values and perspectives. Indigenous non-Western values and skills have often been ignored, derided or distorted by the electronic media. Mainstream paradigms are helped by the mass media; minority or non-Western paradigms are often victimized by the media. Sins of both omission and commission have been committed.

In the age of the electronic media, audio-visual techniques can be mobilized to serve not only Western traditions of higher education, but also indigenous traditions worldwide. A revolution in ideas is needed. The biases of exotica, urbanity, elitism, gender and the generation gap have to be transcended.

It is also worth remembering that the best members of the mass media are, almost invariably, graduates in higher education. And the best informed scholars are those who maintained sophisticated contact with the media. A symbiotic relationship is discernible at this level. It can be tapped for the greater good of society and the human race.

Finally, let us remind ourselves that the West still dominates global flows of information. Indeed, Western information often masquerades as universal knowledge. But several distortions are recurrently at play in this masquerade. News and information have often been transmitted through the distorting lenses of *race, sexism, urbanism, elitism, negativism* and *exotica*. The Western ropetrick continues to be remarkably effective. It is time for non-Westerners to break the spell of their own credulity.

Notes

1. These functions of culture have been explored in detail in Ali A. Mazrui, *The African Condition: A Political Diagnosis* (London and New York: Cambridge University Press, 1980), pp. 47-68; also see Ali A. Mazrui, *Cultural Factors in World Politics* (London and Portsmouth, NH: J. Currey and Heinemann, 1990), pp. 7-8.

2. The Internet, for instance, offers opportunities for people to see news from other sources, rather than be captive to commercial or government sources. For example, according to a *Pew Internet & American Life* Project report, many Americans (almost a quarter) sought images from the Iraq occupation that US networks and newspapers thought were too horrific. More details about this report, and links may be found at http://www.pewinternet.org/PPF/r/130/report_display.asp (Report dated July 8, 2004, accessed July 14, 2004).

3. People are even willing to put up their photographs on the Internet to have people rate them! For one such example, see the site http://www.hotornot.com/ (Accessed July 14, 2004).

4. E-mail, perhaps the most prominent and most used feature of the Internet for communication, is under threat because of spam (junk or commercial e-mail). As John Breyault, Research associate at the Telecommunications Research and Action Center, a nonprofit group in Washington, D.C., said in a news article: The ever-increasing flood of spam is causing consumers to turn away from e-mail as a means of communication. Many people we hear from are contemplating getting off the Internet altogether. See Katie Hafner, "A Change of Habits to Elude Spam's Pall," *The New York Times* (October 23, 2003).

5. According to one analysis, although the northern emirs tried to have schooling open to all, these efforts were not successful because the British Colonial Office was afraid that educated people would be harder to rule; see Peter K. Tibenderana, "The Emirs and the Spread of Western Education in Northern Nigeria, 1910-1946," *Journal of African History* (1983), 24, 4, pp. 517-534.

6. For further reading on this war, consult Zdenek Cervenka, *The Nigerian War, 1967-70: History of The War, Selected Bibliography and Documents* (Frankfurt Am Main: Bernard & Graef, 1971).

7. An overview of the North-South and other cleavages bedeviling Nigeria may be found in *The Economist* (January 15, 2000), pp. 14-15.

8. Relatedly, see D. Quinn Mills, *Buy, Lie, and Sell High: How Investors Lost Out on Enron and the Internet Bubble* (Upper Saddle River, NJ: Financial Times Prentice Hall, 2002).

9. For a brief overview and commentary on the general subject of pornography on the Internet, consult JoAnn di Filippo, "Pornography on the Web," in David Gauntlett, Ed., *Web.Studies : Rewiring Media Studies for the Digital Age* (London; New York : Arnold, co-published in the United States of America by Oxford University Press, 20000, pp. 122-129. The concern about adults preying on minors was part of the reason Microsoft's MSN closed chat rooms in 28 countries in 2003, and nearly a quarter of 550 teens surveyed in 2003 said they had been contacted on-line by a stranger for a meeting in person. See Sebastian Rupley, "Keep Your Kids Safe," *PC Magazine* (August 3, 2004), pp.101-102.

10. Internet dating is one of the few success stories of Internet business. A detailed look at this phenomenon may be found in Jennifer Egan, "Love in the Time of No Time," *New York Times Magazine* (November 23, 2003).

11. See S. Hazarika, "12 Are Killed in New Delhi Protesting 'Satanic Verses,'" *New York Times* (February 25, 1989).

12. See "The Mazrui - Gates Debate," *Africa Update,* (Winter 2000), Vol. VII, Issue 1, accessed online at
http://www.ccsu.edu/AFSTUDY/updtWin2k.htm (accessed July 24, 2004).

13. Some examples of the exchange between Mazrui and Soyinka, see, for instance, the web-sites http://igcs.binghamton.edu/igcs_site/dirton3.htm and www.westafricareview.com/war/vol1.2/soyinka.pdf (accessed July 24, 2004).

14. An August 2001 report by Mike Jensen on "African Country Internet Status Summary Aug 2001" (at http://www3.sn.apc.org/africa/afrmain.htm#Table) revealed that Ethiopia, with a population of about 59 million had only about 2,500 dialup subscriptions to the Internet! (accessed August 4, 2004).

15. White households are more likely (55.7 percent), to own a computer than Black households (32.6 percent) in the United States. Still, for an optimistic outlook on this digital divide, consult the data and conclusions in the fourth in a series on the "digital divide," *Falling Through The Net: Toward Digital Inclusion* at http://www.ntia.doc.gov/ntiahome/fttn00/Falling.htm#2.1, published by the National Telecommunications and Information Administration in October 2000 (accessed August 5, 2004)

16. Political circles have been abuzz in 2004 about Barack Obama, the Kenyan-American political star from Illinois, who is apparently on his way to victory in the Illi-

nois Senate race and becoming the third elected African American in that body since Reconstruction. In an electrifying speech at the 2004 Democratic Boston convention, Obama said: . . .children can't achieve unless we raise their expectations and turn off the television sets and eradicate the slander that says a black youth with a book is acting white. See David Broder, "Democrats Focus on Healing Divisions: Addressing Convention, Newcomers Set Themes," *The Washington Post* (July 28, 2004), p. 1, for more details on the speech.

17. Table H-1 in the National Science Foundation publication *Women, Minorities, and Persons with Disabilities in Science and Engineering: 2004* (NSF 04-317) (http://www.nsf.gov/sbe/srs/wmpd/start.htm, accessed August 14, 2004), shows that in 2000, it was estimated that only 4.4 percent of scientists and engineers in the US labor force were black, and only 3.3 percent in engineering occupations were black. Table H-5 in the same publication reveals that of the approximately 2.03 million math and computer scientists, only about 148,000 were black.

18. See Max Weber, *The Protestant Ethic and the Spirit of Capitalism* (New York: Charles Scribner's Sons, 1958).

19. Francis Bacon, *Advancement of Learning and Novun Organum.* (New York: The Colonial Press,   1899), p. 366.

20. Francis Robinson, "Technology and Religious Change: Islam and the Impact of Print," Inaugural Lecture given March 4, 1992, at Royal Holloway and Bedford New College as Professor of the History of South Asia, University of London. Reprinted in *Modern Asian Studies* 27, 1 (1993): 229-251.

21. *The Wall Street Journal* (February 17, 2000), p. 1.

22. See relatedly, W. B. Wriston, "Bits, bytes, and diplomacy," *Foreign Affairs* 76, 5 (Sep-Oct 1997), pp. 172-182.

23. For more on Islam and the Internet, consult Gary R. Bunt, *Virtually Islamic: Computer-Mediated Communication And Cyber Islamic Environments* (Cardiff: University of Wales Press, 2000).

24. Erskine B. Childers, "Amnesia and Antagonism," in Farish A. Noor, Ed., *Terrorising the Truth: The Shaping of Contemporary Images of Islam and Muslims in Media, Politics and Culture.* (Penang, Malaysia: Just World Trust, 1997), pp. 140-141.

25. Andrew Block and Virginia Weisz have noted: the experience of a half-century since finds Brown's [Brown v. Board of Education, 1954] promise of improved educa-

tional opportunity as painfully out of reach as ever for our most disadvantaged children. Nowhere is this more brutally apparent than in the crisis afflicting high-poverty school systems, where African American males are now more likely to end up in jail or in prison than in college.

Andrew Block and Virginia Weisz, "Choosing Prisoners over Pupils," *The Washington Post* (July 6, 2004), p. 19.

26. For analyses of this decision and implications, consult, for example, the following: Charles J. Ogletree, Jr., *All Deliberate Speed: Reflections on the First Half Century of Brown v. Board of Education* (New York: W. W. Norton, 2004); Derrick Bell, *Silent Covenants: Brown v. Board of Education and the Unfulfilled Hopes for Racial Reform* (Oxford and New York: Oxford University Press, 2004); and Richard Kluger, *Simple Justice: The History of Brown v. Board of Education and Black America's Struggle for Equality* (New York: Vintage Books, 1977, 1975).

27. Simeon Yates, "English in Cyberspace," in Sharon Goodman and David Graddol, Eds., *Redesigning English: New Texts, New Identities* (Milton Keynes, England: Open University; London; New York: Routledge, 1996), pp. 109-110.

28. See Jon Snow, "All the News that Fits on Screen." *Guardian* (London), Sept 19, 1995. But women are catching up; for some discussions, see, for example, Ann Travers, *Writing The Public In Cyberspace: Redefining Inclusion On The Net* (New York : Garland Pub., 2000), pp. 152-155 and Aliza Sherman, *Cybergrrl! : A Woman's Guide To The World Wide Web* (New York: Ballantine Books, 1998).

29. Nasim Butt, *Science and Muslim Societies* (London: Grey Seal, 1991), p. 62.

30. Further discussions on this topic may be found, for example, Sohail Inayatullah, "The Future of Science in the Islamic World," *American Journal of Islamic Social Sciences*, 14 (Fall 1997), pp. 77-81 1997; and for an appraisal of the "Islamization of science," see Aliyu Usman Tilde, "A Critique of Islamization of the Sciences: Its Philosophy and Methodology," American *Journal of Islamic Social Sciences* 6 (September 1989) pp. 201-208.

Chapter 7

Global Media and Changing News Practices

Mohammed Musa, Ph.D.
University of Canterbury, NEW ZEALAND

Introduction

A notable consequence of the post 1990 neo-liberal ascendancy is the emergence of multinational corporations as central actors in nation states. This development has gone hand in hand with the neo-liberal focus on the market system instead of public authority as the new orientation in social life. In the media sector it meant the termination of a public service oriented media and its replacement with a market governed, commercially oriented media. This collective romance with the market system has resulted in the emergence of multinational media corporations that were clearly the international arm of an expanding global capitalist enterprise whose main motive is profit rather than public service.

The outcome of this development is the dominance of public space and discourse by media accountable to profit seeking directors rather than the public. This problem is compounded by the lack of a countervailing force as the public sphere is eroded in most countries.

While media practitioners are always quick to rationalize their actions as the outcome of professional judgment guided by a commitment to professional values, this chapter will argue that such values are increasingly undermined as a result of media's profit orientation. Specifically the chapter inquires into the global media coverage of conflict to point out how market orientation has brought changes in news practices that undermine professional values.

Indeed, in previous wars such as World War II direct censorship undermined journalistic credibility in reporting the conflict. In contemporary wars however, as seen in the Iraq war, indirect censorship has become the norm as media are integrated into the war structure. Both the press pool and the embed system manifest the changing values of news practices but also the incorporation of journalism into a control structure that undermines the very principle of independence and objectivity.

The chapter also argues that whereas Africa is home to over 60% of world ethnic conflicts the global media have underreported such conflicts with serious implications for their perception and resolution. Yet the underreporting of African conflict, the paper argues, is a manifestation of the asymmetries of globalization. While the unprecedented alliance of military, media, and market is resulting in changing news practices the prioritization of certain conflicts rather than others point to the unequal development that characterizes neo-liberal globalization.

Neo-liberal Globalization and the Global Media

Neo-liberal globalization has become a contemporary buzzword or phrase whose proponents argue, will usher prosperity and stability for humanity. Even though the planting of its seeds pre-dates 1990, the emergence of neo-liberalism as a dominant global system came with the disintegration of the Soviet Union and the termination of the Cold War. Neo-liberalism in this era referred to the new thinking or guideline that promoted private businesses and corporations' domination of social affairs with little or no opposition. Governments of nation states become facilitators in the domination of capital. McChesney adds that:

> Neo-liberalism is more than an economic theory, however. It is also a political theory. It posits that business domination of society proceeds most effectively when there is a representation democracy, but only when it is weak and ineffectual polity typified by high degree of depoliticalization, especially among the poor and working class. (2001 p. 10).

Seen this way therefore, the new World Order under globalization is said to promote multinational corporations as the new rulers of the world (Pilger 2002). The removal of trade boundaries between nations of the world turns a hitherto large universe into a global village for convenient capital flow and investment by multinational corporations. This pan capitalism (Tehrenian 1999), according to its advocates, enhances global economic integration that will benefit humanity through unprecedented economic boom. In reality though, major beneficiaries of globalization remain to be the multinational corporations as even the United

Nations acknowledges that the poor of the world are getting poorer in the new era.

Yet it is important to understand the enabling factors that have facilitated and enabled neo-liberal globalization to thrive, namely, global institutions of finance capital such as the World Bank and IMF and the World Trade Organization (WTO.) Regulatory policies by these agencies made member nation states to remove all boundaries to trade but also to ensure deregulation of their economies where governments cease to be the principal player in the economy.

The integration of world economies and the ascendancy of neo-liberal capitalist democracy is also enhanced by sophistication in new communication technologies especially digitization and satellite that have not only made instant communication possible but also made a change from analogue to digital transmission possible. This meant that text, sound and picture can all be delivered through the same vehicle leading proponents to celebrate the elimination of distances of time and space.

Writers such as Fukuyama (1992) have optimistically heralded the era of globalization as one ushering the end of history or ideology where humanity will experience happiness.

The reality of globalization for most Third World countries however, has been intensification of balance of payment deficit, domestication of poverty and general crises of under-development such as illiteracy, ill health and reduced life expectancy so that the average experience for the majority is one of 'hell on earth'. The numerous wars fought around and within such countries are also symbols of such underdevelopment features. For majority of African citizens globalization has merely exacerbated the two-tier structure of society where few enjoy affluence and majority languish in deprivation and poverty.

It could be stated at this point that two distinct pictures have emerged with a central role for the media institutions. First, neo-liberal globalization that has brought huge advantage of new markets and competition elimination for western-based MNCs is good news for Western economies. On the other hand, the development is bad news for a larger proportion of the world that lives in its margins and at its receiving ends.

The central role of the media in this development can be seen as two-fold. First, through advertising and other cultural productions the media create market for Western goods manufactured by the multinational corporations whose increasing size is, according them enormous power of dominance. Second, the picture and impressions of the crises of underdevelopment brewing in the Third World are disseminated and told by these media who are not neutral in the first place, in so far as the unfolding crises are concerned.

For in the era of neo-liberal globalization the world has seen the emergence of what can be described as truly global media. Like other multinational enterprises, these giant media owe their emergence to deregulatory policies by global institutions of Finance capital i.e. the IMF, World Bank and WTO as well as governments around the world that lend support to such measures. The transition from analogue to digital transmission of data has added to the enabling environment for these media to reach global markets. Their investment in sophisticated communication technologies has granted them access to global markets and audiences.

Today, production and distribution of media content from news to advertising and music CD, movies and children television etc, the broad range of material that is aptly referred to as symbolic goods, are dominated by no more than ten giant firms that are based in North America and Europe. These include AOL-Time Warner, Disney and Rupert Murdock's News Corporation. Others within the bracket of global media include Viacom and the German based Bertelsmann.

These mostly Anglo-American media are the giants that promote liberal ideology and market economics around the world. Their overwhelming dominance through investment in latest technology and appropriation of the economy of scale has made it impossible for a viable countervailing force to emerge. Their activity through advertising support has also promoted the rise of commercial broadcasting around the world.

Media Power in Contemporary Discourse

The mass media have always remained the most central source of news and information to most people of the world. Their centrality as news and information sources is increasing for two reasons. First, the appetite for distant news has increased because of what is called global interdependence. Yet majority of world citizens both in the developed and developing world can hardly afford to travel outside their locality. This makes the modern media the most ideal institution or sources of providing the distant news.

Secondly, proliferation of media outlets as well as urbanization and the emergence of internet technology have also enhanced people's media dependence. Who we vote for in an election, what coloration a national foreign policy takes, what resources are allocated to what sector in public service are largely influenced by media information as principal raw material in meaning construction and opinion formation. Earlier studies have long established a relationship between issues considered important by the media and issues that the public also consider important. (See McCombs and Shaw, 1972, Gandy, 1982; MacQuail, 1987). Even though they do not directly tell us what to think, the media are found to direct our minds on what to think about.

Contemporary discourse on media and public opinion is especially concerned with such enormous power of the media for two reasons. First, that by being the major vehicles for advertising transnational goods and services as well as becoming powerful corporations themselves as contemporary trends in mergers and acquisitions show, the media are very important capitalist institutions.

Secondly, being the informational arm of transnational capitalism as well as possessing such cultural power as in the dissemination of symbolic goods makes the media no longer neutral arbiters in the kind of information they disseminate. (See Garnham, 2002; Gitlin, 2002, Murdock and Golding, 2002) The transformation of news, especially crisis news, into infotainment, spin, spectacle, and hype, can not be separated from the transformation of the media into economic empires, a trend that was consolidated by the coming of neo-liberalism as a global system. This was confounded as diversity usually guaranteed through alternative voice or forum of public expression is missing out of the new game plan. News is diluted with entertainment so as to retain a reasonable and sizeable audience for the advertiser.

The concentration of means of public expression and debate in few powerful private hands undermines pluralism both because cost of entry is prohibitive to new and financially weak participants and also because the established media have destroyed a plain field of competition. Yet Keane sees the existence side by side, of such strong private media and other public media as essential basis for pluralism and therefore countervailing effects. This way, Keane argues, private media can act as watchdogs on the State even as the public media perform similar role on private interests.

> Market-influenced media can also function as important countervailing forces in the process of producing and circulating opinions; they are not only economic phenomena, but sites of signification that often run counter to opinion-making monopolies operated by churches, states and professional bodies.(Keane in Boyd-Barret and Newbold. 1997, p. 264)

But the enormous financial power of the private media puts them in an enviable position of setting the terms of competition thereby blurring the dichotomy of public/private.

Changing News Practices and the Reproduction of Hegemony

The economic boom of the post war period in the mid 18th Century has changed the nature of Journalism as professional standards emerged to eliminate the earlier partisanship so that the media can "reach every one" and "offend no one" (See Knight,1985).

Subsequently, developments both within and outside Journalism have continued to undermine detachment from vested interests as professional journalism evoked. The result of such changing news ideology is the reproduction of hegemonic viewpoints in public discourses.

Within journalism itself, the commitment to the principle of objectivity through constant reference to, and reliance on persons of authority as the most reliable sources of news undermines diversity and is inimical to countervailing mechanisms. Critics have argued that this tendency reproduces a skewed version of social reality; that it legitimates powerful voices as the dominant voices and opinions in society (Hall et al., 1978; Schelesinger, 1979, Golding and Elliot, 1978).

In contemporary journalism, investigation as an essential ingredient has been undermined in several ways. First, the rise of press affairs departments within government departments has resulted in official viewpoints finding their way into news bulletins as people in authority transfer the burden of accountability to such Press Officers.

In private establishments Public Relations departments produce Press releases that feed image-making material into media news.

The number of both Press Relations Officers or departments and Public Relations units in private establishment has risen a great deal over the years. This unusual trend has undermined investigative journalism and blurred the dividing line between official position and objective viewpoint.

The threat posed by such developments to democracy and peace in modern societies is very serious indeed. As McChesney (2001) observes:

> If there is ever a point to measure the caliber of a free press, it is at moments like these when the fate of democracy or war and peace hang in the balance. In moments of crises, the media system needs to generate factual accuracy on every thing relevant. It needs to provide a wide range of debate over policy proposals to address the crisis. And it needs to provide the necessary background and context so that citizens can make sense of the problems and determine the best possible solution. (p. 1)

The Construction and Dissemination of Crises News

The claim to impartiality and independence as essential ingredients of professional journalistic values are especially challenged and threatened in reporting military conflicts. Governments as well as military institutions have interest in closing off certain information especially deemed to aid the enemy or affect troops' morale or reduce support for the war. Journalists on the other hand, have interest in gaining access to information that they want to disseminate to the public as audience.

While journalists evoke professional values and their commitment to these as evidence of the conflicting interests between them and government this paper will analyze key issues and developments in conflict reporting that tend to undermine established journalistic values of impartiality, objectivity and detachment and, thereby, blurring the dichotomy between reporters' interest and that of government or armies in times of crises.

Even though we shall argue that factors such as emergence of the press pool, propaganda, embeds, and militainment, etc, have brought changes into journalists' professional ideologies it is not the first time journalism practice is going through changes. Early journalism that predates the 18th century economic boom in Western Europe was partisan and made no claim to values of objectivity and detachment from constituencies of interests. Detachments through tenets of objectivity were evidence of turning point in the history of the profession.

The commitment and claim to professional ideologies and values by journalists serve several purposes since the change that ended partisan journalism of the early 18th century. First, it professionalizes the practice of journalism and deflects public criticism of bias by claiming allegiance to such professional values. Secondly, it reassures audiences in their dependence on journalists and the media as the only ones professionally positioned to inform and educate them from a neutrally disinterested position. Thirdly, the claim to professional ideologies also insulates journalists from sources who would want to manipulate or censor media workers or even challenge unfavorable coverage. Fourthly, and very importantly too, there is a historically strong commercial motivation to the professionalization of journalism. The economic boom that followed the postwar reconstruction in the mid 20th century brought competition among businesses who, all needed to reach out to clients with information about products or services. For the press, it was an opportunity to capture advertising revenue, but that could only be maximized if the audience was not restricted. This need for larger audience was not going to be guaranteed by the prevailing partisan orientation and constituency allegiance of the press. For newspapers to 'reach everyone and offend no one' proprietors came together to device codes of practice and values that professionalized the practice of news reporting through the elimination of partisanship.

However, studies into media production processes have questioned claims of objectivity and impartiality that guide media production. Such studies have, instead, come to opine that contrary to the claim by journalists who 'objectively hold the mirror' for society to see itself, social reality is either 'constructed', 'manufactured', 'decided', 'bent' or 'made-up' etc. (See Golding and Elliot, '78, Gans, '78 Schlesinger, '78 etc).

Other studies whose perspectives especially guide our analysis of changing journalistic values in relation to conflict point to the increasing trend of media concentration into fewer hands for the purpose of enhancing profit through a focus on rating for the benefit of the advertiser (Garnham,1986; Murdock and Golding, 1996; McChesney, 2004).

This paper explores how specific features of journalistic values in processing and reporting conflict such as the rise of the press pool, embedding and militainment, are all leading to the commodification of war through the production and dissemination of war news as spectacle that is, in the final analysis hegemonic and in the general interest of capital.

The press Pool,   Public Relations and Propaganda

In the PR-isation of war news, coalition forces in the two Gulf Wars as well as in Kosovo have created the trends of war reporters' pool where about a hundred or so reporters are given daily briefing by an appointed officer or commander who 'carefully' provides an account of developments on the war.

The experience of United States in the Vietnam War has made the public opinion side of war as important as the battle side of it for two reasons.

First, home support for the war must be kept intact else the growth of anti-war consciousness among the home civilian population will result in political pressure to end the war. Secondly, television images and sounds that are not 'properly managed' can also bring about condemnation of the war and growth of anti-war consciousness. In doing this though, a process of Public Renationalizing of the conflict is employed before the first shot is fired. In line with this, a villain is made of the enemy through a personalization process. This was seen in the two gulf wars as well as the war in Afghanistan where Saddam Hussein and Osama bin Laden were the folk devils that have unleashed deaths and horrendous sufferings on innocent people that must be saved from their wrath. This process of vilification and victim creation as an ingredient of war propaganda is intended to play an important role in the mobilization of civilian consciousness for support of the war.

The discourse of victims to be saved plays on the moral consciousness of the public so that when military spokespersons address journalists using the vocabulary of 'victim' to be saved from a 'villain' it is accepted without much questioning for two reasons. First, the pressure of timeliness as a news value imposes limitations on how much time journalists can waste digging up a piece of information. Second, the information is narrated within a familiar discourse, one that also falls within the understanding and sensibility of the public to whom it will be eventually reported.

What has become routine viewing for audiences around the world who followed the Iraq war through any of the major television networks is the daily press briefing by the coalition forces spokesperson. In this forum correspondents of different media outlets (mostly accredited) are given 'full' briefing of accounts and progress of the war. And because such briefing is made by a military officer everything said must have the stamp of approval of superior officers. The implication of this to investigative reporting, to journalistic values is enormous.

For it is an attempt at managing news in the same way that press relations departments in government parastatals are doing to censor news and shield public officers from accountability (Musa, 1996, Golding and Elliot, 1978).

Yet the press pool in military conflicts has a history that dates back to the First World War. During the First World War, censorship operated through the Press Bureau, set up to provide information favorable to the war effort and to suppress any information that was not. (Freedman, 2004, p. 64)

At the time though journalists reacted to this form of censorship through the emergence of 'unilaterals', correspondents who shunned such press bureaus and investigated the war in their own way but with grievous personal risks. It is true that today's reporting environment is more competitive compared to the one during the world war and, that technologies such as the Internet provide possibilities of alternative perspectives. However, the major networks with the biggest resources and widest outreach succumb to the official sources of news. In both the 1991 Gulf war and the 1998 Kosovo war where NATO forces intervened directly, the pool system was a major news source but also a major means of news management.

The deployment of television in reporting war has enhanced the role of the media in the execution of war because the medium's immediacy coupled with sound and image gives it reliability and impact among the viewing public in times of crises. The treatment of US marines in Somalia in 1990, the portrayal of the atrocities of apartheid in South Africa in the 1980s were both said to be the major turning points in the histories of the crises and struggles in Somalia and South Africa respectively. The abuses of jailed Iraqis in Abu Ghraib by American and British soldiers in the second Gulf War also earned the coalition a further moral deficit.

With all this knowledge as well as the Vietnam experience where US attributed its failure in that war to negative media coverage the stage became set for very careful execution of future wars so that:

> Long term forward planning now includes significant media and political hegemonic strategizing. Warfare planning now builds into its core a media policy. (Louw 2001, 178)

The first Gulf War became the theatre for the unfolding of orchestrated mediazation of war as Saddam Hussein, a hitherto US ally is now vilified and demonized. The commencement of the ground offensive saw effective media management as journalists were formed into pools and, away from the battlefield were periodically fed with information on war proceedings by appointed military spokesperson or PRs and interviews were conducted with military protection so that: Military PRs ensured a 'flow of favorable military sourced information to fill vacuum created by media restrictions (Louw, 2001, p. 178). Even at this point, we must not lose sight of the fact that the PRization of war has an economic dimension that we shall return to later.

Embeds as Death Knell of Objectivity

At this point, it is also important to highlight the second development in the art of war reporting that has enormous consequence on public understanding and perception of war. Called embedded journalism, it refers to the practice where journalists are embedded with fighting troops to bring 'eyewitness' account of battlefield encounters. This feeds to the pressure of live reporting of war as a spectacle.

Moreover, the fact that embedded journalists are protected by the troops they are covering introduces an obvious bias first, of a responsibility to and camaraderie with the troops offering such protection. For when such journalists are embedded (or in bed) with troops their protection, accommodation and general welfare are in the hands of the troops and not their networks. If they don't slant news reports as reciprocal gesture they could do so for fear of the guns surrounding them. The implication of the embedding system on professionalism can not be more graphic than BBC's Gavin Hewitt's disclosure of his experience as an embed when he picked out a target for his troops.

> I shouted across to the captain "that truck over there-I think these guys are going to attack us." I thought the Captain would have sent one of the tanks to try and investigate....eventually the truck went up-boom-like this. And I was absolutely horrified. I thought for a moment that these could have been innocent civilians. I could have made a mistake and at that moment I thought "are we getting too close to this?"...And of course all the unit was delighted. From then on the bonding grew tighter (Hewitt G quoted in Miller, 2004, p. 11)

Moreover, to the extent that journalists are embedded to the coalition troops (in the Iraq war) and not to the Iraqi troops is a violation of the principle of balance that is essential ingredient of the journalistic values.

Secondly, the position in which an embedded journalist moves is the same as that of the troops the journalist is covering. This implies therefore, that the embedded journalists report from the physical angle of the troops and not the enemy's so that in the final analysis the news reported by an embed becomes a skewed version of the reality of war. All this goes to show that beyond the claim of 'eye witness' account that embedding system professes, it is actually an evidence of the incorporation of journalism into official system of control and censorship.

Militainment and the Commodification of War

The routine journalistic pressure of working around dead lines in news production that has become a central feature of contemporary journalism has been intensified in the era of globalization of news. Round-the-clock news production and dissemination which, in television, was started by the CNN has now spread to every continent of the world. The globalization of 24 hour news was made possible by two factors. First, the power and influence of Anglo-American media in setting and exporting professional agenda could be said to play a central role in transplanting this culture beyond western boundaries. Secondly, the export of profit oriented, western commercial model of broadcasting has replaced a public service oriented model. Both factors however, are directly linked with the ascendancy of neo-liberalism as a global system that glorifies the market system in place of public service as the best way of organizing social existence.

The outcome of this development is that 24 hours news is found not only with CNN and BBC but also Star news in Asia, Zee News in India, CTTV in China, Globo News in Latin America, AIT in Nigeria, Al-jazeera in the Middle East and SABC in South Africa etc.

With research indicating that serious programs such as news and current affairs are losing audience to other mainly entertainment-oriented programs there is mounting pressure on such serious programs to recapture their lost audience. This pressure becomes especially immense given the new commercial and profit orientation of the media in a market system. This orientation requires the media to deliver a sizeable but also quality audience to the advertiser. One of the outcomes of this development is the blurring of the distinction between commercial departments and news departments as both operate within an overall profit goal.

Conflict and crises, and especially war, have all the ingredients of news by virtue of combining essential elements of news values such as unusualness, drama, episode and event orientation etc. But to ensure audience rating war news and battlefield military activities generally, now need also be entertaining. Moreover, new trend in mergers and acquisitions have seen the fusion of major news networks with conglomerates with major stakes in the entertainment industry. CNN for instance, under a multi-billion dollar merger is now part of AOL-Time Warner reputed to be the world's biggest media entertainment outfit. In the same light, ABC is said to now be part of the Disney Empire. This development is said to impact on news content where show business and entertainment generally is being prioritized (Bennet, 2003). The effect of this is that quality programming takes the back seat and that media outlets compete in offering more and more entertainment so as to capture audience. Clearly this undermines diversity and choice that should be available to citizens if they are to form rational judgment and perspectives on issues.

The increasing trivialization of news through larger and longer entertainment doses predicated on the desire to deliver audience to the advertiser is reinforced by and reinforces the event orientation of news. In this regard, conflicts and wars are presented in the news devoid of the social context in which they occur. That most of conflicts are happening in Third World countries or are said to be caused by people of Third World origins does not evoke investigation. Instead, the audience is inundated with images of poverty stricken, 'undemocratic cultures' that are threatening the civilized world. The social context of those people's underdevelopment and their violent resistance to all forms of exploitation do not get mentioned. The perspective developed and disseminated by the global media becomes the dominant perspective that is picked up, built upon and elaborated by other genre such as movies, soap opera etc so that people of certain background will always appear in predictable roles as trigger happy, murderers, hijackers and criminals (Sa'id, 1997). And as Bordieu observes, reality through television construction becomes:

> A series of apparently absurd stories that all end up looking the same, endless parades of poverty-stricken countries, sequences of events that, having appeared with no explanation, will disappear with no solution-Zaire today, Bosnia yesterday, the Congo tomorrow. (1998, p. 7)

As television entertainment is delivered to our living rooms the war spectacle is also delivered to us devoid of the blood and termination of lives that characterize wars. In what is now known as a major classic in the militainment melodrama in the second Gulf war, an Iraqi doctor gives a graphic account of the theatrics called the 'rescue of Jessica Lynch' by the American troops. He disclosed that the American troops were fully aware that Private Lynch was in the hospital along with other immobile patients and that, the entire hospital was unarmed but still, the Americans mounted the 'rescue mission' in Hollywood style, cameras, action, direction, etc. 'It was like a movie involving Sylvester Stallone' according to the Iraqi doctor. And in the news all the networks featured 'the rescue of Jessica Lynch' by American troops who, according to President Bush, 'never leave a comrade behind'. Yet, after all the sensation it came to be revealed that Private Lynch was not under threat or danger in the first instance and so, the claim of rescue initially reported to world television audience was a military rehearsed and prepared story and an indication of the implications of embedding to journalism.

African Conflicts in a Changing World Order

The end of the Cold War that was expected to supposedly usher in an era of unipolarity in world politics and international relations has impacted greatly and in different ways on conflicts in Africa.

In the former Soviet Union and Eastern Europe, the cold war era was a relatively more stable period in terms of ethnopolitical conflicts in the sense that a dominant communist ideology had suppressed ethnic rivalries and competitions through a socialized distributive mechanism of basic resources and privileges:

> It was ideology that bound historically hostile people together; now old rivalries have re-emerged, and neighbors have again become antagonists fighting for power, status, and control of adjacent territories. –Communism in its ideal form also instilled a sense of collective responsibility and solidarity that overcame more parochial identities. The transformation of socialist societies into predatory capitalist societies has led to a sense of alienation and isolation and an increased emphasis on narrow group interest and self-interests. This increased sense of isolation has been circumvented by a heightened ethnic awareness and, in some states, a growth in intolerance toward members of others groups (Harff, & Gurr, 2004, p. 10)

The historical landscape of the post Cold War era is one replete with instances of ethnopolitical tensions and conflicts in the former Soviet block and Eastern Europe generally. These include the Russians endless war against Chechnya, the Kosovo, Albanian crisis etc. Ethnic groups that have felt marginalized or discriminated against in one form or another have become politically active. A world survey of such groups puts the post-communist state as second to Africa in the number of such groups seen as potential indicator of ethnopolitical conflict.

The Cold War politics of bipolarity had had a different effect on ethnopolitical conflicts in the African continent. The two hegemonic blocks on which the Cold War hinged, the communist block and the capitalist western alliance, played significant roles in promoting military conflicts on the African continent as both the United States and Soviet Union aided opposite factions in such conflicts both militarily and financially. At the time each power block used the intervention either as a way of checking the expansionist drive of the other or of extending its own influence or both.

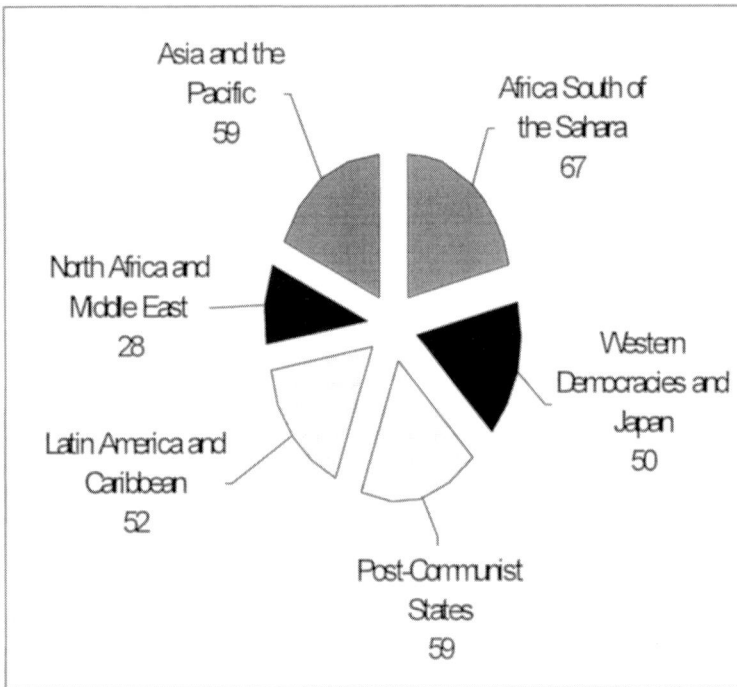

Figure 1: Politically active ethnic groups by region, 2001
Source: Barbara, H. and Gurr, T.R (2004, 4)

Understanding the nature of those conflicts both within the African region and in the international community was, to many people, dependent on media representations of the conflicts. Yet, owing to the nature and character of the leading international media of the cold war era the coverage of such African conflicts was either scanty or lopsided in line with the block hegemonic interest that the reporting media belonged. The effect of this was either the conflicts in Africa were obfuscated or reported devoid of context and therefore improperly understood thus making genuine intervention at their resolution difficult. Those that attempt to report differently paint the conflicts as stemming from indigenous factors of a crises ridden continent and people.

The role of the Cold War power blocks in African conflicts does not end just with military and financial assistance to feuding groups. Historians have argued that a weak state translates into a weak or absent authority to impose order and administer social welfare. And as Carter observes:

> The origins of contemporary intrastate conflicts can be traced to the Cold War when political elites deliberately undermined formal bureaucratic institutions but were nonetheless kept in office by repression and the financial and military support of the superpowers. As these kleptocrats accrued massive personal wealth through state channels, the standard dichotomy between the private and the public realms effectively dissolved. (Carter, 2003, p. 21)

Carter further opines that the deliberate withdrawal of welfare packages like security and economic stability was employed by the rulers, and this, in turn, leads to coercion and corruption. While the method initially weakens the material base of potential challenges others were guaranteed of patronage through continuous loyalty. But the end of the cold war meant a termination of the superpower support and with rising internal pressures outbreaks of civil wars have often been inevitable (Carter, 2003).

Such superpower involvement in African conflicts could be seen in Angola, where in the 1970s FNLA and UNITA received American support and MPLA received Cuban and Soviet support thereby making the war a very protracted one.

In Zaire, (now DRC), Independence and pro-Soviet leader Patrick Lumumba was said to be assassinated with a CIA involvement in 1961. His assassination brought the American favored General Mobutu who (mis)governed the country for three decades. The end of the Cold War left Zairean people massively underdeveloped and the population hugely fractious so that with the Rwandan genocide and the resulting refugee crisis in eastern Zaire the country was left with a weak state. This resulted in the inevitable civil war in 1977 that led to the demise of Mobutu himself.

Beside a weakened state structure in the absence of super power support that obtained during the Cold War a 'unipolar' global order meant that the various 'war lords' nurtured by the Cold War had to resort to the control of export commodities to service military requirements necessary for the sustenance of military combats. Companies from western countries on the other hand, were always at hand to purchase such 'conflict commodities'. This way, the African conflicts were integrated into the post Cold War global political economy.

> Yet rather than positively influencing economic growth and national development these ties may be increasing both the intensity and the duration of violence. In order to maintain world price levels, the DeBeers cartel has had a long and controversial history of buying "conflict diamond" originating from rebel-held territories in countries such as Angola and Sierra-Leone-diamonds purchased overwhelmingly by Western consumers. Likewise, coltan, a crucial mineral used in the production of cell phones and laptop computers, has become a main commodity in the war economy of the DRC (Carter, 2003, p. 32).

But the strategic importance of the African conflicts to the global political economy pales in relation to conflicts in other regions of the world such as Europe and the Middle-East. This is evidenced by the little or no attention from the major world media and the international community generally. The Rwandan genocide that consumed about 800, 000 lives received much less publicity and western intervention compared to conflicts of lesser proportion in other parts of the world. In the same week that thousands of lives were lost in the Liberian conflict in June 2003, it was discovered that a bigger news for the major global networks like CNN and BBC world was the transfer of David Beckham from Manchester United to Real Madrid. As Harff and Gurr (2004, p. 12) observe:

> 'Unlike the situation in Yugoslavia, there was no serious international effort to check the Ethiopian civil war. No major power recognized Eritria as an independent state, international organizations regarded the conflict as an internal matter, and there was no media-inspired publicity.

Crises and conflicts in Africa receive far less global media coverage than those elsewhere such as the Middle East or Europe. The (ir) relevance of such African conflicts to global capital makes them less deserving of prominent coverage. Instead, the resulting refugee crises that could lead to the influx of thousands if not millions, of refugees, to western countries receive more attention because of its implications on the economies of such western countries. Exception to this rule in Africa could be seen in the Niger Delta crisis in Nigeria where the average news consumer in Australia, United States and New Zealand knows of Alhaji Asari Dokubo. For as a result of the crisis that affected oil production in Nigeria the price of the commodity in the global market rose to a record high of US $50 in 2005. Such a conflict would receive so-called international community attention not because of its humanitarian implication but because of its implication on global stock and capital flow.

Conclusion

Wars and conflicts have acquired global dimension by virtue of their coverage by a media system that is also global. These wars and conflicts have also acquired global dimension by virtue and extent of the integration of the region where they are fought, into the global neo-liberal order. The ascendancy of neo-liberal globalization as a dominant social order has also seen the emergence of Anglo-American media to the position of global dominance in the creation and distribution of media content all over the world. The notable consequences of the emergence of these giant multinational media corporations to such global prominence and dominance is among others, the export of a commercial, advert supported broadcasting model as the dominant model, the rise of a global audience as well as homogenization of content to appeal to such audience.

The implication, largely, is that the global media today have become the major sources of news and information for most citizens of the world. They have become early warning systems to small domestic media networks in Africa and other poorer regions of the world.

In a world ridden by wars and conflicts the global media have become ever central in bringing such wars and conflicts to the living rooms. They are also instruments of warfare given the centrality of propaganda in both the build up and execution of the war. In modern warfare, the media and propaganda planning and preparation are said to be as important as the military aspect of it. This dimension about the role of media and propaganda in war and conflicts therefore, makes the study and analyses of the construction of public opinion in electronic warfare very important.

The role of global media in the coverage of the first and second Gulf wars reveals very interesting lessons when compared to their coverage of wars and conflicts in Africa. For as Van der Veer observes:

> It is increasingly clear that media representations are crucial for both the form
> of warfare and the understanding of it. These representations belong to a global
> capitalist system of production, circulation, and consumption in which the
> North is dominant, (2004, p. 4).

In the era of neo-liberal globalization the world is seeing the triumphalism of the market system over public control of the distribution of resources and welfare. The global media as both product and embodiment of the market system have profit as their *raison d'être*. The implication of this in news is a dumbing down and the blurring of distinction between news and commercial departments of these media organizations as both strive to make profit. The outcome is the transformation of news into infotainment so that in reporting war and conflicts both process and background are missing and, in their place, there is emphasis on war as a spectacle. Both press pool and embed system are instances not only of news control and management but also of the production of war news as drama and entertainment for commodification purposes. This undermines professional journalistic values of objectivity and impartiality etc.

While Africa ranks among the world's leading conflict zones, such conflicts receive minimal coverage from the world media. Moreover, whereas most of the conflicts in the continent have their roots in global historical projects such as colonization, cold war politics and super power rivalry or super power induced insurgence etc, the minimal report about them from the global media paint such conflicts as the natural order of fragmented Africans who are prone to ethnic conflicts and feuds. Conflicts elsewhere (Europe and the Middle East) are treated from the journalistic news value of unusualness and therefore news worthy.

The differential attention to conflicts and wars by the global media is a manifestation of the contradictions surrounding the fate of nations in the neo-liberal globalization project. Conflicts spots in Africa that are less relevant to global capital in terms of resources or market get minimal attention or coverage from the global media who are the informational arm of global capital.

Conflicts in the Middle East and other locations in Europe receive wider coverage because of the relevance of such spots to global capital. Conflicts in petroleum rich countries of Africa for example, are more likely to receive global media coverage than those from non-resources endowed locations of the continent.

But it is not African conflicts only that are reported without their historical contexts and roots. In both the first and second gulf wars as well as the Afghanistan war there are indications of a trend in Public Relationising of war for the dual purposes of keeping high morale among the troops as well as maintaining domestic (global) support for the war.

> US-based media firms still overwhelmingly dominate the global information landscape; these firms continued to play the part of war cheerleaders before, during, and after the bombing of Afghanistan (Gross and Costanza-Chock, 2004, p. 4).

Today, a familiar strategy employed by the pentagon in the PRisation of war is the practice of 'embedding' journalists to US troops in Iraq as well as the pool of war reporters who take daily briefing from military spokesperson. This is a major shift from earlier wars such as World War 11 where reporters where subjected to direct censorship.

Media coverage of conflicts was once seen as important in keeping the world well informed about the war. If such information is to be the basis for response and intervention as well as policy decision the conflicts in Africa don't even get reported enough compared to those elsewhere. With their roots often in the imposed historical asymmetries in the distribution of resources, African conflicts are not seen to be central in global capital investment and regeneration and, as Thussu notes:

> As a result of such trends, television news rarely seems to cover the root causes of conflict in countries on the receiving end of neo-liberal 'reforms' which have yet to deliver for majority of the world's population. (2003, p. 130)

The lesson for Africa is that coverage of wars and conflicts by 'for profit media' is generally blurred because of the transformation of news into infotainment. Africa becomes doubly disadvantaged because of its peripheral standing in relation to the globalization agenda.

Although wars and conflicts on the African continent rank among the most devastating in terms of both destruction of infrastructure and loss of lives, yet they receive the least global attention or intervention for a resolution. This, we contend, points to the limitations of interdependence central to the globalization thesis as propagated by its proponents. Such lopsided coverage of African conflicts by the global media shows the asymmetries of neo-liberal globalization.

If citizens around the world rely on news accounts to form opinions and perspectives on conflicts, if such perspectives become bases for public opinion then, such opinion about conflicts and wars in Africa will be blurred and skewed. Yet it is such blurred and skewed public opinion that is supposed to guide national policies.

References

Bennet, W.L. (2003). *News: The politics of illusion, 5th Edition*: New York: Addison Wesley

Bordieu, P. (1998). *On television and Journalism.* London: Pluto Press.

Carter, C. (2003). 'The Political Economy of Conflict and UN Intervention: Rethinking the Critical Cases of Africa' In Ballentine, K & Sherman, J. (eds) *The Political Economy of Armed Conflict: Beyond Greed and Grievance.* Boulder: Lynne Rienner.

Financial Times. London, October 20 & 21, 2000

Freedman, D. 'Misrepresenting war has a long history'. In Miller, D. (ed.). *Tell me lies: Propaganda and media distortion in the attack on Iraq.* Cambridge, Pluto Press.

Fukuyama, F. (1992). *The end of history and the last man.* Avon Books, New York.

.Gans, H. (1979). *Deciding what's news.* New York: Pantheon.

Gandy, O. (1982). *Beyond agenda setting: Information subsidies and public policy.* NJ, Ablex, Norwood.

Gittlin, T. (2002). *Media unlimited: How the torrents of images and sounds overwhelms our lives.* New York. Metropolitan Books.

Grossberg, L. et al. (1998). *Media making: Mass media in a popular culture.* Sage, London.

Gross and Costanza-Shock, (2004) 'The West and the Rest: a drama in two acts and an epilogue'. In van der Veer, P.& Munshi, S. (eds) *Media, war, and terrorism: Responses from the Middle East and Asia.* London: Routledge.

Hall, et al. (1978). *Policing the crisis: Mugging, the state, and law and order.* Palgrave Macmillan, London.

Hall, S. (1993) 'Encoding and Decoding in Television Discourse', In During, S.(Ed.) *The cultural studies reader*, pp. 507-517. London: Routledge.

Harff, B. & Robert T.G. (2004). *Ethnic conflict in world politics.* Colorado: Westview Press.

Keane, J. (1997) 'Democracy and Media: Without Foundations,' in O. Boyd-Barret & C. Newbold. (Eds.). *Approaches to media. A reader.* London: Arnold.

Knight, G. (1982). News and Ideology. *Canadian Journal of Communication 8*(4) 15-41

Louw, E. (2001). *The media and cultural production.* London: Sage:

MacGregor, T. (1997). *Live, Direct and Biased? Making Television News in the Satellite Age.* London: Arnold.

McChesney, R. (2001). Global Media, Neo-liberalism, and Imperialism. Monthly Review, 52(10).

McCombs, M. E. & Shaw, D. L. (1972) 'The Agenda -Setting Function of the Press'. *Public Opinion Quarterly 36*, 176-87.

Miller, D. (2004)   'Information Dominance: The Philosophy of Total Propaganda Control?'. In Y. R. Kamalipour and N. Snow. (eds). War, media and propaganda: A global perspective. Rowman & Littlefield, Lanham.

Musa, M. (1997). From Optimism to Reality: An overview of Third World News Agencies. In P. Golding & P. Harris. (Eds.). *Beyond cultural imperialism: Communication, globalization and the new order.* London: Sage.

Musa, D. (1996). 'The Sleeping Dog Cannot Bark: Media and Mass Disempowerment of Civil Society in Africa'. *African Media Review.* vol. 10 (3).

Pilger, J. (2002). *New Rulers of the world.* New York: Verso Press.

Salisu, M. (2003). *Foreign Direct Investment in Sub-Saharan Africa.* Unpublished paper. Dept. of Economics, University of Lancaster.

Sa'id, E. (1997). *Covering Islam.* Vintage, London.

Schiller, H. (1976). *Communication and cultural domination.* White Plains: International Arts and Science Press..

Schlesinger, P. (1978). *Putting reality together.* Constable, London: BBC News.

Tehrenian, M. (1999). *Global communications and world politics.* Colorado: Lynne Rienner.

Thussu, D. K. (2003). 'Live tv and bloodless deaths: war, infotainment and 24/7 news'. In Thussu, D.K and Freedman, D. (Eds.). *War and the media.* SLondon: Sage.

van der Veer (2004). 'Introduction' in van der Veer, P.& Munshi, S. (eds) *Media, war, and terrorism: Responses from the Middle East and Asia*. London: Routledge.

Chapter 8

Conflict, Globalization and the New World Information and Communication Order

Nosa Owens-Ibie, Ph.D.
&
Abigail O. Ogwezzy, Ph.D.
University of Lagos, NIGERIA

Introduction

In the mid 1960s, Marshall McLuhan, a Canadian cultural scholar, posited that the rise of the electronic media marked a new phase in human history as physical distance would no longer be a barrier, and instantaneous mass communication across the globe would be possible. The outcome was McLuhan's notion of a "global village", where people of the world would be brought closer together as they made their voices heard. McLuhan argued that such information environment compelled commitment and enhanced participation (Croteau and Hoynes, 2000). Essentially, McLuhan wrote about globalization and its expected benefits.

Croteau and Hoynes (2000, p. 331) see globalization as a process that signifies more than environmental interconnectedness. It also includes political globalization, as embodied by the United Nations, and economic interdependence, as seen in the growth of multi-or transnational corporations (Croteau and Hoynes, 2000, p. 331). According to Demers (1999, p. 5):

> A spectre now haunts the world: a global commercial media system dominated
> by a small number of super-powerful, mostly U.S.-based transnational media

corporations. It is a system that works to advance the cause of the global market and promote commercial values, while denigrating journalism and culture not conducive to the immediate bottom line or long-run corporate interests. It is a disaster for anything but the most superficial notion of democracy – a democracy where, to paraphrase John Jay's maxim, those who own the world ought to govern in it

So, the trends in media globalization are marked by distinct ambiguity and contradiction. Some developments seem likely to produce positive changes of the sort envisioned by McLuhan; others are cause for alarm. The distinction, ambiguity and contradiction derive from two central components globalization - the changing role of geography and physical distance, which has resulted in instantaneous communication and interaction over far distance. Another dimension of globalization is the content of communication (Croteau and Hoynes, 2000). As Demers (1999, p. 4) puts it:

Global media don't really care about promoting a diversity of ideas, democratic principles or equality…All they care about is profits. Global media are greedy organizations that are destroying good journalism and democratic values. News and entertainment programming are trivial and more to encourage consumerism and materialism than a robust debate about social inequities and injustice… Global media are a menace to good journalism and democracy

Another school of thought on globalization also opined that:

Global media emerge because national media are incapable of satisfying the information and entertainment needs of an increasingly complex and interdependent world. Furthermore, global media enhance democracy because they have the resources to produce higher quality, more content-diverse products and services (Demers, 1999:5).

Demers (1999, p. 5) further argued that "Because global media are products of or are heavily influenced by Western culture, they help spread values like representative democracy, free speech, equality for women and minorities, and the notion that a diversity of ideas is important…. And global media have the potential to help integrate disparate countries and cultures into a global village, reducing the potential for war or social *conflict* (emphasis ours) and increasing understanding across cultures. In short, global media have the potential to play the role of messiah."

So, it must be admitted though that the international flow of news has received a great deal of attention. Either way, the structure of flow has ensured that the volume of information flow has tended towards unidirectionality.

In explaining this trend Wilbur Schramm said that "almost anything of serious significance that happens in the developed countries is likely to be of interest or concern to smaller countries…"He hinged his argument on the potency of the developed countries manifest in their economic, scientific and industrial might (Opubor, 1976)

This of course was the reality that the world was getting used to till the debate commenced in the 1970s to critically re-examine the state of the information flow situation and seek a redress of the identified imbalances. For sometime after the international debate started, the concept of free flow of information was still interpreted in the context of unrestricted flow even if it meant that only a country was sending all the information while the rest of the world was doing the receiving. The Montréal Meeting of Mass Communication and Society held in 1969 sensitized the world, especially the part of it canvassing for greater balance in information flow, to the lag (UNESCO, 1980). The emphasis in the campaign was no longer for free flow of information but for a new world information order, later, New World Information and Communication Order.

Not that the flow has altered significantly, but the consciousness of the imbalance and national and regional attempts to give an outlet to information from previously disadvantaged countries in the flow process are being stepped-up. The irony being that even in doing this, the disadvantaged states still rely heavily on the goodwill, technology and aid packages of the few states that have traditionally enjoyed advantages over the years and still do.

Alfred Opubor (1976), writing on "The Flow of News in the Black World", has demonstrated the dilemma of the world-wide view on the flow of news. That dilemma is that there is a basic imbalance and exploitation of technological advantages in the flow and manipulation of news, whether intra-nation or international. But the specific situation Opubor dealt with was the December, 1975 football match between Rangers International of Nigeria and the Hafia of Guinea in the final round of the African Cup of Champions Clubs Competition. The match played in Conakry, Guinea at about four O'clock in the afternoon witnessed Nigerians awaiting the live commentary of the match via their radio sets. The wait was in vain as the announcer who also explained that there was no direct communication link between Nigeria and Guinea has said with regrets; "Ladies and Gentlemen, I'm afraid we cannot bring you live commentary on the football match from Guinea. We have been unable to reach our commentators in Conakry" (Opubor, 1976). The match could not be received in Nigeria because of the indirect network of the sub-region's (West Africa in this case) communication process. It was, and remains easier to link Paris with Conakry and Lagos with London than Conakry with Lagos.

Other commentators have highlighted this discrepancy in the flow pattern of international communication and information fare. But in the various attempts to examine these imbalances, efforts have advanced beyond the conceptualization of information only in terms of news flow. The MacBride report notes that such imbalance affects on an ever growing scale, "the collection and diffusion of data necessary for scientific purposes, technological innovations, commercial news, trade development, exploitation of natural resources, meteorological forecasting, military purposes....there is an imbalance regarding strategic information for political and economic decision-making" (MacBride, 1981) . Figure 1 gives a detailed description of the international flow of information.

Trend in the Information Flow Process

A noticeable trend in the flow process, which ironically has tended to focus on news flow, has been the sustaining of colonial and post-colonial links in the volume and direction of flow. Although today's super powers–the United States and the Union of Soviet Socialists Republics (USSR) were not strictly colonial powers in the same mould as Britain and France, they have emerged as vital sources of information that daily spread to different parts of the world. While the United States through an orchestrated policy backed largely by private capital provided by super-loaded transnational concerns continues to break new grounds in terms of range and frontiers for information emanating from the country, the Soviet Union, apart from the advantages enjoyed as a world power whose sneeze must catalyze a cold in many a countries enjoys a special and ideologically influenced relationship with eastern block and other communist regimes and countries that slants information flow in favor this leader of the East.

Again, former colonies had their information machinery structured by their colonizing countries. Such machinery, included manpower, technology, programming in the case of the electronic media and the shape of the newspaper and the entire communication systems. In spite of the acrimony that attended independence struggles, these relationship and dependencies outlived the colonial era. There developed an indigenization tradition that saw the emergent elites taking over the whole structure from the departing colonial administrators. What a great many countries did was to diversify their dependency, depending on the political direction of those in power. Before a good many countries bothered to think about the dangers of the avalanche of information materials from the developed states, they had been overwhelmed and destabilized. How much success can be achieved in reversing this trend, short of a true communication revolution, is what an expectant world looks forward to.

Techno-Human Adaptation of International Flow of Information

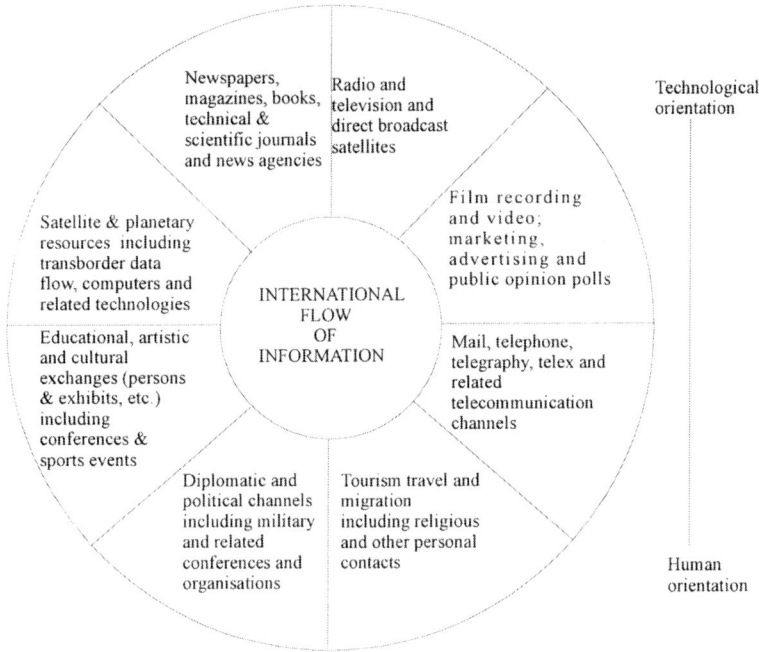

FIGURE 1
Channels and types of international flow of information

The technological and human orientations should be
thought of as complementary, interrelated and adaptive.

Source: Hamid Mowlana. (1985). *International Flow of Information: A Global Report and Analysis*. Paris: UNESCO.

The Subject of Information and Communication Flow

The subject of information and communication flow, in consonance with the increasing interest on it, is attracting a lot of research into its various facets. These perspectives are grouped into five and condensed into three. These, as enunciated by Hamid Mowlana (1985), are the:

1. International relations and systems perspective which deals with the subjects of imperialism, integration, conflict and cooperation, image and perception among and between nations.

2. Communication and development perspective that examine the internal and external communication systems of nations and their political, economic, social and international contexts delving into the balance or otherwise of information flow.

3. Institutional and commercial perspective look at international actors and the impact of political and persuasive messages on the behavior of individuals and nations; propaganda and policy studies as they relate to conflict management.

4. Political economy and structural perspective focuses on national and international communication structures and the political economy of international information flow; elements and factors influencing the process, production and distribution.

5. Technical and legal perspective deal with the technology and techniques of national and international information regulations and standards.

A contraction of these areas of enquiry has been undertaken by Mowlana who in looking at literature on world news flow, highlights two main areas of enquiry which will be dealt with in the section of news flow. These areas are those dealing with actual flow and content of news and the factors that determine such flow of news.

As part of this general treatment, it is instructive to state that the references to information, communication and news, depending on the one deemed most relevant, are an attempt to be as comprehensive in this analysis as possible.

It must be noted that the emphasis on the right to communicate, as distinct from information, by Jean D'Arcy, and successive attempts to highlight the differences between both, in spite of their interdependence, makes it imperative, at least in this chapter, that due recognition must be given to both concepts. Gunnar Garbo (1985, p. 68) defines this interpretative difference between information and communication by stating the "Information may be perceived as the contents of a message from sender to receiver....communication suggests the process of transmission among several participants and the resources this process requires".

What accentuates this difference and buttresses Jean D'Arcy's distinction between both concepts is that either way – whether from the information or communication perspective, the factor of imbalance show marked depth. Not only has the world witnessed a situation where information flow has been slanted heavily against the less developed countries, the latter's right to also communicate their information to these other nations has been virtually non-existent. The relative ignorance of the true state of affairs in African countries among Americans as against the high knowledge ratio of America and American affairs among the average African buttresses this paradox as well.

It would appear that most of the reports on Africa are those on drought, coups, poverty, illiteracy, the liberation struggle in apartheid South Africa, the illegal occupation of Namibia by the racist regime and Nigeria's nascent democracy. All else, it would appear is darkness and some accounts by some Nigerian journalists on study trips to the United States have confirmed this ignorance. The inference would be that channels of communication available to African, Latin American and some Asian and Middle-East countries is inadequate against the superior channels available to these nations which already enjoy an advantage in the information and communication flow situation. With the increasing sophistication of technologies in these more developed the imbalance could probably get worse.

The Flow of International News

The subject of international flow of news is one that has gained a lot of currency so much that it tended to dwarf the wider subject of information and communication flow, until recently. The currency gained by the subject is consistent with the goals of the Universal Declaration of Human Rights which states that "Everyone has the right, to freedom of opinion and expression; this right includes freedom to hold opinions without any interference and to seek, receive and impart information and ideas through any media and regardless of frontiers" (MacBride, 1981, p. 137).

It is in the furtherance of the right to receive and impart information that news has become a trillion-Naira industry, rooted in technological changes of the times, politics and doses of controversy. Studies on the subject are now anchored on two stands; the actual flow and content of news and factors determining such flow (Mowlana, 1985, p. 20). These categories provided a framework through which we attempted a close understanding of the subject.

The first category is subdivided into four. The first looks at the country to country flow and content of news; the second is on the role of the 'dominance-dependency' and 'centre-periphery' model; the third looks at the qualitative nature of news through the images and perceptions contained in content; while the fourth is the 'events-interaction analysis' which interprets the interaction of states or international actors as reflected by the analysis of news data. Factors determining the flow of news include media factors influencing news flow and extra-media factors that determine the content and flow of news (Mowlana, 1985).

Flow and Content of News

A study of flow and content of news between countries and the dominance-dependency model of news flow has a good beginning in a major theoretical construct. Johan Galtung's structural theory of imperialism provides a framework; the centre-periphery hypothesis for examining the vertical pattern of flow. The centre nations are the developed and dominant countries and the periphery nations are the dependent and dominated countries. Galtung's hypothesis has been summarized in four statements:

1. "There is a preponderance of 'centre' news events reported in the world press systems.

2. There is a much larger discrepancy in the news exchange ratios of 'centre' and 'periphery' nations than in exchange ratios of 'centre' nations.

3. 'Centre' news occupies a larger proportion of the foreign news content in the media of 'periphery' nations than the 'periphery' news occupies in the 'centre' nations.

4. There is a relatively little or no flow of news among 'periphery' nations, especially across colonial-based bloc borders" (Mowlana, 1985).

According to Mowlana (1981, pp. 16-17), Herb Adde, using Galtung's model had found that in both 1960 and 1970, the pattern of flow was still feudal, confirming the dominance of the centre nations in the flow pattern. Other studies have either confirmed Galtung's hypothesis or negated it. The overwhelming evidence has pointed to a discrepancy in news flow that has tilted to the advantage of the 'centre', 'North' or 'developed' countries. This is not synonymous with the non-existence of a South-South or periphery-periphery flow. In fact, there is data from a study of twenty-nine countries to be examined later, that throws clearer light on the issues.

The big five news agencies have however continued to maintain a hold on the flow of wire news. The total amount of news produced by the leading four – 32, 850, 000 words per day is many times more than what all the other world agencies put together produce. These big agencies are not only blessed with the wherewithal to station correspondents in most countries or regions of the globe, but have in spite of the establishment of many new national and regional agencies, established largely to counter the perceived negative role of the big ones, remained a major source of news in media in periphery countries. Such sourcing has been both quantitative and qualitative. On the quantitative plane, Nigeria's news agency's daily production of 20, 000 words per day compares unfavorably with AP – 17, 000, 000; UPI – 11, 000, 000; Reuter – 15, 000, 000... Deustche Press Agenture (DPA) of the Federal Republic of Germany – 113, 000; the Italian Agenzia National Stampa Associata (ANSA) – 300, 000; the Telegrafaka Agencija Nove Jugoslavia (Tanjug) of Yugoslavia – 75, 000; and Inter Press Service – 100, 000" (Mowlana, 1985).

The figures also show a marked imbalance between the wire news production of the big four agencies and the European agencies. It is however in the direction of flow of the news generated by these wire services that the imbalance presents a stark discrepancy. The MacBride Report gives these examples:

AP sends out its general world wire service to Asia from New York an average of 90,000 words daily. In return, Asia files 19, 000 words to New York for world wide distribution. UPI's general news wire out of New York to Asia totals some 100,000 words and the file from all points in Asia to New York varies between 40, 000 to 45, 000 daily... AFP's service from Paris to Asia is 30, 000 strong. In addition, some 8, 000 words are collected in Asia and distributed within the region to Asian clients. The same 8, 000 word file is sent back to Paris for incorporation into other world services of AFP .... A study carried out in Venezuela in 1977 revealed that on one particular day the country received 1, 360 news item from external sources, 20.44% of which (278 items) came from North America while it exported through the 10 agency correspondents 71 items, of which only 30 through North American agencies (UPI: 16; AP: 4). In other words, for every 100 news items from the USA received in Venezuela, the country dispatches seven, via AP/UPI. The same study rated the imbalance of domestic compared with international news at 5 to 100 (MacBride, 1981, p. 146).

The big five agencies also cover news they consider of interest to the audience in their country of origin, while simultaneously promoting values central to their societies. Ideological compatibility, regional proximity and colonial orientations play major roles in the volume of news covered in national and international news agencies. In some cases, undue concentration on particular countries, distorts the true picture of happenings in entire countries. This trend led Hal Hendrix, Latin American editor of the Miami News to conclude in his analysis of the flow of news from Latin America on one agency that "if this wire file were the only source of enlightenment for the rest of the world, then Latin America could be considered to consist mainly of Cuba. From several countries there was no news whatsoever during the month. From Bolivia, there came only the announcement of the arrival of Prince Phillips; from Peru, only shots about a plane crash and a bus wreck; from Chile, nothing more than a note that Billy Graham, the evangelist, was conducting his meetings in Santiago" (Schramm, 1963).

One of the more direct results of this inadequate reporting of the periphery nations has been the establishment of news agencies both by agencies based in the industrialized countries to facilitate increased news flow from the dependent to the dominant nations, national and regional agencies and agencies established under the auspices of international organizations. The national agencies are mainly dedicated at least from the level of adjectives, to the use of information for the goals of national development and stemming the tide of distortion and inadequate coverage of national news by correspondents of the big agencies who are patronized by the media of such countries.

While national agencies are now major sources of news, with varying degrees of credibility, what they have not significantly changed is the trend in the reporting of the periphery by the centre. Even agencies like the Inter Press Service, that are supposed to perform balancing acts on the international news flow situation, are faced with the problem of utilization of their news dispatches in the centre countries. The impact of agencies like the Pan-African News Agency (PANA), News Agency Pool of Non-Aligned countries, Caribbean News Agency (CANA), the Latin American Regional Agency (LATIN) and specialized agencies like OPEC News Agency for the Organization of Petroleum Exporting Countries based in Vienna may not be easily quantifiable, but there is no doubt that these among many other 'South' agencies are gradually growing as sources of Southern news to Southern clients, no matter how minimal the flow may seem now.

These agencies may have to be assessed somewhat, along the lines of the possible impact of the newly established South-North News service started by Peter Martin, a former editor and foreign correspondent of Time Magazine, in Hanover, New Hampshire in the USA. This service, which partly makes use of the Associated Press news wire to transmit its stories, aims at sending southern news, packaged by writers from the South, for consumption in the North. The service already distributes six such stories each week to twelve newspapers in the U. S. These include the International Herald Tribune, the Toronto Star, the San Francisco Examiner, the Dallas Herald, the Washington Post, and the Los Angeles Times (*FOCUSAFRICA,* 1986, pp. 11-13). The contributions of such a service to be relevant to the news flow debate will have to be patronized on the long run. But whether it or either similar agencies whenever established can ever upstage the big agencies as a mere 'credible' source of news from the South, is arguable.

However, Serebery-Mohammadi (1985, pp. 39-42) in a study of foreign news reporting in the media of 29 countries including Nigeria, among other findings, throws light on the regions of priority focus of the mass media systems in different parts of the world. Regions are defined as those countries from particular regions, included in the study. The findings were that with the exception of Yugoslavia and Poland, every other country reported more news from their geographical sphere of location than any other region. The United States media concentrated, 26 per cent, on its region's news, give equal attention to the Middle-East and Western Europe while Asia received a high level of attention.

Latin America news in the Latin America media studied, accounted for about 30 per cent, followed by the United States news in the Mexican media, and Western European in the Brazilian and Argentine media. The Middle-East also received substantial attention in the Argentine media.

African news in the African media added up to about 50 per cent of the total news coverage. The Middle-East followed in priority in six out of the seven countries studied, while Western Europe, where the United Kingdom and France – Africa's previous colonial powers, situates, came third.

In the Middle-East, 30 per cent of the news featured had regional origin. Lebanon followed this with Western Europe; Egypt gave equal attention to North America, Africa and Western Europe; while Iran followed with Asia as its next region of priority.

The Asian average witnessed Malaysia giving 65 per cent of its media space to Asian news while Australia's percentage was comparatively low. North American and Western European news was well represented in the Australian media. In the other Asian countries studied, Western Europe and the Middle-East were next in coverage after the Asian region.

In Western Europe, coverage of regional news ranged from 40 to 50 per cent. The Middle-East and North America were next in importance, but the media in the Federal Republic of Germany and Finland paid significant attention to news from Eastern Europe. The exception to the general trend was the Eastern Europe which recorded regional news least. In the Yugoslav and Polish media, Western Europe got as much attention as Eastern Europe.

Specific events at the time of the study played some part in securing coverage of certain areas. The perennial clashes in the Middle-East are one such source of news. Africa, Latin America and to some extent Asia did not come from this study, seem to attract attention in the 'Northern' media. On the other hand, Western Europe and North America received a fair deal of attention in the African, Latin American and Asian media. While this should be indicative of some relationship, based possibly on political goals, between the periphery nations, it further reconfirms the lopsided nature of some news mention of the periphery in the centre media and vice-versa. There is a tendency to report the North than the South in Southern media, while South-South coverage is scanty, although foreign policy objectives of some countries may play a part in fostering the reporting of the South by the South and although the degree of direct governmental control of the media may help to streamline such focus. Based on the first observations, the study detailed above recorded that "Latin America ranks eighth in the African media and Africa ranks sixth in the Latin American" (Se-rebery-Mohammadi, 1985, p. 43).

Another important focus in the study by Sreberny-Mohammadi *et al* (1985, p. 45) is that of the international news reported by the afore-mentioned media systems. It was found that international politics, military and defense and eco-nomics dominated the stories in almost all the national systems.

One important trend that cuts across the international news reporting situa-tion is still the domination of the centre or Northern nations, and of course the transnational companies. African countries have to depend on the big and not-so-big agencies in the centre nations to report on other African countries, Asian countries have to rely on these same sources to report on their neighbors, but Americans rely on themselves to get news on their neighbors. The Soviets, simi-larly, have TASS to blanket their primary area of influence. A study by Peter Golding and Phillip Elliot on the Nigerian broadcast media in 1977 has shown for instance that "the combined input of Reuter, AP, AFP, and VISNEWS as sources of foreign news amounted to 85 per cent" (Mowlana, 1981, p. 23). In some countries, the figure could be higher but in a growing number of others, the figure is less. The latter could be attributed to international news exchange arrangements between national agencies, the practice of media from developing countries stationing correspondents in the centre nations and other centers within their regions. But this is heavily constrained by the resources at the disposal of these media and national agencies, with the result that what obtains is marginal representation vis-à-vis the areas expected to be covered by such correspon-dents.

The flow has however proved to be as important as the content of news. For it is in the area of content that a lot of dust has been raised. In fact, criticism of the flow pattern has been largely predicated on the distortion that has attended the flow over the years has fostered. Such distortion, which has implications for the qualitative perception of news, has had its toll on the interpretation of cultur-al images with the subsequent westernization of whole cultures and their consi-derable mal-acculturation. The MacBride Report provides clues to what consti-tutes distortion in news reporting; Distortion occurs when "events of no real significance are given prominence, partial truths are assembled to form the ap-pearance of a complete truth...when facts are presented in such a way as to cause misinterpretation by implication, where implicit conclusions drawn by the audience are favorable to particular interests...when events are presented in a way that stirs unfounded or exaggerated doubts and fears...when silence is maintained on facts or events presumed to be of no interest to the public" (Mac-Bride, 1981, p. 158).

The criticism of distortion of news leveled against center nations must in no way be interpreted as synonymous with the requirement for total objectivity, which in itself is idealistic. What has simply been happening for long is the problem of unequal standard in the interpretation of what constitutes news in the eyes of the centre nations. The situation has been, and largely remains such that while a wedding, speech by a major or even minor political actor, a discovery, police effort to combat crime, or even the escapades or activities of the wife of a country's leader, qualify to be news in the centre nations, similar items hardly ever are regarded as of news value, if they occur in the periphery nations.

This apart, there is an undue attention on sensation in the news coverage in the periphery nations. The result is that all some news watchers ever get to know about the South are stories of droughts, coups, wars and conflicts and of course, visits to the South by an American president, Soviet leader and the Queen of England, among others. Such undue emphasis on 'negative' news distorts the true picture of happenings in the South and should be seen as contributory to such occurrences as African tourists being asked if Nigeria is in Ghana or some such ludicrous questions. It also calls to question the advantages of the widely listened-to external broadcasting services of centre nations who have African, South (Latin) American and Asian services, to the periphery nations. No doubt, 'they' sell their countries to these periphery nations, but if the amount of news and analysis they carry about the South, no matter now negligible, gets to their home (e.g. the BBC) audience, there won't be as much darkness about the periphery, among the centre nation's population as there seems to exist now.

The lack of depth in the news reported internationally has been another source of distortion. A lot of the news reported says little to background the information being spread in the news. Media in the periphery nations have however not been exempt from the malady of the 'centre' press. Negative news as described above are also predominant while over the years are finding faithfuls in the media of periphery with possible exemptions in countries that operate their media systems with strong ideological or political convictions. This means that while news in the centre nations have been oriented to serving their home audience, the same can not be said of their counterparts in the periphery nations. Appeals to elitist interests, a traditional criticism of the news from the centre nations, is a growing feature of the media in periphery. This growing trend would have contributed to the finding that portrayed Africa as "politically gullible, naïve and immature but also as a continent whose course of action is precariously dependent on the Big Powers" (Mowlana, 1981, p. 27).

Factors Determining News Flow

A useful starting point is in an analysis of the factors that determine the flow of news in the world, would be an examination of the criteria that determines the selection of news. While there is the acknowledgement that the selection of news in the centre nations is based on the desire basically to satisfy the home audience, an insight into the criteria for such selection in the periphery African, Arab, Asian, and Latin American nations in a study Alcino Louis Costa *et al* (1980).

In African countries, criteria for news selection ranged from an option referred to as psycho-political security where prominence is given to news from countries with which close relations are maintained, "existence of community interests" where good news about other countries with similar political, economic, cultural or ideological interests are given prominence in the local media; and "compatibility with imperatives of national policy" where news selection is aimed at legitimizing or promoting positions held by government. Non-governmental communication media appear on the other hand to be concerned with international news that helps to justify positions adopted by them. African news agencies feature essentially, news that enhances the image of African countries.

The Arab countries also have a series of local and alien factors that determine news selection. These include the factors of Arab nationalism, conflict with Israel and the fight against neo-colonial forces, a new world economic order, religion, and the Islamic way of life, oil politics, local and international food problems, development issues, social and administrative reforms and the anti-corruption/bureaucracy drive, women and their rights, family planning, science and technology; and taboos and superstition.

In the Asian countries, political news receives greater emphasis than economic news, while industrially developed countries get more foreign economic coverage than developing countries.

There is a city or urban bias in the coverage of agricultural news. The electronic media is more in the hands of government and pay more attention to rural interests. In the reportage of political news, the Asian media are used as vehicles for political persuasion, exhortation and mobilization. However, there is a segment of the Asian media that is motivated strictly by the consideration of commercial success with little or no consideration for the values of society and the traditional watchdog role of the media. The Latin American media on the other hand has tended to respond to the dictates of market forces typical of free enterprise economies.

On the global level, most of these identified factors help determine the flow of news. This is true, whether the factors of transnational might, the regional or national agencies or the mass media systems in the different periphery and centre nations, are considered.

Media factors that affect and shape the flow of news, have to do with availability, or lack of it, of communication resources. Here, there is as has been noted, an advantage enjoyed by the centre nations and the many private institutions within them. The technological resources at the disposal of the centre nations guarantee for them a geographical reach that the periphery nations do not enjoy. With the increasing sophistication of communication technology, these periphery nations, while becoming part of the 'global village' are increasingly incapacitated in their ability to contribute meaningfully to the international news flow situation. This is in spite of the option of becoming part of or contributing their quota to the international network. While television stations in periphery nations can keep to the agreements on the reception of news film on events around the world, the determination of the information that is fed into such satellite network is the preserve of the centre nations, especially the international corporations.

Another area of noticeable imbalance of communication is the professional manpower available to the different systems for the reporting of news. Because of the superior resources at the disposal of the centre nations, they are able to maintain a network of correspondents in different designated news centers all around the world. Most correspondents are also stationed in the centre nations. They also have the capacity to deploy a corps of highly mobile manpower complete with an arsenal of sophisticated equipment to cover the location of any 'emerging news' that is of international significance or seen as deserving due coverage for the benefit of audiences in the centre nations. While some periphery nations, due may be to the political significance attached to such events, are able to deploy their media personnel to cover such events, they lack the resources to significantly internationalize the reception of news emanating there from. A study in 1975 found that out of 865 correspondents stationed in the United States, there was "none from Black Africa, 23 from Israel, 1 from Pakistan, 23 from Taiwan. Western Europe accounted for more than half of the correspondents, with few from Latin America, the Middle-East or Asia. There was a total absence of foreign correspondents from several countries" (Mowlana, 1981, p. 27). By 1981, the number of foreign correspondents had gone up to 1262 with none still coming from Black Africa. The non-representation of Black Africa has however started to change. The News Agency of Nigeria is now represented in the United States and some other news centers around the world. The ratio of representation of the periphery nations is still relatively small.

The whole issue as regards the factors mentioned already, is economic. These economic factors affect basically all aspects of the production and distribution of news. The lack of a good capital base, made worse by the dwindling resources of the periphery nations and in the face of a global economic recession and mounting debts, makes the task of coping with the demands of a modern communications media, difficult. Affected are the quality, quantity and distribution of news. News gathering and transmission is impaired, remuneration for journalists, payment of telecommunications tariffs and the access of the audience to the news products become problem areas. With this disability, the capacity for competition in a largely free enterprise setting, the type which the TNCs find most suitable, becomes seriously restricted. The implication is evident in the quality of the news products of the national mass media systems that in some cases are forced by circumstances, and against the national quest for indigenization of the media, to imported news products and the resources of the transnational corporations whose advertisement revenue become lifeblood in the face of reduced government subvention. This situation in some cases have been compounded by the increasing foreign exchange difficulties of the local media, who though expected still to continue functioning as agents for the furtherance of given objectives, have to fight for such basics as newsprint, ink, television cameras, tapes, recorders and insufficient vehicles to ensure meaningful coverage and dissemination of news. With an urban-bias that customarily has been associated with the media in the periphery nations, and in view of the economic difficulties, the rural areas are increasingly isolated in the scheme of news coverage. Not because the media are not aware of their responsibilities, but because the resources are not there to sustain the coverage of substantial geographical spread that is the rural. And these rural areas are the location of most of the population the potential audience of the news media. Economic factors therefore represent not only media but extra-media influence on the content and flow of news.

Political considerations are also vital in the determination of the international flow of news. That the entire media set-up is regulated by political forces and the prevailing political climate in national systems is an indication of the importance of this factor. Gate keeping which is standard national and international practice is one such element in the political mix. Gate keeping is not exactly the same thing as censorship. In the first, news content is determined by the need to present news along given editorial directions. This editorial direction could either be determined by the factors internal to the media or external to it. It involves the funneling of news along the many editorial lines it must go through before being fed as news to one or more channels of mass communication. The concept of gate keeping owes its origin to the psychologist Kurt Lewin and operates not only in the mass media but interpersonal channels. Gatekeepers are at national, sub-regional and international levels.

Wilbur Schramm (1963, p. 85) explains how the gate keeping process works. According to him, "The first gatekeeper is the person who sees the news happen. He sees it selectively; notices some things, not others. A second gatekeeper is the reporter who talks to the 'news source...sources...he has to decide which facts to pass along the chain...his editor... must decide how to edit the story... someone at the news services must decide whether it is one of the few stories which, out of many hundreds, will be picked up...in what form and how long it should be. If it does...go overseas...where two news agencies exchange copy...the second news agency must decide whether to pass it along... to cut or rewrite....If the story goes...to...the national news wire, the regional wires, ultimately the newspapers or broadcasting stations...news editors must decide." The chain may be shorter, but while identifying the gate keeper's existence, it is important to stress that the criticism of distortion leveled against the content of news that flows internationally, emanates largely at the level of the gatekeeper.

Reporters may have to rely on the eyewitness, who a good many instance is the first in the line of gatekeepers. The eye of the camera however keeps the gate and enables other gatekeepers to see only things its operators want to be seen. That is another instance where the transnational corporations and the centre nations have an advantage.

Closely related to the gatekeeping function in international news flow is the factor of censorship. Censorship is predicated on the regulation of news content or flow as a result of the intervention of force or authority or the fear of punishment for not falling in tune with the dictates of the censor. The gatekeeper appears a more voluntary actor. The fact though is that gate keeping could be undertaken under censorship, with the individual, group or media channel transmitting only that which is allowed. Censorship is an act in gate keeping.

The determination of what to and not to import is political. This in effect determines what the local audience could watch or read. Controls over the entry or exit of journalists into a country are another factor. Incidences of the expulsion of journalists on charges of sabotage or espionage are a common feature of today's world. Such regulation of the entry of journalist, inevitably affects the reporting of news and therefore its flow. The goals set for the media by the political class represent another important element as they determine the emphasis of the media in terms of the news emphasis and directions.

Socio-cultural factors also play an important role. Culture, religion and traditional beliefs constitute hindrances in the international flow of news. This is largely because of the distinctive character of these factors and the heterogeneous nature of most societies and the resistance of media systems to the cultural and religious influences of all news sources. In a region like the Arab states, religion has contributed to the forging of a common defense to alien influence.

The flow of news is therefore impaired. The lack of local lingua franca in most countries is another socio-cultural constraint as distortion of news content attends attempts to interpret international news in order to reach the wider audience. In the absence of linguistic substitutes in the local communication media, national systems unwittingly function as agents for the transmission of hybrid names and terms that are inevitably built into the linguistic forms of the nations at the receiving end of the news. In the course of transmitting news, stereotypes have been transferred. It has become 'accepted' that words like 'blackmail', and 'blacklist', are no more to be frowned in the wire copy.

Extra-media factors that determine news flow include factors like literacy level which is an indicator of the reach of transmitted news, population and trade which determines the direction of news exchange on the international scene.

Conclusion

This look at the general perspective of information flow should be viewed against the background of its significance for the national communication systems of the developing countries. Whole cultural values, reeling under the deluge of the largely unidirectional flow of world information and communication today face the threat of extinction. The result is that political and traditional communication values are experiencing new phases of distortion which are subtle in some cases and quite apparent in others, may end up turning the world into one robotized geographical contraption with the captains of the ship being the forces which are currently at the root of the present imbalance. This systems if not properly handled might turn McLuhan's idea of a global village to a paradox, which could result in poor perception, between and among nations, perhaps resulting in conflict.

References

Croteau, D. and Hoynes, W. (2000). *Media society: Industries, images, and audiences, 2nd edition.* London: Pine Forge Press

Da Costa, A.L., Aboubakr, Y., Chopra, P., and Matta, F. R. (1980). Sources of information on news values. In *News values and principles of cross-cultural communication.* Paris: UNESCO.

Demers, D. (1999). *Global media: Menace or messiah?* Cresskill, New Jersey: Hampton Press.

FOCUSAFRCICA: News and views from the United States Embassy, Lagos, Vol. 1. 1986, pp. 11 – 13.

Garbo, G. (1985). *A world of difference: The international distribution of information: The media and developing countries.* Paris: UNESCO

MacBride, S. *et al.* (1981). *Many voices, one world.* Ibadan: Ibadan University Press

Mowlana, H. (ed.). (1981). *International flow of news: An annotated bibliography,* pp. 16-17. Paris: UNESCO).

Mowlana, H. (1985). *International flow of information: A global report and analysis:* Paris: UNESCO

Opubor, A. (1976). The flow of news in the black world", originally Broadcast In the Series "Black Society", *Voice of Nigeria,* Lagos.

Sreberny-Mohammadi, A., Nordenstrong, K., Stevenson, R., and Ugboajah, F. (1985). *Foreign news in the media: International reporting in 29 countries.* Paris: UNESCO

Schramm, W. (1963). *The science of communication.* Urbana: University of Illinois Press

Chapter 9

Threat Perceptions and Security in the West African Subregion

Joses Gani Yoroms, Ph.D.
National War College, Abuja, NIGERIA

Introduction

The Economic Community of West Africa States (ECOWAS) marked the 29th year of its existence in the month of May 2004 without any extra ordinary celebration. Unfortunately this expectation was not met because the sub-region has been smeared by insecurity, intractable conflicts and serious environmental degradation. The genocidal conflicts and civil wars have led to population displacement, deconstruction of feminine gender hood, drifting refugee and humanitarian problems. In the process, the regional economic development plan that ECOWAS was established to accomplish suffered stunted growth as attention was diverted to security sector and conflict resolution. This situation is emerging in the period of globalization which is captured as a moment of information economy creating fundamental distinction in the world between fast and slow economies between the North and south respectively (McGowan, 1995; Yoroms, 2000).

In the light this, globalization is seen from the perspectives of developing countries as a process of creating an architectural scaffold of conflict by its perpetrators to perfect their domineering overload and control of others in the international system. In reflecting on the effect of globalization on regional security therefore, this paper attempts to look at, first, global security and threat perceptions in risk society, with particular reference to West Africa. Here, attempt is made to understand regional security in terms of threats and insecurity, which stigmatizes the region as a risk society. Secondly, the paper discusses ECO-

WAS's Security Policy in the light of inadequate regional security arrangement, and how they have affected the issue of security dilemma in the sub-region. Thirdly, the paper examines security cooperation and coordination in ECOWAS, in order to establish how external supports have succeeded to enhance security network in West Africa. The paper finally made some concluding remarks about the whole concept of Globalization and Global security.

Global Security and Threat Perceptions in Risk Society

Threat perception is a conceptual variables underlining factors or circumstances that put individuals or groups of people in a position that they feel their desire and expectations are being undermined in environment where they perceived to be their natural habitats. The levels of their perceptions about threat make them feel unsafe, necessitating the right to self and/or group defense. The basic value for understanding threat perception is survival. In this process, a risk society is created where individuals and groups begin to arm themselves in self-defense. Risk is a process towards crisis, which invariably is a crisis interlaced with conflict. Therefore, risk society includes conflict societies that have suffered discrete crises, which have snowballed into unimaginable conflicts. This is complicated by the rise of globalization where both state and non-state actors are competing for security space to protect their interests and values across the globe.

In the developed world, in fact, global security is couched to reinforce the interest of non-state actors, which while establishing their interests across the globe, are equally protected by their home government. In this case, the interest of the protecting state and that of its non- state actors are symbiotic, in reconstructing and reordering the architecture of global security. The example of the European Union (EU) becoming an octopus in reinforcing the vestiges of Atlantic Charter is important in this respect. Unfortunately, in the developing world, what globalism and global security means is that individuals and groups that have suffered estrangement are beginning to define their bio-social origin by questioning the existing social and economic order.

Therefore, globalism and global security are the lubricants that facilitate with high speed through information technology the penetration of multinational corporations to other parts of the world than ever before. However, for the developing world Global security is seen as a mechanism of consciousness for estranged and marginalized groups to seek redress through the struggle for identities and self-determination, when their mode of production is threatened. In relations to this, therefore, threats perceptions are functional effects of economic, social, political, cultural, environment, gender and religious interface in the society. Individuals and groups faced with these interfaces would have suffered from inequitable distribution of resources, injustice and social disequilibria. As a result they would be certainly tasked psychologically to defend themselves.

It is on the basis of this that one can understand the changing nature of security scenarios in West Africa. The West Africa sub region has been noted to be coup prone society with intermittent crisis and conflict since independence. Even so, this situation did not create any serious devastating scenario as it is now. Hitherto, coup making increasingly became significant in the sub continent when it was discovered that the promises at independence have not been fulfilled. The region continues to experience one party personal rule and military dictatorship. These regimes became repressive as they mismanaged the economy, created architecture of corruption and constitutionalized exclusivist approach to power and denounced representative democracy, accountability and transparent governance. Therefore, coup making, whether radical or conservative, was then intended to change the status quo, by either establishing radical populist rule or authoritarian populist regimes. However, in the end, it was discovered that coup making itself was a function of repression intended to mortgage the struggle of the oppressed from the inbuilt post colonial status quo acquired by the Africa leaders. In fact as at the time the security in the sub region began to be threatened, only The Gambia, Benin, and Senegal had some symbolism of democratic appearances. All the other 12-member states were under one form of dictatorship or the other.

The period of globalization, therefore, succeeded in turning off coup making and military rule scenario of the cold war, opening up channels of contestation and struggle against the militarization of the society. It changed the nature of conflict and further escalated conflict to multi-dimensional levels. The process of globalization stimulated mass populism and rebellions as a counterforce to repression and militarism. As a result of these circumstance non-uniformed political zealots exploited the grievances of the ordinary people to upstage the security system through violent revolutionary- penetrate, to destabilize the subregion. So, at one extreme globalization under the notion of global security enables the transfer of economic interests, cultural technologies and political values of the western world through borderless frontiers to the other parts of the world. At the other extreme of the developing world it created clashes of culture among ethnic groups who are meeting its challenges for the first time, but lack the capacity to exploit its opportunities.

The changing security scenario widened the scope of common security perceptions and threats in West Africa. What is obvious is that the sub region became a bulwark of threats perceived, real and imagined, to include among others, economic-triggered political/ethnic and religious crises, inter-state border-security conflict, cross border crimes, human trafficking, proliferations of mercenaries and militias, spread of small arms and light/soft weapons, abuse of children as child soldiers, environmental degradation and the deconstruction of gender-mainstreaming. Kofi Anan (2004) in his report to the United Nations Security Council captures this thus:

> The increasing use and proliferation of mercenaries, child soldiers and small arms account for much of the instability in the West African subregion. This is not an exhaustive list of such problems. The culture of impunity, the spread of HIV/AIDS, the continued weakening of the security sector, the proliferation of roadblocks, youth unemployment, environmental degradation, social exclusion, remnants of war, mass refugee movements and other forced displacement, inequitable and illicit exploitation of natural resources, weak national institutions and civil society structures, and violation of human rights, including the rights of women, are some of the other serious cross-border problems afflicting many parts of the subregion.

These are fundamental security threats which ECOWAS lacked security structures to tackle.

ECOWAS' Security Policy

It has already been noted that ECOWAS was not originally meant to tackle intractable problem of insecurity, but mainly to address economic problem in the sub region. However, it was difficult meeting the challenges of economic development when conflicts tend to overshadow the process. The security dilemma in the sub-region kicks off with a bizarre of uneventful skirmishes in the outskirt of Liberia in the late December of 1989 (Yoroms, forthcoming). The crisis rendered military concept of state security inconsequential as irregular forces became well armed to overturn authoritarian military and/one party police states. The velocity with which the crisis spread from Liberia to other countries demonstrate the level of frustration, anger and confused state of the suffering majority of the population in West Africa, against leaderships that have squandered opportunities for development. In his prediction, few years after the start of the Liberian conflict, Kaplan noted that West Africa was becoming the symbol of worldwide demographic, environmental and social stress in which criminal anarchy emerges as strategic danger (Kaplan, 1994).

Indeed wild fire of conflict in Liberia spread to Sierra Leone, Guinea Bissau, Guinea, Côte d'Ivoire and consumed the entire manor river region. Though the degree and intensity of insecurity may differ from country to country, the fact remains that the vast majority of ordinary people in West Africa have also been denied their fundamental rights including the lack of adequate access to health care and environmental facilities. As noted, the leadership failed to 'serve as a source of security for and the guardian angels of their citizens' (Jaye, 2003). Rather, they turned the subregion into a risk society, endangering peace, security and development.

In tackling the security problem ECOWAS depended on two main policy processes. The first was to rely upon the Protocol on Non-Aggression (1978) and the Protocol on Mutual Assistance in Defence (1981). The second aspect is to depend on willing actors. Unfortunately, the two legal instruments had outlived their usefulness. And as pointed out by Mohammed Ibn Chambas, the ECOWAS Executive Secretary, the two protocols 'had gross limitations because they were mainly suited to addressing interstate conflicts while what was required was an instrument to deal with intrastate conflict' (Ibn Chamba, 2004). The failure in the application of these ECOWAS security regimes succeeded in throwing up willing actors. These actors, correctly or otherwise, were determined to resolve the conflicts, but they eventually complicated the security dilemma in the sub region. Thus, though threat perceptions were common but approaches to preventing them were contradictory. This led to the protracted conflict in Liberia, which eventually engulfed the other member states.

There are five key political actors in the subregion whose commitment or lack of it defines the scope and trends in the sub-regional security. These are Nigeria, Ghana, Guinea, Senegal and Côte d'Ivoire. In the course of the regional insecurity Nigeria committed substantial resources and armed personnel for the resolution of the conflicts. She lost more than 2,000 soldiers during the war as much as about 39 billion dollars spent to end the conflict up to date (Ezeodum, 2004). Apart from this, Nigeria suffered more in terms of its reputation as her involvement was viewed as hegemonic ambition. In this, Côte d'Ivoire, a co-architect of regional conflicts, together with Burkina Faso, exacerbated and prolongs the conflict to this time. Thus, apart from Boigney's personal interests in the conflict, his involvement was to scuffle Nigeria's hegemonic interests.

It was also appalling that Nigeria did not bother about this but continued to pursue an agenda that remained repugnant to member states. Just as she did in Liberia, Nigeria opted to pursue a military solution by brushing aside "aside the preference of some other states in the sub region for continued diplomatic efforts to resolve the crisis" (Berman & Sams, 2000, pp. 117-118). Côte d'Ivoire was too concerned about scuffling Nigeria's hegemonic interests that she could not address her internal contradiction, as she was later consumed by it. But as Takwa pointed out "the question remains whether any other single West African nation could replace Nigeria in this odious and financially costly task... Nigeria therefore is an indispensable actor to the success of any future sub regional peace and security initiatives, especially the military dimension" (Suifon, 2004).

Though Senegal did not show any serious commitment but her internal conflict in Casmance weakened her role in the sub region in spite of initial assistance provided by the United Sates for her to participate. Nigeria was left alone to count on the support of Ghana, Guinea, The Gambia and Sierra Leone. Unfortunately the political leaderships in The Gambia and Sierra Leone later suffered the consequences of both their actions as well as the necessity of the revolving conflict in the sub region. Sir Dauda Jawara was toppled in a military coup while General Joseph Momoh of Sierra Leone was chased out of power, as his country was plunged into a devastating war. As for Guinea, she has suffered constant intimidation and threats, which resulted in humanitarian crises along her border with Liberia.

Therefore, at the end most of the countries including the key actors either became fatigued or consumed by their internal contradiction that they distanced themselves from active participation in maintaining peace and security in the sub region. In this case, member states also became polarized by their colonial vestiges and identity. Thus, after a decade, beginning from 1989 when the conflict started, ECOWAS had no concrete policy on regional security, as security issues were attended to in ad hoc approach. As the ad hoc approaches undertaken by ECOWAS were being carried out, a long a term planning were also made for creating regional security regime policy.

Meanwhile international organizations like the UN and OAU (predecessor to the African Union, AU) later had no option than to find ways of assisting ECOWAS through United Nations Mission in Liberia (UNMIL) and the United Nations Mission in Sierra Leon (UNAMSIL). The delay was also as a result of the changing trend of conflict in the subregion, which shifted from intra-state to inter-state. This new trend made it difficult for the application of the UN traditional peace keeping doctrine. Therefore, without any instrumental authorization, ECOWAS was compelled to evolve its own means of responding to and resolving the armed conflicts and potential humanitarian catastrophes in the sub region especially in Liberia, Sierra Leone and Guinea Bissau" (Ibn Chamba, 2004). According to Mohammed Chambas, though the policy and actions taken were imperfect, they "were worthy precedents that subsequently served as a model for other regional organizations to initiate peace keeping operations" (ibid). The imperfect policy not withstanding the circumstances made even the US policy makers to "prefer to work with the imperfect institution rather than hope for new ones" (Howe, 2000, p. 165).

In spite of the imperfect and ad hoc approaches in the pursuit of regional security, ECOWAS summit began from 1998 to work in cooperation towards reconstructing new regional security architecture. After several discussions with stakeholders, civil societies and the academia ECOWAS inaugurated in 1999 a Protocol Relating to the Mechanism for Conflict prevention, Management, Resolution peacekeeping and Security. Otherwise known as ECOWAS Mechanism, the objectives are to:

1. Prevent, manage and resolve internal and inter state conflicts.

2. Strengthen cooperation in the area of conflict prevention, early

warning, peace keeping operations, the control of cross border crime, terrorism and proliferation of small arms and anti-personnel mines.

3. Maintain and consolidate peace, security and stability in West Africa.

4. Establish institutions and formulate policies to coordinate humanitarian relief missions.

5. Constitute and deploy a civilian and military force to maintain or restore peace.

6. Protect the environment and take steps to restore the degraded environment.

The Mechanism made provision for supporting organs like the Defence and Security Commission, the Council of Elders, Ecomog (ECOWAS Ceasefire Monitoring Group) as a Standby Force, the Peace and Security Observation System (Early Warning System) (Yoroms, 1999). These organs are structured to ensure political stability in the subregion. As Aning noted the new Mechanism is intended to "institutionalize norms and processes with structures that ensure consultation and collective management of regional security concern" (Aning, 2002). In furtherance to this, ECOWAS had in 2001 established a supplementary Protocol to the Mechanism, which is the protocol on Democracy and Good Governance. The supplementary protocol intends to provide for election monitoring, the role of armed forces, the police and the security forces in a democracy, poverty alleviation and promotion of social dialogue, education, culture, religion, rule of law, women children and youth.

Another important regional security regime policy is the 1998 Moratorium on the importation Exportation and manufacture of Small Arms and Light Weapons in West Africa. Though the Moratorium was initially seen as voluntary, member states of ECOWAS have given serious attention to it, by accepting to establish national small arms units in their various countries to monitor and track down arms proliferations.

Cooperation and Coordination in ECOWAS Security Policy

More than half of the years ECOWAS existed have been spent in tackling conflict than its original mandate to pursue economic development. Never the less, the conflicts have succeeded in shaping ECOWAS to come to terms with reality. ECOWAS has succeeded to put up strong security structures. The initial bond of confrontation between the Anglophone and Francophone, which used to be enacted by dual security policies, has been simmered. For instance the *Ac-*

cord de non Aggression et de Defence (ANAD), which most of the sub regional francophone states have depended upon for the resolution of their conflicts has been abolished. ECOWAS security regimes now remain the only instruments for sustaining security in the subregion. The ECOWAS Mechanism is very elaborate with a well-structured Early Warning System established in four zonal areas of the sub region. The coordinating centre is in Abuja. The zonal centers are Benin, Gambia Monrovia and Ouagadougou

The establishment of code of conduct and the Program for Coordination and Assistance for Security and Development (PCASED) are also intended to strengthen the Moratorium on the Importation, Exportation and Manufacture of Small Arms and Light weapons. This is important to address the problem of arms proliferation in the region which has risen to as much as 8 million with 300,000 child soldiers and 10,000 mercenaries roaming the sub region with these arms threatening peace and stability.

In terms of concretizing defence and security policy ECOWAS has decided to design training and doctrinal command centers in the sub region. For instance the Koulikoro in Mali is designed for tactical training while Kofi Annan international peacekeeping Training Centre, Accra Ghana is to carry out training at tactical level. The National War College Nigeria is scheduled for strategic level command training.

Thus from indications, ECOWAS has solid security structures which member states cooperated among themselves to establish. However, most of these member states are still economically weak and political threatened. Therefore, they still maintain some bilateral relations with external powers to enhance their capacity to develop. Because of this, several support in both economic and military assistance flow into the sub region from the US, EU member states among others. In most cases these assistance do not come early enough. By the time the assistance arrives some great damages would have been done. At the end, the assistance is reactive rather than proactive. In another development most of the assistance benefit UEMOE than ECOWAS. This parity has serious political and security implications for the stability of the region. Therefore, the UN as well as the series of EU 'Common Position on Human rights, democratic Principles, the rule of law and good governance' need enhanced package for the coordination of regional support to ECOWAS.

According to Dawn ECOWAS 'remains a trouble regional organization, not just because of its lack of institutional capacity but also because the conflicts it is called on to mange are those between and within its own members... Therefore, if ECOWAS is to play the ambitious role for it, it will need a sustained, active partnership with, and assistance from, the UN and the EU....Regional preventive strategies must be international in substance" (Dawn, 2003).

ECOWAS and the new Global security Architecture

ECOWAS' involvement in the new global security policy can only be superintended by the ability of the international system to consider conflicts in the sub region as part of threats to Global security and take up the challenges with all seriousness to tackle them rather than see conflicts as regional problems of Africa. If globalization is about tearing down barriers of frontiers those who promote the idea of globalization must be ready to tackle the effect of the process so that opportunities emerging from it might be shared by all that are affected by it. Also, it is important that in constructing the new architecture of Global Security regional organization should be placed properly to address intractable conflicts because of their proximity to conflict environment. The UN and AU for instance should rely more on what ECOWAS can do, rather than allow ECOWAS to wait for authorization from New York or Addis Ababa. This would be time wasting as the processes and feedback are always bureaucratic and cumbersome.

In addition, discrete training to member countries by external power with out ECOWAS consent creates chaotic situation. There is need for standardization of training, doctrine and logistics. External supports in terms of logistics and training should be provided to ECOWAS training centers in Koulikoro, Mali, Accra, Ghana and Abuja Nigeria for tactical, operational and strategic levels of training respectively.

In this way it is possible to construct common security, which would be in line with the concept of global security. Therefore, what ECOWAS require from the Global security is the development of partnership in terms of cooperation, coordinated by ECOWAS. In fact the overall expectation from ECOWAS is partnering for ownership by the regional organizations. That is, partners are expected to develop ECOWAS capabilities and capacities for maintaining regional security.

Conclusion

Globalization is real. But not all regions of the world are prepared for it. If it should benefit all it must peel off the vestiges and contents of imperialism embodied in it. Or else from the slow economic stratum of the third world, it will continue to create clashes of civilizations as being manifested in form of terrorism, conflict and general political instability. This will however, be a problem in providing the architecture for global security in defense of globalization.

References

Anan, K. (2004, March 12). Report of the Secretary General to the Security Council on Ways to Combat Subregional and Cross border problems in West Africa.

Aning, E. (2002, February 27-28). *The New ECOWAS: Democracy and security sector reform in West Africa.* Paper at the Workshop on Security Sector Reform and Democratization in Africa: Comparative Perspectives, ASDR, Accra, Ghana.

Berman, E. G. & Sams, K. E. (2000). *Peacekeeping in Africa: Capabilities and culpabilities.* Geneva and Pretoria: *UNDIR/ISS.*

Dawn, R. (2003). Conflict prevention. *SIPRI year book.* London: Oxford University Press.

Ezeodum, A. U. (2004). Peace support operations in the West African sub region: Implications for the Nigerian economy. *Fellowship Research Dissertation,* National War College, Abuja, Nigeria.

Howe, H. (2000). *Ambiguous order: Military forces in African states.* Boulder: Lynne Rienner.

Ibn Chamba, M. (2004, May 31-June 4). *Major issues and opportunities in the interface between the UN and regional organizations.* Paper presented at the conference on Challenges of Peace Operations, Abuja.

Jaye, T. (2003, August 1). *Zonal assessment of human security dynamics in the Manor River Union including Cote D'Ivoire.* Paper presented at the Seminar on Civil Societies in West Africa.

Kaplan, R. (1994, February). The coming anarchy. *Atlantic Monthly, 273*(2), 44-76.

McGowan, P. J. (1995). Understanding International Relations in the mid-1990s. In C. Landsberg, et al. (eds.), *Mission imperfect: Redirecting South Africa's foreign policy.* Johannesburg: FGD/CPS.

Suifon, T. Z. (2004). ECOWAS' Sub regional Conflict Prevention: Learning through Experience. *WANEP: From the Field, Issue No. 8.*

Yoroms, J. G. (1999). The New Mechanism for Conflict Management in ECOWAS: Issues and Perspective in African Security and Development. *ACCORD Occasional Paper.*

_____ (2000). Global security system in the Twenty-first Century: Whether Nigeria. *India Journal of Politics,*

_____ (forthcoming). Regional conflict and political instability in West Africa. *Monograph.* Kano, Nigeria: Centre for Research and Documentation.

Chapter 10

Virtual Communication and the Role of Diasporic Communities in Conflict Mediation

Bala A. Musa, Ph.D.
Azusa Pacific University, USA

Introduction

From 2003 to mid-2004, *The McGill Report,* a news blog ran by former New York Times reporter and *Bloomberg News* bureau chief, Doug McGill, published a series of articles regarding a genocide being perpetrated against the Anuak people of Ethiopia (Cline & McGill, 2006). Doug McGill, a resident of Minnesota, became aware of the reported genocide through members of the Anuak immigrant community in his town. Subsequently McGill became a one-person champion of the issue. He heard from the Anuak community of Rochester, Minnesota how: "They were having cellular telephone conversations with friends and family in their home villages and were hearing, through their cell phone connections, the sounds of the massacre--shouting and screaming, gunshots, soldiers yelling, and people sobbing and crying" (p. 7). He attended a church meeting where the Anuak Diaspora met to discuss the issue. With the aid of the Knight Foundation, he traveled to Ethiopia and a refugee camp in Sudan to interview eyewitnesses and survivors of the genocide. With time, his reports got picked up by the mainstream media. Human Rights groups took up the cause. His Webb log became a forum for exchange of information and advocacy for the Anuaks and other interested parties, not only in the United States but all over the world.

"A Kenyan Runner Seeks Peace for Her Corner of the World" reads the headline of an article in the *New York Times*. In it the paper reports on the effort by German-based Tegla Laroupe, world marathon winner, to promote peace in her native community through her Tegla Laroupe Peace Foundation. Her commitment to promoting conflict resolution and equipping the youth to acquire education and job skills has attracted other organizations such as the Oxfam Foundation (Gettleman, 2006).

"Everyday, the 2.5 million people chased from their homes in Darfur face the threat of starvation, disease, and rape, while the few lucky enough to remain in their homes risk displacement, torture, and murder." The above message is part of the Save Dafur campaign which includes web, television advertising, and community rallies in far away United States and other countries around the world (*http://action.savedarfur.org/* campaign.jsp?campaign_).

These stories, anecdotal as they may be, illustrate the increasing transnationalization of African conflict transformation initiatives, the role of the African Diaspora, and the role of the media in conflict resolution.

Since the last decade of the 20th century through the beginning half of the first decade of the 21st century, the world has experienced untold number of international, ethnic, religious, political and social conflicts. Many of them have had catastrophic results. From the first Gulf war to the genocides and ethnic cleansings in Bosnia and Rwanda and the current genocides in the Sudan, there have hardly been any calm moments. Liberia and Sierra Leone witnessed gruesome political/ethnic wars. India, Pakistan, the Philippines, Indonesia, and Columbia have also seen decades of conflict between various ethnic and religious factions. The Israeli-Palestinian conflict has defied solution. Irredentist movements in Spain, Canada and Ireland have also been sources of concern. Zimbabwe, the Democratic Republic of Congo, Somalia, and Eritrea have experienced numerous conflicts. The U.S. and allied forces involvement in the second Gulf War, dubbed Operation Iraqi Freedom, has lasted as long as the U.S. was involved in World War II. Besides these wars and conflicts that have received global attention, there have been numerous communal conflicts and silent genocides that have not received world attention despite the massive scale of atrocities involved.

The information revolution and the emergence of global society have produced diametrically opposing forces and trends – "deterritorialization and reterritorialization" (Georgiou, 2006, p. 2) on one hand, and detribalization and retribalization on the other. Global culture has been shaped by both centripetal and centrifugal interaction. It has enabled millions of people to leave their geopolitical homelands and communities yet remain informed and participate actively or vicariously in the affairs of their communities. The role of the Diaspora in conflict transformation in Bosnia, Rwanda, Iraq, and Afghanistan, the Sudan, and

Columbia to mention but a few, have been largely shaped by media depictions of the violence associated with these conflicts.

This chapter examines how the media portrayal and the perception/interpretations of conflicts as well as the role of virtual communities in the transformation of conflict and violence in Africa. It uses historical and cultural/critical methodologies to examine how images of African conflicts have been used by virtual communities to frame and transform conflicts. It looks at the inter-layering of natural ties with virtual ties and the role of mediated images in the new world disorder, which has largely been characterized by intractable ethno-religious, political, economic, and social conflicts. It examines the power of the image in affective framing of these conflicts and discusses the implications for conflict management and transformation in the new environment.

Changes in communication technology have been analogous to demographic and cultural dispersions as well as implosions. Advances in transportation, print, and telecommunication accelerated expansions and explorations among various populations. The interstate highways, railways, air transportation and the mass media gave rise to megacities, suburbs, satellite societies and global metropolis. It also created diasporic communities of various ethnicities and nationalities in far away lands. These include Chinatowns, Little Haiti, Little Havana, Little Ethiopia and Korea Towns in cities and places far away from the homeland.

Globalization and the information revolution have made it possible to connect the various diasporic communities of the world in real time. As Marshall McLuhan (1964) rightly foresaw, electronic communication and globalization have resulted in cultural implosion and retribalization. He argued that new social networks and virtual communities will replace the individuation and sociocultural explosion created by the print revolution. What he did not fore-see was how the traditional "tribal" ties and sentiments were going to be energized in the new global society.

Diasporic/Virtual Communities, Retribalization and Global Conflicts

The identities and realities of diasporic people vary according to context and time. Some are marginal others are integrated into their new communities to varying degrees. People in the Diaspora have different feelings of connection and/or nostalgia toward their homelands. Thus, they have different and evolving identities relative to their sense of identification with their original or new communities.

Virtual communities are groups that interact with one another on an ongoing basis but do so essentially through mediated communicated–particularly the Internet. The typical virtual community is a hyper-real network of minds that are not limited by gender, ethnicity, age, or any other physical and socio-cultural factors (Gunkel & Gunkel, 1997; Dery, 1994). However, as will be shown later, a critical aspect of the communities in reference here is the diasporic communities that combine the elements of the genderless, raceless, classless, disembodied entities with the natural and real identities of the real world, so called. Their cyber- and telepresence are privileged here because of their relationship to the media particularly cybermedia as a constitutive forum (Mitra, 1997a). According to Mitra (1997a), in addition to using the mass media to communicate about issues of mutual interest, these diasporic communities communicate through "community events, ethnic newspapers, occasional national and international gatherings." Therefore, "increasingly, the Internet and the WWW is playing a role in the production of a virtually connected community of people who are producing a cyberidentity for themselves as well as for their country through the variety of discourses on the WWW" (p. 159).

The Save Dafur campaign, for instance, involves a coalition of over three hundred national and international groups such as American Jewish World Service, American Society for Muslim Advancement, Amnesty International USA, Dafur Peace and Development, NAACP, Genocide Intervention Network, National Association of Evangelicals, National Black Church Initiative, etc. Virtual communities that have formed around causes of conflict resolution and peace-building in Africa include both the African Diaspora and other supporters who have no kinship ties to the groups in conflict. Through communication media, they have been linked together into a virtual network of people committed to the same cause. Other virtual sites such as the Global Normads Group provide information including video links on the conflicts in Southern Sudan, the Rwanda crisis, the Iraq war, and other displaced groups.

As mentioned earlier diasporic and virtual communities are characterized by the dialectic of both detribalization and retribalization. Isa (2001) observed that:

> the increasing process of globalization and democratic projects; worsening economic crisis and social injustices and inequalities; the re-emergence of neo-liberal ideology of market reforms and the attendant erosion of state legitimacy and capacity to manage these conflicts [which] have all led to the resurgence of individual groups under new ethnic chauvinism" (p. 1).

Just as natural traditional villages were inhabited by close-knit tribes that had strong personal ties, today's global village is likewise being organized along both old and new "tribal" identities. This author agrees with Christians (2004) and others that "Transnationalism has tribalism's fury." "Electronic implosion" has not dissolved traditional ties, as envisaged by McLuhan, instead it has strengthened them. Carey (1998) likewise underscored the role of the mass media as a driving force of global culture change and internationalization:

Modern communications media allowed individuals to be linked, for the first time, directly to the imagined community of the nation (at least for the nations as large as the United States) without the mediating influence of regional and other local affiliations. Such national media laid the basis for a mass society, understood in its most technical and least ideological sense: the development of a form of social organization in which intermediate associations of community, occupation, and class did not inhibit direct linkage of the individual and primary groups to the state and other nationwide organizations through mass communications (Carey, 1998 p. 30).

Carey (1998) further opined that in addition to the centrifugal dispersal and individuation effect, communication technology has also had a centrifugal effect of transforming "inchoate groups into national but specialized audiences organized around ethnic, occupational, class, religious, racial, and other affiliation interests" (p. 30). Virtual communities consist of old and new tribes that attempt to recruit, mobilize, exclude, and oppose individuals and other groups that threaten or perceived to threaten their interests.

Nevertheless, it is probably the unintended offshoots of these media that are most notable. One such result is the impact on the nature of community and intergroup relations. These media have broken down boundaries as well as built them up. Majid Tehranian (1993), for instance, observed that post-Cold War world order was being shaped by forces of "globalism, regionalism, nationalism, localism, and spiritualism" (p. 197). In his view:

The end of the Cold War, however, has unleashed the centrifugal, ethnic, and tribal forces within nation-states....It has led to the breakup of the former Soviet Union, the world's largest multinational empire, the breakdown of multiethnic patchworks such as Yugoslavia and Iraq, has threatened the break up of other nation-states such as Canada and India, and unleashed racial and ethnic violence in the United States, Israel, South Africa, other multiracial and multiethnic societies (p. 197).

The information revolution has not only created a global village but glocalized villages (Kraidy, 1999). It has both dissolved and strengthened old ties and relationships. The reality of the international community since the information revolution and the end of the Cold War has proved once again that predicting the future of technology and culture change requires both intellectual audacity and blind faith (Carey, 1998). Each time the promises held out by advances in communication technology seemed to have been reaching realization, the outcome has been otherwise than expected. At the heart of modernization and the interrelated advances in technology, social infrastructure, and cultural institutions is the dream of a better society. Although there is no express contract detailing what the better world or human utopia would look like, there are certain universal human aspirations. This constitutes the social contract that people share as citizens of the globe. According to Christians (2004), "citizens of the world have cosmopolitan duties to the globe." In his view, "Beyond our self interest, we are responsible for the flourishing of human beings generally (solidarity), acceptance within limits of the ways people understand the good (pluralism), and for conciliatory approaches to conflict (way of peace)" (p. 9).

Virtual communities of the Indian Diaspora use the media to maintain contact with one another and discuss issues of mutual interest. The virtual forum often provides an avenue for discussing issues relating to the homeland. Unfortunately, the conflicts of the real or larger society are carried into the virtual community as well. Virtual communities extend the divisions and fragmentations of the larger culture. (Mitra, 1997b). Diasporic communication includes conventional media (radio, television, or journalism) and neo-traditional media (pilgrimages, religious occasions, family rituals, etc. (Dayan, 1998). The natural inclination is to expect greater understanding and cooperation with increase in communication and interaction between various people. The reality has been otherwise.

According to Williamson & Pierson (2003), "groups like the Ku Klux Klan (KKK), Neo-Nazis, Racist Skinheads, Christian Identity, Black-Separatist, and Neo-Confederates, have found a fertile new medium in cyberspace" (p. 250).

Sometimes the roles of the Diaspora or "external republics" as Seaton (1999) calls them can be detrimental to conflict transformation and peacebuilding. According to Seaton:

> A new factor in modern conflicts, however, is the existence of 'external republics': the groups of immigrants who remain fiercely committed to the communities they have come from, and the ways of life they have left behind. Nationalism—at a distance—is a contemporary phenomenon, and one especially dependent on the media. It is often more virulent than the home-grown variety and it has become a powerfully destabilizing force in some of the conflicts seen as 'ethnic' in origin.... Migrants became members of their new communities, but this did not diminish their attachment to the regions from where they had come, although it did change and the nature of that attachment. (p. 46).

The adoption and application of new media have not been the exclusive preserve of antisocial groups. Many prosocial groups also have also used to media to advance worthy causes.

Peace processes

Although the preceding discourse on African conflicts have emphasized violent, even genocidal, other forms of communal, political, and social conflicts cut across the African landscape. Violent and catastrophic conflicts receive the most attention because they result in failed states like Somalia; mass murders like the genocides in Rwanda and Dafur; the civil wars in Liberia and Sierra Leone. However, political conflicts in Zimbabwe, Togo, and Côte D'Ivoire have equally traumatic effects on the lives of the masses in those countries. While failed states receive global attention because of the power vacuum and the tendency of the international societies to recognize states as primary political groupings, failed communities tend to go unnoticed. In reality failed communities, usually as a result of communal conflicts, are more perennial because they are rooted in the people's identity (Isa, 2001). Even in relatively stable countries the effect of frequent communal conflicts which result:

> in political competition and struggle for political power in Nigeria, is violent destruction of lives and property to tunes of billions of nairas (Nigerian currency), stagnation of economic activities, social disorder, and refugee problems, such as in the recent Kaduna crisis, February, 2000; Lagos, Imo, Anambra and the Niger Delta area (Isa, 2001, p. 1; See also Peoples, 2004).

The same can be said of the Congo, Chad, Burundi, Mozambique, Togo, Morocco, Algeria, and a host of other African countries. Added to these are structural conflicts manifested in human right abuses, injustice, poverty, inequality, and nepotism. Peace processes include all efforts to stop or reverse these trends. These include creating awareness about a conflict, the framing of the issue, conflict mediation and intervention initiative–whether bilateral or multilateral, conflict prevention efforts, capacity building, and a wide range of activities related to diffusing conflict.

By nature, the media are known to be key players in conflict because conflict is always news worthy. Not so with peace-building and conflict transformation. Media can potentially advance peace processes through their ability to define and articulate the issues for internal and external groups, shape the tone of the debate or negotiation, legitimize or delegitimize a particular group or faction in conflict, and influence how parties in conflict act or react (Wolfsfeld, 2004). Generally the media have not been viewed as using this capacity responsibly. Worlfsfeld suggests that because peace processes are slow and tedious, they attract less attention from the media than violence and manifest conflicts. This is because the media are drawn to the sensational and the dramatic (Musa, 2006a). By emphasizing episodes of clashes between factions in a conflict and showing graphic images of victims of wars, media are criticized for fueling conflict rather than promoting peace. While others have attempted to debate whether the media should be objective reporters or peace advocates (Cramer, 1994; Seib, 2002; Musa, 2004; Mwesige, 2004; Richards & King, 2000; Gilboa, 2005), it is outside the scope of this discourse to engage that debate.

Although diasporic and virtual communities rely on the media for informa-tion, they also add another dimension to conflicts. New media enable them to be *prosumers* of information, not just consumers. The World Wide Web, cell phones, text messaging, and other alternative media enable them gain access to a variety of information and in participating in online and community discussions they help influence the media agenda on conflict, directly or indirectly. How members of the Anuak community in Minnesota got the story of the conflict in their home country, Ethiopia, to a web blogger and then to mainstream media and other agencies is a case in point.

Media and Meta-narratives of African Conflicts

The rest of this study is rhetorical analysis of meta-narratives through which African conflicts have been framed and depicted. It is biased toward visual framing because of the increasing dominance of images in contemporary media content. Particularly in reporting conflicts graphics play very powerful roles, which shall be examined shortly. Research has shown that diasporic and virtual communities use media images to record, store, and transmit collective memory (Dayan, 1998; Musa, 2006b) Upadhyaya, 2006). Media images perform a range of rhetorical functions from informing and agenda-setting to issue framing, per-suasion, and even manipulating (Messaris, 1997). This rhetorical critic also adopts *emic* analysis–pointing the light inward by looking at media routines and issue framing, as well as an *etic* analysis by looking at media portrayals of Afri-ca's conflicts.

Through (visual) framing, media set the agenda for diasporic communities, while these communities use media information to frame conflict narratives. Mostly this involves affective framing or second level agenda-setting (Coleman & Banning, 2006; McCombs & Ghanem, 2001). Global conflicts are complex enough even when they are explained with words. When images appeal more to our emotions forcing us to process the information through a peripheral rather than a central route, they further limit our understanding of the issues.

The media set the public agenda by influencing what the public thinks about. This is done primarily through portraying those issues as important by the amount of attention, and prominence they are given. Framing relates to the as-pects of the news or information the media choose to play up or the way the narrative positions (pegs) a story. According to Entman (1993):

> Framing essentially involves selection and salience. To frame is to select some aspects of a perceived reality and make them more salient in a communicating context, in such a way as to promote a particular definition, casual interpreta-tion, moral evaluation, and/or treatment recommendation for the item it de-scribes (p. 52).

Researchers hold conflicting views on the cause-effect relationship between media agenda, public agenda, and policy agenda. Those who subscribe to the validity of the so called "CNN Effect" or "CNN factor" in agenda setting argue that media agenda drives both public and policy agenda. Critics of this view invoke empirical data that show public and policy agenda driving media agenda (Fan, Brosius, & Kepplinger, 1994; Iyenger & Simon, 1993; Livingston & Eachus, 1995).

Globalization and the proliferation of diasporic and virtual communities are partly associated with various phases of modernity. In this context, modernity refers to the change associated with the progress of the human spirit and its manifestations in social, cultural, spiritual, and physical change. It is trend rooted in the enlightenment revolution and the expansion of Westernization and Eurocentric episteme. Modernity became a worldwide factor due to commercial and religious explorations, colonization and, now, as a result of the wave of globalization. In looking at modern conflicts, we will examine the various dimensions of and responses to modernity as central forces behind contemporary conflicts. These include pre-anti, hyper, and post-modernity.

In most cases, where world attention has been brought to bear on a particular conflict, television and other media images and content have been the powerful tools of concientization. There is an added dimension in this era of many-to-many communication. This involves the multiple sources of information, particularly images of war and conflict. Unlike when society relied almost exclusive on big corporate media to report on wars and conflicts, many individuals and groups are now able to create, collect, and disseminate information to the world from personal cell phones and computers. Online fora, group listservs, chartrooms, news groups, and cybercommunity web sites combine visual images with textual narrative to tell their stories. With the arrival of U-tube and even before, the idea that "the whole world is watching" is no longer a mere claim.

Some characteristics of media framing of conflict that make it relevant to conflict transformation are worth noting. Many of these frames are determined by news routine rather than professional or organizational decision on how to peg a story. Such frames include:

The affective frame–Media content, particularly news images, have the power to appeal to people's emotions and feelings. Words tend to require more central route processing as described in Elaborartion Likelihood Model. According to this model, information that is elaborated on is usually processed through the central route involving more critical thinking and engagement on the part of the recipient. Information that is not elaborated upon is mostly processed through the peripheral route (Griffin, 2000). Empirical tests of this model using pictures and videos found that "Visual images that are not elaborated on are processed as peripheral cues, which have their greatest influence when a person is not very involved in an issue". ... and that peripheral cues have a greater impact when the message was presented on video tape rather than writing" (Coleman & Banning, 2006 p. 315; Petty & Cacioppo (1986).

Images have the ability to invoke sympathy, anger, or disgust by the graphic or vivid description of pain, suffering, joy, or any other reality. Though human beings what to pride themselves on being rational, evidence has shown that people are moved more by feeling than by reason.

The intuitive frame–It seems an oxymoron to use the words "framing" and "credible" together. Framing connotes slanting or pegging. If the decision on how to peg a story is subjective, how then can it be trusted? The problem is further compounded in cyber communication where it is difficult to establish the authenticity of a source not to talk of the message. Nevertheless, people are accustomed to the idea that "seeing is believing." Reporters, bloggers, advocates, all want to "substantiate" their arguments with visual images. Eye-witness report is always considered believable. With digital manipulation, it is possible to simulate almost any image a person wants. Yet people find the visual more captivating.

The episodic frame–News reports of conflicts are generally episodic (Musa, 1999, 2004). This is due mostly to the news routine of media organizations. Pictures capture the images before them very well. They however don't explain the context unless someone provides it. The causes and contexts of most conflicts are complex and multilayered. Pictures can hardly give the needed context. To understand an issue more clearly, one needs to know the history behind it. The episodic frame sells the serious observer short in that one may not get the larger context of the event by looking at the picture.

The scopophilic frame–It looks more at the object rather than the person. A dialogic approach would be more informative, dignifying, and engaging frame. The pictures of victims frame them as passive, weak, and uncreative. Likewise aggressors present themselves or are presented as strong and in control. Scopophilic images make the audience observe rather than know or identify with (Lidchi, 1999). Most images of African conflicts show refugees who are helpless, malnourished, and destitute. Lidchi considers that a form of objectifying and dehumanizing.

The aesthetic frame–Image-driven media privilege aesthetics over ethics (Christians, 2004, Baudrillard, 1983). According to Baran and Davis (2000), "Stories are often complex combinations of visual and verbal content–all too often the visual information is so powerful that it overwhelms the verbal" (p. 271). Because of information explosion and overload, those who have particular agenda to highlight certain conflicts feel a need to make their narratives scream loud in other to stand out from the clutter. This sometimes leads to finding and using the most shocking image. This is coupled with the fact that society has continually been desensitized to violence by excessive exposure. Therefore, it seems the more graphic the image the more suitable. Also, because online communication is seen as niche communication, images that would not be considered ethical to show on network television or cable for that matter are routinely shown on the Internet. Case in point is the beheading of kidnap victims by terrorist groups, suicide videos, and images of the prison abuse at Abu Ghraib.

The predominance of these frames over time has created certain meta-narratives on the nature, causes, and possible approaches to African conflicts. These include

The meta-narrative of premodernity–Western media often present Africa's conflicts as conflicts of premodernity (Atkinson, 1999; Musa, 1999; Wall, 1997a, 1997b.) African and other Third World conflicts are portrayed as conflicts fueled by primitive and barbaric impulses as opposed to rational strategic political or economic motives. Western media focused on images of uncivilized natives engaged in frenzied killings in Liberia, Rwanda, and Somalia thus portraying the conflicts as senseless.

Representation of these kinds of conflicts have also been driven by the "trend toward directing news to the 'lowest common denominator', by using simple stories and easily understandable images, is combined with nature of news reporting, as fast-moving and predominantly space-filling, to produce a situation where sensationalism rules, and little indepth political analysis is developed" (Atkinson, 1999 p. 104; see also Musa, 1990, 2006).

The meta-narrative of anti-modernity–Much of the religious conflicts from the Iranian revolution to religious riots in Nigeria and today's terrorist attacks are portrayed as culture clashes between the forces of modernity and antimodernity. The conflict the engulfed most of the Moslem world following the cartoon of the Prophet Mohammed in a Danish newspaper reflects this impulse.

The meta-narrative of post-modernity–The riots in 2006 involving immigrants from North Africa in France and immigrants from the Arab world in Australia reflect the force of post-modernity. Likewise the train bombings in London which has been attributed to homegrown terrorism in the Western world reflect the force of post-modernity, such as the discontent among young people who have been driven to despair and nihilism due to frustrations of unfulfilled dreams. While McLuhan (1964) envisaged implosion as abolishing fragmentation and ruling the global village, Baudrillard (1983) in a postmodernist, somewhat nihilist fashion, reads implosion as increasing fragmentation, abolishing meaning, the social reality itself and establishing a state of absolute non-communication, where the media saturate the environment, with seductive images and spectacles. In the later view, implosion is seen as a radical contracting phenomenon which overtakes postmodernity at every level (Kolar-Panov, 1997, p. 30).

The meta-narrative of hypermodernity–Many countries experience crises deriving from rapid modernization has led to cultural dislocation. Hypermodernity has led to crises of rising expectations and intergenerational conflict. Structural conflicts in Africa have been seen as deriving from greed, overconsumption, and rapid Westernization.

The meta-narrative of Countermodernity–The reign of terror unleashed by Idi Amin of Uganda, the Chadian revolution of Goukouni Wadeyi, the many religious riots that have occurred in Northern Nigeria and as protests against Western influence fit this meta-narrative. They are portrayed counter reactions to the failure or ills of modernization.

Diasporic and virtual communities cut across each of these strands and are affected by all these forces of modern conflicts. Instead of being unproblematic –given, merely 'factual'–a Diaspora is always an intellectual construction, tied to a given narrative. Like other types of communities, but more so than most, Diaspora is an incarnation of existing discourses, interpretants of such discourses, echoes or anticipations of historical projects. They are 'imagined communities' *par excellence,* and they can be imagined in a number of possible, sometimes conflicting ways (Dayan, 1998, p. 110).

Diasporic communities that tend to be anti- or counter modernist hold certain nostalgia about an imagery homeland or era with conservative values of honor, integrity, propriety, and peace. These often have religious and nationalist undertones. In the absence of direct personal contact with the communities they identify with, diasporic communities hold onto images of the communities they knew in the past even if the realities have changed. Dominant narratives of homelands as ideal communities provide referents for individuals trying to establish their moral compass in a global society.

In conflict situations, there are always competing narratives. As indicated earlier, Africa's conflict are caught in the intersection between micro narratives of local history and the macro or meta-narratives of globalization and the many phases modernity. Africa as a whole is still on the margins of the information revolution. There are different perspectives on how Africa and other developing countries ought to respond to the westernization/modernization model of development, which many see as contributing to the conflicts in Africa. Detailed treatise of the viewpoints on appropriate paradigms of development and paths toward peace and stability are beyond the scope of this essay. Suffices to say that a community's narrative of change in an era of globalization has direct bearing on whether or not that community helps to foster peace or escalate existing conflicts.

Diasporic and virtual communities, whom Seaton (1999) describes as citizens of "external republics" (p. 48) are potentially powerful forces for promoting rhetoric that can either help resolve or escalate any conflict based on the choices and roles they play. Distance changes the perspectives of observers and participants in conflict. Diasporic and virtual communities occupy a physical and psychological space that enables them to see the realities of particular conflicts differently from those in the immediate space of the conflict who are victims of violence, aggressors, or displaced persons. Being removed from the physical site of conflicts influences the perspectives from which one observes a conflict. On one hand, one has the opportunity to analyze the situation without the pressure to react instantly for personal safety reasons. It can be assumed that it affords one the privilege of a more cool-headed response. However, there is also the danger of one missing the gravity and urgency of a tragic situation until it is too late to act. This has been the criticism of the international community's response to the genocides in Rwanda, Bosnia, Darfur, and elsewhere.

Based on the subtexts of the described meta-narratives of African conflicts in an era of global communication, two significant communication approaches come to the fore. Virtual communities and diasporic communities do not all have the same agenda or motives. At the very least, one can distinguish between prosocial agents of peace and antisocial warmongers. For each group, access to the media means different things. Examples of antisocial use of the media by virtual communities have been identified earlier. It is worth mentioning still that the internet and cyberspace remains a strong tool for propaganda and hatemongering among antisocial virtual groups. Media forums that promote antisocial narratives and perspectives tend to dehumanize the other, fuel notions of victimhood and calls for revenge. In many of the major conflicts around the world, narratives of good group and bad people tend to dominate. There is always the tendency to paint the in-group in a positive and glowing light while portraying the outgroup in a negative light. Gerbner (1991) opines that these narratives breed certain labels which in turn produce particular actions and reactions. In his view negative perceptions and portrayals of the "other" is at the root of the acts of violence and dehumanization that groups visit on each other. According to him:

> These portrayals, including the choice of labels, serve as projective devices that isolate acts and people from meaningful contexts and set them up to be stigmatized and victimized.... Calling some people barbarians makes it easier to act barbarically toward them. Presuming some people to be criminals, permits dealing them in a ways otherwise considered criminal. Labeling a large group "terrorists" seems to justify terrorizing them. Declaring nations as enemies makes it legitimate to attack and kill them. Calling some people crazy or insane makes it possible to suspend rules of rationality and decency (Gerbner, 1991, pp. 3-4).

This has played out time and again ethnic, religious, and communal conflicts in Africa and other parts of the world (Musa, 2000, 1990). From the holocaust in Western Europe, the genocides in the Balkans, Asia, and Africa to today's terrorist attacks and the war on terrorism, the breakdown in communication and community often starts with narratives that portray the other group as evil. Even well-intentioned people and groups have fallen prey to the narrative and portrayal of Africa and the Third World as premodern. This has made them to perceive conflicts, wars, coups, disasters, and human rights abuse in those regions as endemic and inevitable. The consequence has been a lack of the will or motivation to act, even in cases where minimal intervention would have made a significant difference.

A prosocial application of today's global communication media to influence conflicts in Africa and the international community would call for a dialogic and communitarian approach. Members of diasporic and virtual communities, as global citizens are best positioned to create the atmosphere and culture necessary for dialogue. There exposure to third cultures, mostly advanced democracies, however loaded the term, enables them to draw from cultures of dialogue rather than violence, to encourage tolerance for opposition, and to advance the tenets of grassroots participation and freedom of expression that serve to diffuse conflict and violence. The dream of a global village can only be realized if virtual society evolves into through community. That requires exchanging narratives that promote hate and division for shared realities of mutual interest and mutual humanity. Access to and control of communication technology will be used to promote exchange of ideas, expression of grievances, and true dialogue. There will be need to remember even painful pasts but not for the purpose of vilifying the other. New narratives that encourage reconciliation, forgiveness, and healing will have to be created to bring about a new culture of peace and unity.

Conclusion

How a conflict is framed informs the public response to it. For instance, conflicts depicted as premodern as considered as non-negotiable because of the irrationality of the underlying forces or the disputing factions. Other conflicts are seen as requiring only military or humanitarian solutions. Because of globalization and the rise of virtual communities modern conflict have been glocalized and taking on multiple complex dimensions. Visual frames dominate because today's culture is image-driven, however the medium can hardly capture the complex nature of these conflicts. Multimedia has the potential to promote dialogue among people at a distance and involve neutral parties who would otherwise not be aware or interested in a particular conflict. The ability to use its resources effectively will be the difference between a peaceful and united global village and a fragment world of warring communities. "The proliferation and freedom in information and communication flows made possible by communication technology such as video (and satellite television and the Internet, etc.) allow those organizations to have access to a choice of regional traditions, languages, dialects and cultures and create a basis for more than one way to 'belong'" (Kolar-Panov, 1997, p. 30).

Diasporic communities have the special privilege of being cultural boundary spanners. They can serve as advocates and agents of conflict transformation. Their knowledge of and contacts in the African communities in conflict afford them a better understanding of the historical backgrounds of the local conflicts. They have the means to mobilize external resources toward conflict resolution and community building. Virtual communities and proxy tribal members should seek to promote understanding and peace rather than take sides with particular factions in conflict. Cybernedia are not limited by time and space. Therefore they can transcend the constraints that have forced traditional media to adopt episodic, aesthetic, or scopophilic frames. Virtual communities have the means to enlarge the meta-narratives that influence the perception and approaches to conflict transformation and peace processes in Africa.

Reference

Atkinson, P. (1999). Representations of conflict in the Western media. In T. Skelton & T. Allen, *Culture and global change*, 102-108. New York: Routeledge.

Baran, S. J. & Davis, D. K. (2000). *Mass communication theory: Foundations, ferment and future*. Belmont, CA: Wadsworth.

Baudrillard, J. (1983). *Simulations*, trans. P. Foss, P. Patton and P. Beitchman. New York: Semiotext.

Carey, J . W. (1998). The Internet and the end of the national communication system: Uncertain predictions of an uncertain future. *Journalism & Mass Communication Quarterly, 75*(1), 28-34.

Christians, C. G. (2004). *Universals and their discontents.* Paper presented at the International Conference on Communication Ethics and Conflict, Calvin College, October, 11-13.

Cline, A. R. & McGill, D. (2006). *Death in Gambella: What many heard, what one man saw, and why the news media missed it.* Paper presented at the Colloquium on Mass Media Ethics, Minneapolis, MN, October 14-16.

Coleman, R. & Banning, S. (2006). Network TV news' affective framing of presidential candidates: Evidence for a second-level agenda-setting effect through visual framing. *Journalism and Mass Communication Quarterly, 83*(2), 313-328.

Cramer, C. E. (1994). Ethical problems of mass murder coverage in the mass media. *Journal of Mass Media Ethics, 9*(1), 26-42.

Dayan, D. (1998). Particularistic media and diasporic communications, in T. Liebes & J. Curra n (Eds.). *Media, Ritual and Identity*, pp. 103-113. New York: Routledge.

Dery, M. (1994). Flame wars. In M. Dery (Ed.), *Flame wars: The discourse of cyberculture*, (pp. 1-6). Durham: Duke University Press.

Entman, R. M. (1993). Framing: Toward clarification of a fractured paradigm. *Journal of Communication, 43*(4), 51-58.

Fan, D. P., Brosius, H., & Kepplinger, H. M. (1994). Predictions of public agenda from television coverage. *Journal of Broadcasting & Electronic Media, 38*(2), 163-177.

Georgiou, M. (2006). *Diaspora, identity and the media: Diasporic transnationalism and mediated spatialities.* Cresskill, NJ: Hampton Press, Inc.

Gerbner, G. (1991). Symbolic functions of violence and terror. In Y. Alexander & R. G. Picard (eds.), *In the camera's eye: News coverage of terrorist events* (pp. 3-9). New York: Brassy.

Gettleman, J. (2006, November 18). A Kenyan runner seeks peace for her corner of the world. *New York Times*, p. A4.

Gilboa, E. (2005). Media-broker diplomacy: When journalists become mediators. *Critical Studies in Media Communication, 22*(2), 99-120.

Griffin, E. (2000). *A first look at communication theory.* Boston: McGraw-Hill.

Gunkel, D. J. & Gunkel, A. H. (1997). Virtual geographies: The new worlds of cyberspace. *Critical Studies in Mass Communication, 14,* 123-137.

http://action.savedarfur.org/campaign.jsp?campaign_KEY=5191&track=google_ads. Accessed December 2, 2006.

Isa, M. K. (2001). *The state and institutional responses to ethnic conflict in Nigeria: The case of Jukun/Chamba and Kuteb communal conflicts of Takum Local Government, Taraba State.* Most Ethno-Net Africa Publications. Africa at Crossroads: Complex Political Emergencies in the 21st Century, UNESCO/ENA. http://www.ethnonet-africa.org/pubs/crossroadskabir.htm. Accessed May, 18th, 2006.

Iyenger, S. & Simon, A. (1993). News coverage of the Gulf crisis and public opinion: A study of agenda-setting, priming, and framing. *Communication Research, 20*(3), 365-383.

Kolar-Panov, D. (1997). *Video, war and the diasporic imagination.* New York: Routledge.

Kraidy, M. M. (1999). The global, the local and the hybrid: A native ethnography of glocalization. *Critical Studies in Mass Communication, 16*(4), 456-476.

Lidch, H. (1999). Finding the right image: British development NGOs and regulation of imagery. In T. Skelton & T. Allen (Eds.), *Culture and global change* (pp. 87-101). New York: Routledge.

Livingston, S. & Eachus, T. (1995). Humanitarian crisis and U.S. foreign policy: Somalia and the CNN Effect reconsidered. *Political Communication, 12,* 413-429.

McCombs, M. E. & Ghanem, S. (2001). The convergence of agenda setting and framing, in S. D. Reese, et al. (Eds.), *Framing Public Life: Perspectives on Media and Our Understanding of the World,* 67-82. New Jersey: Earlbaum.

McLuhan, M.. (1964). *Understanding media: The extensions of man,* 2nd ed. New York: New American Library.

Messaris, P. (1997). *Visual persuasion: The role of images in advertising.* Thousand Oaks, CA: Sage.

Mitra, A. (1997a). Diasporic web sites: Ingroup and outgroup discourse. *Critical Studies in Mass Communication, 14,* 158-181.

Mitra, A. (1997b). Virtual community: Looking for India on the Internet. In S. G. Jones (Ed.), *Virtual culture: Identity and communication in cybersociety* (pp. 55-79). Thousand Oak: Sage.

Morley, D. & Robins, K. (1995). *Spaces of identity: Global media, electronic landscapes and cultural boundaries.* New York: Routledge.

Musa, B. A. (1990). The mass media and socio-political crisis in Nigeria. In N. Alkali, J. Domatob, & A. Jika (Eds.), *African media issues* (p. 148-157). Enugu, Nigeria: Delta Publications.

_____ (1999). *Retribalization and conflict management in the new world (dis)order: The media, diplomacy and framing of domestic implosions in Bosnia and Rwanda.* Doctoral Dissertation, Regent University, 1999. UMI Dissertation Services, 9921561.

_____ (2000). Pluralism and prior restraint on religious communication in Nigeria: Policy versus praxis. In J. Thierstein & Y. R. Kamalipour (eds.), *Religion, law, and freedom: A global perspective* (pp. 98-111). Westport, CT: Praeger.

_____ (2004). *Journalistic ethics and conflict reporting: A critique of objectivity, advocacy, and social responsibility.* Paper presented at the National Faculty Leadership Conference. Washington, D.C., June 24-27.

_____ (2006a). News as infotainment. In B. A. Musa & C. J. Price (Eds.), *Emerging issues in contemporary journalism,* (pp. 131-155). Lewiston, NY: Edwin Mellen Press.

_____ (2006b). *Virtual communities, media images and the transformation of modern conflicts.* Paper presented at the National Communication Annual Convention, San Antonio, TX, November 16-17.

Mwesige, P. G. (2004). Disseminators, advocates and watchdogs: A profile of Ugandan journalists in the new millennium. *Journalism, 5*(1), 69-96.

Papacharissi, Z. (2005). The real-virtual dichotomy in online interaction: New media uses and consequences revisited. In P. J. Kalbfleisch (Ed.), *Communication Year Book, 25,* 215-237. Thousand Oaks, CA: Sage.

Petty R. E. & Cacioppo, J. T. (1986). *Communication and persuasion: Central and peripheral routes to attitude change.* New York: Springer-Verlag.

Peoples, C. D. (2004). Mediating peace, or mandating conflict? How ethnic-based policies impact interethnic relations. *Journal of Political and Military Sociology, Vol. 32/2,* 167-184.

Richards, T. & King, B. (2000). *Canadian Journal of Communication, 25,* 479-496.

Rasmussen, J. L. (1997). Peacemaking in the twenty-first century: New rules, new role, new actors. In I. W. Zartman & J. L. Rasmussen (Eds.), *Peacemaking in international conflict: Methods and techniques* (pp. 23-50). Washington, D.C.: United States Institute of Peace.

Seaton, J. (1999). The new "ethnic" wars and the media. In T. Allen & J. Seaton (eds.), *The media of conflict: War reporting and the representations of ethnic violence,* pp. 43-63. New York: Zed Books.

Seib, P. (2002). *The Global Journalist: News and Conscience in a World of Conflict.* Lanham, MD: Rowman & Littlefield Pub.

Upadhyaya, B. (2006). *Home videos, Indian Diaspora and (construction of meaning) of Celebration of religious festivals and performance of religious rituals.* Paper presented at the National Communication Association Annual Convention, San Antonio, TX, November 16-19.

Wall, M. A. (1997a). A 'pernicious new strain of the old Nazi virus" and an "orgy of tribal slaughter": A comparison of US news magazine coverage of the crises in Bosnia and Rwanda. *Gazette, 59,* 411-428.

Wall, M. A. (1997b). The Bosnia crisis: An analysis of news magazine coverage. *Gazette, 59,* 121-134.

Williamson, L. & Pierson, E. (2003). The rhetoric of hate on the Internet: Hateporn's challenge to modern media ethics. *Journal of Mass Media Ethics, 18*(3&4), 250-267.

Part 3: Conflict Strategies

Chapter 11

Harnessing the Power of Traditional and Modern Media Systems to Avert Conflicts in Africa

Ritchard T. M'Bayo, Ph.D.
American University of Nigeria, NIGERIA

Kehbuma Langmia, Ph.D.
Bowie State University, USA

Oloruntola Sunday & Ifeoma Amobi
University of Lagos, NIGERIA

Mass communication, in a word, is neither good nor bad; it is simply a force and, like any force, it can be used either for good or for bad purpose (Aldus Huxley, 1958)

Aldus Huxley's premonition about the dual purpose of the media has been quite instructive over the years. Communication technology as an instrument of good and evil is a theme that resonates in many contemporary research about the media. Media researchers have focused on this theme extensively in the discussion of the *functions* and *dysfunctions* of mass communication such as the mass media as either facilitators of peace or instigators of conflict. When media performance leads to desirable societal goals and outcomes the media are said to be functional; when they produce undesirable goals and outcomes, they are dysfunctional. In the hands of autocratic governments mass media systems have been used as weapons of oppression and propaganda as in Adolf Hitler's Germany, or as channels for the dissemination of hate messages as in the 1994 Rwanda genocide. Still, others have used them either to foment crises of all sorts or to avert disasters and conflict. Contemporary societies in an era of global conflicts and terrorism are faced daily with poignant lessons about the banality of good and evil perpetuated through the use of communication gadgets. For example, it is difficult to imagine our world without the mobile telephone. With its value added features such as messaging capability and inbuilt digital photographic systems, its potentials in conflict and crisis situations are limitless. Yet, it is the same gadget that is used to ignite explosive devices that have shattered jumbo jets into bits and pieces of debris in midair or reduced underground trains into pieces of mangled metals. In this chapter our focus is on the functional applications of the various forms of communication, including African traditional systems, to avert conflicts in Africa.

Traditional Communication Systems

Chiovoloni Moreno defines traditional communication systems as all organized processes of production and exchange of information managed by rural communities utilizing tools such as traditional theatre, masks, and puppet performances, tales, proverbs, riddles and songs which are seen as cultural and endogenous responses to different community needs for information, education, social protest and entertainment. All communication processes based on media, which are not created and managed by the rural community themselves, such as radio, video and television are not perceived as traditional.[1]

Jussawalla and Hughes (1984) see traditional communication systems as channels embedded within the traditional mores of a people and contributing significantly to their history and culture. (Akpabio, 2003, p. 2). Ansu-Kyeremeh sees it as any form of endogenous communication system, which by virtue of its origin form and integration into a specific culture, serves as a channel for messages in a way and manner that requires the utilization of the values, symbolism, institution and ethos of the host culture through its unique qualities and attributes.

Ansu-Kyeremeh (1998) as well as Wang and Dissanayake (1984) see traditional media as interpersonal channels and networks of communication such as the Indonesian Banjar, the Korean Mothers club and the Hui or Chinese loaning

---

[1] (Http://www.metafro.be/leisa).

club. Ugboajah (1985) refers to them as "Oramedia" and uses folk media, traditional media, informal media and indigenous media interchangeably.

Similarly, these writers see traditional media as informal channels of communication, deriving their authority and strength from the cultural mores, traditions and customs of the people they serve and utilizing symbols and tools such as village group discussions, council of elders, women's groups, puppet theatre, music, songs, dance, etc.

Music, song and dance use instruments which serve as accompaniment and disseminators of information. These include the wooden drums, ritual rattle, wood block, metal gong, xylophone, hand shakers, pot drums, skin drums, whistles, deer horn, ivory tusk and reed pipe. Among the many functions of these instruments is the use of the wooden drum to warn citizens of grave danger; the ivory tusk is used to settle quarrels and offer final word on contending issues. Music in its various manifestations communicate diverse messages; for example, it was used extensively in the liberation struggles in many African countries.

The Leketio, a pregnancy belt studded with cowry and used by the Massai of Kenya, is a symbol of peace; Urucaca, a type of grass commonly found in various parts of Rwanda, Burundi, Western Uganda and Northern Tanzania is also a symbol of peace, while the palm frond and broom in Nigeria communicate both quarrel and settlement. Similarly, other symbols of peace such as food, water and brew are used as elements that complete the process of reconciliation.

Women are key players in promoting a culture of peace in traditional Africa. They are often seen as the transmitters of cultural values to their progeny and to future generations through the use of artistic operations such as songs, dance and folk tales. They act as intermediaries in conflict situations, facilitating communication and peace negotiations. They are also used as bridge building blocks between hostile or fighting communities, notably through inter-community marriages whereby a daughter of one community is given in marriage to another community as a way of sealing an alliance for peace and reconciliation.

Role of Traditional Media in Conflict Resolution in Africa

Osaghae and Robinson (2005, p. 1) have observed that Africa has the uncanny reputation of being the world's leading theatre of conflict, war, poverty and instability. Hence, it is not surprising that scholars of ethnicity and conflict management regard the continent as a major laboratory for experimentation and theory building on the subject.

Though conflict is an inevitable component of human interactions, the way a society is organized can create both the root causes of conflict and the conditions in which it is likely to occur. Any society in which some people are treated unequally and unjustly is likely to erupt into conflict.

There is a tendency for scholars to perceive all African states as conflict-ridden. Unfortunately, with the persistent violence and seemingly intractable crises in these countries, many of them live up to this image.

From the notorious genocide and ethnic cleansings in Rwanda, Burundi, Angola and Sudan, the civil wars in Liberia, Sierra Leone, the Democratic Republic of Congo, Somalia and Côte d'Ivoire to the minority uprisings in Nigeria's oil rich Niger Delta region and the separatist agitation in Cameroon and Senegal, Africa manifests an image of violence, turbulence and chaos, a continent riddled with bitter conflicts.

Some of these conflicts date back to the colonial periods when many African countries fought bitter wars to gain independence from their colonial rulers, particularly in Kenya, Algeria, Zimbabwe, the Congo and Angola (Http://www.cidse.org); the pre-colonial era was characterized by communal conflicts, some of which took the form of land and property disputes. However, Africa has since independence recorded over 70 military coups while the last decade of the 20th century witnessed increased violence and chaos in many African countries.

The prevalence and intensity of these conflicts in Africa have become of grave interest to scholars, governments and stakeholders alike, as they remain intractable, almost impossible to predict and difficult to manage. Though a measure of success has been recorded in countries like South Africa, Ethiopia, Botswana through sub-regional approaches using the Economic Community of West African States (ECOWAS), Southern African Development Community (SADC), Inter-governmental Authority on Development (IGAD) and the African Union (AU), a dismal picture of failure, inability and helplessness is generally painted. This has forced a rethinking of current approaches to conflict resolution, throwing up new challenges and demanding innovative and alternative approaches and perspectives.

This is why some analysts are advocating a return to the use of traditional media in conflict resolution. Since communication is at the center of human existence, African traditional media, despite their perceived and real limitations such as limited reach, have proved to be effective in several contexts. For instance, Moemeka (1981) found that the rural population of former Bendel (Edo) state in the South-South of Nigeria depended more on traditional media such as *social forums*, *town-crier*, *village market* and *village school*, than on newspapers, radio or television, in their response to development projects (p. 46). The lessons from these projects could be valuable in conflict situations as well.

The Role of Modern Media in Conflict Resolution

Modern media include the traditional forms of mass communication (print and electronic–newspapers, radio, television, etc.), and the new media–the Internet and World Wide Web. The newspaper and the radio in the early fifties were instrumental in disseminating information about armed conflicts, border disputes, civil strives and other human predicaments. They sought to play the mediating role of bringing factions to the negotiating table or as the case maybe, fuel armed conflicts (Loewenstein, 2004). Quite often, mass media systems, unlike other forms of human communication, are used as tools for propaganda to perpetuate and advance the agenda of the government or the militia. This is what has been responsible for the sometimes scathing attacks levied at the media. The multiplicity of the modern communication media should therefore play a more significant role in bringing various opposing factions for peaceful negotiations aimed at achieving lasting peace.

Nowadays with the influx of diverse forms of the media, the media should serve as the gadfly of the society, uniting rather than putting a wedge between opposing factions, and playing the role of the arbiter. This is where the birth of media plurality should be celebrated rather than be condemned. Plurality ushers in the much needed diversity and more importantly access by various groups. Africa can, and is already benefitting tremendously from the use of the multiple forms of communication to harness peaceful co-existence rather than fanning the flames of war. These media outlets like cellular phones, facsimile, laptops, ipods, iphones, Internet, PCs, cable and satellite TV and other wireless forms of communication are now connecting people in all geographic locations, those in the rural areas as well as those in the urban centers. The more people communicate among themselves about their problems and potential conflicts, the more they will be able to forestall the escalation of such conflicts or prevent them from occurring in the first place. With plurality of media channels, and a politically conducive climate that encourages the independence of the media, the right to free expression of ideas, etc., will greatly enhance efforts to resolve regional, civil, border and international conflict.

Online Communication Systems

The newspaper and the radio are considered the oldest forms of mass communication. The fact that they have been in existence for scores of years is proof of their continuous importance. However, with the birth of cable television in the 1950s (Goolsbee and Petrin, 2004) human communication took on new dimensions. New target audiences and alternative viewpoints could be seen and heard from various media outlets. Nowadays, not only the intrusive presence of cable television is felt world wide, online communication is gaining much grounds.

The Internet with features like online news, streaming media, text-messaging, blogging, tele-conferencing, video-conferencing and wireless PCS with portable digital transmissions and retransmissions have not only improved interpersonal and mass communication productions, but they have provided new ample opportunities for information diffusion. These new channels of communication can now be used particularly in volatile conflict-ridden communities in Africa and could play a significant role in improving the lives of people caught in difficult situations. Puddephatt (2003) argues that "the media also provide information, act as a watchdog on all those who have power and offer a forum for intense public debate about the choices facing a society" (p. 110). For instance, in Africa, there is no easy solution to the problem facing the people of the Darfur region of Sudan. The two rival factions, Sudanese government and the Janjaweed militia on the one hand, and the International community on the other are finding it difficult to carry on meaningful communication in the search for a peaceful settlement to the conflict that has already claimed thousands of lives. The media, and in this case, the internet can be of vital importance. Blogs, chat room discussion sites, teleconferencing on and about Africans and Africans in the Diaspora should harness all their energy through this "independent" media channel to call attention for unconditional intervention from the International community. In other words, the various forms of he media can be used to mobilize global public opinion to bear upon the situation in Sudan. A sustained public opinion can yield peace dividends in such a situation.

Ebeling (2003) has equally shown the importance of the new media in resolving old and new conflicts particularly in developing countries. He comments on how this has been a success in the past in Nigeria. Ken Saro Wiwa, a political activist was brutally murdered for organizing a riot against the government of Nigeria for exploiting the local indigenes of their oil wealth. A lot of protests and violence erupted that resulted in several deaths. Nigerians in the Diaspora used the web as a rallying forum to quell the conflict because the international pressure on the Abacha government did not succeed to resolve the impasse. Ebeling (2003, p. 104) posits that:

> Although international protests did not prevent Saro-Wiwa's death, they did sensitize and mobilize not only Nigerian Diaspora but also the larger African Diaspora and other international communities to scrutinize Western corporations involved in exploitative business practices in Africa. Additionally, as more and more African, Caribbean, African American, and black European newspapers and journals become available online-through their web sites or through portals such as AllAfrica.com-scholars, students, laypeople, and activists can directly access news articles on and produced in the black world, rather than those filtered by Western mainstream media.

The Internet therefore provides much hope for Africans as exemplified by the actions of Nigerians and other Africans in the Diaspora.

The Internet has also been used by the government of Denmark to create a forum where the citizens, government officials and the opposition can come together in a physical public sphere to dialogue and to seek solutions to emerging conflicts (Jensen, 2003). In arguing for the Internet as a powerful influence on the democratic process in African, some writers have suggested that:

> The Internet's greatest strengths, however, is its ability to support simultaneous, interactive communications among many people. Unlike the telephone, which primarily supports one-to-one communications, or radio and television, where information flows in only one direction, from a single source to an audience that can only listen passively, the net allows information to flow back and forth among millions of sources at practically the same time (Ott & Rosser, 2000, p. 142-143)

Television Systems

In as much as the Internet has been instrumental in bringing peace activists and other conflict-ridden factions to the virtual table of debate, television studios continue to play significant roles in rallying conflict experts to discuss ways of bringing peace to Africa. In the same way that Kellner (1990) argued for the meaningful role television played in the United States during the 1960s civil strives, Africans can also use television and other new media systems to resolve the never-ending regional and national conflicts inflicting the continent. Fortunately, the number of private television stations and channels continues grow. These can be used for harnessing peace initiatives in the continent. Opposing factions, say in Darfur, Côte d'Ivoire, Congo, Zimbabwe, Nigeria, Ethiopia and Eritrea could be brought to the negotiating table virtually or face-to-face by the media. The kind of messages sent through the various media, the gestures, the feedback from those caught in the midst of deadly violence would make the media the reliable source for peaceful negotiations. The rather redundant messages of threat, violence, fear and revenge that characterize government-sponsored propagandistic media systems would gradually give way to a variety of sources and a diversity of views for promoting harmony and unity among people. This way, the new media technology would be beneficial to the people who most often than not were accustomed to asphyxiation from a monopolistic media system.

Olumu (2005) provides information in Nigeria where some programs on television are being made to unite the people. The television program *The Academy*, is an offshoot from an organization called the Common Ground Productions (CGP): "The Organization is using drama series, which will promote mutual respect, tolerance and understanding and create harmony from all the differences in the nation" (p. 1). This harmony constituted the main theme of the role of the media in conflict resolution at the Kenya-Nairobi Conference in August 2006. Mohamed Sahnoun, the special envoy of then UN Secretary General,

Kofi Annan, remarked that the media can harness its energy and bring the message of hope to the people and governments (Daily Nation, August 2006). With the multiplicity of media in Africa, conflict resolution should now be a matter of willingness not availability. It is true that access to some media system is difficult in some parts of Africa. In that case traditional forms of communication could be harnessed for that purpose.

Newspapers and government-sponsored radio systems are becoming redundant mechanisms to resolve belligerent parties involved in conflict. The newspaper and government sponsored-radio are heavily censored. They are there to promote government agenda. When private newspapers and radios do not defend the side of the government in place, the station or production companies are heavily censored or temporarily shot down. This was the case with some private newspapers like *The Messenger, The Mutation* and *L'Expression* in Cameroon during the early days of multipartism in 1990. With globalization and the unfolding digital media revolution around the world, the new media systems can play significant virtual role by linking peace negotiators without government censorship. Eribo and Tanjong (2002) argue that in this day and age "the new popular media must not only inform but also provide a platform for debate on ideas and issues affecting the commonweal" (p. 29). One of the main issues affecting the commonweal especially in Africa is how to resolve tribal, ethnic, regional and national conflicts that are threatening to tear the continent apart. The media should be at the center for initiating positive change in human interrelationships around the continent.

Integrating Traditional Communication and Modern Media to Avert Conflicts

Akpabio (2003) contends that whether one is considering the Eurocentric clan of irrelevance of traditional communication or "the passing of traditional societies" argument, the uncontestable fact is that traditional communication has continued to march on; politicians seeking elective offices and dissemination of development messages cannot ignore it. When combined with the modern mass media, the traditional communication complements modern communication in achieving the desired objectives such as increase in knowledge and attitude change.

And, because of their ability to reach large populations over a large area, the mass media with their information and education functions have the responsibility not only to ventilate the atmosphere for peace but also to prevent the outbreak of conflicts. Thus, for greater effect, there is a need to blend the traditional communication with modern media to avert conflict.

It has been established that Africans have traditional communication systems aimed at conflict resolution and prevention of conflict. However, the need to integrate these and modern media to avert conflicts has become imperative. In doing this, the role of community broadcasting cannot be overemphasized. According to one writer (Sunday, 2006), community broadcasting will:

> Help to promote the cultural values of the community, serve as an instrument for preserving indigenous languages and cultural identities, accelerate the achievement of the social and cultural objectives of broadcasting in the country of operation and it remains the most credible platform for the marginalized sections of the society to air their views about issues that affect their lives, and development priorities. Therefore, community broadcasting will no doubt be a credible avenue to promote programs aimed at averting conflicts.

Hieber (1999) buttressed this when she observed:

> Promoting tolerance and restraint, dispelling rumors, humanizing the other side, providing a forum for solutions to conflicts, are all roles the media can play as peace-builder. But to do so successfully, practitioners, traditionally lone wolves, need to work closely with other professionals to make the most building potential

This may require partnership with local broadcasters, or by engaging local staff, or by establishing operation agreements with community representatives.

In Nigeria, there are various traditional communication systems aimed at preventing conflicts at individual, community and national levels. Most of these have been incorporated into the national media. These include: *Gboro mi ro* (*Listen to my case*) a television program that discusses and settles issues and matters that can lead to conflict. Others are *Peoples Palaver* also a television program which brings people with diverse experiences to discuss and offer solutions to matters like a typical council of elders in a village setting.

When violence resurfaced in the streets of Liberia, the Liberian Capital, in September 1998, Talking Drum Studio (TDS) embarked on a drama series which highlighted the social, economic and political impact of the war and encouraged opposing forces to use dialogue as the best means for settling conflicts. The studio featured drama and talk show which shifted the focus of the listeners from the fears and apprehension of war to how to engage in more rewarding activities for a better, peaceful future (Common Ground Approach to Media (http://www.sfcg.org/info/articles/egptric2.htm).

Search for common ground is an example of the integration of traditional communication and modern media to avert conflict. With its uniquely African identity flavor and feel, the series takes viewers behind the headlines into the heart of conflict. Whether it is a village Kgotla (council of elders) mediating a land dispute in the former Zaire, or the Truth and Reconciliation Commission in South Africa, each episode demonstrates that good story telling does not have to glorify conflict for its own sake. That an agreement can be as dramatic as any soap opera. At the same time, the series challenges the view that Africa is incapable of solving its own problems" (http://www.stcg.org/programmes/cgp/cgp-television.html).

In the waning days of the Mubotu regime, people in Kinshasa returned to traditional mechanisms to resolve conflicts. There was a tribal court in which the plaintiff, the accused, the lawyers, judge, and jury put their dispute into songs and dance–and the whole community accepted.

From Ethiopia, Inter-Africa Group on UNICEF's behalf, broadcasts a peace program into Somalia on a daily basis. The programs make specific links between peace, protection of women and children, and religious transitions. A UNESCO symposium on Somalia Peace and Reconciliation urged more media programs to present positive images of components of peace building such as traditional conciliation mechanisms and human rights.

Video Dialogues in South Africa is a series of profiles of South African rural communities in transition, each focused around a particular conflict issue (for example, land rights, local government, or educational reform), critical to the community but with ramifications for the country. The purpose is to create forums with local peace committees to further public debate, dialogue, and the management, if not resolution, of conflict within the communities. Community profiles around specific and contentious issues are screened within the communities themselves.

There are numerous forms of traditional communication techniques in the continent. Techniques like using drums, horn, rituals, songs and music are as forms of communications. They could be integrated with the modern forms of communication to resolve conflicts among people. These traditional forms of communications predate the newspaper and radio. Traditional ethnic societies relied heavily on the norms and traditions of their forbears to bring about peace and harmony in the society. The chief's courtyard used to be the rallying ground to resolve disputes with the people. Drums were used to summon people to the King's palace for special announcements. Law breakers were heavily punished or reprimanded as the case maybe in public. The society was formed in such a way that people were made to avoid public ignominy by abiding by the traditions and customs of the land. The emergence of modern media should therefore be a symbiosis for enhancing effective communication necessary to avert growing conflicts in Africa.

A bipolar communication process in Africa could be effective in redressing inter-tribal, civil, and international conflicts that seem to be ravaging the continent. Modern mass communication with all its technological characteristics is very effective among literate urban dwellers. It may not be very efficient especially with the rural poor and illiterate populace. In that case the traditional forms of communication like drumming, music, and dance could be integrated within the framework of radio and television broadcast for the people. This way it may provide opportunities for bringing people together to brainstorm on their daily problems and potential conflicts.

In the case where modern media facilities are difficult to access, especially in regions where natural conditions do not allow signals to reach or where the people cannot afford the new forms of communication, traditional forms play active roles to assemble the people. Mushengyezi (2003) buttressed this concern:

> Modern mass media, then, have remained largely inaccessible to the majority of Ugandan communities not just of the low literacy level, but also because of the lack of hardware, software, and supporting infrastructure of computer-accessed communication. Consequently, these media cannot be seen as essential to communication in predominantly rural societies. (p. 108).

Hence, it is imperative for the two media systems to merge in order to satisfy the needs of everyone. The idea of adapting new media technologies with already existing forms of communications like using songs and music can be an essential tool to grasp the attention of the public. In this case the media cease to isolate themselves from those especially at the grassroots who neither read nor write. This is what is being done in Afghanistan where the modern media have coexisted with the local media of communication to look for ways to resolve the more than 22 years of civil war in that country (Rowan, 2002).

Elite media - digital radio, cable, satellite, Internet, etc. - are what abound now in most developing countries. Without the integration of the traditional forms of communication, there will be few success stories and many missed opportunities for using the power of communication to avert conflicts.

Application of Traditional Media in Conflict Situations: Selected Cases

Analysts have reiterated the importance of African traditional communication systems, observing that one cannot dispense with these traditional approaches any more because they embody a lot of African culture that show that Africans also used to counsel and resolve conflict peacefully. They note that these methods are simple, flexible, and universally and inexpensively accessible, and that they pose no language problem since they are easy to understand and apply. They are often relevant in their structure and content to host audiences and are interpersonal, bringing about total reconciliation and healing. In addition, they promote the image and self esteem of those involved and reveal and re-emphasise especially to the youths the role and significance of elders in society who are often relegated to the background by factors such as poverty, illiteracy, etc. (http://www.usaid.or.ug). These various symbols and patterns of the traditional media are used in different ways to resolve conflict in parts of Africa. Let us look at some specific applications of the traditional communication systems in selected African countries.

Nigeria

In Nigeria, various devices are used for the dissemination of messages. These include the wooden drum used to alert citizens of grave danger, the bell called *ngbiringba* (in Igbo), *agogo* in Yoruba and *Kararawa* in Hausa, used to get attention while settling a dispute, while the Ivory tusk, gourd and reed pipe are used in the South-Eastern part of Nigeria to settle quarrels, place injunctions on disputed land and property and offer final word on issues of controversy (Akpabio, 2003, p.18). Traditional African music communicates diverse messages. It has been used by artists such as Fela Ransome Kuti, Lucky Dube, and Sony Okosun, to aid liberation struggles in countries like South Africa and to condemn inequalities, injustices, corruption, etc.

Elements, symbols and icons are also used to communicate or pass across messages. As Doob (1961) submits, symbols arouse responses very similar to those evoked by reality itself. The broom, for instance, communicates quarrel and settlement, while the white chalk or *nzu* in Igbo, *ndom* in Ibibio, *Orhue* in Bini is used to cleanse a defiled house or a woman suspected to have committed adultery. The young unopened palm frond of the palm tree called *Mariwo* by the Yorubas and *omu* by the Igbos has tremendous communication capacities. It is used to summon people to meetings by enclosing it in their invitation letters, declaring lands in disputed "no go areas", serving as a symbol of traditional authority and a reminder that disobedience will result in dire consequences. It is also used to ostracize and restrict movement of offenders, indicates the presence of a shrine, alert a general public about certain routes that are temporarily off limits, signifies land in disputes, refrains factions in conflicts from continuing in their feuds, ostracize witches, wizards and deviants, indicates the urgency with which messages should be treated and warn individuals engaging in anti-social activities.

Other illustrative use of traditional media to address conflicts in Africa include the sending of salt and pepper by one town to another. It means the two towns have misunderstanding and the sending town is ready for war. If the receiving town wants peaceful settlement of the dispute, it will choose salt and not the pepper. Similarly, the sending of bow and arrow by one town to another is a message to the receiving town to prepare for war. To tell the sending town that they are not ready for war, the receiving town will then send emissary to go and plead for peace. In case somebody has committed a grievous offence that could warrant death penalty as punishment in a town, the offender will be given Ewe the leaf of a tree called *Ape* to go and give to the king of the town. This symbolizes a plea on behalf of the person to be forgiven. Also, if one friend sends a keg of palm wine to another friend early in the morning or in the evening it symbolizes a desire to mend a fence between the two friends, without allowing a third party to know about it. If the friend accepts the palm wine it means the matter has been settled. Also, if a father-in-law sends a reddish local beauty cream called *Osun* in Yoruba land to a son-in-law, it means their daughter has offended her husband and she was at fault and the father-in-law is asking the husband to forgive his wife and accept her back. On the other hand, if the husband's family sends six cowries to the wife, it means that there is a misunderstanding between the wife and the husband, and the latter is at fault. The cowries symbolize a plea by the husband to the wife to forgive him and return home (Opatodun, 1986).

In Ibibio land in the South-South of Nigeria *Nnuk Enin* made out of elephant tusk, with a hole at its tail end through which a message is blown, is regarded as the most dignified royal medium of communication. It has a sacred and definitive function in traditional communication. Its importance also lies in the fact that is rarely used except in very serious circumstances such as settling quarrels, placing injunctions on disputed lands or property and offering final word or judgments on issues. The medium on its own does not communicate in different languages and this makes it possible for its messages to be easily understood and related to events that are actually associated with their use.

The spoken word helps to inform and shape the attitudes and behavior of members of the community. It is one of the fundamental aspects of the African soil as it sometimes keeps old men for months under the palaver tree settling disputes. The Kabba people in Kogi State in Nigeria have specific proverbs, idioms and maxims aimed at conflict prevention and resolution. Among these is the saying, *"Abeja ya ghe hi a paragha"* meaning *"Even if we disagree, it must not degenerate to bloodshed."* Another axiom says that *"Arinu mo bi ole, oni o be ghe gba omale"* meaning *"One who does not get angry when offended is a coward, but the one who refuses to be pacified is a bastard"* (Jimoh, 2005).

The council of elders, the Igwe-in-council made up of the Igwe or Obi (King) and Ndichies (red cap chiefs), is the highest traditional decision-making body among the Igbos of South Eastern Nigeria. This body, which derives its authority from the culture, tradition and custom of the people, has the final word during conflict resolution. It often settles communal conflicts, land disputes, etc, has its equivalent in the Northern part of the country, headed by the Emir or Sultan, and in the West and Midwest by the Oba.

Rwanda

The *Agacada* which derives from the word *Urucaca*, an evergreen grass found in various parts of Rwanda, Burundi, Western Uganda and Northern Tanzania and symbolizing peace, is a mechanism used to resolve conflict in Rwanda. When there is a problem within the clan, family or neighborhood, the elders gather at the site and each warring party is asked to present its case. The elders then mediate and the guilty party is asked to buy a pot of local brew for the elders. The guilty party is also fined and cautioned by the elders, thus resolving the conflict. Today, the government of Rwanda has adopted elements of this method of conflict resolution, in dealing with some of the 1994 genocide cases, rather than resorting to the international or Arusha tribunals. (http://www.usaid.org).

Tanzania

In Tanzania, the council of elders plays a prominent role in conflict resolution. The council assembles the feuding parties to give their sides of the case. The council then takes steps to establish the facts and then proffer a solution. A meeting for reconciliation is convened and the parties involved are summoned together with the witnesses. Each of the two parties takes a calabash of water and sits on haunches in front of the crowd and then sips from it, promising to abide by the decision made by the council of elders. Sometimes the elders, after deliberating on issues, organize ritual ceremonies for resolving the conflict with God and their smaller god called Mahoka. (http://www.usaid.org).

Mali

The traditional puppet theatre in Mali is not only used as an entertaining and educational medium, but also as a channel for resolving conflicts. The Malinke community of the Bougouni region uses this channel to solve internal age-determined and generational conflicts. In the daytime, puppets (tiefe do) present the point of view of the youths, while the nocturnal puppets (sufe do) provide the elders' point of view and answer to questions and problems raised by the younger people. This channel affords the younger generation opportunity to express their needs and problems to the entire community while serving as an alarm bell. It also helps the village elders to assess the depth and spread of the problem in order to decide on a course of action or solution. Gordon (1986) observes that the puppeteers act out private situations or struggles between people, criticize the society in a way that people cannot always safely do and can also be used to address delicate matters of life and social conflict issues that otherwise would not be treated openly by people (http://www.metafro.be/leisa).

Burundi

Though in the traditional setting, a woman is recognized as having an advisory position, behind the scenes, especially where her husband is concerned, women have been known to play major roles in conflict resolution, strengthening solidarity and social harmony in Burundi. A number of methods are used depending on the circumstances. The crisis that exploded in 1993 was seen by Burundians especially women as the result of the catastrophic collapse of the moral and social values such as the *Ubuchingantabe* (mutual help and solidarity, honesty, respect for the sanctity of life and the secular unity of the Burundi), which had been the foundation of Burundian society (UNESCO, 2003, p. 31).

In the traditional Burundi society women are regarded as the driving force behind the family's relationship with its neighbour. They were held to have no families, since they are destined to live and fulfill themselves within other people's which they would regard as their own. They married and gave birth to children of other ethnic groups. They are regarded as symbols of peace and were supposed to forge alliances and strengthen unity. In conflict situations they acted in their advisory roles, counseling their peers where it involves women or acting through their husbands where the disagreement is between men. They set up their own council consisting of a group of wise and respected women known as Inararibunye (those who have seen many things) who in case of conflicts especially among women held hearings of the parties in an isolated spot, known as Mukatabesha (the place where lies are told) and after deliberation, passed judgment, laying down a course of behavior, especially for the guilty party (UNESCO, 2003, p. 20).

In cases of armed conflict they intervened in an advisory capacity through their husbands. They have been sheltering victims of the crisis, at times breastfeeding very young children whose mothers had been killed, providing food, clothing and medicines and setting up income-generating activities.

There are also reports of women called Queen mothers who acted as regents when the kings were still too young to reign or when they were away. One Queen mother who stood out for her remarkable contribution to conflict resolution was Ririkumutima who helped a man threatened with eviction by king Mwezi under the sway of evil courtiers. The Queen mother insisted that the case go before the Bashingantabe and at the end of the day she won. The Bashingantabe is the traditional elders' council consisting of men in Burundi. It is the highest decision making body; it also mediates in conflicts situations. Cases beyond the Inararibunye are referred to this body.

Kenya

Conflict resolution in Kenya especially among two ethnic groups is usually not a one time event. It takes place serially, building on and affirming peace symbols with rituals related to the community's experiences and memories acquired from the past generations (http://www.usaid.org.ug). Peace concepts and symbols are used in this process such as the Osotua (the Maasai word for peace), which connotes a gift out of relationship or the umbilical cord, which symbolizes the first relationship between mother and child. When the umbilical cord is cut at birth, a grass is tied on either side so that the mother and child may separate in peace and continue to have a good relationship. This grass is today a symbol of peace. Whenever there is a fight and a Maasai picks up the grass, the fighting stops because they believe they all come from one womb. There is also the pregnancy belt called *Leketio* among the Pokot and other tribes in Kenya. This belt is studded with cowry shells worn by pregnant women and believed to support life. When the Pokot are fighting and a mother removes her pregnancy belt and puts it between the men, the fighting must be stopped irrespective of whether or not she is a biological mother in that community.

Trees are also living symbols of peace making in Kenya. When the Maasai people are making peace, they sit under the shade of a particular tree referred to as *Oloip*. Before this is done, all warring parties must drop their weapons. However, when a murder has been committed, the people sit under a dead tree, to resolve the grave situation.

Conclusion

Conflict is an inevitable component of human interaction, which becomes intractable when a society is inequitably organized. In the pre-colonial era, traditional media were key elements in promoting societal harmony, forestalling and resolving conflicts. Traditional media using patterns and tools such as music, song, dance, and puppetry, council of elders, women groups, village schools, village markets and symbols such as grass, palm fronds, leketio or pregnancy belt, salt, pepper, water, food, etc. played a significant role in this process. With the passing of traditional society to modernity, these channels, which are acclaimed by scholars to have been very effective, were subjugated by modern media to near obscurity. The massive failures of the modern media have prompted scholars and stakeholders alike to call for a return of the traditional media as a potent tool in the process of conflict resolution in Africa.

Fortunately, the boundary defying new media, because of their integrative capacity, flexibility and portability, and the trend toward the flattening of the communicative processes from vertical to horizontal models, provide limitless possibilities for participation and exchange among people in society, and for opportunities to integrate traditional and modern forms of communication.

References

Akpabio, E. (2003). *African communication system: An introductory text*. Lagos, Nigeria: BPrint Publications.

Ansu-Kyeremeh, K. (1998). Indigenous communication in Africa: A conceptual framework. In Ansu-Kyeremeh, (editor). *Perspectives on Indigenous Communication in Africa*, vol. 1. Legon, Ghana: School of Communication Studies Printing Press.

Chiovoloni, M. (1994). The interactive power of local and traditional communication systems. Retrieved February 5, 2007, from http://www.metafro.be/leisa.

Conflict Resolution. Retrieved February 10, 2007, from http://www.en.wikipedia.org.

Doob, L. W. (1961). *Communication in Africa: A search for boundaries*. New Haven: Yale University Press.

Ebeling, M. (2003). The new dawn: Black agency in cyberspace. *Radical History Review, 87,* 96-108.

Eghosa, O. & Robinson, G. Porter, E, Schnabel, A. & Smith, M. (2005). *Researching Conflicts in Africa: Insights and Experiences*. New York: United Nations University Press.

Eribo, F. and Tanjong, E. (eds). (2002). *Journalism and mass communication in Africa: Cameroon*. Lanham: Lexington Books.

Global News Wire. (2006). Kenya Nairobi conference debates role of media in conflict resolution. Retrived from: *http://cassel.founders.howard.edu:2060/universe/print*

Goolsbee, A. & Petrin, A. (2004). *Econometrica, 72* (2), 351-381.

Heiber, L. (1999). Broadcasting Peace building – The Lifeline Media Experience; Publication of the European centre for Prevention, including searching for Peace Publications and our Conflict Prevention newsletter.

Hokororo, A.M (2001). African traditional methods in Tanzania: A case study of the Wamakua Wamwera, Wamkonde and Wayao. Retrieved February 5, 2007, from http://www.usaid.or.ug.

Jensen, J. (2003). Virtual democratic dialogue? Bringing together citizens and politicians. *Information Polity*, 8, 29-47.

Jimoh, J. (2005). *Traditional ways of handling conflicts/disputes in Kabba community of Kogi State, Nigeria*. (unpublished)

Kamuhangire, E. (2001). African traditional methods in Rwanda: A case study of the Agacaca method of conflict resolution amongst the Banyarwanda. Retrieved February 5, 2007, from http://www.usaid.or.ug.

Liberia: The Conflict context. Retrieved February 8, 2007, from http://www.international-alert.org.

Loewestein, A. (2005). Reflections on Dafur: A personal and political account. *The Brown Journal of World Affairs,11(2),*235-241.

Moemeka, A. (1981). *Local radio: Education for development*. Zaria, Nigeria: Ahmadu Bello University Press.

Mushengyizi, A. (2003). Rethinking indigenous media: rituals, 'talking' drums

Morrison, J. (2001). AIDS education in Africa: The uses of traditional performance. Retrieved February 5, 2007, from http://www.academic.sun.ac.za/journalism/news.

Nigeria: The Conflict context. Retrieved February 8, 2007, from http://www.international-alert.org.

Ntahobari, J. & Ndayiziga, B. (2003). *The role of Burundian women in the peaceful settlement of conflicts. In women and peace in Africa: Case studies on traditional conflict resolution practices*. Paris, France: UNESCO

Opadotun, O. (1986). Aroko: Awon ami ati iro ibanisoro l'aye ijelo. Ibadan, Nigeria: Vantage Publishers.

Ott, D & Rosser, M. (2000). The electronic republic? The role of the Internet in promoting democracy in Africa. *Democratization, 7* (1), 137-156.

Olumu, C. (2005). Resolving conflicts through entertainment. Retrieved from: *http://cassell.founders.howard.edu:* 2060/universe/printdoc.

Peace building and conflict resolution/prevention. In Towards true partnership: EU-Africa Summit. A CIDSE position paper. Retrieved February 8, 2007, from http://www.cidse.org.

Puddephatt, A. (2003). After the war is over.... *Index On Censorship, 32(4),* 110-115.

and orality as forms of public communication in Uganda. *Journal of African Cultural Studies,* 16 (1), 107-117.

Rowan, M. (2002). Modern mass media and traditional communication in Afghanistan. *Political Communication,* 19 (2), 155-170.

Small arms and light weapons in West Africa. Retrieved February 8, 2007, from http://www.international-alert.org.

Sunday A. O, (2007). The Imperative of Community Broadcasting. In R. M'Bayo, (editor). *Contemporary issues in Communication and Society.* Lagos, Nigeria: Unilag Press (Forthcoming).

Sultan, S. (2001). African traditional methods in Kenya: A case study of the Pokot and Maasai peace building cultures. Retrieved February 5, 2007, from http://www.usaid.or.ug.

Television/Radio: Africa Search for Common Ground retrieved February 5, 2007, from http://www.sfcg.org/programmes/cgp/cgp_television.html.

Ugboajah, F. O. (1985). Oramedia in Africa. In F. O. Ugboajah, (2d.). Mass communication, culture, and society in West Africa, pp. 165-176. London: Hans Zell.

West Africa. (2007). The conflict context. Retrieved February 8, 2007, from http://www.international-alert.org.

Chapter 12

Conflict and Conflict Resolution in African Folklore

Christine Oduor-Ombaka, Ph.D.
Maseno University, KENYA

This chapter discusses various forms of conflicts and conflict resolution as reflected in the African folklore, that is, folk literature or 'literature orally transmitted' (Finnegan 1970, Lovell 1972). Folklore includes folktales, myths, legends, poetry, songs and stories told in song –the Ballard. Folklore does not exclude music or proverbs or sayings of the wise, nor does it neglect customs, popular beliefs and superstitions and what Utley (1968) describes as 'the way of life associated with people and subcultures we call folk'

Typically, folklore includes oral genre which may be spoken, sung or dramatized or even written by an individual who is a folk product (Lovell, 1972). They are also passed down from one generation to the next and deal with accounts of events which are true to life or false, or fiction. They highlight human vices – or the things which make for the joys and sorrows of the people. Sometimes the issues raised in the folktale, myth, legend or song are made on the sport based on the creativity of the artist who has to fulfill definite purposes: to inform, educate and entertain. The artist informs the people on the significance of particular event in life.

As part of oral literature, folklore also reflects feelings and tastes that are communal rather than personal. Always in solution, its creation is never completed; at every moment in history, it exists not in one form but in many. In the highly appreciative definitions, folklores are 'echoes of the heartbeats of the vast folk, and in them are preserved feelings, beliefs and habits of antiquity' (Lovell 1972).

However, a good deal of what is now being said about folklore and the oral performance in Africa, applies equally to opera or pantomime or popular music or hymns and religious rituals in other parts of the world. Very few of them would be performed as words a lone without music and dancing and drumming. Thus, folklore, in the context of this chapter, has been kept alive perpetuated and preserved by word of mouth and dramatization from generation to generation. Today, a good number of them are being preserved through the written word, video tapes and CD ROMS while still continuing as an oral art. In many ways, folklore acts as a vehicle of communication conveying cultural values, passing on wisdom, morality, philosophy, history, knowledge and skills of a given people. For this reason it can be viewed as a conservative art educating and reinforcing in members of the society appropriate ways they should act, feel, behave and think. Thus, in folklore, one can understand a people's perceptions and worldview on events of the 'real world'. For African folklore is didactic. It is functional and comments upon the whole range of human experience; folktales, myths, legends, trickster stories, poems, songs, satire, allegories and epic all depict various forms of conflicts in human society and the strategies of coping and settling disputes especially when certain actions infringe the rights of others.

African writers who have attempted to re-create African cultural life in fictions either in its contemporary or historical setting, have often chosen to do so through the oral traditions of African people because it best expresses their reality and sensibility. It is, therefore, common to find that oral traditions continue to exist side by side with literary tradition (Obiechina, 1975). Modern writers have incorporated folklore into their literary works, which have developed a great deal. Obiochina observes that whether in the tales of Amos Tutuala, in the novels of Chinua Achebe, in the plays of Clark and Sonyinka or in the poems of Okigbo, these modern writers have drawn on African folklore, which have survived in Africa despite the introduction of European literary tradition.

An analysis of inter-tribal wars in Africa through folklore is important in reflecting a growing awareness of a formula for successful conflict resolution and peace-building efforts, to which the African experience can contribute greatly considering the fact that the continent has been plagued with internal civil wars and ethnic conflicts for generations. The questions we need to ask are: How have war and related conflicts been depicted in African folklore and with what resolutions? What are the methods of cooperation and costs of not cooperating? For conflict or disputes to be settled between and among groups, there has to be rules for settlement and reconciliation. In the words of Maier (1965, p. 127), 'there has to be laws in terms of an institution, the procedure of compensation and reconciliation'. In other words, there has to be a real basis for an internal settlement, where the parties want peace rather than war and compromise rather than continued conflict. A way has to be found in which the major conflicting parties can simultaneously achieve essential elements of what they want. Does African folklore offer any teaching on conflict and conflict resolution?

Ombaka (1998) argues that war and military violence have remained uniquely topical themes in the arts and literature generally and folklore in particular because war evokes strong emotions arising from gruesome human massacres, physical suffering, and mental anguish that war victims experience during and after the war. The effects of war on civilians are fundamentally some of the moving images of war that have created imprints in the human psyche and have continued to haunt the imagination of folklorists and other creative artists. Folklorists have often explored war themes, symbolically and satirically, to provide didactic lessons to their communities to improve human relations providing the wider framework, which serves to urge leadership towards compromise as well as assisting in the development of democratic practices and institutions.

War folklore paint a grim picture of violence in African communities despite the fact that African people are known to be deeply conscious of peace, justice and progress, and have everywhere consistently pressed for the suppression of all forms of oppression; respect for the territorial integrity of states; and called for establishment of communal economic order and ultimately the institution of progressive general disarmament against the background of deeply rooted cultural norms and religion.

It is clear from the African tales discussed in this chapter that in the past, African folklorists, or artists, for that matter, did arrive at the threshold of pain where they began to feel the impact of human conflict and the muscle of political authority in their own communities such that they had to come out with tales that depicted their experiences, the joys and sorrows of the people for folklore grows straight out of the needs of the people who find it fit and perfect form of explaining events that they do not understand. Using different forms of oral narratives including fables, song and poetry, traditional folklorists seem to glorify and celebrate war. For instance, many of them depict warriors boasting about their strength and incredible military tactics in ways that personify them as the conquerors, never the conquered. They compose praise songs to honor their exploits and power. With some form of moral punch line, which demonstrates well the African storyteller's use of tales as a vehicle to teach human societies correct social values, responsibility, humility and a sense of justice, folklorists often create ideas around which political leaders, chiefs and heads of clan construct and sustain social institutions. So important the historical perspectives some of them are that they act as personal memoirs confronting tyranny, through the use of imagination. Due to their historical importance, some oral narratives have now been written and used as anecdotes in written novels or produced in films as the final step in the long process of "improvement" from their earlier forms of oral narrative.

Although the messages they convey to their listeners are similar to those found in written materials, folklore retains to some extent its oral composition. This confirms the hypothesis that orally composed literature is distinguishable from written literature on the basis of its form rather than its content. In terms of style of presentation, it typically has traditional elements called formulas—a group of words which is regularly employed under the same metrical conditions to express a given time phrase. Such fixed epithets as "A long time a go" or "once upon a time" have always been recognized as characteristic of oral narrative.

Several scholars (Finnegan, 1976; Miruka, 1994; Odaga, 1984) argue that in traditional Africa, folktales were commonly told in the evening after a hard days work accompanied by mime and frequently music. They were, and still are, important medium of entertainment and instruction woven from the substance of human experience, and very often realistic and down-to-earth. They maintain that, today, African folklore remains a vigorous art, rooted in rural communities but flourishing too in the cities. Going by the various positions adopted so far by scholars of folklore in many cultures in Africa, skilled storytellers would memorize and captivate audiences with their stories of war and adventure and of relationship with the gods.

One of the most interesting mythical-historical dramatizations of a war genre is found in the story of Luanda Magere among the Luo people of Western Kenya (Omtatah, 1991). This is a folk legend about inter-tribal war that took place "a long time ago" between the Luo community of Western Kenya and the Langi people of Rift Valley in Kenya.

It is a story that magnifies the chaos and destruction of two communities fighting to dominate the other and subjugating its victims to slavery and torture. For years, Magere, the superhuman Luo warrior, caused death and mayhem and brought the Lango people to their feet, taking away their land and other natural resources to achieve political and economic control in the region. Not only did Magere rob the Lango of their land but also enslaved their men, women and children. Usually, as the war ragged putting a heavy toll on the Lango people, Magere, a man with a mysterious body of a rock that could not be physically harmed, baffled the enemy. He would sit calmly under a tree and piped away as he watched how his army was progressing in the battlefield.

But the moment he saw his army being overpowered by the enemy, he would leap into the battlefield and, in no time, exterminate almost the entire Lango tribe. The inter-tribal terror between the Luo and the Lango can be understood within the context of domination and other dictatorial systems dominating the world today. The whole development of war, as depicted in this legend, can be traced back to the concept of "Domination", the conviction that one part of mankind has the right to force its will upon the rest of the world and subject them to slavery and oppression (Andics, 1969). The theory of domination was based on the principle of violence as an instrument of conquest and government, which lies at the very heart of the system invented by Lenin and perfected by Stalin and Hitler. They believed that only by violence could a minority achieve power, and only through terror could they retain it. If they lost the power to control the people, there would be no peace and progress.

Indeed, it is narrated that the Lango people wanted very much to end the war, as it had put such a heavy toll on them socially, economically and politically. They wanted a shared solution which supports self-determination within regional integration and unity. Without this, they argued, they were going to be badly affected if greater attention was not given to tackle the war. Thus, in the interest of peace, stability and prosperity, the Lango people vowed to work for common measures for their protection at all levels, so that everyone in the community could enjoy a safer and healthier future.

Indeed, as any human being, the Lango wanted to enjoy a decent standard of life, which required adequate food, clothing, shelter, water, health and general well being. The strategy to be adopted to put an end to this war and its impact on the people was as challenging as it was creative in devising an appropriate policy and practical interventions on behalf of the community. But the question was: How could a man with a wife and children, with blood flowing in his veins, have the body of a rock? Where was his flesh, which could be speared so as to kill him? What types of community reconciliation processes were to be adopted to bring lasting peace in the two warring communities? These were some of the questions that needed to be addressed for peace to prevail in the land.

According to this folklore, Magere was to be given a beautiful woman to marry--a woman who would spy on him and find out where his human flesh actually lay so that she could report back to her community. Her role was that of espionage. Women, in those early days, were used as peacemakers given away in marriage to the enemy to settle disputes and bring everlasting friendship between warring communities.

Several months later, Magere launched a deadly wave of terror over his enemies. He massacred the Langos again en mass and came home to the celebration and honor from his people. The Luo people gave him a hero's welcome with song and dance. Praise songs were composed in his honor making him swell with pride. But after sometimes he fell ill with a terrible headache. It was, then, that he asked his new wife to cut his forehead from his shadow and draw out bad blood that he believed was the cause of this excruciating headache. But his first wife objected to having the new wife perform the task lest she discovered the secret of where Magere's supernatural powers lay. But Magere, who loved his second wife most dearly, would not hear of it. As soon as the Lango wife cut his forehead and bad blood oozed out, she knew, instantly, where Magee's mighty strength lay. At night, she sneaked to her motherland to report to her people.

It was not long before Magere was in the battlefield again massacring the Lango soldiers when suddenly one of the Lango warriors stealthily and carefully planted his spear in Magee's shadow killing him instantly. The mystery is that his body turned into a poisonous stone where hunters, to this day, sharpen their arrows when going hunting. But more importantly, the battle came to an end with women playing a key role in the demilitarization of these two warring communities. In this folklore, we not only observe the effects of armed conflict on the Lango community but also the practice of intervention in which women were used as agents of 'foreign espionage' or collaborators to get inside the enemy camp and learn more about them to strike better.

Beautiful women have often been used to help destroy the aggressor so that peace can prevail in warring communities. It is a strategy used in most of James Bond's films where beautiful and sexy women are made to use their bodies to seduce the enemy in order to cunningly extract information that is used to destroy him. Espionage is normally used in such situations and if the woman's intensions are discovered, she may be killed creating more room for the war to escalate. Indeed, like the biblical epic of the mighty Samson and Delilah, Samson, the strong man, was robbed of his powers once his cunning wife, Delilah, lured him into shaving his head making him lose his power and getting killed by the philistines. Delilah, like Magere's Lango wife, was a conspirator who had tricked her partner to the enemy becoming a member of a ring bent on bringing about the downfall of a superpower enemy.

Inter-ethnic conflicts in traditional Africa and many parts of the world usually arose because of political expansion or struggle for power as depicted, once again, in the epic *Shaka the Zulu* (Mapanje and White, 1983). As in the legend, *Luanda Magere*, the poet praises and glorifies the Zulu king as a great warrior who brings down his enemy without much effort. Shaka is described as strong, powerful and ferocious. People fear him because of his ferocity in causing mass destruction. The poet recounts, with particular admiration, the many communities and clans Shaka has ferociously destroyed and vandalized in an all-out attack in record time.

The poet describes Shaka admiringly with destructive and violet images. He is depicted as 'He who is like a madman', 'the ferocious one of Senzangakhona', 'He who is as dark as the bile of a goat', 'the spear that is red on the handle'. He is like 'fire', 'lion' and 'viper'. Shaka is also as swift as 'a hawk' in his military attack and so 'illusive' that his opponents cannot capture and subdue him. The poet admires him for having bravely fought many wars, conquered and brought economic and political crisis in the land of the enemy. He continues to emphasize that Shaka's meticulous and ferocious strategies and successful raids are not only devastating but unmatched by any other warrior in living memory. Shaka has fought and defeated Buthelezi clan, attacked Sondaba of Mthanda, Macingwane at Ngonyameni and Mangcengeza of the Mbatha clan. He 'devoured' Nomahlanjana son of Zwide of the Maphelas, Mtimona son of Gaqa of the Maphelas, Mpondo-phumela-kwezinde of the Maphelas, Sikloloba-singamabele of Zwide's people. The list of those he conquered, subdued or killed is long.

Shaka is so strategic that he keeps his enemy in a state of 'excitement'. The effects of the wars brought so much suffering to the people such that they were reduced to the state of 'beggars' and 'homeless criminals' (p. 27)

The ensuring poverty of the land and homelessness as the aftermath of war depicts Shaka's regime as tolerating no ceasefire but reinforcing and giving him legitimacy to plunder the land and a platform and visibility to destroy and manipulate the situation at will as a warlord. As a powerful leader in this historical time in South Africa, Shaka was left largely to his own devices as he had successfully managed to emerge as a dominant power destroying the unity of the human family in the region. But the issue here is that militarization of Africa that started 'a long time ago' and continues to this day as witnessed in many parts of Africa will not guarantee peace and security in the region. It is justice and upholding democratic ideals that will save Africa from war and militarization.

Another Nigerian poem, *Onikoyi, the Warrior King,* in the same anthology, depicts Onikoyi just as ferocious as Shaka and Magere. Like 'a vulture' or an 'eagle' or a 'hawk' parching on a baobab tree or sitting on the silk cotton tree, Onikoyi 'flaps' down to attack his enemy. He moves swiftly and efficiently. He, too, is personified as a vulture or a 'man eater' –one who will 'devour' his enemy in record time and cause untold suffering. He 'loves nothing but war'. To him war is like a hobby such that when others relax and 'drink wine, he drinks blood instead. 'When others plant yams, he is planting heads. When others reap fruits, he is reaping dead warriors" (pp. 124-125).

The needless horror and death Onikoyi, the king, brings upon his enemy are praised and glorified through powerful expressions and figures of speech. The people are depicted as helpless victims of the atrocities caused by the invading warrior King. This poem is, certainly, a mirror of African life in pre-literate societies. A time dominated by political instability and civil strife before the coming of Europeans indicating that even though some pre-literate societies had political systems, they did not have rules for controlling violence or bringing it to an end in the way it is done today through international mediation and peace-keeping through the United Nations. What it shows, however, is that poets as the mouthpiece of the society are also historians who recall and record past histories as creatively and true to life as possibly. On the other hand, they enjoy and celebrate war meaning that war is good, right and proper and should be encouraged in the society. Breaches of human rights including insecurity and wanton destruction are offences against humanity but such offences can be atoned by restriction to any individual in authority and must be dealt with by punishing the individual for inflicting the atrocities in the society. For instance, Onikoyi's large-scale destruction is an offence too serious to be made good by compensating the masses he has selfishly massacred. Such an action can be controlled and curbed through diplomatic channels or through conventions or treaties or by making use of natural law–the law of nations to promote the universal common good.

This is necessary because tribal wars in Africa need international interventions. Actions by local autocratic leaders have failed because leaders do not agree to dialogue and suggest settlement for common good. They may use diplomatic channels or sign conventions and treaties by following rules and regulations of nations. But more often than not such laws are inadequate and don't commit leaders to stop atrocities. Instead, they make a leader to think that outsiders are interfering with him and accuse the locals for collaborating with foreigners. This attitude on the part of African leaders has often led to much loss of life and extensive displacement of people, many of whom become refugees in and outside their own communities.

As in this poem, Onikoyi needs to be punished for Human Rights violation. While this poem maybe referred to as a praise poem found in many African communities, it catalogues the many ills and predicament Africa faced under their tribal warriors and kings without condemning the kings for their atrocities. They are part of inter-group atrocities which many African states suffer from today. Although Onikoyi, like other kings and warriors discussed in this chapter remain responsible for the crimes committed and ought to be punished for Human Rights violation, he is praised in song and dance for the injuries he has caused in the land. In Yoruba, such praise songs are called *Oriki*; in Zulu *Izlgbongo* (Mapanje and White 1983, Jahn, 1968). In the Luo community praise songs are called *Pakruok* describing the deeds and character of an individual usually a chief, warrior or a god.

A major factor about praise poems/songs and the folklore tradition is that they continue to be genres not only for individual heroes but also for groups. The words and names in the song could be altered to suite different individuals in different circumstances. In other words, they can be remodeled and reworked by singers after singers until the impress and significance of the original composer disappear. The process of communal re-creation depends, however, upon the accepted set of words and clichés. Often, it is recast in terms of familiar problems and conflicts within the culture, which may include corruption, greed, pride including prejudice against orphans, girl-children or 'outsiders' or 'strangers'. Thus, to the Africans, song, poetry and rhythm both in the traditional past and modern times, today, are not composed for the sake of it but for enacting social processes that are functional in the society in which they are take place and motivating and encouraging warriors and the general public to engage in war and bring honor and glory to their communities.

Inter-tribal wars, oppression, discrimination, hunger and poverty were not of the people's own choosing. Communities got involved in wars because their leaders, aggressive, arrogant and greedy, thirsted for war sinking their people deeply into the quagmire. Modern African history has been marked by sporadic eruptions of civil strife across the continent as Ayittey (1992) and Achebe (1983) in particular state that 'civil war gave Nigeria a perfect and legitimate excuse to cast the Igbo in the role of treasonable felon, a wrecker of the nation' (p.45) in reference to the Biafra war of the 1970s. There were people in Gowon's cabinet who wanted their 'pound of flesh'. But Gowon discouraged vengeance and brought the war to an end. People were fighting social, political and economic ills because they had been made to live and experience them by their leaders.

When leaders cause war and untold suffering among their tribes, it is their people who must be mobilized to fight them collectively rather than individually before they can settle down to the fruitful ways of peace. Indeed, only the Africans and perhaps African Americans in the United States have made significant contribution to the musical tradition by modifying songs to express racial conflict they experience in their societies. It means that the most general approach to the explanation of group violence based on communal cleavages is to interpret it within the context of broader theories of political violence of the kinds reviewed in the poems above. Not only do these poems emphasize inequalities among groups but that the greater the inequalities, the more likely the victims of war are to take collective action (Deng and Zartman, 1991). Denial of the opportunity to reduce war and conflict is a particularly potent source of grievance. But once no practical solution to their grievances is forthcoming, the aggrieved people (consoling and referring to themselves as 'soldiers') fall back to religion. They look forward to the gods to save them from war or relieve them of the predicament they face in the world.

They feel there is faith in future bliss to which every person affected by the war look forward to and which is intended not for them but for future generation. The people see themselves as soldiers relying on 'God of war' as their protector. For instance, in *Things Fall Apart,* one of the earlier novels in which Achebe weaves his story with everyday folktales, legends and myths as well as proverbs, traditional maximum and cryptic anecdotes, indicate the writer's awareness of the importance of folklore in African culture and the messages they convey with respect to conflict and conflict resolution in human society.

Depicting traditional culture before the coming of the imperialists, Achebe respectively recreates the experience of the Igbo people in the 'age of innocence'. He is able to re-create the past with the art of a traditional storyteller. The novel, very much folklorist in style focuses on the theme of war and heroism personified in *Okonkwo* his protagonist. In three major epochs–the purely traditional phase, the period of invasion by European colonial powers, and the capture of Igbo land, we read of various conflicts and their resolutions from traditional perspective.

First, *Okonkwo* is depicted as a brave and daring young warrior of the people of Umofia. He is 'manly' and, in many ways ferocious almost like *Luanda Magere*, *Shaka* the Zulu and *Okutoyi* the warrior in the legends and poems described above. We are told that as a young man of eighteen he had brought honor to his village by throwing Amalinze the cat. (Amalinze was the unchallengeable wrestler, for several years in nine villages, from Umuofia to Mbaino). At this early age, 'he had taken two tittles and had shown incredible prowess in two inter-tribal wars' (p.6). Young as he was, *Okonkwo* had already brought five human heads home from various inter-ethnic wars and was considered one of the greatest men of his time. As the elders said, '*Okonkwo* had washed his hands and so he ate with kings and elders'.

Because of his elevated status, he was appointed by the community to go to Mbaino as a war emissary and seek compensation for the war Mbaino people had waged against Umofians. Portrayed as 'a man of action, a man of war', he symbolized strength and bravery–a role model whose impressive acts of heroism and fearlessness had earned him fame and a distinguished place in the community. Achebe further portrays Umofia clan as 'militaristic' and 'fearless' in nature. Having been provoked by the cold-blooded murder of the wife of one of the clan members (*Ogbuefi Udo*) by the people of Mbaino, Umofians were ready for war. They felt provoked and 'thrust for blood'. But the Oracle of the Hills and Caves averted it, arguing that the people had no just cause for war. In other words, the Oracles called for disarmament and warned Umofians against engaging in a war that was likely to be seen as a senseless war–'a war of blame'. Since the Gods had spoken against engaging in war, none had the moral right to engage in it. For successful conflict resolution, the external community had to offer the necessary resources, particularly in the post-conflict, peace-building phase.

Prominent personalities were used as war emissaries. Okonkwo, a man of tittles and elevated status was asked to play such a role and to seek compensation from Mbaino people for injuries caused to the Umofians. The intention was to atone the Earth Goddess for the murder of Udo's wife and to strengthen peace and reconciliation with the people of Mbaino. Mbaino people were only too glad to pay compensation to avoid the impending war at all costs for they were aware of the age-old belief held in the community that Umofians possessed powerful magic and medicine that were thought to be the most potent of all.

Thus, the Mbaino people accepted to pay compensation in the form of a virgin woman given away to Udo, as a direct replacement for his slain wife–the murder that had caused the war. The ill-fated *Ikemefuna* was given away to the community to sacrifice to avoid further war and bloodshed as the traditional gods demanded. The chief aim in this peaceful and compensatory negotiation was to achieve improved relations between the two clans. But more importantly was the belief in the oracles, magic, and medicine that were important mythical systems used to bring peace between and among warring communities.

To a great extent, the Umofians are portrayed as non-violent. To them, violence was ruefully the only answer to the persistent harms and brutalities of the wicked people in the society. It means that in pre-colonial era, Africans managed their own affairs and administered justices among themselves. They felt that in a situation where war was eminent, they could consult their gods–the oracles. In this respect, the Umofians could only engage in war so long as the Oracles and the god of war approved it. As a non-violent society, the Umofians dedicated a special week for observing peace, which was observed to improve human relations in the family and community levels. Fighting, quarrelling or displaying violent behavior was avoided at all costs as people learnt the importance of commitment to peacekeeping and living in harmony with fellow humans.

Conflict with nature was also avoided for it was believed that "darkness held a vague terror for these people, even the bravest among them. Children were warned not to whistle at night for fear of evil spirits. Dangerous animals became even more sinister and uncanny in the dark. A snake was never called by its name at night, because it would hear. It was called a 'string'" (p. 7)

The desire to be at peace with nature and the rest of the universe was critical to human survival. As people wanted explanations of why they suffer misfortunes and diseases which make them ill, or why their crops fail, convinced that these problems do not happen haphazardly but selectively. They were able to explain their misfortunes occurring due to providence, ill luck or witchcraft. They took the blame and said the victim of misfortune must have committed a crime for which the gods were angry and punishing him. They, therefore, sought within their communities a person who had the power to reverse the misfortune. They thought of someone with whom they had quarreled, and suspected of the evil deed. Thus, witchcraft as a theory of causes of misfortunes was related to personal relations between the sufferer and his fellows, and to a theory of moral judgments as to what was good or bad.

When a person suffered misfortune, which he could not remedy, such as *Okonkwo's* misfortune of the killing of *Ezeudu's* son on *Ezeudu's* funeral, people accepted it as a crime caused by bad luck but also one which had to be punished. Beliefs and cultural norms were in place to help manage such misfortunes or provide solutions for already existing problems. They were believed to be more likely to result in a relatively peaceful transition, in which a critical mass of human survival were negotiated and retained. Religion, cultural beliefs and superstition were conduit for reconciliation with the evil forces in the environment in which men and women and children lived and interacted.

In *Things Fall Apart*, conflict whose effects were broad and adverse attracted considerable devotion to the *Week of Peace* and as people with a high sense of human predicament and destiny, the Umofians found religion important and necessary for keeping peace with neighbors. Anyone found to violate religious beliefs and norms especially during the *Week of Peace* was heavily punished by being made to pay a fine to pacify the *Earth Goddess*. Thus, when *Okonkwo* repudiated this, when he beat up his wife, *Ojiugo*, he was warned and made to pay a fine. Custom prescribed the methods of administering justice so that punishment was not in excess of the offence. All these are fundamental to folklore, which borrows heavily from the political, economic, and cultural struggle of that momentous upheaval in the history of the African people.

Indeed, both Achebe and Ngugi, and many of the first generation of African writers and poets of the time, tended to derive their inspiration from traditional lore, indigenous customs, and the oral traditions to demonstrate that Africans, like other races of the world, had a distinguished culture of which they were proud. In an interview with Lindfors (1971), Achebe said:

> You would have thought it was obvious that everybody had a past, but there were people who came to Africa and said, 'You have no history, you have no civilization, you have no culture, and you have no religion....' Well, you know, we didn't just drop from the sky. We, too, had our own history, traditions, cultures, and civilizations. It is not possible for one culture to come to another and say, 'I am the way, the truth, and the life; there is nothing else but me'. If you say this, you are guilty of irreverence or arrogance. You are also stupid. And this is really my concern' (pp. 1-2).

African writers of the 1960s wrote amidst challenges from white supremacists, who claimed that Africa had no history to be proud of except primitiveness and backwardness. Viewed from these perspectives, early African writers and poets became protest artists who, in keeping with their roles as committed artists, were mainly concerned with the unfair violence waged against their race.

Achebe's story about the people of Umuofia and the events that followed in the latter half of the nineteenth century emphasized the historical conflicts that African communities faced with the arrival of the whiteman.

From the story of *Things Fall Apart,* we observe the state of hostility as it was in traditional times. Although individuals committed crimes against one another, the commonest method of settling conflicts was by arbitration—a method whereby one person or group of persons are invited to adjudicate cases of interpersonal conflict including domestic violence and disagreements. Arbitration was always held with the consent of the persons involved in the conflict, for it is only then that settlement can be achieved.

The *egwugus* were such arbitrators or councilors who took the lead in solving disputes. We, therefore, note that the Umofians had a code of conduct, which compelled them to keep peace and live in harmony with one another, failure to which punishment, and retribution was to fall on the aggressor. As Obiechina (1975, p. 202) argues, these norms of behavior, customary beliefs, attitudes and values had come down to them with as little modification as possible from the immemorial past. All-important aspects of cultural life were protected by religious sentiments, and great store was set on social conformity. The existence of a traditional culture depends on the existence of a community, that is, the kind of society in which there is intimate face-to-face relationship and co-operation among people and who as a result experience what C.H. Cooley calls 'a certain fusion of individualities in a common whole''.

Therefore, when individuals commit crimes against humanity, they are punished as part of justice and Human Rights in the community. This is made clear when *Okonkwo* is sent to his motherland for nine years for killing *Ezeudu's* son inadvertently during the burial ceremony of *Ezeudu* himself. *Okonkwo's* gun had exploded during a funeral celebration and a piece of iron had pierced the boy's heart. According to the people's custom, *Okonkwo* had polluted the land. Consequently, his homestead had to be demolished and valuable property including animals set on fire, as he and his family fled to his motherland. It was a crime against the earth goddess to kill a clansman even if it was inadvertently done. According to Igbo traditions, a man who had committed such a crime had to flee from the land and his home and property destroyed.

The question many elderly men asked including *Obierika* was: 'Why: should a man suffer so grievously for an offence he has committed inadvertently?' It was the justice of the earth goddess even though the people questioned the fairness of this law inflicted on *Okwonkwo*. They observed that the punishment inflicted on *Okonkwo* did not seem to be commensurate with the crime he had committed. Even though they complained, 'the Earth had decreed that *Okonkwo's* crime was an offence on the land and justice had to be done accordingly. If the clan did not exact punishment against *Okonkwo*, the great goddess would loosen her wrath on all the land and not just on the offender. Everyone would suffer as the elders said, 'if one finger brought oil, it soiled the other' (p. 17). In essence, it seems that the judicial system could not be challenged and a person's social status was not to be taken into account either. The full law of the land was enforced compelling the people to live in harmony with each other.

While the law existed to regulate human relationships, we must admit that the ultimate solution to human conflicts also lay in the willingness of humankind to obey the enforcement of those laws. Cultural norms and regulations were of inestimable value in achieving peace, or bringing about an end to fears, prejudice, pride, and irrationality, which were the barriers to a truly integrated society. But peace, non-violence, and integration were only partial, though necessary steps toward the final goal, which societies sought to realize in the face of daily confrontations.

However, traditional folklorists and modern writers in Africa noted with great concern that though there were internal conflicts and ambivalence in the traditional past, Africa also enjoyed relative peace. This peace was beginning to fall apart as a result of the onslaught of colonialism and military conquest that depleted Africa to its very roots. As chroniclers of their time, writers did not hesitate to capture violent confrontation that was characteristic of this colonial process in their creative writings.

In *Things Fall Apart,* for instance, we are informed that *Abame* had virtually been reduced to ashes on one market day by the imperialists. Achebe narrates that the whiteman arrived and killed the people en mass in retaliation of the murder of one of them–a missionary. In one of their organized punitive expeditions, the whitemen opened fire and exterminated the entire people of Abame who were not only taken unawares but were themselves unarmed. Abame was obliterated. It was subsequently annexed as the people lost their land to the whiteman. From then onward, the Igbo people had to obey the European laws and social systems, which encouraged the philosophy of violence and domination.

Similarly, in Gikuyu land, Ngugi wa Thiongo, in *The River Between* narrates that the coming of the Whiteman (butterflies) was just as destructive as anywhere else in Africa. When they arrived, they robbed the people of their God-given land and posed a great threat to the people's source of livelihood. Already, they had captured Nairobi, Muranga, Siriana Missionary Centre, Kiambu, and Tumutumu and were gradually moving further inland to capture more land while displacing the people and destroying their cultural life in the process.

Later the issue of land became a major theme in Maumau oral literature. Maina wa Kinyatti (1980), in his anthology *Thunder from the Mountains,* records racial conflict through political and patriotic songs which the movement used as a weapon to politicize and sensitize Kenyans to take up arms and expel the hostile British people from their land. The song/poems being of historical importance reveal an authentic inspiration from the popular vernacular songs of the people documented in this anthology. First, songs aimed at familiarizing Kenyans with the political goals and heroism of *Mau Mau* and in Kinyatti's words they 'heightened the people's consciousness against the forces of foreign occupiers and, in the process, prepared them for an armed struggle. These songs were sung at Kenya African Union (KAU) rallies, in independent schools and churches, in the homes of the ordinary people, in guerrilla bases, in detention camps and in prisons' (p ix).

In the angry, stabbing lines, the poet-politician lamented about the stolen land and other crimes related to oppression and cultural assimilation. The demands for land, the call to arms, the heroism of battle, the horror of imprisonment and the treachery of the collaborators are major conflicts that Africans experienced in the process of colonialism. Without land to satisfy their material needs, the African people were doomed to a miserable existence as squatters. The transfer of ancestral lands (a religious inheritance from their ancestors and peoples' life blood) provoked the people to take up arms and resist colonial domination.

In *Weep Not, Child,* Ngugi asks, 'Where did the land go? While several poems in Maina wa Kinyatti's collection including *You White People Are Foreigners in Our Country* and *Struggle for our Land,* make the war for land almost a religious war especially when they appealed to god 'Ngai' and their ancestors to protect them during this war of injustice and exploitation. The poet encourage the people to fight the enemy until the country is liberated and add that the land problem had been predicted by the community's prophets and seers, in particular, Chege. He had seen that conflict and hatred would increase and friendship diminish with the coming of the whiteman' *(p. 31).*

The poets in this anthology, appeal to 'Ngai', God the creator of Mount Kenya as well as Mumbi and Gikuyu, Chege, Mwangi and Waiyaki respected ancestors of the community to help the movement win the war against British oppressors who like 'beasts in sheep's clothing' pretended to lead them into the light. Very much like the popular trickster story where the theme of deception is played by a cunning mischievous character that assumes a false personality and uses it to exploit others or reap certain gains from the victims of his deception. The white man in this anthology is depicted as engaging in similar dirty intrigues. They stole the land given to the Agikuyu by their gods and do not want to give it back causing perpetual racial war and injustice.

In this anthology, are numerous references to the slave-like conditions, the brutalities of colonialism, and recurring themes of conflict and insecurity. The poems criticize an unjust society. –a society where much of the injustices continued to prevail even within a law-abiding nation. People who continue to commit atrocities in the land are depicted as in a contest between a man and another: The poets were concerned with addressing specific moral problems at both the personal and the social levels. For instance, shouldn't traitors and home guards be punished for seeking to undermine the efforts of freedom fighters and the power to enforce change? It is observed in the works of both Achebe and Ngugi that strict justice was almost a religion as far as ideology was concerned. .

Africans had a law of reparation. Under this law if a person killed, or betrayed the community retribution was bound to fall upon him/her and retribution was believed to affect not only the offender but also the entire family of the offender.

The African poet seemed to spend more time highlighting   punishment for those who violate human life than reward for those who protected it. The most courageous and downright warning went to traitors and members of the master race as the poet makes early warning that those who have betrayed the people will be heavily punished as internal justice is in place to deal with them and that there is no exception. Poets emphasize the natural justice that existed in African culture for aggressors and conflict creators when gross violations of Human Rights take place. In particular, the poem *The Traitor to Our Cause* draws on the land issue as a source of conflict and long-standing history of struggle with the colonialists. He comes up with a solution: revenge. They would pay for their treachery when the white man returns to his county after independence.

Traitors and collaborators would have to be punished when black leaders take over power. The people would revenge against them for betraying their cause. In other words, the philosophy of '*tit-for-tat*' was justified as a natural justice for traitors rather than forgiveness and reconciliation. This is depicted in the poems *Prisons Are Terrible Places'* and *The Betrayer.* Both the poems remind traitors that they would be crying for mercy when the white man leaves the country.

The fact that these poets are naturally sensitive to the injustices inflicted on their communities demonstrate that not only are they eulogizing the heroism of the *Mau Mau* freedom fighters and singing their praises for their distinguished role in destroying the enemy forces, they do contribute to the important pool of information about conflict and conflict resolution—a resolution led by the oppressed African themselves determined to liberate their country from foreign domination. Those who have been trading in injustice and benefiting from it as traitors or collaborators, will finally get what they deserve—isolation. As sellouts, and 'worthless animals', the poets predict their doom.

Songs such as: *Struggle for Our Land, Why Sell Your Land? The General Cry in Gikuyu land'* and a host of others in this anthology call upon the patriotic masses to wage war against foreign enemy and its local allies. Majority of poems in this collection are mass songs, which were composed before the British declared war on the people during the Mau emergency of 1952. These songs were used by the *Mau Mau Movement* to politicize and educate the general population about the nature of the British colonialism in order to win their support for the armed struggle. They express the African people's hatred towards colonialists and their 'local boys' (p. ix).

The works of these poets embody the peoples' values and attitudes in freedom and respect for human rights. But more importantly, their deep seated beliefs in religion, mythical systems and consciousness of their historical life, collective outlook and ethics, in their legends and folk-tales and other forms of oral culture. They highlight racial conflict with its effects on the people's social, economic and political well-being. These are conflicts whose settlement can only come about when the oppressed are liberated to run their own affairs.

The major themes running through these works are the demands of the people for the return of their stolen land and for freedom and recognition of their dignity, and culture as a people. Kinyatti (1980) further explained that these poems 'highlight the long social, economic and political crisis the Africans faced in the camps and in prisons. The poems express the people's bitterness against the 'Home Guard' traitors who were hunting, spying on and torturing their compatriots in the camps and who superintended their eviction from the settlers' plantations'. Clearly, these are works of oral literature, which focus on human conflicts and survival. They indicate that the issue of land, during colonial time, brought great conflicts between the rulers and the ruled as poets urged the oppressed Africans to take up arms and fight for their motherland. *Struggle for Our Land,* incites the people to seize their stolen land back from the white colonialists because land was not only their god-given resource but also a source of livelihood that was to be natured and protected for posterity. Political reform by itself was not enough. It had also to incorporate mechanisms for fair and equitable distribution of wealth within races. This would radically ensure responsibility and effective peace-building.

Mau Mau poets and praise singers became stern advocates of war against colonialists. They saw war and bloodshed against the Whiteman as a means to get back their land with the oral medium remaining very important in the education and sensitization of the majority of Africans.

It must be stressed that the oral medium was also commonly used in South Africa during their struggle against apartheid. The African people, the victims of oppressive apartheid regime demonstrated a spirit of armed resistance and a commitment to war and bloodshed as a means to bringing peace, good governance and development to the people in general. This commitment was very strong in Angola, Mozambique, and Guinea where apartheid regime had caused so much destruction to the people.

According to the literary output of the region poets came to express anger and ferocity as found in Dicken's anthology, *When Bullets Begin to Flower*--a collection of militant poems against colonialists. Artists expressed their grievances and pledged to take up arms to liberate themselves because they were oppressed and inhumanly treated. Poems such as "*Contract Workers*" and "A *Militant's Poem*" pledged revenge and warned that the people would open all the prisons, set free all the African prisoners and destroy all the colonial tyrants in order to gain independence and be at peace with one another. .

Within the process of militarization of African literature, folktales, poetry and the novel, artists came to express a common issue: the issue of land and the need to take up arms and fight oppression. Their works were associated with the revolutionary movements. Thousands of Black leaders such as Steve Biko, the Black Consciousness idealist whose sad story is captured in the film *Cry Freedom* is captivating. The brutal murder of Soweto children in 1970 is also echoed in musical videos such as *Sarafina* and *Graceland*.

By the second half of the twentieth century after gaining independence from the outrageous and brutal systems of colonial domination, war in Africa never ceased. The African masses generally believed that political independence would automatically bring peace and solve their economic woes. African leaders, they expected, were going to bring an end to various conflicts and injustices they had suffered under colonial rule and see to it that all citizens would enjoy fundamental liberties. Thus the African masses, celebrated their freedom with unbound euphoria which Mugo (1978), a Kenyan poet, was to express in her poem *We will Rise and Build a Nation*. In this poem, she describes the African masses as having been very happy and excited in rebuilding their countries after the departure of colonialists and had trusted their leaders and "garlanded them with embracing hearts". (p. 68).

But it was a great irony that this excitement was short lived. For immediately after independence, there were great exploitation, poor leadership, political assassination and all manner of atrocities. Wars and military coups ensued one after another causing untold suffering in ways similar to the kind of intertribal wars and bloodshed recorded in African folktales, legends and myths. New African leaders engaged their citizens in shameless bloodshed and mass destruction despite having assured them of good governance, peace, and prosperity. Scanning through the literary works of the post –independence era, one is inclined to see more conflicts taking place between the state and its people. There are problems of poverty, corruption, degradation, tribalism, dictatorship and abuse of power in such works as Achebe's *A man of The People, No Longer At Ease,* Ngugi's *Petals of Blood,* Amar's *The Beautiful ones are not Yet Born* and the like.

Later, the Biafra war broke out in 1962, novelists of the Biafra War emerged such as Cyprian Ekwensi's *Survive The Peace,* Kalu Okapi's, *Biafra Testament,* Achebe's *Girls at War and Other stories* and his collection of poems *Beware Soul Brothers,* Okpewho's *The Last Duty,* Eddie Iroh's *Toads of War* and *Forty-Eight Guns for the General* and many other war artists in this category. Artists of both oral and written medium were interested in exposing the impact of war on the masses and the physical landscape so that new states could take initiatives to bring peace and justice in the land that was being badly destroyed because of greed for power and tribal hatred. Like the 'Ogre' in John Uganda's play *The floods,* African leaders were simply 'monsters' ready to devour their people.

In this play, Ruganda characterized the head of state (Buogo) as the 'Ogre'. He uses his soldiers to create chaos in Uganda-a country whose politics, at the time of independence, looked much brighter and was commonly referred to as the 'Pearl of Africa'. Idi Amin's regime destroyed the country through systematic murder, assassinations and disappearance of political leaders, military destruction, lawlessness, and crackdown of human rights in post-colonial Uganda.

Concerned with the political tyranny during Idi Amin's regime, *Ruganda* dramatizes this unforgettable historical event in the hope of sensitizing the people to unite and overthrow the system so that peace could prevail. Many people fled the land in terror to avoid being seized 'like goats for the slaughter house'. The play shows the hypocrisy of African leaders who claimed to have brought 'the gift of peace to the people of Africa after the colonialists left while, in actual fact, they had not found the peace to offer their citizens. Instead, there had been shameful military lawlessness, as the soldiers who should protect the citizens become the enemy of the people, plundering the country's resources, raping women and killing innocent people at will. We are told of lorry loads of civilians driven to death over cliffs at the point of bayonets and of bodies of those massacred cruelly thrown to the crocodiles in Lake Victoria to be devoured.

One is, therefore, reminded of the animal stories in Africa—in particular, the 'Ogre' or 'monster' stories (*Beasts and Giants*). The ogre a grotesque and frightening monster is usually capable of transforming himself into humans and other forms changing his voice and appearance in order to lure his victims and devour them. He kills people indiscriminately and by impersonating himself, he is able to trap his victims safely. Similarly, the trickster stories of the cunning Hare, *Anansi the Spider*, *The Jackal*, *The Fox* and *The Monkey* represent the cunning, boastful and exploitative characters in the society. They always resort to tricking and duping other bigger animals to achieve their selfish goals. But underneath the stories are moral lessons to be learnt by the listeners and readers. The lessons centre on different kinds of conflict and successful resolution and peace-building efforts.

For instance, there can be rewards for brave fighters or faithful servants and severe punishment ranging from vengeance for an act which everyone agrees is wrong, including defending and asserting one's rights, order that the damage done be made good, sanctions against accessing certain resources, and death of the cunning individual or the offender. Animal stories are usually about human vices, which are satirized, and virtues extolled without directly pointing to specific individuals whose behaviors correspond to those characters in the tale. These trickster stories are not only familiar in most part of Africa and the rest of the world but act as a vehicle of communicating how peace, reconciliation and settlement are arrived at among warring individuals and communities. More typically, they are used to educate and reinforce, in members of the society, appropriate ways to respect the right of others and to live in harmony with neighbors.

Those who are greedy or gluttonous, exploitative, proud, lazy or deliberately set out to deceive and ridicule others like the cunning Hare, are often punished by death or fall victim to their own pranks. Sometimes, they may bring about good to their victims without intending it. Yet in some instances, the trickster is a culture hero or a transformer, who may use his wits to destroy monsters that kill or terrorize the community by bringing about its death. In some cases, after the cruel and destructive Ogre (*ondiek* or *apul apul* as they are referred to in the Luo community) has been killed, the young man and woman victims of the tyranny of the Ogre get married and live happily thereafter. Peace and harmony are restored in the land. All these are aspects of government, since all the basic responsibility of individuals in a state is to maintain law and order in what would otherwise be a hostile society.

References

Achebe, C. (1958). *Things fall apart*. Nairobi: Heinemann Kenya

Achebe, C. (1983). *The trouble with Nigeria.* Nairobi: East African Educational Publishers Ltd.

Ayittey, G. B. (1992). *Africa betrayed.* New York: St. Martin's Press

Deng, F. M. and Zartman, W. (1991). *Conflict resolution in Africa.* Washington DC: The Brooking Institution

Duane, O. B. (2004). *African myths and legends.* London: Brockhampton Press

Finnegan, R. (1970). *Oral literature in Africa.* Nairobi: Oxford University Press.

Jennings, J. D. and Hoebel, A. (1966). *Readings in Anthropology.* New York McGraw-Hill, Inc.

Jahn, J. (1968). *Neo-African literature: A history of Black writing.* New York: Grove Press, Inc.

Lovell, J. (1972). *Black song: The forge and the flames.* New York: The Macmillan.

Mair, L. (1965). *An introduction to social anthropology.* Oxford: Clarendon Press

Mapanje, Jack & White, L. (1983). *Oral poetry from Africa.* Esses: Longman Group Ltd.

Miruka, O. (1994). *Encounter with oral literature.* Nairobi: East African Educational Publishers

Mugo, M. G. (1978). *Visions of Africa.* Nairobi: Kenya Literature Bureau

Obiechina, E. (1975). Culture, *tradition and society in the West African novel.* London: Cambridge University Press

Odaga, A. B. (1984). *Yesterday's today: The study of oral literature:* Nairobi Lake Publishers & Enterprises

Omtatah, O. (1991). *Luanda Magere.* Nairobi: Heinemann Kenya

Okpewho, I. (1983). *Myth in Africa.* London: Cambridge University Press

Ombaka, C. (1998) War and environment in African literature. In Murphy, P. D. (ed) *Literature of nature* London: Fitzroy Dearborn Publishers

Utley, F. E. (1980). Definition of folklore. In Tristram Coffin, editor, American *folklore.* Voice of America Forum series. United States International Communication Agency.

wa Kinyatti, M. (ed.). (1980). *Thunder from the mountains: Mau Mau patriotic songs.*
London: Zed Press.

Chapter 13

The Press as Tools and Casualties of Political Conflicts in Nigeria

Abiodun Salawu, Ph.D.
University of Lagos, NIGERIA

Sola Isola
Redeemer's University, NIGERIA

Introduction

In addition to playing the role of a watch-dog against the excesses of the ruling class and assisting in setting agenda for good governance, the media also provides the platform for political actors to exchange rhetorical assaults whenever they are in conflict. Beyond playing the role of chronicler of those conflicts, the media invariably get dragged into these conflicts and in the process often lose their status as a veritable and an unbiased public institution. This trend was evident in most of the 19th and early 20th centuries which were the political budding years, when Nigeria experienced various kinds of political systems including colonialism, 'militocracy', and democracy.

This experience has adversely affected the media, constituting a serious limitation to its journey toward professionalism. Often, because of involvement in political conflicts, the press lost credibility at various times, lost its freedom and the right to publish at other times and most importantly lost skilled personnel to other lucrative sectors of the economy. Consequently, even though journalism is among the earliest professions in Nigeria, it tends to be the least in terms of possession of ingredients of professionalism. This situation cannot be separated from social, political and economic crises witnessed in the polity at one time or the other.

This chapter attempts to explore the historical antecedents of the Nigerian press and its involvement in political and social conflicts which have limited its performance. Recommendations are made on ways by which the press could emerge stronger to contribute positively to political development, peace building and conflict reduction in Nigeria in the 21st century.

A Review of Literature: Mass media and conflict

Tichenor *et al* (1980, p. 17) note that social conflict is a principal ingredient of much newspaper content since conflict is a central component in community life and social change. Tehranian (1996, p. 3) explains this further by saying that the media are naturally attracted to conflict. He elaborates: "conflict is the bread and butter of journalism Conflict sells" (p. 3). Arno *et al.* (1984, p. 2) assert: "I would go so far to assert that news is defined by its conflict focus and that there is nothing deplorable about the fact."

The media is justified in reporting conflicts because it has the responsibility of recording events as they unfold, part of which is conflict. In other words, conflict is a part of reality and the media has the task of portraying reality. In fact, the provision of information about conflict in the media is a step towards resolution. Tichenor *et al.* (1980, p. 2) provides an insight:

> There is the traditional viewpoint that resolution of social problems is related to inputs of information. Accordingly, if a system is sufficiently saturated with information, a general understanding of the topic will develop within the system. Once understanding is at hand, resolution is assumed to be at hand.

Viewed differently, newspapers' and other media's reports of conflict are said to be contributory to the legitimating of the conflict (Nnaemeka, 1996). Olorunyomi (2000, p. 5), with background knowledge of the genocide in Rwanda, further, contends that the media can act as an accomplice to genocide not only through its indifference but also through active collaboration. He asserts: "In every communal or ethnic conflict, the positions of the media can significantly impact the outcome".

Olorunyomi (2000, p. 7) again notes that the problem associated with media coverage of diversity or conflict is not normative, but rather ontological. He argues:

> To isolate the problems associated with covering diversity as simple matters of norms is to suggest that only endogenous factors influence the practice of the media. The fact of diversity in concrete editorial terms always assumes a plu-

ralism that also includes the exogenous variables of ownership, employees, content and sources. (Olorunyomi, 2000 p. 6)

He, thus, counsels that the media's capacity to respond to its own structural weaknesses would strengthen its capacity to better promote tolerance and help manage diversity in the communities they serve and beyond.

Internal diversity in media organizations or not, individual media owners and journalists need to appreciate the tensions between globalization and primordial feelings and between the notions of totality and heterogeneity (Olorunyomi 2005, p.5).

In a number of places, it has been asserted that wars and conflicts are becoming tailored for the media (Mogekwu, 2005, p. 86; Engelhardt, 1991). The Gulf War, for instance, was prosecuted as an almost made-for-television war. Mogekwu remarked that war has begun to assume the nature of entertainment which people (usually far removed from the scene of the conflict) look forward to everyday – just like soap opera addicts would look forward to interacting with their favorite characters on screen and follow the plots as they unfold. He asserts: "war as total television is gradually falling under the same genre as reality television – a la SURVIVOR" (Mogekwu, 2005, p. 87).

Colonial Period: The Press on a Nationalist Cause

Journalism is one of the oldest professions in Nigeria. The first newspaper, *Iwe Irohin*, came into existence in the country in 1859, a clear 55 years before the emergence of Nigeria as a geographical entity. Initially, *Iwe Irohin* was set up as a missionary endeavor by Rev. Henry Townsend, a missionary of protestant stock (Duyile, 1987; Omu, 1965). The content was mainly about the happenings in the ecclesia environment and of converting the people of Abeokuta, a prominent town in the Yoruba South west and her environ into Christianity. The publisher actually stated in the first edition of the paper that the paper was aimed at inculcating the habit of reading in the people and to propagate the gospel as widely as possible in the then dark part of Africa[1]. Having gathered some experience in the trade in his brother's printing business in England, Rev. Townsend was able to manage the newspaper sufficiently to cover his cost and he subsequently included translated version in the local language in the contents. This initiative catapulted the newspaper into prominence in the pre-colonial environment and soon the paper was read next to the Bible for the gospel as well as other contents about the socio-economic life of the people which crept gradually into the paper.

Reverend Townsend recognized the potentials in his newspaper to fight political causes and this he plunged hastily into. First, he deployed the contents of the publication into the anti-slavery struggle, which was a popular cause in

Africa, Europe and America then. In strongly worded editorials, the paper spoke against illicit trade in slavery, which was still going on in some part of the West African coast and other inhuman treatments of people engaged in by both Europeans and the local people. This hit the right chord among the local readers who perceived the paper as fighting for a cause that could lead to eradication of a malaise which was then seen as truncating the development of humanity. In strongly worded editorials, the paper campaigned strongly against illicit slavery which was still going on in some part of West Africa.

Next, *Iwe Irohin* went into the economic terrain where it reported news about produce trades, movement of goods and merchant ships from Europe to West Africa, prices of commodities and even carried advertisements of products and businesses that could strengthen interactions between Africans and Europeans who by then had already established trading posts in the West African coasts and were moving into the hinterland to engage in trading with the local people. This plunge also hit the right chord among the local people and it further boosted the popularity of *Iwe Irohin*. However, the newspaper began to criticize the unfair trading practices being engaged in by the European business community at the detriment of the local people. This drew the attention of the British crown governor, who was in charge of the colony of Lagos which was close to Abeokuta. At first, Rev Townsend received a mild warning from the governor and was advised to tone down the extent of his criticism of these negative trade practices. It was recorded that later, Rev. Townsend was actually invited over to London for a sterner warning because of his obduracy. This was also good enough for the readers of *Iwe Irohin* and the newspaper's credibility actually shot up, even though by then, the colonial administration's mandate was restricted only to Lagos and *Iwe Irohin* was actually operating away from this territory. Only its influence and readership was spreading to Lagos, and so there was nothing the crown governor could do in terms of censoring the contents or restricting the newspaper's reach.

Iwe Irohin's death knell was however sounded when it dabbled into the local political conflicts between the Egba and the Ibadan people, arising from a disputation over the control of the trading routes which linked the two territories with Lagos. This kind of civil conflicts was common in the Yorubaland at that period. The recurrent bloody tribal wars were actually one of the reasons adduced by the British for extending their colonial mandate to the Yoruba hinterland in order to curb the prevalent internecine bloody encounters among the Yoruba. The newspaper was accused by the Egba, who were hosting the newspaper, of taking side with their enemy in that conflict. As a result, the offices and printing press of the newspaper were sacked and vandalized and the publisher, Rev. Townsend fled *Egbaland*. Although the newspaper was said to have been revived after the crises, it never remained as it was originally. The closure of *Iwe Irohin* meant loss of livelihood to its publisher, workers and numerous others who benefited from the operations of the newspaper. This event signified the beginning of a trend in journalism in Nigeria which had extended into the contemporary times.

The press is an important ingredient in the democratic governance process, and, as such, has the responsibility of mediating between the rulers and the go-verned (Habermas, 1989)[2]. Essentially, it should be the watchdog against the excesses of the ruling class and must often be seen to be championing the good of all in an unbiased way. Also the press must learn the skill of balancing acts in political conflicts and in contestation for power and resources, in order not to lose the reputation of being an unbiased umpire in the political environment. This unfortunately is a lesson the Nigerian press failed to learn and which has remained an albatross to the development of the press up until the present time.

The colonial period in Nigeria marked another phase during which the press, though was very active in the political environment, witnessed a lot of stunted growth. Between 1880 and 1837, about 81 newspaper titles were estab-lished in Nigeria (Idowu, 2001). Most of these did not survive for long due mainly to hostile political and economic operating environment. However, the few who survived for a while made marks in the socio political terrain. Most prominent among these was the *Lagos Weekly Record* published by John Payne Jackson, who later handed the publication to his son, Thomas Horatio Jackson (Omu, 1965). The paper was very powerful since its inception in 1890 until 1930 when it ceased publishing[3]. It came into being before the amalgamation of the Northern and Southern Nigeria, which took place in 1914, and played prom-inent role in the early resistance against colonialism, including the British co-lonial policies in its various protectorates in West Africa. The then governor of Northern region, Lord Lugard, who effected the amalgamation of the Northern and Southern Nigeria, received a lot of bashes from the *Weekly Record* for his atrocious administrative style.

The activism of *Lagos Weekly Record* led to the promulgation of the first press gagging law in Nigeria - the Seditious Offences Ordinance of 1909. The editor of the *Weekly Record* was the first victim of the law and he was jailed as a result of his criticism of some of the colonial administration policies. When the paper remained adamant and refused to soften its hard stance on public matters, the colonial government ordered the stoppage of all its foreign advertisement subscriptions which put the publication into a precarious economic situation. Although it survived this siege, it never had it smooth again. It however became the nursery for breeding radical and fearless tribe of journalists in Nigeria.

In the twilight years of the *Lagos Weekly Record,* another vibrant newspa-per, the *Daily News,* owned and managed by the leading nationalist, Herbert Macaulay, emerged. *Daily News* became instantly famous for its vehement op-position to the various colonial constitutions and policies. *The Lagos Times* was another newspaper that was very significant among the militant and nationalistic press in Nigeria. Uche (1989, p. 93) recorded that the newspaper started the first pitched press war between the Nigerian nationalists fighting for independence and the British colonial administrators when it editorialized:

> We are not clamoring for immediate independence...but it should always be borne in mind that the present order of things will not last forever. A time will come when the colonies on the West Coast will be left to regulate their own internal and external affairs (cf. Coker, 1968, p. 32).

The arrival of Dr Nnamdi Azikiwe's *West African Pilot* boosted this agitation. Young Azikiwe, who was educated in America, brought in new savvy to the practice of journalism because of his exposure to the ideals of liberal democracy in the west. The publication met, almost instantly, serious opposition from the government, who put several hurdles in place for the paper. It was required to provide sureties to stand for the renewal of its registration, which most of the educated elites were not ready to do because of obvious risks. At a time, the paper was prevented from remitting required funds overseas for subscription to foreign wire services, which was an important content source for the paper. The doggedness and determination of Azikiwe was the only reason why the newspaper operated successfully in that era and motivated other papers to go along in spite of the hostilities in the operating environment.

The Nigerian Media and the Nation's Civil War

Perhaps, the greatest siege against the press in Nigeria was the emergence of regional and partisan press, which came about shortly before political independence. It is however important to note that regionalization or tribalism was not peculiar to the press. The broadcast media in Nigeria were also actively involved. It is also instructive to note that the mass media abstracted from the nature of the formation and the structure of the nation's political parties. The mass media were regionally or tribally based. The result, according to Uche (1989: xviii) was that the mass media of the regions became the megaphones of political interest articulation of each of the regions within the federation. This pattern of mass media structure and control constituted a breeding ground for political irresponsibility that inevitably culminated in ghastly national accidents (coups and a civil war). As already indicated, the tribally-based politics of the country did not leave the press untouched. This tribal orientation of the press contributed, in no small way, to the outbreak of the nation's civil war of 1967 to 1970. Each of the former regions of the country had its own press, and all the media joined their regional governments to engage in bitter political polemics (Uche, 1989, p. xxi). As an illustration, Uche recalled a story dispatched from Lagos by a foreign correspondent about the terrible crisis that characterized the 1964 general elections in the Western Region of Nigeria:

> In the populous Eastern Region, whose political powers are aligned with the opposition Action Group in the West, key city councils adopted ordinances banning papers that stayed neutral or actively backed the Western Government's return to power.

This group includes the Federal Government-owned *Morning Post*, the Western Government-owned *Daily Sketch* and the independent *Daily Express* and the *Daily Times*–Nigeria's most widely read paper. The net effect of the ordinances has been to block the entrance of these papers into the Eastern Region by either air or road.

In retaliation, city councils in the West have made it a crime not only to read pro-opposition *Pilot*, *Telegraph* and *Daily Tribune* but also to tune in the Eastern Region radio. If caught errant newspaper readers and radio listeners are subject to a year's imprisonment. The East has imposed no such penalties. But purple-uniformed political thugs have set up road blocks, searched cars for the "wrong" papers, and beaten the occupants who possessed them (cf. *New York Times*, Nov. 20, 1965).

Similarly, the following discussions that took place among a former Nigerian military head of state, Yakubu Gowon, the former Igbo (Biafran) leader, Chukwuemeka Ojukwu, and some other Nigerian military leaders at Aburi, Ghana, during a conference held to nip the then impending civil war in the bud illustrate the implications of the regionalization of the media and terrible performance of the press during those crisis periods (Uche, 1989, pp. 99 - 100):

> *Lt.-Col. Gowon*: On the Government Information Media I think all the Government Information Media in the country have done terribly bad (sic). Emeka would say the *New Nigerian* has been very unkind to the East.

> *Lt. Col. Ojukwu*: And the *Post* which I pay for.

> *Lt. Col. Gowon*: Sometimes I feel my problem is not with anyone but the *Outlook*.

> *Lt. Col. Ojukwu*: All the other information media have done a lot. When the Information Media in a country completely closed their eyes to what was happening, I think it is a dangerous thing.

> *Major Johnson*: Let us agree it is the situation.

> *Lt. Col. Ejoor*: All of them have committed one crime or the other.

Lt. Col. Hassan: The *Outlook* is the worst of them.

Lt. Col. Ojukwu: The *Outlook* is not the worst, the *Post* which we all in fact pay for is the worst followed closely by the *New Nigerian*.
Mr. T. Omo-Bare: Let us make a general statement on all of them, no distinction.

Lt. Col. Gowon: I think we agreed that all Government Information Media should desist from making inflammatory publications that would worsen the situation in the
country (cf.John de St. Jore, 1972, p. 345).

Parochialism and Partisanship in the Nigerian Press

The establishment of *Nigerian Tribune* also invigorated the tribal press war (Omu, 1996). The paper was established by Chief Obafemi Awolowo, a leading political figure and leader of the Action Group party, which had its stronghold in the South West of Nigeria. The paper was actually established to champion the sectional interests of the Yoruba ethnic group in the political terrain and it never hides its mission. This caused immense devastation to the nationalist posture of press struggle and brought ethnic coloration to the political struggle[4]. This trend became a cankerworm which has defied solution in the Nigerian political terrain till date. Other regions of the country where various political parties held sway followed on the example of the Action Group party of the western region by starting their various regional newspapers. At the commencement of self rule in the country, electronic media came into the scene and again, the western regional government blazed the trail by establishing the first television station. A radio station had earlier been established by the federal government under the National Broadcasting Service, though. By independence, Dr Nnamdi Azikiwe's *West African Pilot* had been turned into a megaphone of his National Council of Nigeria Citizens (NCNC) political party, another regional party with a strong hold in the East.

The first real attempt by government to venture into owning and running a newspaper was the establishment of *Gaskiya Tafi Kwabo* by the government of the Northern region. This paper was established in 1937 mainly to counter the influence of the Southern newspapers among citizens of Northern Nigeria. Government ownership eventually bloomed after independence as a result of divisions in the political ranks in the various regions which led to the establishment of *Sketch* in the West, *Daily Star* in the East and *New Nigeria* in the North. A former editor of the New Nigerian was reported to have said that the Nothern government found it necessary to establish the newspaper to (i) get across the views of the Nothern elite and mobilize them in order to achieve its goals; (ii) fight the Nothern case in all disputes at the centre (Daura, 1971, pp. 39-40).

The attainment of the nation's independence in 1960 did not change the character of the press. Even the Federal Government-owned press, the *Morning Post* was not immune to the pursuit of tribal and sectional interest in preference to the goal of national unity, identity and integration. It was this parochialism that led to the death of the Post (in early 1973). Uche (1989, p. 99) recalled that the *Post* 'died' because it took its audience for a ride. It failed to recognize that it had a nationally-based audience..." The only newspaper which was neutral and most prosperous after independence was the privately owned *Daily Times*. There was a semblance of professionalism in the *Daily Times* for its neutrality, which enabled journalists within the organization to build careers. However, the acquisition of *Daily Times* years later by the federal military government led to the gradual decline of the organization. Uche (1989, p. 101) remarked that the *Times*, over the years, had grown to be the largest circulating newspaper in Nigeria due to its neutrality and non-allegiance to any political party until during the Second Republic when the Shagari administration converted it into a party propaganda organ. Presently, even when the organization has been privatized, it is still grappling to survive.

It is remarkable to note that the only visible trampling on the press freedom in the post-independence first republic was the restrictions imposed on certain newspapers with political bias from circulating in certain regions by the regional governments. Notable among this was the limitation imposed on *Nigerian Tribune* from circulating in certain parts of the Northern region and similar retaliatory policies by other regional governments against newspapers perceived as being in the opposition. The greatest siege against the press came during the long military dictatorships in Nigeria which spanned about 28 years. From the first to the last of the various military regimes, the press witnessed arrests, incarcerations, jailing and killing of journalists, promulgation of obnoxious press decrees, banning and unbanning of news media organizations, forced and voluntary exile of journalists[5]. In all of these incidences promising careers were stunted in the press, people became jobless and promising brains were lost to other professions. Compared to other sectors of the Nigerian economy, the media sector attracted the least investment during this period for reasons of insecurity of investments.

Significantly, the press got itself heavily involved in the politics of the Nigeria's Second Republic. It was both a tool and an important casualty of the political conflict of the period. The *National Concord*, founded on March 1, 1980, by a Nigerian multi-millionaire and chairman of the powerful American ITT for the Middle-East and African zone, had an influential impact on the nation's politics of the time. Uche (1989, p. 103) noted that the National Concord came to existence in order to protect the political interests of the then ruling National Party of Nigeria (NPN) as well as to disseminate the ideals of the party, NPN, in a most convincing manner. Its founding followed the controversy, antagonism and bitterness the 1979 general elections had generated. The emergence of the *National Concord* added greater confusion to Nigeria's political intrigues.

In furtherance of his political ambition within the ruling NPN, the Concord's publisher, late Chief M.K.O. Abiola, launched a virulent attack with his newspaper reports and editorials on the leader of the opposition party, the Unity Party of Nigeria (UPN), late Chief Obafemi Awolowo who happened to hail from the same region with him. Among other things, the newspaper exposed Awolowo's acquisition of 360 plots of land from some peasants in the reservation areas of Maroko village of Lagos at a paltry price of $1.5 million. For this stance of the newspaper, its patronage in the Southwestern part of Nigeria, the region both the publisher and Chief Awolowo belonged to, was very low. This was because of the larger-than-life image of Awolowo in the region. This response to the newspaper in the region meant a financial loss to the newspaper as the region is home the highest percentage of the literate population in the country. Yet, the newspaper was undaunted as its wealthy publisher continued to fund it and, thus, continued the pursuit of its political ambition.

The story however changed when the newspaper did not succeed in realizing his ambition of being the NPN's presidential candidate in 1983. In reaction, he quit NPN and formal politicking, but the newspaper continued to dabble into political frays. One important feature of the newspaper after the quitting of the NPN by its publisher was to make u-turn in its political stance. It started supporting the presidential candidature of the erstwhile enemy of his publisher, Chief Awolowo while also attacking the incumbent president of Nigeria, and the renominated presidential candidate of NPN, Alhaji Shehu Shagari. Uche (1989, p. 106) noted:

> The credibility of the *National Concord* as an authoritative, respectable and non-tribal newspaper began to erode when it made a surprising U-turn to support the presidential candidature of Awolowo whom it had set out to discredit and destroy politically...

At the time of this political switch-over of the *National Concord*, some political thugs were suspected to have set ablaze the newspaper's house that housed its newsprints. The genera belief was that some politicians who were being frustrated by *Concord*'s editorials and news coverage, decided to burn down the entire newsprints so that the newspaper would have nothing to print on as the NPN central government would not grant it import licence to enable it place orders a for newsprints (Uche, 1989, p. 108).

The newspaper was also faced with another challenge when it dabbled into religious controversy occasioned by the then proposed Nigeria's membership of the Organization of Islamic Conference (OIC). For the fact that its publisher was a Muslim, the newspaper stoutly campaigned for the nation's membership of the organization; and in the process shutting out the Christian opposition views expressed in both editorial and advertorial forms.   The Christian community reacted to this stance of the newspaper by stopping to read and patronize it.

A number of other newspapers established for political reasons in the Nigeria's second republic (1979-1983) entered the political frays and became a casualty, especially after the termination of the republic in 1983 through a military putsch. Such newspapers included Advocate, founded by the national chairman of the National Party of Nigeria, Chief Adisa Akinloye; People's Voice, founded by Niyi Oniororo; and Broom, founded by Godwin Daboh.

The Court's Bard and the Crusading Press

Some other newspapers suffered the problem of credibility, and thus were shunned by the public because of their publishers' involvement with unpopular governments, and the newspapers' stance on political issues. Such included *Third Eye*, whose publisher was known to be a contractor of the Ibrahim Babangida military government (that annulled the June 12, 1993 presidential election, widely adjudged to be free and fair), and *Monitor*, founded by another contractor, this time of the General Sani Abacha government, and a military apologist.

Yet, there were other newspapers that just emerged to join a political fray for crusading purpose. That was actually the case with many publications that emerged between 1993 and 1994 in pursuit of the struggle for the actualization of the presidential mandate of Chief M.K.O Abiola, the man widely believed to have won the annulled June 12, 1993 presidential election. Abiola's *Concord* group of newspapers was finally suffocated out of circulation by the Sani Abacha military junta during the struggle for June 12.   Some other media houses suffered the punishment of closure for different lengths of time during the June 12 crisis as they were regarded by the junta as the opposition media. Such included *Punch, The Guardian, Sketch, Tribune*, and Ogun State Broadcasting Corporation (now known as Gateway Radio and Television).

Individual journalists also suffered various fates in the hands of the junta. Some were killed, some jailed, some detained, some hounded into exiles, while some even had their pregnant wives detained in place of unreachable husbands.

The press is much freer in the current democratic political dispensation. However, investment in the media is still very low compared with other sectors and this has been adduced to the concentration of the media contents only on political issues. However, there tends to be a constant struggle between the press and politicians in which the press appears to be the ultimate loser. Politicians often court members of the media whenever they are struggling to gain power or get into political offices. During this time, they describe the press as partners in progress. However, as soon as they get into office, they begin to cast suspicious look at the press and there are often temptations to trample on press freedom.

While the media would insist on performing the role of watch dog against the excesses of the ruling class, politicians often view the press as a distraction, which has to be tackled in order to progress. It then becomes a cat and dog fight. Because of this close interlink with politics and constant intervention in political conflicts, the media sector, has attracted the least investment and syndicated funds among all sectors of the economy since the commencement of the present dispensation in 1999. Judging by investment into the communication, banking and oil sectors for instance, investment into the media had been poor. No newspaper or broadcasting organization is currently listed on the Nigerian stock exchange; they only report the activities there. That accounts for the reasons why the media is witnessing perhaps the highest turnover of staff, constantly loosing its personnel to other sectors of the economy as public relations and information officers.

This trend has also posed big ethical challenges to journalists who continue to operate in the same environment with other professionals who earn better income and enjoy better career prospects. There are constant temptations to compromise and sell their conscience for material gains. Without trying to excuse the journalist for flouting professional ethics especially as regards the issues of reward and financial matters, the economic challenges of practicing as a journalist in Nigeria is so overwhelming that it is only the strong willed individuals who are determined to make a semblance of career in the media that remains in the same media organization for upward of 5 years. Others are lost into politics and other economic endeavors. This hampers the quality of media output and instigates low patronage from the public. The total circulation figure of about 50 national and regional dailies circulating in Nigeria is less than 200,000 copies – in a population of over 120 million with about 65% literacy rate!

Conclusion

One way the press can establish professionalism and ascertain its future in Nigeria is to develop a sound business model. This requires that it frees itself from political entanglements and serve as a purely unbiased umpire of political events. By identifying the salient interests of the audience and catering to those interests outside of politics, the press would occupy an enviable place in the polity. In order to succeed, a newspaper needs to be guided by a clear vision and focused editorial policy. In addition, such press establishment must be committed to management methods that are clearly and entirely professional and adopt the best practices in enduring democracies across the world.

A trace of these elements is already emerging among the newspapers that have maintained neutrality in the political arena. They are the ones being patronized the most by advertisers and whose circulation has been consistent. They are the ones that attract and sustain good quality professionals over a fairly longer period and whose objectivity has been unquestionable in the present democratic dispensation. They could serve as the model for a future press for Nigeria.

Notes

1.   See the account of the establishment of the newspaper in Nigeria, its purpose and operations in Duyile (1987) and Omu (1965).

2.   Habermas (1989) explained the role of the press as a public sphere, but also argued that such role is being eroded by the culture of consumerism.

3.   Omu (1965) provides a more detailed account of the activities of The Jacksons in the journalism scene during the colonial era, the difficulties they faced and the impacts they made in opposing the policies of the colonial administration in Nigeria.
4.   Omu (1996) provides an incisive explanation of the ethnic and political rivalry which brought about division in the rank of newspaper owners and prevented the press from adequately preparing the people for the challenges of independence during this period.
5.   The accounts of the repression of the press during the military regimes in Nigeria is provided in more detail by Lanre Idowu's article, 'Path to Sustainable Greatness', in 2001 edition of *Media World Yearbook.*

Reference

Arno, A. and Dissanayake, W. (1984). *The news media in national and international conflict.* London: A Westview Special Study.
Coker, I. (1968). *Landmarks of the Nigerian Press.* Lagos.
Daura, M. (1971). Editing a government newspaper in Nigeria In O.
      Stokke, (ed.). *Reporting Africa.* New York: African Publishing Corporation.
Duyile, D. (1987). *Makers of Nigerian Press.* Lagos: Gong Communication Ltd.
Habermas, J. (1989). *The structural transformation of the public sphere.* Cambridge: Polity.
Idowu, L. (2001). Path to sustainable greatness. In *Media world yearbook, 2001.* Lagos: Diamond Publication Ltd.
John de St. Jorre. (1972). *The Nigerian civil war.* London: Hodder and Stoughton Ltd.
Mogekwu, M. (2005). Media and peacebuilding in Africa: The Imperative of a reorientation'. In *Journal of African and Social Sciences and Humanities Studies,* vol.1, no.1, pp. 79-98.
Nnaemeka, T. I. (1976). Issue legitimation, mass media functions and public knowledge of issues. Ph.D. dissertation, University of Minnesota.
Olorunyomi, D. (2000). Conceptual issues in media and conflict. In *Covering*

diversity: A resource and training manual for African journalists. Washington: The Panos Institute; New York: Centre for War, Peace and the News Media; Lagos: Independent Journalism Centre.

Omu, F. (1965). *Nigerian newspaper press, 1859 – 1937: A study in origin, growth and influence.* Ph.D. dissertation, University of Ibadan, Ibadan, Nigeria.

Omu, F. (1996). Journalism in Nigeria: A historical overview. In O. Dare and A. Uyo, (eds.). *Journalism in Nigeria: Issues and perspectives.* Lagos: NUJ, Lagos Council.

Tehranian, M. (1996). Communication and conflict. In *Media Development*, 4. Vol. XLIII.

Tichenor, P. J., G. A. Donohue and C. N. Olien (1980). *Community Conflict and the Press.* London: SAGE Publications.

Uche, L. (1989). *Mass media, People and Politics in Nigeria.* New Delhi: Concept Publishing Company.

Chapter 14

The Mass Media and the Establishment of Peace as Path to Sustainable Development in Africa

Matt Mogekwu, Ph.D.
Bowie State University, USA

Introduction

Since the 1960s, attention has been focused, in terms of research and debate, on the issue of development and how to deal with it. This ostensibly followed the 1961 United Nations General Assembly resolution that the 1960s would be termed the *Development Decade*–a period in which the world community would devote itself to the problem of generating, in less developed countries that constituted two-thirds of the world population, a process of accelerated economic growth that could, in time, tilt the world's less affluent out of grinding poverty and provide the wherewithal for a marked improvement in the quality of life of the world's people (Millikan, 1973). Furthermore, in 1970, during the 25th anniversary of the founding of the UN, the General Assembly voted unanimously to proclaim the second *International Development Decade*, using the International Development Strategy as guideline. This strategy document was a large - scale perspective and action plan that was to lead to drastically improved standard of living of the world's poor, living outside of the modern economy (Mogekwu, 1995).

Thus, the issue of development has been on the international agenda at the highest level for quite some time and a lot of work has gone into establishing theories about it. At first, there was the competitive market theory that derived from the framework of conventional economics in which human labor and other inputs would be used to produce goods and services that would be valued by consumers and, thereby, generate growth. By the late 1970s, another perspective of development had emerged which was referred to as the Basic Human Needs (BHN) approach (Leipziger 1981). From this perspective, poverty–a very important element of underdevelopment–was seen as the inability to meet certain basic human needs on the part of identifiable groups of human beings. It was characterized by hunger and malnutrition, ill health and lack of education, safe drinking water sanitation and decent shelter. Therefore, a vital aspect of the elimination of poverty would consist of securing access to these goods and services by the poor so that people have the opportunity to lead lives free from hunger, disease and deprivation.

Earlier, Lerner (1958) in The Passing of Traditional Society had essentially equated development with modernity in which a Traditional–Modern continuum existed along which a country would be said to move as it developed. There was the need to discard most of traditional ways and values and embrace modernity if a nation was to be seen as developed. Many communication researchers/theorists bought this perspective. They argued that communication was an independent variable in the development process which, itself, must be situated around modernization. As Shore (1980) noted, the "needs achievement' of McLelland (1961), the externally induced diffusion of innovation of Everette Rogers (1977) or the other "modern" attributes suggested by Schramm (1964), Pye (1963), and Inkeles and Smith (1974), all tended to define, operationalize and measure the objectives of development with the largely individual psychological characteristics that were assumed in the modernization theory of the times. But even then, many scholars sounded a note of warning regarding the promotion of communication as almost a necessary and sufficient condition for development. For instance, Felstchausen (1968) noted:

> The tendency to equate communications problems with problems in disseminating (technical) information has led many... to virtually ignore social and institutional structures in promoting development. This is even the case in areas where field workers and educators realize that information alone cannot change social conditions. Such caution was meant to direct attention to the need to set the importance of communication within a larger context.

Felstchausen's advice that we situate the importance of communication "within a larger context" is the driving force of this chapter.

As we moved into the 1980s, scientists, politicians, researchers and all other scholars seemed to realize that the way "development" as a concept was being studied and defined would give the impression that it was an end-point, when, in fact, it is a process–that is supposed to be ongoing- and as such, needs to be kept going. Therefore, the qualifier, "sustainable", became imperative. Hence the emphasis now on "sustainable development" in which *sustainability* becomes a key concept.

This paper looks at sustainable development in Africa and argues that for it to be achieved, the precondition of peace has to be established as a clear path to that goal and that the mass media play, or ought to play, a vital role in the establishment of such condition. It examines issues such as conflicts, population problems, diseases, and poor governance as important variables in the consideration of peace in the continent and argues that the mass media have crucial roles to play in identifying and diffusing elements in them that would directly or indirectly inhibit the establishment of peace.

The thrust of this discourse is to underline both the relationship between mass media and peace and the strong link between peace and development and thus underscore the multi-functional role of the mass media in the development process, and thus situate the importance of communication within a larger context.

Sustainable Development

Development is a multi-faceted concept which tends to mean different things to different people. The International Broadcast Institute in Cologne in 1973 defined development as the improvement of the well-being of the individual and the betterment of the quality of his or her life (Moemeka 1996). Everette Rogers, in the process of developing theories regarding development and communication, had defined development as a widely participatory process of social change and material adjustment for the majority of the people through their gaining greater control over their environment (Rogers 1975). This implies greater equality, freedom to make choices and pursue individual and collective goals and the availability of the wherewithal to carry out such pursuits.

The Basic Needs approach to development that was noted earlier, hinges on the supply and demand of basic needs and the appropriate institutional arrangements for access and delivery.

As early as the 1960s, Inayatulla (1967) focussed on the many aspects of development when he defined it as change towards patterns of society that allow better realization of human values, that allow a society greater power over its environment and over its own political destiny, and that enables its individuals to gain increased control over themselves.

Moemeka (1996) has noted that although development as a concept means different things to different people, the various viewpoints are not necessarily mutually exclusive. Indeed, for him, they are interwoven, and together stress the fact development is a normative concept in that existing conditions are no longer conducive to human dignity and socio-economic advancement. He concludes:

> Therefore, development, though seen from different angles, means one basic thing to all people, a change for the better in both human, cultural, socioeconomic and political conditions of the individual and, consequently of the society....More importantly, it is a matter of increased knowledge and skills, growth of a new consciousness, expansion of the human mind, the uplifting of the human spirit and the fusion of human confidence.

Development can only be meaningful and appreciated if all concerned have a hand in it. Therefore, there has always been an emphasis on everyone participating. Hence, participatory development.

But beyond this, an important element of development is that it should be sustained. Achieving a level of self/social improvement and sliding back, for whatever reason, to the status quo ante is an exercise in futility as much as it is a dangerous source of frustration. Therefore, in the last decade, emphasis has been placed on the sustainability of whatever is achieved in the process of attaining a higher quality of life.

The notion of sustainable development was popularized by the Brundtland Commission (1987) report which stressed the need for development that "meets the needs of the present without compromising the ability of future generations to meet their own needs." According to the report:

> Sustainable development is a process of change in which exploitation of resources, the direction of investments, the reorientation of technology development, and institutional change are all in harmony and enhance both current and future potential to meet human needs and aspirations. (WCED, 1987 p.290)

Just as the concept of development attracted various definitions, sustainable development has also been defined or explained from various perspectives. Karshenas (1994) defined it in terms of the pattern of structural change in natural and man-made capital stock (including human capital and technological capabilities), which ensures the feasibility of, at least, a minimum socially desired rate of growth in the long run.

In the late 1990s, the Tory (UK) government produced several definitions of sustainable development as part of the UK's strategy for development. In 1994 its Department of Environment noted that sustainable development" does not mean having less economic development: on the contrary, a healthy economy is better able to generate resources to meet people's needs, and new investment and environmental improvement often go hand in hand. Nor does it mean that every aspect of the present environment should be preserved at all costs. What it requires is that decisions throughout society are taken with proper regard to their environmental impact" (Doe, 1994, p. 7). Three years later, the Department's Planning Policy Guideline defined sustainable development as seeking "to deliver the objective of achieving, now and in the future, economic development to secure higher living standards while protecting and enhancing the environment" (Doe, 1997, p.3). The Labor Administration that took over in 1997 focused mainly on three components of sustainable development: (1) the environment, (2) economic growth, and (3) social progress (Sewel, 1997, p. 4).

Steps were, therefore, taken to integrate these issues "which are inextricably linked in the quest for sustainable development."

Later, the government came up with its own definition although still in line with that of its predecessor:

Sustainable development is a very simple idea. It is about ensuring a better quality of life for everyone, now and for generations to come. To achieve this, (it) is concerned with achieving economic growth, in the form of higher living standards, while protecting, and where possible, enhancing the environment ...and making sure that these economic and environmental benefits are available to everyone, not just to a privileged few (DETR, 1998, p. 4).

It is, thus, a generally accepted posture to relate sustainability to the environment in ecological terms–recognizing the finite nature of environmental resources. The concept is that in order for (biological) resources to exist, they must reproduce. That reproduction rate is the key to sustainable development. The resource collection rate cannot exceed resource reproduction else failure occurs (Schaefle, 2002).

If we again go back to the (1997) UK government emphasis, sustainable development relates equally to the three domains of economy, environment and society. These, incidentally, were the areas that were focused on during the last World Summit on Sustainable Development (WSSD) held in Johannesburg, South Africa in August/September 2002.

It is argued that future generations should have the same right to a healthy environment as us. But sustainable development means more than conservation. A healthy economy is just as essential in satisfying our material and non- material needs as preserving the natural foundations of life. And only a society that displays a degree of solidarity is able to distribute its goods and opportunities fairly, preserve that society's values and efficiently and effectively organize the use of natural resources.

But the question that arises from all of these is whether sustainable development can occur in a vacuum. Whether we are talking about the economy, or the environment or the society, there is a necessary condition for success to be achieved. This has to do more with the society than with anything else. This necessary condition is *peace*.

Incidentally, this condition is assumed or taken for granted and such oversight could be very problematic. A social environment that is devoid of peace cannot sustain any development and yet debates and discussions of sustainable development take it as *given.*

In Africa, the absence of peace in most areas would thwart any efforts at sustainable development. Conflicts retard economic growth, destroy the environment in a physical sense–and therefore, the resources therein, and destabilize social formations and cohesion.

It then becomes imperative for us to seek to identify the place of such vital element and see how mass media can be used to establish and promote it to provide an enabling and conducive environment for all the three arms of sustainable development to work in concert.

Peace in Africa

Peace is a word that is uttered "as a matter of course", like "love" and "truth" and similar concepts. Its usage is so commonplace that little effort has been put into coming out with its conceptual definition. Morales (2002) notes that one of the surprising aspects related to peace studies is that despite the recurrent reference to the term "peace" in journals, magazines, and textbooks is that few initiatives are devoted to the definition of the concept itself, and as such, peace has been factually and conceptually linked to war. Most variants of perceptions of peace must include the absence of war. But Albert Einstein once noted that peace is not merely the absence of war but the presence of justice, of law, of order – in short of government. Linking peace to war seems to be a negative approach to defining and understanding the concept. Attempts are now being made to look at peace from different perspectives. The work of Leo Sandy and Ray Perkins, Jr., (1992) on the nature of peace and its implications for peace education, has looked at peace from different dimensions and suggested that one way of clearing the confusion over terms is to define types of peace and war. According to them there can be hot war, cold war, hot peace and cold peace. However, of interest to this discourse is the notion of hot peace and cold peace.

They explain that in cold peace, there is almost a neutral view of a previous enemy. There is little mutual hostility but there is also a lack of mutually beneficial interactions aimed at developing trust, interdependence and collaboration. By contrast, hot peace is explained as involving active collaborative efforts designed to build bridges between and among past and present adversaries. This involves searching for common ground and the development of new non-human enemies which could include human rights abuses, air and water pollution, dwindling energy resources, the destruction of the ozone layer, famine, poverty and ignorance. They argue that the object of hot peace is the proliferation of cooperative relations and mutually beneficial outcomes. Hot peace thinking is supposed to imagine peace and the abolition of war.

We are urged to think of peace by accentuating the positive like Trostle did in the early nineties. Placed within a positive context, he defined peace as a state of well-being that is characterized by trust, compassion and justice. In this state, "we can be encouraged to explore as well as celebrate our diversity, and search for the good in each other without the concern for personal pain and sacrifice ... It provides us a chance to look at ourselves and others as part of the human family, part of one world" (Sandy and Perkins, 1992).

Therefore, peace, here, is not limited to the absence of war and/conflict. Rather, it is seen to be linked to all actions and events that would help eliminate or ameliorate tension, anxiety, societal confusion and lack of focus, various forms of deprivation and inhibition, lack of self-confidence, absence of inspiration and similar circumstances that would generate any form of dissonance among a people. It is a condition that should pervade an environment in such a way that people are able to concentrate on the here, now and the future, are disposed to recognize and appreciate what exists in the environment and how they can be utilized for self development. If such a condition does not exist, all talks about development or the sustainability of same would be a farce.

Peace can be seen as the antithesis of exploitation, marginalization and oppression. It should be found in the protection and support of the rights of all.

The problem of the absence of peace is not peculiar to any region of the world, or continent or group. Over the years, peace had eluded people in Northern Ireland as those in Sri Lanka. India and Pakistan are not at peace with each other over territories just like Ethiopia and Eritrea. The turmoil in the Balkans is still fresh in our memory. The Middle East today is literally on fire. The Great Lakes region of Africa has not been at ease for a long while. Rwanda, Burundi and the Democratic Republic of the Congo are still seething. Iraq has been invaded by the US and the "coalition of the willing" and death on the streets is an everyday occurrence. The Basque separatists are alive and well in Spain as the fundamentalist Islamic party is in Algeria.

Everywhere we look; peace has been threatened or continues to be threatened. It has remained elusive for many people for a while. However, some parts of the world have a greater share of this situation than others.

One of the distinguishing characteristics of the African continent is the prevalence of conflict and turmoil at local, national and intra/international levels. This has been the picture since the advent of political independence in the 1960s. We have suffered through periods of coups, famine, hunger, violence, poor/bad governance, disease, deprivation, squalor, lack of education and health facilities and other basic infra-structural needs. All of these have led to stagnation in our development process, a situation under which we cannot speak of sustainability.

From this range of "negatives" we can distil a few variables that can be discussed in terms of how they help to eliminate or endanger peace and used as a backdrop against which the role of mass media can be better understood in the sustainability of development. These would include conflicts, politics and poor governance, population problems, and poor health.

Conflicts

Conflict is the peace problematique (Mogekwu, 2000). To deal with conflict we must understand its nature and character and in so doing, we concern our-selves with the causes of conflict, its dynamics and its effect on communities, societies and nations. Although it has been argued that the resolution of conflict is "only a minimalist condition" for the achievement of peace (Hansen, 1987), it is still a significant effort in that direction.

There have been many attempts to define conflict and conflict situations. Coser (1956) defines conflict as a struggle over values and claims to scarce sta-tus, power and resources in which the aims of the opponents are to neutralize, injure and eliminate their rivals. In 1973, Kriesberg defined social conflict as a relationship between two or more parties who believe they have incompatible goals. As Anstey (1991) notes, this definition centers on two issues: relation-ships and the fact that conflict is rooted in people's beliefs about goals as op-posed to objective facts. Anstey then offers a two-part definition of conflict that essentially differentiates between *latent* and *manifest* conflict:

> Conflict exists in a relationship when parties believe that their aspirations can-not be achieved simultaneously, or perceive a divergence in their values, needs and interests (latent conflict) and purposely employ their power in an effort to defeat, neutralize, or eliminate each other to protect or further their interests in the interaction (manifest conflict).

Anstey's definition is useful because it explains most of the conflict situa-tions that have plagued Africa. They derived from issues such as ethnicity, reli-gious intolerance, race, class/economic conflict, ideology, generation gap, and territorial claims and disputes. Each of these, alone or in concert with others, has been responsible for the various conflict experiences in the continent.

The truth is that conflict tends to perpetuate an environment that is devoid of stability and security and, therefore not enabling for sustained development. Conflict, with its attendant violence and chaos would not allow for a gradual advance or growth through progressive changes. It does not inspire investment of material or human effort for productivity and development.

Adebayo Adedeji (1992) lamented that instability, both political and socio-economic, had become a chronic feature of Africa's problematic political econ-omy. According to him:

The persistent instability constitutes a disabling environment for
...transformation, and for the basic continuity of policies and programs needed
to achieve other pertinent development goals.

Conflict deprives a nation or people of the stability that provides the relative constancy of an environment within which a slow dynamic ought to evolve through a normal and harmonious interplay of social, economic, political and cultural factors without major disturbance (Fall, 1992). Stability forms part of (political) evolution as opposed to revolution. It places special emphasis on the principle that social progress, development and peace in general, if they are to be viable and durable, must take place within a certain continuum and harmony. Fall adds that stability provides an air and feeling of durability and firmness of purpose. It confers a degree of constancy that can provide a foundation for the building of trust, because one perceives in a stable environment a firmness in purpose and character. Conflict, which breeds instability, negates all that.

Akin to stability is security which is a state of being without care or anxiety that guarantees safety and freedom from danger and helps build confidence. As Fall (1992), again, points out, security and stability have a logical relationship with each other and with development to the extent that combined, they form a basic condition for, and advancement, development. Social and political turmoil and upheavals jeopardize stability, pose a threat to security, disturb the circumstances for economic production and force the channeling of social energies and economic into directions other than development.

It would not be necessary to go into seeking explanations for the instability and insecurity that have derived from the conflicts in Africa in this discourse. It would suffice to note, however, that they do not augur well for peace.

Although the other variables of poor governance, population problems and poor health problems are not in themselves conflict situations, they are still akin to conflict to the extent that they have the potential to precipitate tensions and anxieties that can ultimately lead to conflict.

Politics and Poor Governance

African leaders have for long ignored the basic principles of good governance which are accountability and transparency. Politics has been a game of who can best exploit ethnic, religious, racial or tribal divisions and loyalties for the achievement of electoral goals and leadership positions. The winner-take-all syndrome and the president-for-life propensity have become glaring features of the politics in the continent. Headship of a state was seen as a divine right and as such the office holder does not often see the need to explain his actions or inactions to the "electorate" nor does he think he owes anyone any apologies for any manifest ineptitude.

For many of Africa's leaders, precipitating a crisis is usually a handy technique for diverting attention from the main ills of government. They sustain themselves in power through all kinds of devices, often resorting to intimidation and ruthlessness as a defense mechanism to cover up their inadequacies. Often, a small clique would wield enormous power over the rest of society, leaving the latter with a feeling of frustration and despondency. It, thus, becomes difficult to avoid the kind of corruption that has become the norm in many states.

Even where democracy is said to be practiced, it often is a mockery of the concept. Participatory democracy is yet to be entrenched except to the extent that people are goaded to cast votes for predetermined "winners".

There are heads of states who want to perpetuate themselves in office by resorting to the engineering of the constitution. Examples of this scenario abound in the continent.

When poor governance becomes unbearable, the masses react and the consequences could be catastrophic – going back again to the issue of conflict.

Population Problems

The pattern of development in many (African) countries has been such that urbanization, with its consequent rural–urban migration has precipitated population problems that are becoming a menace to the society. Without necessarily going into the theories and concepts of demographic changes, it has become obvious that many of the countries in the continent have not been able to contain this menace. The result is that urban areas are teeming with youths, in particular, who come in search of the good life. Not finding it, they resort to all kinds of unwholesome behaviors that contribute to insecurity.

In addition to the migration issues, population problems also include fertility and mortality rates and how these affect the political economy of states. Many African countries have high fertility rates as well as high mortality rate- whether it is infant, maternal or general, that they have not been able to deal with effectively. Whereas high fertility rates impact on the effective distribution of available resources, high mortality rates tend to diminish human resources that are required for development purposes. A country's Gross Domestic Product and per capita income are often affected by the way population problems are handled. Poverty is usually a by-product of any mismanagement. Besides, the environment itself suffers if uncontrolled population growth is unleashed on finite environmental and other natural resources, leading to an inability to sustain whatever development is planned or envisaged.

Poor Health

This is linked directly or indirectly to the issues mentioned above. Ill health would occur when an individual is not able to provide for himself the basic and necessary nutritional requirements for the sustenance of life. Lack of food can derive from poverty which, in turn, could be a fallout of population problems or the consequence of conflict that established an atmosphere of insecurity and instability that could deprive one of the freedom to fend for oneself. The rural-urban migration has led to very serious squalid conditions in cities in the form of townships and shanty towns that are essentially breeding grounds for various illnesses and poor hygiene.

Diseases and other forms of health deprivations are serious hindrances to growth and development. The scourge of HIV/AIDS in the continent is now public knowledge and a great cause for concern. High mortality rate in the continent is not unconnected to poor health conditions.

Either because of poor management or poor financial profiles, many African countries have become vulnerable to various epidemics such as cholera, malaria, river blindness, meningitis and other opportunistic diseases related to HIV. These have negatively impacted on the various economies.

Poor health is a threat to peace because it ends up eliminating the state of well-being of individuals.

All the variables discussed so far are not exhaustive, by any standards, regarding what elements contribute to conflict or absence of peace. Many more could be identified depending on how far one wants to go. This is not necessary here. The important point is to attempt to establish how they are linked and therefore, how they can be dealt with.

One common denominator in these variables discussed so far is the human being who is at the receiving end of conflict, poor health, and poor governance and is the focal point of population problems. Therefore, human beings should be the target of strategies to deal with the situation.

No single strategy can offer a panacea for the problems identified. All designs can only contribute to an overarching strategy, each filling a particular niche. But the fundamental issue that cannot be ignored is the need for peace to prevail in any environment before any strategies can be applied. This is where the mass media, more than many other sectors, can play a very significant role.

Mass Media and the Establishment of Peace

The mass media have the greatest potential to deal with the human mind to bring about change in attitude and behavior, create awareness and push people to action along a particular course, for a given cause.

When we examine the issue of conflict, we would see that just as the media are capable of aiding and abetting the exacerbation of conflict, they can be equally effective in contributing to the containment of such conflict. The role of the mass media in the conflict situation in Rwanda is now a classical scenario of how the media can help exacerbate conflict situations. The use, by the Hutus, of the Radio Milles Collines to whip up hatred against the Tutsis and the role of the extremist Hutu newspaper *Kangura* in inflaming passions that led to the eventual massacre of over half a million people in Rwanda (Mogekwu, 2000) is a case in point. The same situations could be found in other parts of the continent such as Nigeria where ethnic sentiments are whipped up by politicized media to establish conflict situations that are then exploited by unscrupulous politicians. In fact, Nichols and McChesney (2005) have expressed concern at how the American media deliberately create enabling environments for conflict by selling wars, spinning elections and destroying democracy.

In fact, some conflicts are "made-for-media" as attention seeking strategies. We have seen examples in Somalia in the abduction of Red Cross workers who were detained with the threat of death that turned out to be a publicity stunt. Similarly, when an extremist organization carries out a bomb attack on a target and calls the media to claim responsibility, it is a media-centered attention seeking stunt.

The media can equally contribute to peace in a structured way by helping out in the area of political socialization, health campaigns and cultural reorientation.

The mass media have played a role in bringing about change in society and have been credited with accelerating the rate of development in various parts of the world. Conflict that derives from poor governance or political irresponsibility can be related to the level of political socialization and participation. The extent to which a people are politically socialized would have a bearing on their political awareness and appreciation of political circumstances. Not every member of a society understands its political system or how it is supposed to work. Such a knowledge gap creates its own problems. Usually, only a handful of the political elite know the details of their country's political system. They, in turn, use the relatively ignorant majority for their own goals, exploiting other circumstances that may not even be directly related to politics–such as ethnicity, religion and the like. Some would argue that the fundamental issue in such political exploitation is economic, that because of the prevalence of poverty in most African societies, the political elite can resort to the use of money as bait. This could be true but only to the extent that the bait is only for their votes but not their minds. Politically speaking, these minds are still virgin lands for positive political education. And that is where the media come in.

The media's role here is two-fold: to diffuse the impact of those elements of division that are exploited by politicians to cause conflict, and to help increase political awareness of civil society especially at the grassroots level.

First, the media should be willing and ready to disseminate sufficient information about the various diverse groups in the society, emphasizing areas of similarity among groups and playing down the kinds of differences that promote conflict. This responsibility can be managed not only through the selection of news and news events, but also in specially designed programs such as soap operas and special documentaries rather than promoting programs that reinforce (negative) stereotypes.

In addition to entertainment, television could, for instance, organize discussion programs in which pertinent issues regarding the fostering of unity are dealt with. When these discussions are given adequate publicity, the mass media would be bringing about awareness that is necessary to deal with, and resist the various attempts at exploitation. In essence, therefore, the media can act as very effective facilitators in the creation of awareness and in the provision and establishment of enabling environments in which minds can be purged of emotions and false notions that help distort them and promote conflict and chaos.

Secondly, political education is a crucial area where the mass media can have a significant impact. For many of Africa's rural (and even urban) dwellers, modern political systems that have been adopted in Africa are still alien and as such the people do not understand what is really going on. If we take (western) democracy, for instance, we would appreciate that there is a high level of ignorance about how it is supposed to work. Even the political elite sometimes only pretend to understand.

Left in their political ignorance, people, at times, tend to be reluctant to participate in any meaningful way in politics. Therefore, the goal of political education via the mass media is to broaden the political awareness of the populace, increase their ability to discern political circumstances, and resist exploitation by the power elite, and thus reduce their vulnerability as pawns and tools for the fomentation of trouble.

Similarly, the media should be in a position to help empower the populace to challenge political authority, and political leaders who are misbehaving. One of the most important institutions for error detection and error correction is the mass media. The media should take up this challenge and act as the true watchdog of society. If errors are identified early enough, larger crises can be nipped in the bud to the credit of the media and the good of society. Besides, when the press in a country is known for such ability and effectiveness, it will constitute a force of deterrence in political affairs - forcing leaders to watch their actions and to perform in line with probity, transparency and accountability. This would reduce the tendency to precipitate crises and conflicts as a cover-up for the misconduct (Mogekwu, 1995).

Population problems as well as problems of poor health and diseases can also be dealt with by the mass media in the form of well structured media campaigns to bring about awareness. When people are aware of the consequences of high fertility rates and poor hygiene on their lives, they would be more likely to adopt attitudes and behaviors that would lead to the amelioration of the problems. The mass media can purposefully engage in mass mobilization for social justice, self reliance, economic emancipation and better life for all. But in doing this, the following must be noted: that we cannot afford to alienate the audience by either the medium we use or the level of communication we employ. Any miscalculation in these areas could be counter-productive. By engaging in mass mobilization, the media would be concerned with the alignment of the thoughts and feelings of a mass or population in such a way that members of that population can go along towards a given goal.

Generally, when the mass media work consistently on the minds of the people to equip them with the instrument of knowledge and awareness, they are empowering them to take hold of their environment, utilize it as best as they can for the improvement of their lives and escape the cycle of violence that derive from the absence of such empowerment. The noted peace scholar, Majid Tehranian continues to advocate "peace journalism" as a path to peace and ultimate development. In a speech to the biennial conference of the International Peace Research Association in Calgary, Canada, in June 2006, Tehranian noted that the opposite of peace journalism is not "war journalism" but "muddled journalism" where information is presented with so little context that it is practically useless.

Conclusion

The role which communication plays in the development process has long captured the interest of communication researchers for decades. Many have unfortunately and inadvertently dealt with the issue as a linear relationship in which development appears to end at a point. But as we go further into the new millennium, it has become necessary to begin to envisage development as a continuous process that needs a favorable environment to perpetuate itself so that sustainability can be achieved. Development that cannot be sustained might as well not be embarked upon.

The aim of this paper has been to suggest that communication scholars should begin to focus on designing strategies for enhancing the environment in which development takes place. In doing this, various variables can be identified to provide focus for research. Peace has been identified here. There are definitely others. By the time all of them are put together, we would have contributed, probably more than most other disciplines, to the optimization of the environment necessary for the sustainability of development.

References

Adedeji, A. (1992). Africa in a world in transition: Laying the foundation for security, stability, structural transformation and cooperation. In O. Obasanjo and F.G.N. Mesaha. (eds.). *Africa: Rise to challenge*. New York: AFL

Anstey, M. (1991). *Negotiating conflict: Insights and skills for negotiators and peacemakers*. South Africa: Juta.

Brundtland Commission, (1987). *Our common future* (World Commission on Environment ad Development) Oxford: Oxford University Press.

Coser, L. (1956). *The functions of social conflict*. New York: Free Press.

DoE. (UK). (1994). *Sustainable development: The UK strategy*, Cmnd 2426, London, HMSO

DoE. (UK). (1997). *Planning policy guidance 1 (Revised) General policy and principles*. London, HMSO.

Fall, I. (1992) "Stability in Africa: A critical analysis and options for the future," In O. Obasanjo and F.G.N. Mesha (eds.). *Africa: Rise to challenge*. New York: AFL

Felstchausen, H. (1968). Economic knowledge, participation and farmer decision – making in a developed and an undeveloped country, *International Journal of Agrarian Affairs, 5, No. 4.*

Hansen, E. (ed) (1987). *Africa: Perspectives on peace and development*. London: Zed Books.

Inayatullah, S. (1967) "The nature of development", quoted by Hamdan Bin Adnan, et al. (1980) Introduction to development communication. Honolulu: East West Center.

Inkeles, A. and Smith, D. (1974). *Becoming modern: Individual change in six developing countries*. Cambridge, Mass: Harvard University Press.

Karshenas, M. (1994). "Environment, technology and employment: Towards a new definition of sustainable development", *Development and change, 25 (4).*

Kriesberg, L. (1973). *The sociology of social conflicts*. Englewoods, NJ: Prentice Hall.

Leipziger, D. M. (1981). *Basis needs and development*. Cambridge, Mass: O G and H Publishers.

Lerner, D. (1958). *The passing of traditional society*. Glencoe, ILL: Free Press.

McLelland, D. (1961). *The achieving society*. NY: Van Neostrand.

Millikan, M. (1973). "A strategy of development" in *The case for Development: 6 Studies* by the United Nations Centre for Economic and Social Information. New York: Praeger.

Moemeka, A. (1996) "Perspectives on development communication", In C. Okigbo (ed) *Development communication principles*. Nairobi: ACCE.

Mogekwu, M. (1995). "Media, stability and security: Imperatives for sustainable development in Africa," in C. Okigbo (ed.). *Media and sustainable development*. Nairobi: ACCE.

_____ (2000). "Media and the establishment of regional peace in Africa," in O. S. Spring (ed.), *Peace studies from a global perspective*. India: Maadhyam Books Services.

Morales, M. (2002). "Energy for sustainable development: The road from Stockholm to Johannesburg", *Renewal energy for development*, Vol.15, no.1/2.

Nichols, J. and McChesney, W. (2005) Tragedy and farce: How the American media sell wars, spin elections and destroy democracy. Norton & Co. Inc.

Pye, L. (ed.). (1963). Communication *and political development.* Princeton, NJ: Princeton University Press.

Rogers, E. (1977). "Network Analysis of the Diffusion of Family Planning Innovation" in W. Holland and S. Reinhardt (eds.). *Social networks: Surveys, advances and commentaries.* NY: Academic Press.

Schramm, W. (1964). *Mass media and national development.* Stanford, CA: Stanford University Press.

Lord Sewel. (1997). Central and local government in accord. Speech to the conference "Sustaining Change: Local Agenda 21 in Scotland, Edinburgh.

Shore, L. (1980). "Mass media for development: A re-examination of access, exposure and impact." In E. McAnany (ed) *Communication in the rural third world: The role of information in development.* New York: Praeger.

Tehranian, M. (2006). Patterns of conflict, paths to peace. Speech to the IPRA conference, Calgary, Canada.

Trostle, T. (1992) Personal correspondence in Sandy, L. and Perkins, R. The nature of peace and its implications for peace education. (www.oz.plymouth.edu/-/sandy/peacedef.html - sourced Feb 21, 2006)

Part 4: Africa in an Era of Global Conflicts

Chapter 15

The Mass Media and Ethnic Conflict in West Africa

Emeka J. Okoli, Ph.D.
Norfolk State University, USA

Introduction

Race particularly troubles urban America---our centers of business, industry, education, music, art and culture where the nation's destiny in the 21st century will play out. Indeed, racial mistrust is likely to grow in significance as America's minority population swells, new racial and ethnic rivalries emerge...let none mistake the news media's role. Journalism helps shape how racially diverse people think of each other and how public policy on race-related issues are formulated. (Gissler, 1994, p. 123)

Gissler seems to have captured the core of a perennial problem in America and the power of the media to shape people's responses to the issues. Although this paper is primarily concerned with the press and ethnic conflicts in West Africa, recent events around the globe have shown that ethnic conflicts are not limited to Africa. Examples of open ethnic rivalry abound in Bosnia, Great Britain, Iraq, former Soviet Union, to mention just a few. Ethnic conflict abounds in such "civilized" democracies like the United States of America and Canada. The difference between the later type of conflict and the former is the presence of a very strong control mechanism within the American and Canadian societies that discourages any manifestation of conflict.

Conflict in the West African subregion like that in United States arises when peoples with divergent agendas are forced to share from a limited resource base. In such situations, ethnic interests overshadow national interests (Okoli, 1995). It differs, however, from ethnic conflicts in the U.S. in two major aspects. First, the conflicts in West Africa have international dimensions. Second, many countries in West Africa, like their counterparts in the rest of Africa, are under non-democratically elected governments.

Western Media and Conflict in West Africa

Up till the end of the World War II, news coverage of the African continent was defined more by great white hunters or missionaries leading savages to the light -- Hollywood's enduring stereotype -- rather than by reasoned or informed reportage. The outset of the cold war dramatically changed that picture. Peering through the prism of that Manichean struggle, Western media fell in lockstep behind . . . the West's "strategic interests" on the global chessboard . . . abandoning any pretence of objective analysis (Lardner, 1993. p. 97).

Lardner regretted that despite the passage of time, the image of Africa as a continent of the apes swinging from trees and lions running free in the wilderness; a land occupied by savages incapable of managing their affairs still lurks in the recesses of newsrooms in the West. This image shows up in the issues that attract Western media attention: war in Liberia, famine in Ethiopia, the rivalry between warlords in Somalia, the despots in power. The list seems endless. Lardner suggests that this negative portrayal of Africa and African issues serves Western "strategic interests". He faults the American media for their inability to extricate themselves from the diplomatic maneuverings of their government that set up and funded despots all over Africa as a check on the Soviet expansionist efforts on the continent during the Cold War era. The Western media, very much like their counterparts under African "despots", took sides with their governments' covert operations in Africa. With the dismantling of the Soviet Union, however, the Western governments are "trying to rid themselves of petty dictators who fed for a quarter century off the epic U.S.-Soviet struggle". Says Lardner:

> Like their governments, the Western media also have sought historical distance from collateral damage in the aftermath of the Cold War. A ready example is Somalia . . . Before he was finally chased out of Mogadishu . . . earstwhile Somali tyrant Siad Barre routinely played both sides of the ideological divide. . . acquiring from both billions of dollars in weapons. (p. 97)

Needless to say that this dictatorship funded by the West for "strategic reasons" fuelled ethnic imbalance that continued long after the ouster of Mr. Barre. This same scenario can readily be replayed in Liberia, Angola, Sudan, Mozambique and many other spots in Africa. Lardner rightly wonders why the Western media never mentions such undercurrent causal factors to the sensational newsreels that flow out of Africa. He wonders if this is not a case of deliberate unwillingness to acknowledge historical causality that would embarrass the Western countries whose "strategic interests" the media has worked so hard to protect. Lardner cites another case of "media historical myopia" in Zaire's Mobutu Sese Seko:

> Mobutu…was installed in power by the CIA in the wake of the Congo crisis in the early 1960s. His longevity, although now threatened, was sustained at critical moments in the last three decades by the direct intervention of European and U.S. military and intelligence collaborations. Now a Cold War relic, he is often portrayed by the Western media as just a generic, hometown African dictator, but the historical record tells a different tale. (p. 97)

Says Jack F. Matlock, Jr., a veteran foreign service officer and former U.S. ambassador to the Soviet Union in an interview with *Media Study Journal* Editor, Edward C. Pease on the interplay between press and policy information during the Cold War era, "there was no question in most media executives' minds or correspondents' minds what the issues of the Cold War were. For the most part, they were on the right side of them. We were all on the same side" (Pease, 1993, p. 51). Indeed, the Western media have always been on the same side as their governments. This can explain why 'news' from and about Africa is usually slanted toward what Lardner calls "the tedious cycle of murderous, bumbling despots, wars and assorted disasters of Biblical proportions."

As long as the West had use for the so-called despots in Africa, the Western media could see nothing wrong with despotism. They seem oblivious of the impact of the leadership of the likes of Mobutu on the people they pretend to govern. They seem too eager to either forget or to totally ignore the Western diplomatic maneuverings that caused the current slew of problems in Africa. Examples abound in France, Germany, and other European countries where the media chooses to ignore historical factors that lie behind current issues. This writer must add that this media amnesia is still a part of that grand plan to protect the "strategic interests" of the Western policy makers. African journalists, like their counterparts in the West, also face the challenges of the balance of the high roads of objective reporting and the attractions of parochial interests.

The Mass Media and Ethnic Conflict in West Africa: The Nigerian Example

The government of a country is a major factor in determining the media environment within that country. Lewin (1936) suggests that the environment in which communicative acts take place influences both the interactants and the outcome of the interaction. This means that one's behavior at any time is a function of who one is and the environment in which the interaction is taking place.

Khun (1975) echoes the same thought when he posits that "human beings are controlled systems behaving in an environment" (p.112). It follows then that to fully appreciate the role of the media in the West African environment, the researcher needs to understand the dynamics within that environment. Within the West African subregion, the media faces challenges in three broad areas:

(1) Government/Governed Conflict

A government that seems insensitive to the needs and aspirations of the governed. A government like that in Zaire and many parts of Africa where the policies of the government are tailored to favor Western interests rather than the aspirations of the governed. In such environments it is easy to see how an individual can run a nation like a personal enterprise and anybody who voices dissatisfaction is ill-treated and censored.

(2) Government/Media Conflict

Owing to the commitment of the media to impartially inform and educate the people and considering the fact that government interests are at cross-purposes with those of the citizens, the press is constantly in conflict with the ruling party.

(3) Government/Ethnic/Media Conflict

Owing to the very unique structure of African societies, ethnicity becomes a factor that further complicates the government-media-governed relationships. In most African countries, the primary allegiance of the journalist is to his/her ethnic group. This affiliation has the potential of affecting the journalist's ability to walk the high roads of ethical, objective management of news.

Although the focus of this paper is West Africa, this writer will examine the media in Nigeria. Nigeria, because of its size and the complex dynamics at work within that environment, can be readily replicated in all the other countries in the region. The journalist in Nigeria, like his/her counterpart in Cameroon, Liberia, Ghana, Togo, or Sierra Leone, struggles with a government that seems apathetic to the needs of the country (Huband, 1993) and the painful struggle of having to choose between ethnic interests, personal safety, and the dictates of objectivity (Puri, 1994). To understand the role of the media in a pluralistic environment like Nigeria requires that the researcher first studies the Nigerian environment itself. It is the position of this writer that any study on the media in Nigeria, or in fact any other country in West Africa, must factor in the ethnic and cultural dynamics at work in the area. Nigeria is home to virtually all the native races of Africa. With a population of over 120 million comprising more than 250 ethnic groups, Nigeria is a suitable base for the study of ethnicity and its impact on communication within an environment. The Nigerian press is strong and consists of 40 or more dailies, each with a Sunday edition. Dare (1996) lists some 20 weeklies devoted to business, sports, and entertainment, six weekly news magazines and about a dozen other periodicals of acceptable quality. He, however, laments that although some of the weekly news magazines, like *Tell* and *Newswatch,* have won international awards for quality, the Nigerian press still has to deal with "profound regional and ideological differences". Says he, "religion and ethnicity are . . . significant factors in press outlook. . . .In all three regions, what operates for the most part is an instrumental press that tends to espouse causes that advance the interests of its proprietors or their ethnic groups, oftentimes with scant regard for the larger public interest".

In a pluralistic society like Nigeria, each ethnic group seems to have clearly definable identity that differentiates it from all the other groups. These defining features have managed to survive any pull toward assimilation. A visitor to Nigeria will have no problems noticing the differences between the Hausas of the North, the Yorubas of the West, and the Igbos of the East. Each of these groups occupies a territory that it considers to be its own by right of first occupancy and inheritance. Nonmembers of a given group who have lived and worked for several decades in the territory of the group are still considered to be aliens. In most rural areas, such aliens may not acquire outright title to land (*Encyclopedia Britannica*).

Researchers on Nigeria readily agree that allegiance to the tribe is much stronger than that to Nigeria as a state (Musa, 1994; Ugboaja, 1980). Francis (in Osei-Kwame, 1980, p. 22) argued that multiplicity of tribes or ethnic groups in a nation like Nigeria poses a major problem because in most instances, the identification of the individual to his/her tribe or ethnic grouping is much stronger than that to the state. The problem is that at heart, the various people groups see themselves first as Hausas, Igbos, Yorubas and Binis (Mgbejume, 1991, p. 55). They respond to national issues, not as Nigerians but according to their ethnic affiliation. The factors that drive Nigerians are totally different from those that drive the Americans. The Nigerian polity does not seem ready to compromise the benefits of a closely-knit ethnic group for national promises that may never be realized.

How does the ethnic composition of Nigeria influence the Nigerian media? This writer would argue that the no-win front readily presents itself to the researcher who examines only the surface structure of things in Nigeria. It is the position of this paper that factoring the realities of the deep structure of the Nigerian society in the equation would reveal a totally different dynamic than has hitherto been reported by researchers. Let us begin by asking some basic questions. Is it possible that the performance of the press in Nigeria has its roots in the ethnic dynamics? Is it also possible that ownership of the media and politics in Nigeria are ethnically driven? Would it be stretching the issue too far to sug-

gest that journalists in Nigeria are pressured by their ethnic affiliation to abandon the high roads of professional practice for the pursuit of ethnic interests?
The answers to these questions seem to be the keys that would lead one to the
dynamics at work in Nigeria and, in fact, most other African societies.

For a start, it is necessary to indicate the possibility that owing to the power
element of the deep structure in Nigeria, the press may be used as a willing tool
in the hands of politicians and military officers whose agendas are, in the main,
ethnic. It is also possible that the main actors in both the government and the
media in Nigeria may be members of the same ethnic group. This suspicion
appears to be strengthened by the fact that since gaining independence in 1960,
Nigeria has had eight heads of state, two presidents, and one prime minister. Of
these rulers, the North, which is predominantly Islamic in orientation has produced five military and two civilian rulers (a total of 70% representation), the
East provided one military and one civilian leader, while the West came in third
with one leader who has ruled both as a military and civilian ruler. Further examination shows that elements from the North have ruled the country through a
combination of military and civilian administrations for at least 29 of the 47
years since independence. Without sounding alarmist, one wonders if a mechanism exists at the deeper levels of the nation's reality that ensures that leadership comes from the northern region.

Although the military tries to position itself as a messianic group that would
deliver Nigeria from her woes, researchers (Kieh and Agbese, 1993, p. 417)
contend that the "primordial entities of ethnicity, religion, and region of origin
of the general Nigerian society are reproduced within the armed forces." They
cite the example of General Ibrahim Babangida in appointing three Muslims
from the north as service chiefs for the three arms of the military in 1989. The
authors hinted at the protest by the Christians who felt marginalized by the appointments. This example of Babangida can be readily duplicated in almost
every key appointment in each of the governments at the center.

The situation is no different at the state levels. Davis et al. (1971, p. 42)
argue:

> Because loyalty to the tribe played such an important role, political parties
> within each region were organized mainly along tribal lines. The party of the
> largest tribe in each region became the majority party. Its leaders dominated
> the region's government.

If the government which controls all the elements of coercion also champions parochial ethnic interests, it follows then that the policies of these governments are ethnic in orientation. Put another way, these policies that appear
"national" and "in the public interest" at the surface level of reality are indeed
carefully veiled ethnic maneuvering to hold on to power at all costs. Consider-

ing the power inherent in government and the media and the fact that the prima-ry allegiance of Nigerians is to the tribe, it seems possible that members of the same ethnic group in both the government and the media would cooperate in protecting the interest of their ethnic group and use force and available means of coercion to silence the media from the other groups.

This brings us to the issue of ownership of the media and its impact on free speech in Nigeria. By 1985 there were 15 dailies in Nigeria, 10 of which are owned by the government (Edeani, 1985, p.47). The federal government of Ni-geria owns the *New Nigerian* newspapers - a major organ that speaks authorita-tively for northern interests. The federal government also controls 60% of the shares of *The Daily Times* (Mgbejume, 1991, p. 54). Edeani describes *The Dai-ly Times* as "the country's most financially successful and most influential daily newspaper" (p. 47). On ownership of radio, Edeani (pp. 47- 48) laments that the governments now own the broadcasting industry in its entirety:

Each state is linked to the Federal Radio Corporation of Nigeria (FRCN), the federal broadcasting network in Lagos, by a regional transmission station which feeds smaller stations in the states . . . . the federal government [owns] . . . all short-wave radio stations . . . as well as all 'powerful' medium-wave sta-tions, leaving the states with less powerful medium-wave broadcasting facili-ties.

Television broadcasting did not escape the powerful government control either. Through the agency of the Nigerian Television Authority (NTA), the government now fully controls not only the issuance of licenses but also pro-gramming through television. Edeani (p. 48) also worries that the government owns the only news-gathering agency - the News Agency of Nigeria (NAN) - authorized to "collect news from inside and outside Nigeria and distribute it at a fee to the news media and other interested subscribers." As is evident, the gov-ernment's interest in the media goes beyond the stated and usually touted re-sponsibility of government to protect and serve public interest. One would sus-pect, given the realities of the Nigerian socio-political environment, that owner-ship of the media is being used as "a vehicle of political control" by the various interest groups that make up the government (Edeani, 1985, p. 48). de Beer, Kasoma, Megwa, and Steyn (1995, p. 234) note:

Governments used the press to inform the masses about what they thought the masses should know and whom they should support. Mass communication . . . has been used as a tool for political power and influence rather than for disse-minating public information and opinion to enhance political choices and hence democracy for the people.

Considering the powerful nature of the media, it is easy to see how they can be used to serve ethnic interests. Researchers agree that in countries like Nigeria, the media tends to become mouth pieces of those who own them (Sobowale, 1985; Edeani, 1985). Sobowale argues that "instead of performing the functions of surveying the environment . . . and transmitting culture . . . the media are turned into indispensable tools for retaining power by those controlling them" (p. 94). It follows that if media owners, who champion ethnic positions, control what is published or positions taken by journalists on major national issues, then these journalists have compromised their commitment to unbiased reporting and become advocates of ethnic positions. Musa (1994) argues that:

> the role of the mass media in several national crises Nigeria has always found itself whether political or religious has been less than commendable. This is because the media appear to be factionalized along the divisive ethnic, religious, and geographical lines of the society. They tend to amplify the tensions by pandering to the primordial interests rather than selling a peace agenda.

The 1973 census in Nigeria is one such major issue in which public opinion was divided along ethnic lines. This census was important because of its economic and political implications. It was clear to all Nigerians that political power and economic benefits in the country would be distributed according to the census figures. Ugboaja (1985) examined the news appearing in some newspapers owned by individuals, the state and federal governments on four conflict-generating issues of development. One of these issues was the 1973 census. He found that this issue turned out to be a "cold war" between the north and the south (particularly the southwest) of the country in terms of the attention given to the issue. It is necessary to note here that the north is predominantly Hausa; the southwest, Yoruba; and the east is Igbo. On this census issue, therefore, the race was between the ruling Hausa tribe and the rival Yoruba tribe. The Igbos apparently were still suffering from the devastating civil war (1967 - 1970) to be able to compete in this arena. Ugboaja (1985, p. 228) noted that "the fact that a newspaper belonged to the government or to the private sector was no longer material to individual medium's performance. What was important was the controversy under debate, its implication and the attitude of the constituency affected by it". This statement by Ugboaja moves the debate beyond that of control of the media for the interest of Nigeria as a nation by government (state or federal, military or civilian) to considerations that are purely ethnic. Any wonder then, why the various ethnic groups in Nigeria would rather fight than let themselves be upstaged on issues that they consider vital to their existence. Since ownership of the media runs along ethno-political lines, Ugboaja's (p. 234) findings are considered pertinent:

Data have shown that the south-western papers (Daily Sketch and Nigerian Tribune) and the northern paper (New Nigerian) were deeply involved in the census issue. This is because the issue affected their localities in a controversial way. The disputable 1973 census figures showed that the northern states gained considerably in population over the southern states of Nigeria, and that the Western State decreased....Nigerian Tribune representing the southern constituency, whose population decreased, showed anti-government behavior on the issue, whereas New Nigerian representing the northern states whose population increased was neutral editorially speaking.

From the foregoing, it seems necessary to caution against examination of this and, in fact, any issue that concerns Nigeria from any perspective that does not factor in the realities of the Nigerian society. This study shows the need to consider the basic assumptions at the deep levels of the environment that inform the surface-level realities that are usually reported on by researchers who neither have the understanding nor the patience needed to decipher the subtle but more powerful dynamics within the deep structures. As indicated in this paper, factoring the realities of the deep structures into the apparent en passe in the relationship between the pen and the sword in Nigeria might provide answers which may lead to deeper understanding of the media in developing societies around the world.

References

Barkindo, B. M., (1985). The Mandara astride the Nigeria-Cameroon Border. In A. I. Asiwaju (Ed.), *Partitioned Africans: Ethnic Relations Across Africa's International Boundaries 1884-1984.* New York: St. Martins Press.

Conrad, C. (1983). Organizational Power: Faces and Symbolic Forms. In L. L. Putnam & M. E. Pacanowsky (Eds.), *Communication and organizations: An interpretive approach.* Newbury Park, CA: Sage.

de Beer, A. S., Kasoma, F. P., Megwa, E. R., and Steyn, E. (1995). Sub-Saharan Africa. In John C. Merrill (Ed.) *Global Journalism: Survey of International Communication.* New York: Longman Publishers

Davis, L., Arnoff, M., Blough, J., Hunkins, F., & Ramsey, C. (1971). *Nigeria.* New York: American Book Company

Deetz, S. A., & Kersten, A. (1983). Critical models in interpretive research. In L. L. Putnam & M. E. Pacanowsky (Eds.).

Edeani, F. (1985) Press Ownership and Control in Nigeria. In Frank O. Ubgoajah, (Ed.). *Mass Communication, Culture and Society in West Africa.* New York: Han Zell Publishers.

Encyclopedia Britannica 1993

Gissler, S. (1994) Newspapers' quest for Racial Candor. In E. Dennis (Ed.) *Media Studies Journal, 8 (3)*

Esman, M. (1989). "Political and Psychological Factors in Ethnic Conflict." In Joseph V. Montville (ed.) *Conflict and Peacemaking in Multiethnic Societies.* Massachusetts: Lexington Books

Khun, A. (1975). Social organization. In B. D. Ruben & J. Y. Kim (Eds.), *General systems theory and human communication.* Rochelle Park, NJ: Hayden.

Kieh, G. & Agbese, P. (1993). From Politics Back to the Barracks in Nigeria: A Theoretical Model. *Journal of Peace, 30.*

Lardner, T. (1993). Rewriting the tale of the "Dark Continent". *Media Studies Journal, 7(4).*

Lewin, K., (1936). *Principles of topological psychology.* New York: McGraw-Hill.

Mgbejume, O. (1990). Breaking Ethnic Barriers: A Communication Model. *Africa Media Review, 4, 72-*82.

Mgbejume, (1991). Constraints on Mass media Policies in Nigeria. *Africa Media Review, 5, 47-*57.

Musa, B. (1994). *Pluralism and the Bloc-Press Phenomenon in Nigeria: Implications for National Development.* Unpublished manuscript.

Oliver, R. & Fage, J. D. (1988). *A Short History of Africa.* New York: Viking Pengium, Inc.

Osei-Kwame, P. (1980). *A New conceptual Model for the Study of Political Integration in Africa.* Washington, D. C.: University Press of America

Pacanowsky, M.E. & O'Donnell-Trujillo, N. (1982). Communication and organizational cultures. *Western Journal of Speech Communication, 46,* 115–130.

Paden, J. N., (1990). National System Development and Conflict Resolution in Nigeria. In Joseph V. Montville (ed.)

Pandey, J. (1992). The Environment, culture, and behavior. In William B. Gudykunst & Young Yum Kim (Eds.), *Readings on Communicating with Strangers.* Newbury Park, CA: Sage.

Ra'anan, U. (1989). The Nation-State fallacy. In Joseph V. Montville (ed.)

Schein, E. (1992). *Organizational culture and leadership.* San Francisco, CA: Jossey-Bass.

Sobowale, I. (1985). Influence of Ownership of Nigerian Newspaper Coverage on National Issues. In Onuora Nwuneli, (Ed). *Mass Communication in Nigeria: A Book of Reading.* Enugu: Fourth Dimension Publishers.

Ugboaja, F. O. (1985). *Mass Communication, Culture and Society in West Africa.* New York: Han Zell Publishers, 1985.

Van Fleet, D. D. (1991). Behavior *in organizations.* Dallas, TX: Houghton Mifflin.

Chapter 16

Social Conflict, Communication, and Youth in Tanzania

Nicholls K. Boas, Ph.D.
Morgan State University, USA

Introduction

Tanzania is envied by most people of Africa. It is fortunate in not having a history of civil violence and political extremism since attaining its independence from Britain in 1961. The country has vast mineral resources, which are now being fully exploited. The extraction of mineral resources will provide the government with revenues needed to support development programs in Tanzania. As one of the key variables for advancing development, resource allocations to support, for example, quality education among the poor majority youth must be given the highest priority in Tanzania's development programs.

The priority of providing quality education to poor majority youth is necessary in Tanzania simply because it would be a fair method of minimizing social conflict between the "haves" and "have not." This classification has rapidly emerged in Tanzania since the reintroduction of the multiparty democratic system in 1992. In fact, expanding educational opportunities for the poor majority youth seems to be the right dosage if Tanzania is to move away from a low to middle-income nation as stipulated in "Development Vision 2025." This government development plan seems crucial in trying to close the gap between the rich and poor in Tanzania; and as a result, social conflicts, which tend to breed social ills such as crime, the use of illegal drugs, the escalation of political and economic instability, may be minimized in the country.

Social conflict in Tanzania can best be understood by applying the analysis of the "conflict paradigm," which suggests that social behavior could be seen as the process of conflict: the attempt to dominate others and to avoid being dominated. In his explanation, Babbie (2000) points out that Karl Max used the conflict model to examine the ways capitalism produced oppression of workers by those who owned the facilities of productions. Indeed the model, which focuses on the macro-level, offers an analysis of the relationship between individuals and society in regard to the struggle among economic classes. It has also proved to be fruitful outside the frames of purely economic analyses. For example, within the conflict model, Simmel (1858-1918) was interested in small-scale conflicts. He noted that conflicts among members of a tightly knit group tended to be more intense than those among people who did not share feelings of belonging and intimacy. While conflicts are common phenomena in societies, it seems reasonable to suggest that they ought to be minimized if political and economic stability, for example, in Tanzania, are to be achieved in order to realize a government plan titled "Development Vision 2025."

Central to the discussion of social conflict in Tanzania are communication and youth. These variables are significant in understanding the analysis of how social ills have escalated in urban centers as well as in rural areas in Tanzania during the one-party authoritarian rule and after the reintroduction of democratic system of governance. To a great extent, the Tanzanian youth of 21st century seem to have an enormous task of advancing tomorrow's development, which is aimed at uplifting the living standards of the masses. It has often been stated that, the youth of today are the brigades of advancing tomorrow's societal development programs; and as such, the responsibilities of preparing them to assume tomorrow's tasks of development appear to rest on Tanzania's societal institutions including the government, NGO's, local communities, private enterprises, religious organizations, and many others.

As noted, social conflict is characterized by certain ideas about communication and society. Communication within the conflict paradigm is often the lightening rod of human conflicts and a catalyst for human social change. Therefore, communication is, indeed, essential to resolving human conflicts. Communication per se is analyzed as an on-going process that has no end insight. It enables individuals to interact as they share and exchange information about their social life.

This chapter is descriptive, theoretical, and practical in approach. It attempts to explore social conflict in Tanzania in regard to communication and youth. On the descriptive level, the paper attempts to examine the facts about social conflict; that is, who are involved in social conflict. Theoretically, the paper looks at various explanations about social conflict. And on the practical scale, the paper explores what needs to be done to minimize social conflict in Tanzania.

Social Conflict

Societies, like economies, have "leading indicators" which give great insight into the future. While these are not infallible predictors, they are generally helpful in judging direction. They are not always right, but they are usually close. They do not predict, but they forecast. Social conflicts, as leading indicators, may forecast a political upheaval between the "powerful" and the "powerless" or between the "haves" and "have-nots," for example, in Tanzania.

In their analysis, Eitzen and Zinn (2000) state that there are objective realities to social conflicts. These, according to them, include: (1) conditions in society such as poverty and institutional culture that induce material or psychic suffering for certain majority segment of the population; (2) socio-cultural phenomena that prevent a significant number of societal participants from developing and using their full potential; and (3) discrepancies between what a society is supposed to stand for (equality of opportunities, justice, democracy) and the actual conditions in which many of its people live. These elements mentioned by the authors seem to be societal conditions that harm the majority segment of the population; and therefore, are societal problems.

Since the reintroduction of multiparty political democracy in Tanzania in 1992, the country has now emerged into two distinct population strata–the "haves" and the "have nots"–a phenomenon that was nonexistent during Nyerere's one-party rule (1965-1992). This population classification helps to explain group bond between those few who are powerful and economically superior; and those who are majority powerless and economically poor in Tanzania. Humans are a group-bound species, who tend to cheer and die for their groups. Our ancestral history prepares us to feed and protect ourselves to live in groups. Therefore, our self-concept and our sense of who we are contain not just our personal identity but also our social identity.

The group definition of who we are, for instance, our economic social status or political party affiliation, implies a definition of who we are not. Thus, the mere experience of being formed into groups can promote ingroup bias (Myers, 2000). For example, the fast emerging group classification in Tanzania that is based on economic status, after the reintroduction of multiparty politics, appears to create a "we" versus "them" mentality. This classification, which is now visible in the country than it was during the one-party rule, could, in the future, prohibit social group interaction between the "haves and "have nots."

As indicated in the literature, the conflict paradigm often focuses on class, gender, and ethnic struggle. This paradigm, for example, offers a theoretical framework of examining the classification of the "haves" and "have-nots" and the impact it may have on the Tanzanian society. For example, it has been noted that after dismantling socialism, the "haves"- a classification that was invisible during the one-party rule in Tanzania - have access to economic opportunities and are better placed to influence public policies. Their status has enabled them to control resources and acquire more wealth for them and their families. The acquisition of wealth, by in large, has provided to the wealthy a significant resource advantage to pay, for example, the high costs for educating their children in better schools, both in Tanzania and abroad. This, indeed, is one of the major social issues capable of creating economic and political instability in the country. The disparity in wealth raises a serious issue in Tanzanian society because it puts, for example, the poor majority youth in dire situation to successfully complete their educational programs in order to pursue career opportunities in the country and the world at large.

Ujamaa Fails to Create Egalitarian Society

The inequality between the few fortunate youth and the majority less fortunate youth in Tanzania appears to have the historical link to the constitutional amendment of 1965, which was used by President Julius Nyerere and his government as a bedrock to institute the failed Ujamaa project. This constitutional amendment established the one-party political rule, indicating clearly that it was illegal to create any other political party in the country. The amendment enabled the late President Nyerere to create the Ujamaa development program based on socialistic economic principles. Ujamaa is a Swahili word which means "familyhood." Since the Ujamaa struck a familiar traditional chord of reciprocity, Nyerere seemed to have thought that by using the word, Tanzanians would easily adopt the Ujamaa program aimed at advancing socioeconomic development that is aligned with the ideology of socialism.

Carried out on the basis of a one-way communication approach (sender-receiver with no feedback), the Ujamaa program included the party's desire to enhance rural development and to create an egalitarian Tanzanian society. Within the program, there was also a notion which hinged on stopping completely the accumulation of private wealth by individuals. During that era, Tanzania seemed to have begun slowly the march to dismantle the class phenomenon of the "haves" and "have nots." Indeed, the Ujamaa doctrine made individuals refrain from being ostentatious of their wealth because they feared of being investigated by the government of how they acquired wealth.

The Ujamaa program seemed ideal because it focused on attempting to minimize social conflicts between the wealthy and the poor. Based on egalitarian approach, the program aimed at distributing the wealth and resources equally to the masses in an effort to advance their social life. By design, the government's intention, under the one-party rule, was to create a classless society, where each individual could have equal access to all local or national resources. In that era, the masses were required to implement government directives and support the government public policy; in turn, the government's responsibility was to make sure that social services, such as education, healthcare and others were freely provided to people of all walks of life. Under this political arrangement, many youth, for example, got free education that enabled them to read and write. Indeed, under the one-party political rule, social conflicts based on the class structure of the "have" and "have nots" was minimally visible.

For sure, what emerged during the era of one-party rule centered on the consolidation of power on the part of the government. This strategy was critical in the sense that it gave the government a leverage to manipulate and control the masses who were required to adopt the Ujamaa program. So, in that era of one-party political rule, "power" was examined in two distinct classifications - "powerful" (government) and "powerless" (masses). Under the theory of socialism in Tanzania, the masses were required to obey and carry out all directives given out by the government. In fact, power was not evenly distributed in the country.

In a political context, power, according to Bertsch, et al (1986), means the ability to influence the behavior of others. It has the capacity to change or influence policy outcomes in society. As such, the distribution of power between the citizens and the government is a pressing policy issue in all nation-state. To a great extent, if harmony is to prevail, power in a society must be distributed effectively between the people and the government. This distribution of power, of course, can only be achieved through a two-way communication process (sender-receiver with feedback), which is democratic in nature. Unfortunately, this was not the case in Tanzania when the government was implementing its Ujamaa development program under the authoritarian rule.

In the rural Ujamaa communities, for example, government directives required individuals to work "collectively" as they farmed and harvested crops from their land. The crops, in principle, were to be shared by all individuals in the community. Indeed, the Ujamaa "collective" principle was foreign; it altered the traditional way of how people worked in the rural areas. As a result, it created social conflict between modernity and traditional values in the society.

The traditional concept of Ujamaa in Tanzania is based on reciprocity among individuals. Under the theory of reciprocity, people in a community may collectively help a person to cultivate land, plant seeds, and harvest crops. As appreciation of their help, those who worked in the farm are treated to a feast prepared by the one who was helped by the community. The harvested crops are only shared by the members in the immediate family unit and not with the community. However, under Nyerere's principles of collective participation, many individuals in the Ujamaa communities never enjoyed the fruits of their labor. Distribution of harvested crops to family members of the community was unfairly done by powerful village leaders. As a result, collective performance in the Ujamaa communities declined.

The declining performance of collective participation was preceded by a sour government action of removing individuals by force from their land of ancestors to newly created Ujamma communities by the government. This action was intended to bring rural scattered individuals into communities where the government would easily provide basic services such as water, electricity, schools and healthcare. The government's action was specifically targeted towards spearheading socialistic economic development under the Ujamaa philosophy of trying to create an egalitarian society in Tanzania. This action was, by nature, a violation of human rights that created a conflict between the government and the masses.

The removal of individuals from their land of ancestors was a bad experience simply because it did not allow people to fully practice their traditional values and rituals in their societies. In fact, excluding traditional values in the implementation of the Ujamaa program stifled development in rural communities. This was contrary to Western Europe, where in England, for example, people continued to cherish traditional values of respecting the monarch as the emergence of Industrial Revolution spearheaded development.

The violation of traditional values in implementing the Ujamma development program created difficulties for the government to convince the masses to adopt the socialistic economic principles of Ujamaa. In order to minimize social conflicts and to make the masses adopt the Ujamaa, the government devised a series of the one-way communication approaches that began with persuasive communication--a basic method of influencing one another in a society. In analyzing the process, Infante, et al (1990) explain that at its most basic level, persuasion may be thought of attitude change toward one's proposal, which results from a message designed to alter beliefs about the proposal. A proposal is a recommended course of action. For instance, enacting and implementing the Ujamaa program was a recommended course of action by authorities to turn Tanzania into an egalitarian society. In this approach of persuasive communication, Boas (1995) explains that, authorities broadcasted quite often Nyerere's speeches on government controlled radio (Radio Tanzania), telling the masses the benefits of accepting the Ujamaa.

As time progressed, the government became jittery because the masses reacted slowly in adopting the Ujamaa. As a result, the government devised another communication strategy–inducement, which was added to persuasive communication. In this communication plan, aid in emergencies such as floods or droughts was given first to those who joined the Ujamaa communities. It is interesting to note that, even with inducement being added by 1973, McHenry (1979) explains that, only 15.5 percent of rural population had been brought into the Ujamaa communities, an ideology that started in 1962. This trend frustrated authorities and as a result, Nyerere finally announced that all individuals who lived in widely scattered rural areas would have to move into Ujamaa communities by the end of 1976.

Nyerere's announcement was the beginning of the final phase of communication strategy–forced communication or coercion. In this strategy, after the government realized that persuasive communication with inducement failed, it resorted to using physical force to remove and relocate rural individuals to new areas planned to start Ujamaa communities. In the end, Nyerere's effort to establish an egalitarian society under the Ujamaa program crumbled. In fact, it was one of the major issues that created social conflict that Tanzania had never witnessed since it attained its independence from Britain in 1961.

Personal Freedom Violated

The abandonment of the Ujamaa project seemed to foster a sense of protecting one's freedom to pursue what appears to be a self-fulfilling prophesy. Indeed, the implementation of the Ujamaa program created a cleavage between the powerful and the powerless in that the powerless (masses) were denied the right to exercise their freedom of choice. Coupled with the violation of personal freedom, the abandonment of the Ujamaa project seems to hinge on two critical factors: the loss of ancestral land; and the foreign component of collective participation in the Ujamaa development program. These factors appeared to have energized the rural masses to return to land of their ancestors, where individuals could, once again, use personal freedom to practice and cherish the traditional way of life they accustomed to.

As it has been noted that personal freedom, during the implementation of the Ujamaa, was expected to be surrendered to the powerful (government) as the powerless (masses) carried out government directives to implement the Ujamaa. This restraint made individuals react accordingly in order to safeguard their personal freedom. Indeed, the return of rural individuals to their ancestral land revolves around "reactance" theory in social psychology, which explores personal freedom in regard to how individuals think, act, and relate to others. In fact, social psychology is micro in nature as opposed to sociology which is macro, for example, studying the behavior of a group. In general, social psychological theory of reactance stipulates that individuals value their sense of freedom and self-efficacy (Baer, et. al., 1980). Based on this theory, it seems that when social pressure becomes so blatant it often threatens people's sense of freedom; and as such, individuals tend to rebel.

In any society, personal freedom to practices traditional values is important simply because it brings a sense of historical linkage of how individuals identify with their communities or groups.   For example, African people tend not to live outside their communities simply because those communities provide a safe net for individual's survival and security. As safe nets, communities tend to provide a platform where cultural values are learned and passed on to youth. Indeed, even though the Ujamaa died quietly as multiparty politics reemerged in 1992, its ideology seemed to have been destructive in tearing down personal freedom that enabled people to freely practice traditional cultural values and norms in their rural communities.

In exploring individual behavior, social psychological theory of reactance points out that attempts to restrict a person's freedom often produces a "boomerang effect", which for instance, occurred during a massive abandonment of the Ujamaa program. At this juncture, it appears fitting to discuss the "boomerang effect" that made individuals abandon the Ujamaa program and how the failure of the program, in the end, created a significant gap between the "haves" and "have-nots," under the multiparty rule in Tanzania.

The Emergence of New Class Strata

To a great degree, the "boomerang effect" hinged on two critical factors - resistance and abandonment of the Ujamaa program. These factors, among others, were critical internal elements that set the stage for Tanzania to return to a multiparty system that has now created new class stratification in the country. The "boomerang effect" on the Ujamaa program took effect at the time when authoritarian leaders throughout Africa began to lose legitimate power because they faced economic crises in their respective countries. In addition, the African leaders' predicament was also compounded by external factors, which contributed significantly to the demise of the one-party rule in Africa. For instance, the fall of communism and socialism respectively in Russia and Eastern Europe had a chilling effect in Tanzania and the rest of Africa. Many African socialist leaders such as Nyerere of Tanzania lost important partners in Eastern Europe, who turned their backs on socialism in Africa in favor of democracy. As a result of internal and external factors that did not favor the one party authoritarian rule, democratization swept through the African continent in the 1980's and early 1990's.

Faced with no other alternatives, the African socialist leaders initiated democratic reform in their nations (Boas, 2000). In Tanzania, the democratic reform enabled rural individuals to regain their lost freedom that was stifled under the one-party rule. The failure of Ujamaa seemed to have made Nyerere to relinquish his presidency in 1985 on his own accord. As he stepped down from the presidency, Nyerere remained the chairman of the supreme ruling political party CCM (Chama Cha Mapinduzi) under one-party rule in Tanzania. In that capacity, as the Chairman, Nyerere embarked on a political move to reform the constitution in order to reestablish, once again, multiparty political democracy in the country.

The return of democratic rule altered significantly the politics and economic dynamics in Tanzania. Once again, it created a free-market economy in which individuals began to accumulate private wealth without fear of being investigated by the government of how they acquired that wealth. Taking advantage of multiparty political system, a handful of elites, including those placed in the position of authority in the government and its agencies began to amass wealth through dubious means. Quite openly, the masses in Tanzania now began to see a handful of elites owning new houses and bungalows, new cars, new bank accounts in foreign currency, and new big businesses they never had during the one-party rule. Indeed, this wealth enabled the handful elites to send their children to good private schools in the country and abroad, while the majority lacked the means to help their children pursue quality higher education. As a result of this phenomenon, a new class of the "haves" and "have not" emerged in this era of multiparty politics, threatening the political stability of Tanzania.

The free market economy is a notion that is embedded in the principles of democratic values, which tend to revolve around protecting individual's freedoms. So, personal freedom that came with the reintroduction of democratic rule enabled the exodus of the poor rural majority youth to migrate to urban centers in order to attain a better standard of living.

The influx of rural youth to urban centers was nonexistent during the implementation of the Ujamaa program. By design, the youth were manipulated by policies of the one-party rule to become the brigades of carrying out the Ujamaa program, after completing the required 7 years of primary education. The majority youth did not get secondary school education because the government stated that it had limited enrollment and lacked resources to accommodate all. As a result, through persuasive communication, the government urged the rural youth to stay and help their communities to implement the policies of advancing the Ujamaa development program. It was an effort by the government to dissuade the rural youth to seek employment in the cities.

The migration of rural youth in urban centers in this era of multiparty politics has impacted the Tanzanian society as a whole. As rural youth flocked to various urban centers, essential services such as housing, water, education, healthcare, and many other services were inadequate to support a large number of people at once. The government unpreparedness to deal with the influx of rural youth, coupled with high unemployment, resulted in exacerbating social ills that included, among others, crime, prostitution, the spread of HIV/AIDS, the sale of illegal drugs and so on. Stifled by Ujamaa policies to acquire higher education, the poor majority youth, who knew only how to read and write, became unproductive in urban centers and a burden to the Tanzanian society.

Indeed, for one to become productive, Maslow's theory of hierarchy points out that an individual is supposed to satisfy the basic survival needs. The hierarchy of needs has five levels, which include physiology, security, belonging, esteem, and self-actualization. Maslow perceived individuals as being driven by a layered hierarchy of needs. To move up to each successive level, the needs of the previous level must be met. The initial layer of needs include the essential physiological requirements of food and shelter, the foundation of physical survival. Once the needs are met, concerns of the second level can be considered– the need for security, and safety from the external threats. In fact, when the needs of the first and second level are satisfied, only then does Maslow see the human being as focusing on the happiness factors such as developing friendship, love relationship, and building up a sense of affiliation by being concerned with social interaction. At that point, the individual becomes concerned with self-esteem and gaining esteem from others. The final motivational pinnacle is self-actualization, which is a need to reach full potential through maximum use of skills and abilities (Redmond & Tragger, 1998). In general, one can't be concerned with anything except rudimentary survival, until survival is ensured.

The theory of hierarchy of needs, in fact, provides a springboard for the analysis of the predicament of the rural youth, who have flooded Tanzanian urban centers to better their lives. This proposition of hierarchy of needs seems real in Tanzania in that the youth in urban centers who lack knowledge and skills are left with no opportunities to better their standards of living. As a result, youth are now using unconventional ways such as crime to support their livelihood in urban centers. One of the major reasons for this trend appears to suggest that the educational system, under the one-party rule, failed to adequately prepare rural poor majority youth to acquire quality higher education that would have given them the advantage of pursuing a better productive life.

The disparity of achieving higher education between fortunate youth and the unfortunate poor majority youth is widespread in Tanzania. As one of the key variables to enhance development and modernization in Tanzania, education must be given a high priority to, enable youth to receive equal opportunity in pursuing quality higher education that supersedes the idea of just providing 7 years of primary education. This approach, in the end, may not only minimize the social conflict between the "haves" and "have not" in Tanzania, but also would enhance the majority poor youth with analytical and critical thinking skills, enabling them to become planners of moving forward their socioeconomic development programs in the country.

Development Vision 2025 indicates that Tanzania will have an educated and learned society by year 2025. This society will be one that embraces empowerment, creativity, innovation, and entrepreneurship. In addition, Vision 2025 anticipates that Tanzania will have graduated from a least developed nation to a middle-income country by the year 2025. While this vision appears optimistic, it fails to show how the poor majority youth can secure resources to allow them to attain higher education, which will enable them to compete nationally and globally on the issues of development. To this end, education in Tanzania needs to be redefined by taking a broader view, which incorporates a plan to provide quality higher education to the poor majority youth. This approach appears not only focused on minimizing the social conflict between the "haves" and "have-nots," but it will also help Tanzania to achieve its goals as outlined in Development Vision 2025.

Indeed, in its 2000 report on "Poverty Reduction Strategy Paper" (PRSP), the government seems to acknowledge that the majority youth from poor families are more likely to be less educated. The report indicates that illiteracy among the poor increased, while the school enrollment rates among the poor majority children ages 7 to 9 decreased from 82 percent in1983 to 80 percent in1993. In response, the government came forth with suggestions of how to address the declining number of youth enrolling in schools. It suggested to raise primary enrollment to 85 percent and to increase the transition rate to secondary school from 15 to 21 percent. While these suggestions are worthy undertakings, the thrust must also include a plan which would give opportunities to poor majority youth to pursue education beyond secondary school. The task of creating opportunities for the poor majority youth to acquire higher education should not rest only on government's shoulders, but also on all societal institutions. This collective effort in trying to provide higher quality education to poor youth is necessary for advancing development and achieving the goals of Development Vision 2025 in Tanzania.

It seems rational to suggest that, in order to realize the objectives of Development Vision 2025, Tanzanian society needs to convene a proposed "National Youth Conference on Education" to outline concrete strategies of how to advance a national agenda by providing quality education to poor majority youth. Since this is a societal issue, institutions such as the government, private businesses, NGO's and others can work together to convene a forum that would offer meaningful dialogue to deliberate ways in which high educational opportunities can be accessible to poor majority youth in Tanzania.

The proposal for enhancing higher educational opportunities, for example, may include a plan to establish a "National Fund Program" that offers scholarships in a form of grants or loans to less fortunate poor majority youth, who are academically sound, but can not continue to pursue higher education because of they lack financial resources. In addition, the national fund may be used to expand vocational training centers, which would provide knowledge and various trade skills required in the market labor force. After successfully completing higher education, the youth can repay the loan in various ways, such as working for specific hours in community projects or paying a certain amount of money from their salaries when they secure employment.

The suggested National Youth Conference on Education is, indeed, characterized by the concept of communication, which offers an interactional communication process for critically debating and finally arriving at an acceptable decision about how to help the poor majority acquire higher quality education. This suggested National Youth Conference on Education has a theoretical link to systems theory of communication, which originated from the biological general systems theory. Developed by Von Bentalanffy (1962), general systems theory suggests that if interdependent units are connected, they form a coherent whole. If the system is lacking other parts, then it is incomplete. As a system, if the National Youth Conference on Education is to succeed in creating policies, which will ensure that poor majority youth receive higher quality education, then independent societal institutions must participate in educational policy deliberations that are aimed at realizing the goals of Development Vision 2025 in Tanzania. This collective participation in a two-way communication process is democratic in that it makes the system coherent and capable of arriving at fair decisions about education for the youth in the country.

To enhance Development Vision 2025, hiring qualified teachers, instructors, or professors and to be able to retain them is quite a crucial task that needs careful planning. As efforts are being made collectively to provide quality higher education to poor majority youth, educators must be motivated by receiving competitive pay, good benefits, and other incentives as a mechanism of making them stay on their teaching job. Given the opportunity to be treated fairly, Tanzanian educators can help to mold the poor majority youth to become productive in advancing development in the country.

Fairness is central to making educators in Tanzania help in the task of spearheading development in the country. It seems obvious that when educators do not believe that things are equitable, by nature, they will move to restore the balance by decreasing, for example, their work performance in schools. This analysis about work performance is related to equity theory in which the basic assumption about it is that workers compare their tasks and rewards with the tasks and rewards of workers around them. They then develop perceptions based on that comparison of whether they are fairly treated (Redmond and Tragger, 1998). Based on this theory, it seems reasonable to suggest that if educators in Tanzania find out that there is inequity in their workplace, they may withdraw their best performance of educating the youth. It is, therefore, important for the authorities to see that inequity among educators is dealt with effectively in order to deter the declining work performance. Indeed, deterrence to stop the decline of work performance among educators is necessary if the Tanzania is to produce an educated and learned society that is capable of competing globally in advancing development.

Communication literature explains that individuals are agents of development in their communities and in a nation as a whole. This proposition seems to have evolved and worked successfully in the Western world were individuals had the freedom to pursue their own development and some became wealthy. This theory of development was altered in Tanzania, where the government, under the one-party rule, became the agent of development in the Ujamaa program. Modern development in Tanzania requires individuals to acquire skills and knowledge in order to effectively share and exchange information about their development. In this perspective, communication, once again, is seen as central to the task of advancing development.

Development communication, as explained by Moemeka (1989), is an art and science of human communication applied to the speedy transformation of a country and the masses into economic growth, modernization, and industrialization. In exchanging ideas or information development, communication per se, is seen as an interactive process, which works in a circular, dynamic and an ongoing way. Indeed, as an art and science, the interactive human communication played a significant role in formulating Development Vision 2025, aimed at lifting the standard of living in Tanzania. The new development plan was created in an atmosphere, which embraced democratic values in that various societal groups were able to freely communicate their ideas about development in Tanzania.

As a component of communication development, the access to higher educational opportunities for the poor majority youth is quite important in trying to reduce the 75 percent of Tanzanians who live in poverty, spending less than one euro a day. Sociological studies have documented that poverty breed poverty; and as results, it creates an endless family poverty circle. In this circle, poverty may persist generation after generation because individuals tend to lack educational opportunities necessary to help them shape knowledge and skills to better their lives.

Being in poverty circle is not necessarily the result of laziness and personal failure; it could be a failure of the system to adequately address the factors that perpetually hinder poor families to move out of the poverty circle. One of the major factors which may seem to gradually break down the walls of poverty in Tanzania is to come up with a well calculated effort that offers opportunities to poor majority youth to receive quality higher education as a significant variable required to enhance development. Indeed, this proposition is a crucial factor for minimizing social conflict between the "haves" and "have-nots" in Tanzania--a class phenomenon that has emerged rapidly in the country, after the reintroduction of democratic rule in 1992.

Conclusion

The classification that has emerged between the "haves" and "have-nots" after the return of multiparty democracy poses as one of the major social conflicts that threaten economic and political instability in Tanzania. This classification, which was nonexistent, during Nyerere's one-party rule, is now vivid exposing unequal patterns of social life between the rich and poor. Tanzania is now witnessing a trend of individuals, who tend to identify themselves within the groups of "have" and "have-nots" in terms, for example, where people send their children to school, places where people live or socialize.

Investing in education, especially for the poor majority youth in Tanzania, will create a backbone for improving the country's economy; and thereby, reduce poverty among individuals. The basic faith in education is based on the assumption that a country, which embraces democratic principles such as Tanzania, requires an educated citizenry so that individuals can participate intelligently in public policies aimed at injecting ideas capable of sustain development issues in the country. Characterized by communication, the suggested proposed National Youth Conference on Education seems to provide a significant platform for participants to develop strategies, which will ensure that educational opportunities are directed more to the disadvantaged majority youth. This strategy may minimize poverty among individuals; and in turn, create an economically and politically stable Tanzania.

The costs of poverty in Tanzania are enormous. Those within the poverty category are most likely to receive inferior education, live in poor housing, be malnourished, and have health problems. Instead of viewing people in poverty as lazy or as criminals, the society, for example in Tanzania, should examine the system, which may have contributed to the conditions of poverty. In their analysis, Eitzen and Zinn (2000) explain that there are two underlying reasons that are linked to poverty. First, most of the poor are impoverished for structural reasons, not personal ones as is commonly believed. That is, the essence of poverty is inequality–in wealth and in educational opportunities. The second reason is important when people take up the possible solution to end poverty–for example, Tanzania needs to give the highest priority in allocating resources for the poor majority youth so that they can acquire quality higher education both in Tanzania and abroad.

Central to the underlying reasons that are linked to poverty is communication. In this perspective, communication ought to be dynamic in creating transparency and accountability between the leaders and the public as they tackle poverty issues. This strategy would most likely create a suitable environment for promoting educational opportunities to youth. Communication is essential in development; and therefore, in order to realize the goals of Development Vision 2025, communication with a feedback channel must be effectively planned. This communication is capable of ensuring participation of societal institutions, which have the responsibility of seeing that the poor majority youth are given opportunities to acquire quality higher education. Providing opportunities for the poor majority youths to acquire higher education is critical not only in eradicating poverty among individuals, but also in minimizing social conflict that has quickly emerged between the "haves" and "have-nots" since the 1992 reintroduction of multiparty democratic rule in Tanzania.

References

Babbie, E. (2001). *The practice of social research.* Belmont, CA: Wadsworth.

Baer, R., Hinkle, S., Smith, K., & Fenton, M. (1980). Reactance as a function of actual versus projected autonomy. *Journal of Personality and Social Psychology.* 38, 416–422.

Bertalanffy, L. (1962).   General systems theory: A critical review. *General_systems theory,* 7, 1-20

Bertsch, G., Clark, R.P., & Wood, D.M. (1986. *Comparing political_system_and policy_in three_worlds.* New York, NY: John Wiley & Sons.

Boas, N. K. (1995). The role of the media in the enactment and implementation of the Arusha Declaration Policy in Tanzania: 1967–1977. Unpublished Doctoral Dissertation. Howard University, Washington, DC.

_____ (2000) Press and politics: The Tanzanian experience. In R.T. M'Bayo, C. Onwumechili, R. N. Nwanko (Eds.). *Press and politics in Africa* (p. 269-284). Lewiston, NY: The Edwin Mellen Press.

Eitzen, D.S., & Zinn, M.B. (2000). *Social problems.* Boston, MA: Allyn & Bacon.

Infante, D.A., Womack, D.F., & Rancer, A.S. (1990). *Building communication theory.* Prospect Heights, IL: Waveland Press, Inc.

McHenry, Jr., D.E. (1979). The struggle for rural socialism in Tanzania. In C.G. Rosberg & T.M.Callaghy (Eds.) Socialism *sub-saharan Africa: A new assessment.* (p41). Berkeley, CA: Institute of International Studies, University of California.

Moemeka, A.A. (1989). Perspectives on development communication. *Africa Media Review.* 3, (3), 1-14.

Myers, D.G. (2000). *Exploring social psychology.* New York, NY: McGraw-Hill Co.

Redmond, J., & Tragger, R. (1998). *Balancing on the wire the art of managing media organization.* Boulder, CO: Coursewise Publishing Co.

Chapter 17

Negotiating the Thorny Road of Conflict as Nigeria opens its Communications Market to Private Interests

Chuka Onwumechili, Ph.D.
Bowie State University, USA

Conflict discourse on Africa has narrowly focused on national and international wars. The communication aspects usually investigate issues of war prevention, dialogue, and peace. At times, the discourse has included media culpability as in the case of the Rwandan genocide. The justification for this, in most cases, has been based on the frequency of wars and the adverse effects of wars on a large number of Africans.

However, it is clear that there are other types of conflicts in Africa that are worthy of attention. Over the last few decades, the continent has been in the midst of major economic transition with potential for a lasting impact. This transition has involved conflicts between the introductions of a liberal market system and the resistance to that system by existing government monopolies. Communication systems have been at the center of this economic conflict in several states. Nigeria is one of these states where the conflict flared and a protracted negotiation towards a successful solution continues to take place.

This chapter focuses on the discussion of the Nigerian case focusing particular attention on telephony and broadcasting. It begins with a description of the conflict background and the beginnings of negotiation. It also discusses periodic solutions that mark the negotiations. Furthermore, it describes the simmering struggles, in spite of the periodic solutions, as well as the various arenas of on-going negotiations.

Background

The Nigerian communications industry was monopolized by the state except in the print sector where private interests were allowed to exist. The state had tight control of the broadcast and telecommunications sectors from the period of Nigeria's political independence in 1960. The state justified its control by citing state security concerns and its need to control the media agenda and focus it on the important goal of national development. In addition, the state's relationship with the communications media followed the structure previously developed and maintained by the colonial government.

The colonial government had controlled both telephony and the broadcast media but left the print sector competitive while using the laws of sedition and libel to check any print media excesses. The government also argued that it needed to control the broadcast media, particularly radio, which was effective in mobilizing both the literate and illiterate masses. Media Rights Agenda (2001) noted an additional goal of the government which was to secure radio in order to make it difficult for coup makers to seize it during crises and to prevent its use by opponents and critics to attack the government.

However, while control was justifiable for quite some time, it was increasingly challenged from several quarters, particularly after industry upheavals in Europe. First, the business class began to pressure the government to open access to the communications market. The business class believed that broadcast and telephony provided sources of profits and they sought to capitalize on opportunities in a liberalized market (Onwumechili, 1996; Ajia, 1994). Second, the citizen elite, tired of the boring fare of local programming, began to seek alternative programming from foreign sources. These two challenges led to a conflict with the government. It is also important to note the role of international financial institutions that intensely pressured the government into concessions. We will elaborate on each of these key issues in the next section.

Monopoly and Liberalization

The struggle between the dialectic of government monopoly and market liberalization exploded into the open following the widespread ideological upheavals in Europe and the emerging structural changes in the global communications industry. In a sense, the adoption of a capitalist economy meant the liberalization of markets including those of communications. East Europe had begun to change ideologically from communism to capitalist structures following the uprising and demonstrations from its frustrated and economically de-prived citizens (McGrath, 2002; Prowe, 1998). From the late 1970s to the early 1980s, the transitions took place in several countries like Poland, Romania, Cze-choslovakia, among other states. In the Soviet Union, the union broke into sepa-rate independent states and the formerly separated Germany broke down a his-toric wall to merge into a single capitalist state (Prowe, 1998). These historical events were keenly watched and it had become clear that the age-old struggle for dominance between communism and capitalism had been firmly resolved in favor of the latter. The effect became central in the internal conflict in Nigeria's communications sector.

The international crisis of ideology was not the only harbinger of change for Nigeria. At about the same time, new communications technologies and new industry thinking had begun to also revolutionize communications technologies worldwide. For instance, the rise of MCI in the United States and its successful supply of effective and efficient transmission of business data for private inter-ests between St. Louis and Chicago eventually led to the break up of AT & T monopoly. In the broadcast arena, the spread of communications satellite servic-es led to the creation of super stations such as TNT and WGN which produced a variety of programming and uplinked them to cable stations in the United States leading to the first nationwide challenge to network television. In Britain, the government moved quickly to allow Mercury into the market to compete with British Telecommunications (BT), effectively moving from a monopoly to a duopoly (Bartle, 2002; Waverman & Sirel, 1997; Sandholtz, 1993).

These market reforms in the global communications industry also spread to Africa. Ghana and Burkina Faso, for instance, were some of the early nations to institute a communications reform and move towards allowing private interests to compete (Onwumechili, 1996; Gross, 1995). In none of those markets was the struggle towards a reform an easy process. Nigeria provides a classic example of the conflict, the negotiations that follow and then a move towards a solution. Ultimately, the new technologies created more options for consumers and en-couraged market liberalization.

Conflict in Nigeria's Communications Sector

In Nigeria, both developments in ideology and new technologies created conflicts with the existing status-quo in the communications field (Onwumechili and Uzomah, 2007). As we noted earlier, the international tilt towards liberaliza-tion had energized and emboldened the business class in Nigeria to press for state concessions in the local communications industry. Onwumechili (1996), Ogundimu (1996), and Ajia (1994) have all noted the pressure for change that came from the industry professionals, journalists, and the business class. This directly pitted them against the ruling military class. The situation was both dire and problematic for the ruling military class. The class continued to believe in the tight control of communications but this position was increasingly tenuous as the Nigerian elite began to access foreign programming from new satellite technologies that the military could not control. Not only were these programs accessible, the business class began to re-sell them in videotapes to the middle and lower class who could not afford satellite dish antennas. At one stage, an exasperated Minister of Information threatened to arrest and jail anyone caught downlinking programs through satellite dish antennas (Akwule, 1992). However, there were thousands of homes with such antennas in the early 1990s in the major cities such as Kano and Lagos (Bourgault, 1995; Panos, 1993). Of course, the government and the ruling military class sought desperately to maintain the status quo for several reasons including security and blocking the opposition from access to the broadcast media.

Another conflict existed but this time between the government and international financial institutions. Nigeria was experiencing monumental economic hardship. The country had accumulated a large debt which would eventually balloon to over $30 billion (The World Bank, 1994). The way out appeared to be further borrowing from financial institutions in order to assuage the needs of the masses. However, the international financial institutions such as the International Monetary Fund (IMF) and the World Bank were not confident about Nigeria's abilities to pay back the loans or the country's motivation to stem the economic crises. Therefore, the institutions balked and instead they instituted several conditions (Faruqee, 1994). The conditions included the introduction of a structural adjustment program (SAP) which included plans for the removal of state subsidies, state divestment, privatization, devaluation, and trade liberalization (Okome, undated; Obansa, 2005). The divestment condition included a removal of government interest from public services. One of the key areas where Nigeria needed to divest was the huge communications service area. Onwumechili (2003) points out that the World Bank had suspended a 1990 loan of $225 million for telecommunications in Nigeria and requested reforms in the industry. However, SAP adversely affected the poor. Additionally, such a situation was difficult to sustain because of the massive unrest that followed and the potential of toppling the government.

The Negotiations

The resolution of the conflicts followed a negotiated process. Earlier, the conflict had appeared stalemated in the domestic front for several reasons: (1) the government's failure to back its threat up with adverse action against violators, and (2) the government's apparent view that the global crises of ideology and the impact of the technological development were fads which would eventually go away.

There were issues that came to the fore during the negotiation period. For instance, it became clear that the elite group was not monolithic and there existed a variety of interests within the group. One of these subgroups did not seek to satisfy any business interest. Instead, it sought to satisfy its own entertainment interest. This was the subgroup that sought alternative programming from the usual dour fare provided by the government owned broadcast media. The second subgroup was mainly the business elite whose interest was largely rooted in the quest for new markets and profits. While this group secretly pressured the government to open the communications markets to competition, it gradually forced openings in other areas. For instance, the group took advantage of an exception in the law which allowed the Nigerian National Petroleum Corporation (NNPC) to provide its own communications network. This strategic move by this class allowed the local financial institutions to quickly develop and operate their own communication networks using VSAT systems and, thus, bypasses the national provider, Nigerian Telecommunications Limited (NITEL). The government was cornered and had been put on its back heels.

On the international front, the government chose to thread very carefully and for good reasons. It was clear that intransigence on its part could lead to its own demise amid public unrest and protests against the economic climate. Therefore, the government encouraged public and media debate as a way of seeking a possible solution to the challenging conditions provided by the international financial organizations. The debate by scholars and journalists were invariably informative but the government continued to be intensely concerned about its own ability to self preserve. The public showed that it had become addicted to the government's provision of public services and was prepared to resist any withdrawal of such services.

It was clear from the above developments that the conflicts between the government and the elite class on the one hand, and between the government and the international financial institutions on the other had reached a head and the quiet negotiation that had set in was either going to end with an acceptable agreement among all parties or it could dissipate into a full blown conflict with possibilities of an anarchy where no regulation was adequate to oversee the market on the domestic front or a toppling of the government.

The Deals and the Control of Conflict

Eventually, deals were reached to douse the conflicts (See Figure 1). One, the government issued two decrees in 1992 as an accommodation strategy that profoundly did the trick. The first was the Decree No. 75 which established the

NCC and second was Decree No. 38[1] which established the NBC. Second, the government moved to respond to the demands of the international financial institutions. Below we discuss both decrees No. 75 and No. 38 before focusing our attention on the response to the international financial institutions.

The NCC Decree

The NCC decree invariably settled the increasing conflict between who had the rights to provide telephone and telecommunications services in the country. As we noted above, these rights had belonged to the nation's public monopoly – the Nigerian Telecommunications Limited (NITEL) but it was increasingly infringed by the private interests who sought and obtained exceptions that allowed the NNPC as well as some financial institutions to provide their own network services.

The decree established the NCC as the market regulator and then opened the market to private competition. Ajayi, Salawu, and Raji (1999) note that the decree requires the NCC to do the following:

1. Licensing telecommunications operators
2. Overseeing quality of service provided by the operators
3. Setting terms for network interconnection

The decree opened the market to private competitors but the establishment of the NCC introduced regulatory oversight that was now far more coordinated with the use of licensing requirements. In addition, the government retained control of NITEL, at the same time, granting it advantages such as free GSM license for which its competitors had paid close to $300 million each. Then it reserved the national fixed telephony service for NITEL and only allowed a second national operator (SNO) in 2003, more than a decade after Decree No. 75 was initially promulgated.

---

[1] Decree No. 38 was later amended by Decree No. 55 of 1999 which introduced stricter control of the NBC by the government. Decree No. 55 added a member of the Ministry of Information and another from the State Security on the regulatory Commission.

Figure 1: Modeling the Conflict Issues

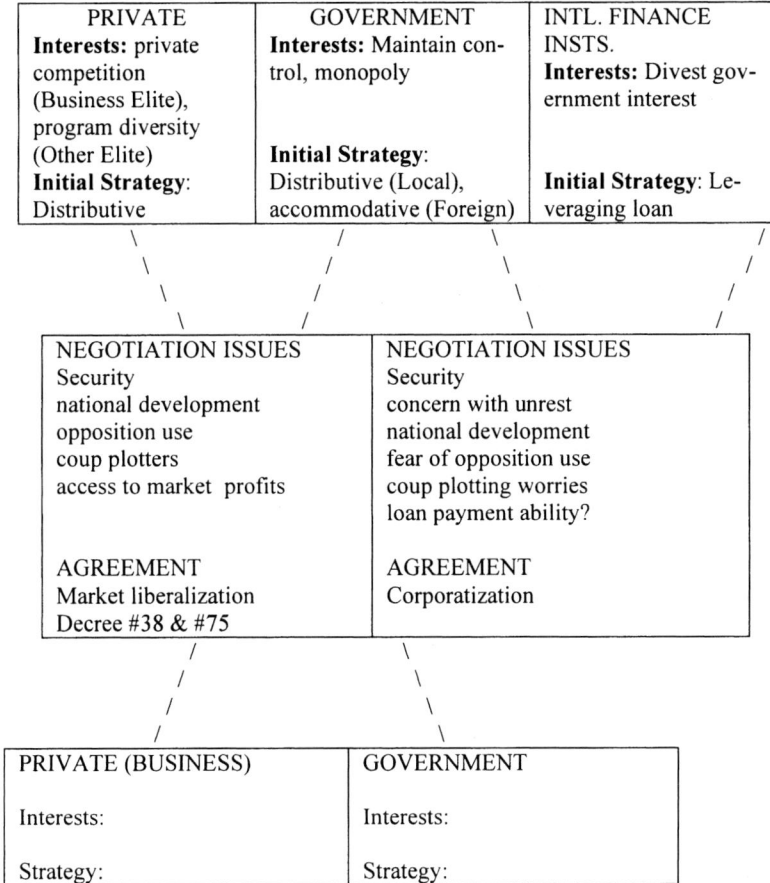

PRIVATE **Interests:** private competition (Business Elite), program diversity (Other Elite) **Initial Strategy:** Distributive	GOVERNMENT **Interests:** Maintain control, monopoly **Initial Strategy:** Distributive (Local), accommodative (Foreign)	INTL. FINANCE INSTS. **Interests:** Divest government interest **Initial Strategy**: Leveraging loan

NEGOTIATION ISSUES Security national development opposition use coup plotters access to market profits AGREEMENT Market liberalization Decree #38 & #75	NEGOTIATION ISSUES Security concern with unrest national development fear of opposition use coup plotting worries loan payment ability? AGREEMENT Corporatization

PRIVATE (BUSINESS) Interests: Strategy:	GOVERNMENT Interests: Strategy:

NBC Decree

As noted earlier, the conflict in the broadcast sector was even more marked. There were no earlier concessions provided to private or business interests in the guise of exceptions such as was provided to the NNPC and financial institutions in the case of telephone and data transmission. In lieu of concessions, an un-coordinated group of private interests responded by: (1) illegally accessing for-eign programming and (2) videotaping such programming and reselling them for profit. The government, in spite of issuing threats, failed to control these activi-ties which it considered "unsavory."

The government eventually accommodated this group with the enactment of the Nigerian Broadcast Commission (NBC) Decree No. 38. The decree was a tacit concession to pressures from private interests. The decree, for the first time, made it legal for private ownership of broadcast stations in the country. In fact, the concessions were far reaching. For instance, it also allowed the establish-ment of wireless cable systems which were allowed to redistribute foreign pro-gramming to meet the entertainment interests of the private elite who earlier had illegally accessed such programming. However, it provided these concessions with the hope that its simultaneous establishment of the NBC as the market reg-ulator would ultimately assure the protection of government interests. These interests included protection against subversive programming and the assurance that local content was reflected in the broadcast services. For instance, the NBC established a minimum percentage of programming that must reflect local con-tent for both providers of regular television broadcasting and wireless cable.

Importantly, the NBC assured the government of the continued control of the national airwaves by not licensing a nationwide provider of radio broadcast-ing. In essence, the Federal Radio Corporation of Nigeria (FRCN) and the Nige-rian Television Authority (NTA), which remained government-owned stations, continued to hold sway at the national level. Licenses to private providers were limited to local and regional levels. This act was important particularly in the case of radio, which remains the most accessible medium in the country because its reach stretches into the rural areas where other mass media are largely non-existent.

The Deal with the International Financial Institutions

The government did not immediately move to divest complete state interest in telecommunications nor did it allow private interest. Instead, it first sought to use corporatization strategies as a midway move to satisfy the wishes of the in-ternational financial institutions while maintaining control of the public services. This compromise strategy appeared to meet the request of the international fi-nancial institutions. The government was no longer going to fund national broadcasting and telecommunications as demanded by the institutions but it continued to control both broadcasting and telecommunications.

Ongoing Conflict and Negotiations

The two military decrees establishing both the NCC and the NBC as regulators of parts of the communications sector clearly brought order to the sector and served as settlement of the conflicts within the sector. However, the settlement was far from permanent. Instead, as later events demonstrated, the conflict emerged as dynamic. In essence, the decrees served as the framework through which conflict could be ameliorated, not entirely solved, and there indeed continue to be room to repair the regulatory system in order to have a better chance of managing conflict.

One critical reason for the emerging conflict was that the government provided concessions on the one hand with the decrees, but sought to abridge the same concessions with the other hand. Obviously, the government found itself in a process of hesitation which was to be interpreted as deliberate.

The government's denial of full concession was assured because both the NBC and the NCC were not fully independent by law. Each commission had its top management serving under the pleasure of the President and the commissions were agencies of the government's Ministry of Information. Below we discuss some of these conflicts by separating them into two major categories: (a) conflicts in the telecommunications sector, and (b) conflicts in the broadcast sector.

Telecommunications Sector

There are three major flashes of conflict within the telecommunications sector. These are focused on electric power generation, fair competition, and loan facilities. The government is directly involved in the negotiations for the first two and has made an important an important concession on the third.

Electric power generation is a key issue as this is virtually absent in the rural areas where many potential consumers of communications services are resident. The private providers of telephone services, for instance, have repeatedly urged the government to speed up the process of providing electricity access beyond the urban areas and to assure reliable electricity service within the urban areas. Private providers are already forced to install two standby generators for every telephone switch in the urban centers where power is irregular and they are concerned about having to expend a huge outlay of funds in the rural areas where power is nonexistent. The government has acknowledged the problem but has been slow to act. Notably, in late 2005 the government signed into law the

EPSR Act as way to reform electricity service but this is yet to make a significant impact (Ikeonu, undated).

Fair competition has been another major issue and it has risen to the fore with the government's announced sale of NITEL to a group of investors under the name Transnational Corporation (Transcorp) Plc. Private competitors are concerned because several of these investors are associated with the government. In fact, only recently the President's Trust Fund, Obasanjo Holdings, was forced to denounce 200 million shares in the company when its investment became public. Obviously, private competitors are not certain that the NCC can maintain independence and fairness in disputes that may involve Transcorp. Moreover, the NCC, for a long period, was slow to act when NITEL (then fully owned by the government) failed to provide interconnection facilities to private competitors in the telephone market.

The conflict related to loans is essentially one between the telecommunications companies and the financial institutions. One aspect of the conflict is poor access to loans and the other is the inconvenient loan terms. Often the capital required to operate large communications companies is huge and difficult for several Nigerian banks to provide. For instance, the cost of GSM licensing was $300 million each. This has forced several of these companies to seek loans from foreign banking conglomerates. However, it is more difficult to secure foreign loans without heavily capitalized foreign partners. In any case, the recent consolidation of banking institutions in Nigeria may help solve this problem[2] (Okagbue & Aliko, 2004). Additionally, while short term development for telecommunications companies is pegged at 24 months and long term at 60 months, financial institutions typically provide six months term for short term loans and 36 months for long term (Ojo, Ekwealor, Amah, and Okwuke, 2005). This conflict in the definition of terms has inconvenienced and complicated planning for the telecommunications companies.

Broadcast Sector

Conflict in the broadcast sector is numerous but we will discuss a few of them in this section. The conflicts surround the points listed below:

1. Disparity in license fees for private and government-owned systems
2. Unfair regulation of the industry
3. Transparency in the licensing process
4. Requirements for local content
5. Freedom of broadcast

---

[2] The Central Bank Governor, Mr. Soludo, ordered banks to be capitalized at N25 billion ($190 million) each by December 2005 or face dissolution.

Each of the above issues is vigorously contested. For instance, the NBC provisions had created a different licensing fee for government stations of $500 and from $15,000 to $30,000 for private stations in the urban areas. Note that these fees also apply to poorly funded and small community stations (e.g. college stations) in the urban areas. Unfortunately, privately owned stations have to compete for the same advertisement funds with government stations and yet they are not allowed to broadcast to the entire nation as the government-owned stations are. This has made it difficult for private stations to stay financially afloat. Consequently, as many as 19 radio and television stations had their licenses revoked for nonpayment in October 1999[3] (Media Rights Agenda, 2001).

In addition, private stations, through the Independent Broadcasting Association of Nigeria (IBAN), have continued to voice opposition to unfair decisions made by the supposedly independent NBC. Among their concerns was a celebrated case in 2000 when the NBC barred Channels Television from retransmitting the European Soccer Championship (Euro2000) programming from TVAfrica following a protest by the government-owned NTA which had failed to secure the same rights from TVAfrica. NBC claimed that TVAfrica, a South African station, was not licensed in Nigeria and thus its programming could not be transmitted in Nigeria. Yet, NBC did nothing about the NTA, which was retransmitting music from South African based Channel O to Nigeria. Channel O was not licensed in Nigeria. In any case, there is no where in Decree No. 38 or its amendment in Decree No. 55 where a foreign producer is required to register in Nigeria before its program can be transmitted in Nigeria.

Transparency in the broadcast licensing process has also been a source of conflict for quite some time. To be correct, the NBC allows a transparent process, including a public hearing prior to license renewals. However, no such process is available before the initial licensing. Instead, the initial licensing process is shrouded in mystery and private interests are convinced that this is intentionally designed to present advantages to those who are pro-government and to deny those who are not. After all, the NBC is limited by law to make recommendations to the President who can ultimately deny licensing.

Providers are also unhappy about the requirements for including local content in their programming. The current rule is 20% and 60% local content in cable television and terrestrial television respectively (Questech Media, 2004). However, it has been very difficult and expensive for private stations to meet this requirement. It is much cheaper to use foreign programs than to produce local ones. Questech Media (2004) reports that it costs about $500 per hour to purchase a foreign soap and $5,000 an hour to produce a local one. However,

---

[3] These stations owed NBC $720,000 license fees in arrears.

the NBC and the Nigerian government are adamant about this provision. They insist that stations broadcasting in Nigeria and to Nigerians must meet the requirement to reflect local content in their programs. Several stations have violated this provision and the NBC has acted to punish such violators. In any case, Nigerian television stations have increasingly made accommodations here by increasing their local content by 45% between 1994 and 2002 (Questech Media, 2004) and the over $230 million local movie industry has encouraged a wireless cable channel (M-NET) to establish the African Magic Channel to show African movies. The conflict on local content continues to exist and negotiations about the required percentage of such content are ongoing.

Freedom to broadcast in Nigeria has been studied by several scholars (Ogbondah, 2003; Onwumechili and Nwokeafor, 2000; and Ekwelie, 1979). There is a litany of arrests, manhandling, and detention of broadcast journalists as well as broadcast station closures that are all related to the struggle for journalists to broadcast freely and the government's intent to curtail such freedom. Media Rights Agenda (2001) points out that the 1999 amendment Decree No. 55 was designed by the then Minister of Information, Chief Nwodo, to increase government's control over the NBC. More adverse was the government's direct use of the State Security Service (SSS) to intimidate private broadcasters whom it deemed a "security risk." In most cases, "security risk" was loosely defined and included broadcasting programs that highlighted government malfeasance but had little or nothing to do with explicit attempts to instigate an overthrow of the government. The SSS not only forcefully closed an erring station, but it also arrested the station's broadcasters and management personnel. In some cases, the NBC was active in station closings citing one reason or the other. Other incidences include the NBC's partial shutdown of Freedom Radio in Kano in 2006 because it broadcast anti-third term programs, the shutdown of Glory FM of Yenagoa in 2005 for its support of Governor Dipreye Alamieyeseigha who was embroiled in a corruption fight with a government agency and in October 2005 the NBC forced the African Independent Television (AIT) off the air for daring to report the crash location of Bellview Airline (Ajani, Amaizi, Ehigiator, and Oyadongha, 2005; and Nwadiogbu and Taidi, 2006). Prior to the liberalization of the broadcast industry, conflict was rare between broadcasters and the government. Instead, the struggle had been concentrated in the print journalism area where private ownership of newspapers and magazines existed. However, liberalization extended private ownership to the broadcast area and a fierce conflict has been extended to the broadcast sector.

Conclusion

The ascendance of global conflicts is not only situated in international wars, ethnic and class strife, or similar events. Conflict is more widespread and includes ideological, technological, and industry upheavals. These conflicts have been played out in Africa as well, and the Nigerian case demonstrates this. The communications sector in Nigeria is one of such area where the conflict between monopolization and liberalization came to the fore. It involved conflicts between the government and private interests on one hand, and government and international financial institutions on the other. In the end, private interest forced concessions from the government, while the government (using corporatization) compromised with the international financial institutions.

It also demonstrates how the government used various negotiation strategies including accommodation and compromise options to seek solutions. Distributive or competitive strategies were also used. However, conflicts are dynamic and in the Nigerian case they have emerged in new forms. These forms include those that have persisted and modified over time and others that have emerged from the decrees which had been promulgated to deal with the conflicts in the first place.

In conclusion, this chapter has attempted to provide a succinct history of the conflicts in the Nigerian communications sector. It is a way to remind us of how global ideological and technological changes have impacted Nigeria's communications sector and how ongoing conflicts are leading to further negotiations within the sector.

References

Akwule, R. (1992). *Global telecommunication: The technology, administration, and politics.* Boston: Focal Press.

Ajani, J, E. Amaizi, K. Ehigiator, & S. Oyadongha. (2005, Dec. 1). Bayelsa radio shut. (Available online). *Http://www. Cpj.org/news.*

Ajayi, G., R. Salawu, and T. Raji. (1999). Nigeria: After a century of telecommunications, what next? In E. Noam (Ed.), *Telecommunications in Africa* (pp. 163-177). New York: Oxford University Press.

Ajia, O. (1994). Deregulation and the changing landscape of broadcasting in Nigeria. Paper presented at the ACCE Conference in Accra, Ghana, October 16 – 23.

Bartle, I. (2002). When institutions no longer matter: Reform of telecommunications and electricity in Germany, France, and Britain. *Journal of Public Policy, 22,* 1-27.

Bourgault, L. (1995). Nigeria. In L. Gross (Ed.), *The international world of electronic media* (pp. 233-252). New York: McGraw-Hill.

Ekwelie, S. (1979). The beginnings of self-censorship in Nigeria's press and mass media. Gazette, 22(3), 219-232.

Faruqee, R. (1994). Nigeria: Ownership abandoned. In I. Husain and R. Faruqee (Eds.), *Adjustment in Africa: Lessons from country case studies* (pp. 238-285). Washington, DC: The World Bank.

Gross, L. (1995). Overview of Africa. In L. Gross (Ed.), *The international world of electronic media* (pp. 224-231). New York: McGraw-Hill.

Ikeonu, I. (undated). The Nigerian Electric Power Sector Reform: Establishing an effective licensing framework as a tool for attracting investment. (Available online). *Http:// www. ip3.org/pub/*

McGrath, T. (2002). From communism to capitalism: Liberalization, learning, and the long road. *International Studies Review, 4(3)*, 167.

Media Rights Agenda. (2001, February). *Broadcasting in Nigeria: Unlocking the airwaves (A report on the framework for broadcasting and telecommunications in Nigeria).* London, UK: Lancaster House.

National Broadcasting Commission (NBC) Decree. (1992). *Decree No. 38 (24th August, 1992). Supplement to the Official Gazette Extraordinary No.33, Vol. 79, 4th September 1992 – Part A.* Lagos, Nigeria: The Ministry of Information and Culture Printing Division.

Nwadiogbu, A., and Taidi, Y. (2006, June 16). Again, security agents storm AIT: Arrest presenter Gbenga Aruleba. (Available online). *Http:// www. Newage.com/*

Obansa, S. (2005). Impact of the Structural Adjustment Program (SAP) on Nigeria's economy. Africa Update, XII (2). (Available online). *Http:// www. ccsu.edu/ Afstudy/*

Ogbondah, C. (2003). State-press relations in Nigeria (1993-1998): *Human rights and democratic development.* Ibadan, Nigeria: Spectrum Books Limited.

Ogundimu, F. (1996). Private enterprise broadcasting and accelerating dependency: Case studies from Nigeria and Uganda. Paper presented at the AEJMC Convention in Anaheim, CA, August 10-13.

Ojo, A., O. Ekwealor, Amah, J. and Okwuke, E. (2005, January 1). Telecommunications: The past is another country. (Available online). *Http:// www. Newage.com.*

Okagbue, S. and Aliko, T. (2004, December 10). Banking sector reform in Nigeria. *International Legal News: An International Lawyers Network Publication, 1(2).*

Okome, M. (undated). The politics of implementing the Structural Adjustment Program (SAP) in Nigeria. (Available online). *Http: // www. africaresource.com/*

Onwumechili, C. (2003). *Reform, organizational players, and technological developments in African telecommunications: An update.* New York: Edwin Mellen Press.

_____ (1996). Privatization of the electronic media in Nigeria. The *Howard Journal of Communications, 7(4)*, 365 – 372.

Onwumechili, C. and C. Nwokeafor. (2000). Predicting Nigerian mass media in a democratic era: An escape from Pandora's box. In R. M'Bayo, C. Onwumechili, and R. Nwanko (Eds.), *Press and politics in Africa* (pp. 185-205). Lewiston, NY: The Edwin Mellen Press.

Onwumechili, C. and Uzomah, U. (2007). Evaluating the regulation of the Nigerian broadcasting industry: Are expectations being met? Paper presented at the Eastern Communication Association (ECA) Conference in Providence, Rhode Island, April 25 – 29.

Panos Institute. (1993). *Radio pluralism in West Africa: Burkina Faso, Gambia, Mali, Senegal, Sierra Leone, Nigeria, Ghana.* Paris: Institut Panos.

Prowe, D. (1998). Dissolution: The crisis of communism and the end of East Germany. *The American Historical Review, 103(4)*, 1274 – 1275.

Questech Media Ltd. (2004). *Nigerian broadcast regulations impact analysis.* (Available online). Http:// www. nbc-nig.org/research2.asp/

Sandholtz, W. (1993). Institutions and collective action: The new telecommunications in Western Europe. *World Politics, 45(2),* 242-270.

Waverman, L., and Sirel, E. (1997). European telecommunications markets on the verge of full liberalization. *The Journal of Economic Perspectives, 11(4),* 113-126.

The World Bank. (1994). *World development report: Infrastructure for development.* New York: Oxford University Press.

Chapter 18

Global Communication Media and the Replication of International Conflicts in Northern Nigeria

Ogu Sunny Enemaku, Ph.D.
University Of Lagos, NIGERIA

Introduction

The Gulf war of 1991 marked a watershed in the ability of the media to bring to people in different parts of the world vivid images and sounds of events as they unfold. For several weeks, the U.S.-based Cable News Network (CNN) beamed to the world US-led air attacks on Baghdad, Kuwait and other military targets in the Persian Gulf. This gradually developed into what Peter Arnett, one of CNN's war correspondents in Iraq later described as "the most severe bombing in military history" (CNN, 2001, p. 2) The mission of the allied forces was to force Iraq out of Kuwait. Iraq, under the leadership of Saddam Hussein, had forcibly annexed Kuwait, declaring that country to be a province of Iraq. As the bombardment of Baghdad and Iraqi strongholds in Kuwait continued, Iraq launched its retaliatory scud missiles into Saudi Arabia and Israel, but most of the missiles were intercepted mid air by America's Patriot missiles. Images of these as well as those of Iraqi soldiers, who overwhelmed by the weight of the U.S.-led coalition forces, surrendered en masse were also transmitted clearly. Within a short period, Saddam Hussein, the then Iraqi President, surrendered and the first phase of the Gulf war came to an abrupt, anti-climactic end.

For many media watchers, one of the most significant events in this phase of the war was the exhibition of the power of the media, which as it were, had never been as orchestrated. To Stech (1994, p.1), CNN's coverage of what became known as Gulf War 1 was "…unique and completely redefined live satellite television news". Consequently, as the war progressed, rich people in Nigeria bought satellite dishes to enable them watch the spectacle, and those who did not buy while the war lasted bought, even after the war, to have access to satellite broadcasting stations which beamed news and entertainment programs from different parts of Europe and America. Owning a satellite dish became a status symbol, and such dishes adorned the houses of affluent people in choice areas of Lagos, Abuja, Kano, Ibadan, Enugu, Kaduna, Port Harcourt and other prominent towns and cities across Nigeria.

Another turning point in the manifestation of the power of satellite broadcasting was in October 2001 when the United States and her allies launched an attack on the Taliban government in Afghanistan after the September 11 2001 terrorist attacks on American targets. For Nigerians, perhaps the most remarkable development in this phase was the realization that international conflicts could cause local uprising. Since the United States, perceived to be a Christian nation, was attacking Afghanistan, a Muslim nation, protests against the United States and her allies began in some Asian countries and rapidly spread to northern Nigeria. Starting from October 13, 2001, over a hundred people, mainly non-Muslims in northern Nigeria were killed, while churches and other property belonging to them were razed (Lewis 2002, p.1). This marked the formal beginning of the domestication of such international conflicts in Nigeria, and since then, it has become a fad. As soon as any international 'religious' conflict is transmitted by the media, the next (il)logical step now is to have such conflicts replicated in Nigeria. This chapter examines this negative development with the following questions in mind:

1.   What is the role of the media in the replication of international conflicts in Nigeria?

2.   What factors make it easy for such international conflicts to be replicated in Nigeria?

3.   What can be done to reverse this trend and promote peace and harmony among Nigeria's heterogeneous groups?

The Role of the Media in Society: An Overview

There are various roles expected of the media in the society. According to Folarin (2000, p.102) the earliest functional theories of mass communication derived from a sociological perspective. As far back as 1948, Harrold Lasswell had identified three important roles of the media in society, namely surveillance of the environment (that is, the news function); correlation of parts of the environment (that is, the opinion, editorial or propaganda function) and the cultural transmission function (that is, transmission of cultural heritage from generation to generation). More than a decade later, Charles Wright added the entertainment function.

A look at the correlation function of the global media indicates that they make available to their readers, viewers and listeners (as the case may be) information about what happens in different societies, whether good or bad. The global media have, for a long time, been under persistent attacks for the flaws observed in the way they report events from some societies. For example, the United Nations Educational, Scientific and Cultural Organization (UNESCO), in 1977 set up the MacBride Commission to "...undertake a review of all the problems of communication in contemporary society" following complaints by developing countries about imbalance in information flow between them and the technologically advanced nations as well as perceived negative approach to events in the developing countries. The commission, in its report observed that:

Distortions of news...occur when inaccuracies or untruths replace authentic facts; or when a slanted interpretation is woven into the news reports...through the use of pejorative adjectives and stereotypes. This occurs where events of no real importance are given prominence and when the superficial or the irrelevant are interwoven with facts of real significance (MacBride, 1980, pp.157-158).

Several decades after the foregoing trend was reported, complaints abound that the global media are still replete with such tendencies (Uche, 1996, and Enemaku, 2003). Even from the advanced societies, there are complaints that most media organizations skew news report to align with their nations' interests, especially in times of war. In the words of Hibbard and Keenleyside (1995):

In times of international crisis, it is characteristic of societies to fall in behind their governments and leaders, and for their peoples to adhere, in effect, to the old adage 'my country, right or wrong'. In such circumstances, it is also not unusual for the media of states, whatever their private reservations to lend broad support to the policies of their governments and thus play a role in building societal support for whatever measures their government opt to take to resolve the crisis (p. 2).

If the media which are expected to provide factual, objective and balanced news reports and analyses, especially in times of international crisis, are entrapped by the tendency to lend "broad support" for their states, then international news reports, under such circumstances, cannot be entirely relied upon. Indeed, it may tend to confirm the old assumption that truth is the first victim of war. And if this becomes the trend, why should people continue to patronize the global media, rather than other local news sources, especially in times of such international conflicts?

The correlation function of the media refers to the process whereby the media provide background information and interpretations as well as sample public opinion. This often makes public opinion to gravitate towards a given direction, thereby promoting social harmony. This function is also often interpreted as the propaganda function. At the level of the global media, this role needs to be handled with a great sense of responsibility. Diversity is a hallmark of the international audiences that watch or listen to broadcast programs, and any attempt by global media stations to correlate public opinion in favor of their nations of origin could alienate segments of the audience and spark off accusations of bias, which, on the long run, will neither be in the best interest of the station, nor be in the interest of the journalistic profession.

The CNN and the Qatar-based Arabic station, *Al Jazeera*, have been in the forefront of allegations of being biased in favor of the West and the Arab world respectively (Hibbard and Keenleyside, 1995; Fleischer, 2001; and Carnegie, 2002). As at February 2006, a CNN anchor, Lou Dobbs was being accused of becoming a crusader instead of being a journalist and for allegedly failing to distinguish between news and personal opinion (Bauder, 2006). The business journalist, Dobbs, had doggedly criticized the U.S. government over plans to sell off six U.S. ports to a company from the United Arabs Emirate. As a result of Dobbs' relentless crusade on the matter, the U.S public, including the congress, was attracted and the deal had to be reviewed, but critics said the efforts of Dobbs went beyond the limits of journalism. In reply, Dobbs said he had no regrets doing what he did because the national security of his country was involved, and that he did what his audience expected him to do. The question that arises then is whether a reporter for a global media station should be preoccupied with only the national security of his own country or the global security implications of his position on such an international issue. Another critical question is if the reporter considers the people of the United Arabs Emirate as being part of his audience, or if Americans are the only audience he recognizes.

Transmission of culture, a third function of the media, is very important, especially at the global level, because of the allegations of cultural marginalization which are at the base of the clamor for a new world information and communication order by developing countries (MacBride, 1980; Uche, 1996). While cultural programs from the advanced countries are regularly transmitted to the people of the developing societies, most of the developing societies lack the capacity to get their cultural programs across to the people of the advanced countries. This implies that cultural transmission is skewed against the developing countries. Indeed, in many developing countries, there are concerns over the preponderance of western (especially American) culture, particularly among the youths, and the attendant decline in the popularity of local or indigenous cultural heritage among this category of citizens. The global communication media need to promote balance in the transmission of cultural heritage from the North to the South and vice versa.

Like the other functions of the media in the global context, the entertainment function has come under serious criticism. The main criticism is that western type entertainment which is increasingly becoming popular among the youths of the Third World, lowers public taste and is replete with indecency, pornography, revelry, among others. The supposedly more decent entertainment forms from developing societies, it is alleged, do not enjoy much popularity on global media stations since such stations are largely based in societies that are believed to be more familiar with banal or vulgar forms of entertainment (Uche, 1996).

Although there are other social functions attributed to the media, the foregoing suffices for our present discourse. However, it is necessary to highlight such other functions of the media. These include the agenda setting function by which the media are expected to identify important issues that should form the topic of public discourse at any given time; the economic integration function by which the media are expected to provide economic and business news; the development function, by which the media are expected to promote social development by providing the kind of knowledge required for development and championing the cause of attitudinal and behavioral changes toward patterns that emphasize development in its broadest sense. This is particularly so in developing societies. Many additional roles are ascribed to the media in society. For example, the media are also expected to promote social harmony and global security.

To what extent have the international media performed the foregoing roles in modern society? This is arguable, but if criticism against the global media is anything to go by, then such stations still have along way to go in meeting the needs of the global community, especially the developing societies. It is believed, for example, that the global media privilege entertainment above development because such stations are based in societies where problems of underdevelopment rarely exist. As indicated earlier on, it is also believed that the global media stations privilege the security of their home countries over and above the safety and security of the rest of the world. This last criticism is of critical importance to this paper.

Does the Security of "Other" Societies Matter to the Global Media?

Would the global satellite broadcasting stations transmit programs or carry other messages if they suspect that such would likely inflame passions or cause social upheavals and disruptions in the western world? Would such media houses be so concerned about the security interest of the developing nations that they would persistently draw attention to likely threats as Dobbs did for the United States? If the United States was going to buy ports in the United Arabs Emirate, would the CNN or Dobbs be that concerned as to persistently draw international attention to it? These questions are arguable, but it is likely that the global media stations would desist from or be cautious in transmitting messages or programs that could inflame passions in the West. Such stations and reporter may also not be too concerned if the strategic interests of the west are not in any way imperiled by security issues in other countries. Both Dobbs and the CNN may not be too worried about an impending U.S take over of ports in the United Arabs Emirate, because the Arab State is not as near as the U.S (proximity factor); the Arab state is not as "strategic" as the U.S., and perhaps, the U.A.E. is not as "important" as the United States.

In news coverage, the issues beckoning on the reporter are so many that try as he may, he is usually unable to cover all of them. Moreover, the media is often unable to transmit or cover all stories filed by journalists. Journalists, including the reporters and the editors are trained to use certain key elements in determining which news item should be reported and which should not. It is evident that some of the lapses in global media coverage of events emanate from the application of such criteria of news judgment.

In an era of globalization and technological advancement, the security concern of the global media should not just be that of their immediate locations. Security breaches no longer respect geographical boundaries, and this is reflected in rapid spread of the massive protests which greeted the Muhammad cartoons published in a Danish newspaper in 2006. The ability of the Al Qaeda network, a group of terrorists, largely from developing countries, to hit targets in the U.S, Britain and other advanced countries with precision, also shows that security concerns of the global media need to extend beyond their immediate locations.

Replication of International Conflicts in Nigeria

In October 2001, U.S. troops attacked Afghanistan following the failure of the Taliban government to co-operate with the U.S. in the effort to bring to book the Al Qaeda operatives suspected of having led the September 11, 2001 (9/11) terrorist attacks on targets in the United States. The Al Qaeda network had its main base and training camps in Afghanistan. Most of the suspects in the 9/11 attacks, including the prime suspect and leader of the Al Qaeda network, Osama Bin Laden, were suspected to be hiding in the rugged and seemingly impenetrable mountainous areas around Afghanistan's border with Pakistan. A few days after the U.S military campaign in Afghanistan commenced (precisely on Friday, October 12, 2001) a group of Nigerian Muslims gathered in Kano, in the largely Islamic part of northern Nigeria, to protest the U.S action, displaying images of Osama Bin Laden and praising his heroic *jihad* against American 'infidels' (Lewis, 2002 and Enemaku, 2003). They were addressed by some Muslim leaders who were said to have condemned the attack by the American forces. The character of what had started as a peaceful protest began to change as street urchins, known as 'Almajiri' in local parlance, joined the train. The protest degenerated, as churches were set ablaze and Christians were viciously attacked and killed. At the end of the violence, over a hundred people, mostly Christians, lay dead on the streets of Kano.

Two years later, following long and heated but unsuccessful debates by the UN Security Council, the U.S. and her allies launched military attacks at targets in Iraq with a view to toppling the regime of President Saddam Hussein. The attack was the culmination of several months of face off between the U.S and her allies on one hand, and Iraq on the other. The U.S and her allies accused President Saddam Hussein of having amassed weapons of mass destruction; harboring camps for the training of Al Qaeda terrorists and hosting some of the terrorists incriminated in the 9/11 attacks. Several countries, including some Arab countries had tried to avert a military confrontation by appealing to the Iraqi leader to co-operate with UN weapon inspectors. France and her allies tried to prevent the war by mobilizing international public opinion against the impending military action (Duffy, 2006).Eventually, reason failed and warfare commenced.

No sooner had the attacks on Iraq dubbed by the media as Gulf War II started than Christians in parts of northern Nigeria came under violent attacks from groups of Islamic militants. Although there had been some protests on the streets of a number of Arab countries against the war, what happened in Northern Nigeria was more vicious and more ferocious. Churches and Christians were again attacked, but this time, some Christians, not wanting to be caught unawares, had prepared for the war. In the ensuing street battle, hundreds of Nigerians, including women, children and the aged were killed.

In December 2003, a student-led Islamic sect called *Al Sunna Wal Jamma*, launched an armed uprising with the aim of "setting up a Taliban-style" Muslim state in northern Nigeria (IRIN, 2004). Starting their "campaign" from Kanamma, a town in Yobe State, the insurgents, who had first set up camp near the Nigeria-Niger border, launched an offensive against the police, killing three policemen in Kanamma and the nearby town of Geidam in the process. The Executive Governor of Yobe State, Alhaji Bukar Abba Ibrahim, who had tried previously to peacefully disband the group without success, had no option than to invite the Nigerian Army, seeing that the police had been overwhelmed. At the end of the insurrection, over eighteen people, mostly Islamic militants were killed. Some members of the estimated 200-member group escaped and later regrouped.

The Nigerian "Taliban" had not had enough. Eight months after the showdown with soldiers in Yobe State, sixty members of the group launched a guerrilla-style attack on a police patrol near Gwoza, around Nigeria's border with Cameroon. After 40 hours of confrontation with law enforcement agencies, 28 of them were killed. Speaking with the international press, the group's leader who had taken the cognomen '*Tashen Ilimi,* (meaning new knowledge)' explained that the real name of his group was *Mujahideen* (meaning 'the fighters'), and that the group was only performing its Islamic duty of fighting to overthrow secular government so as to enthrone an Islamic government in Nigeria as the Taliban did in Afghanistan (Goujon and Abubakar, 2006).

In any case, the climax came in February 2006 and it will for a long time remain fresh in the memory of many people across the globe. A Denmark newspaper had published some cartoons of the Prophet Muhammed which many Muslims considered to be offensive. Across the Muslim world, there were anti-Danish protests, but when Nigerian Muslims decided to protest, the northern Christians became the first victims as churches were burnt and Christians were killed in various northern Nigerian cities, starting from Maiduguri and spreading fast to other towns. Unfortunately, Christians in the South Eastern Nigerian commercial city of Onitsha, many of whose relations had been killed in the protests in northern Nigeria, on seeing the corpses of their kinsmen being brought home for burial, launched reprisal attacks on a number of Muslims. By the time the crises died down, hundreds of Nigerians, both Muslims and Christians, had been killed by what was a domestic replication of an international issue.

The scenarios above are not the only instances in which international conflicts have been replicated in Nigeria by misguided elements, but for the present purpose, these will constitute the central focus.

What makes it Possible for International Conflicts to be Replicated in Nigeria?

Nigeria is one country that personifies the African paradox. It is so richly blessed with natural resources, but unresolved national issues, corruption as well as bad and irresponsible political leadership have emasculated and halted Nigeria's rise as a modern nation. Ordinary Nigerians are still among the poorest people on earth, while politicians, the top military hierarchy and others who have benefited from the spoils of office rank among the richest people on the continent. In spite of billions of dollars generated from the country's sale of crude oil, basic infrastructure such as water, roads, healthcare, public transport, and electricity are in shambles, yet former and serving political office holders have built mansions in far away cities such as New York, London, and Paris, in addition to fat bank accounts in Switzerland and other foreign countries. Religion seems to be the only hope of the average Nigerian who is frustrated by poverty and failed promises. Therefore, religious leaders hold an important place in the life of the average Nigerian. Issues that should be handled by civil authorities are taken to religious leaders who are either misguided or who themselves are frustrated by the Nigerian situation. The ordinary Nigerian, therefore, becomes an easy prey in the hands of religious leaders and can be used to achieve selfish goals.

Commenting on the domestication of international conflicts on Nigerian soil by Islamic militants in northern Nigeria, a commentator wrote:

> Dissident Islamists are a significant force in countries such as Nigeria, where there is a ready social foundation, deep inequities, and a broad failure of governance. Conditions that foster radicalism- poverty, unemployment, social dislocation, cultural polarization, and a large pool of disaffected young men- are evident in abundance. Among Muslims, social grievances often find religious expression through fundamentalist appeals to piety, or through Islamist challenges to the political status quo (Lewis, 2002, p.2).

The northern part of Nigeria is known to be severely underdeveloped in terms of educational and economic development. For example, the Nigerian Poverty Incidence map 1996 produced by the Federal Office of Statistics (reproduced in UNFPA, 2005, p. 14) shows that most states in the northern part of the country have poverty rates ranging between 63.6 to 95.1 whereas the rate for most states in the south was put at 43.0 to 63.5 .Although northern military and political leaders are very influential and have held political power for a greater period of Nigeria's independence, such power and influence have not been used to accelerate the educational and economic transformation of that part of the country. There are also many Muslims in South western Nigeria, but their response to international religious issues differ, apparently because of their relatively higher level of education, greater economic opportunities, and the higher number of Christians in their midst. For example, Muslim youths in Lagos, Nigeria's former capital also protested against the Muhammed cartoons, but rather than vent their spleen on other hapless citizens as the northern protesters did, they went straight to the seat of the state government at Alausa, Ikeja, where the state governor, Senator Ahmed Bola Tinubu received them. The protesting Muslims, under the aegis of the Muslim Students Society of Nigeria (MSSN) demanded for an apology on behalf of Nigerian Muslims, from the Danish government and asked the Federal Government of Nigeria to immediately recall Nigerian ambassadors from Denmark and Norway (Daily Independent, 2006). They did not kill burn, maim, loot or molest as was the case in northern Nigeria.

Why Would Nigerian Muslims Replicate International Conflicts in their Fatherland?

A review of the foregoing scenarios would indicate that international conflicts are not simply replicated in Nigeria by misguided Islamic youths; they are done with worse and more deadly consequences. There are various explanations for this, including Nigeria's social foundation, deep inequities and a broad failure of governance mentioned above. However, from the media angle this phenomenon would fall under what is broadly categorized as unintended effects of the media.

One of the defining characteristics of the media is that they target large and heterogeneous audiences located in far-flung places. The audiences are mostly made up of people with divergent psychographic as well as demographic characteristics. With such a background, responses to media messages and images projected by the media are expectedly diverse. A media message that would receive approbation among a segment of the audience could generate violence among members of another segment.

Sundar (1999) confronted a situation that gave a hint that the media could indeed, produce effects that are divorced from the expected. Sundar testified before the U.S House of Representatives on the issue of potential psychological effects of anti-drug media. He explained that unintended effects of the media are responsible for the increase of drug use even though research had shown that anti-drug public service announcements were enormously successful in reaching their target audiences. In his theoretical explorations, he came across the variable "conative curiosity" which could further explicate the observed trend. In summarizing the exploratory study, Sundar wrote:

> This exploratory study brought to the fore the potential of PSAs (Public Service Announcements) to arouse curiosity, but our data did not specify the exact theoretical mechanism by which exposure to PSAs affects one's level of curiosity…Others have suggested that this could be a 'forbidden fruit' effect, i.e., the tendency among adolescents to be drawn towards that which is forbidden (p. 7).

Although the above study by Sundar's team explored only Public Service Announcements which constitute a tiny segment of media messages, the findings could give an inkling into what could give Muslim youths in northern Nigeria the effrontery to confront law enforcement agencies, attack Christians, and burn down churches; all acts which are forbidden by Nigerian law. Although there are several theoretical explanations within the realm of sociology, religion, political science and even psychology, the present analysis focuses on the realm of communication and media studies.

McQuail (2005) acknowledges the suggestion that the media can variously provoke a riot, create a culture of rioting, provide lessons on how to riot, and spread disturbance from place to place. He, however, contends that the evidence for or against such a suggestion is thin and fragmentary. He explains that there is some evidence that the media can contribute by simply signaling the occurrence and location of a riot event; by publicizing incidents which are themselves causes of riot behavior, or by giving advance publicity to the likely occurrence of rioting. In his words:

> In general, it seems likely that the media do have a capacity to define the nature of events, and even if they are ultimately 'on the side' of established order they can unintentionally increase the degree of polarization in particular cases. While the media have not been shown to be a primary or main cause of rioting....they may influence the timing or form of riot behavior (p. 489).

McQuail adds further that in our own time, mobilization to collective action seems likely to be conducted by mobile phone or the internet rather than as an unintended effect from the mass media. Among the Islamic youths of northern Nigeria, mobile telephone and internet use may not be as pronounced as it is in the United States, due to economic, technological and social factors. Therefore, these may not be acceptable as the most likely means of mobilization for collective action. It is important, therefore, to look at the role of opinion leaders. The social categories and social relations perspectives as well as the N-step flow theory of mass media effects may offer some explanation about the role of the mass media in situations such as the one under focus.

The social categories perspective assumes that members of any identifiable social category are likely to seek out similar communication messages, which they also would likely react to, more or less similarly. Such a social category may be defined by age, educational level, economic status, religious affiliation, among others. Thus, given an opportunity, teenagers, youth, adolescents, and other categories of media users are likely to seek out particular kinds of media messages and re-act to them in more or less the same way. This, of course, depends on several factors and also takes cognizance of the fact that individual differences may exist within such social categories.

Although media reports indicate that the Muslim youths, as opposed to the elderly ones, are the ones behind persistent religious violence in northern Nigeria. However, there is no conclusive evidence that only youths have been involved in the persistent violence, more so since the protests are usually preceded by rallies addressed by Islamic religious leaders who may not necessarily be youthful.

The social relations perspective, on the other hand, posits that people's reactions to media messages are usually defined by their informal social relationships with 'significant others' who may be their family members, employers, religious leaders, classmates, colleagues at work, among others. It is most likely that 'significant others' such as the Ulama or Islamic religious leaders provide the impetus for religious violence in northern Nigeria. Therefore media messages, alone, are not likely to be the main reason for the replication of international conflicts at the local or national level.

The N-step flow theory also provides an important theoretical framework for the analysis of the issue under focus. Folarin (1998) explains that the N-step (formerly two-step) flow theory developed from two parallel sources, namely the Erie County research in the USA which yielded the social categories and social relations perspectives, and studies of rural sociology, with particular reference to the diffusion and adoption of agricultural innovations. The two main issues from the studies that are immediately relevant are: (1) Many people have very limited exposure to the mass media and (2) such people obtain much of their information second hand. Folarin explains that from these findings, the researchers developed the hypothesis of the "Two-Step Flow of Communication." It was discovered in addition, according to Folarin that those who had got the information firsthand were not simply passing on the information but were also helping to shape and interpret it. They were, therefore, called the opinion leaders. Thus, he says, opinion leadership became recognized as an additional intervening variable between the mass mediated message and audience response. In his words, "The two-step flow theory was later modified to multi-step or N-step flow theory, since opinion leaders also have opinion leaders and so on ad infinitum" (p. 60).

Media reports indicate that before the first set of killings started in Maiduguri on Saturday, February 18, 2006, the Muslim Ulama, under the umbrella of the Borno Muslim Forum, had addressed a public rally on the personality of Prophet Muhammed at the Ramat Square, Maiduguri. The rally, which was meant to protest the cartoons, later turned into an orgy of blood letting. This implies that the media messages, acting alone, perhaps would not have led to the uprising. The address by the Muslim leaders was most likely to have been the catalyst that propelled the rioters into action.

In conclusion, the extent to which international crises are replicated in northern Nigerian towns and cities is associated with the degree to which Islamic religious leaders interpret from or add to the media messages. Therefore, media messages, acting alone, are incapable of generating the extent of violence and destruction noticed in that part of the country over the years.

The Media and Social Responsibility

The social responsibility theory of the press has influenced media decisions and conduct in the free world for several decades. McQuail (2005, p.175) summarizes the five key points in the theory as follows:

1. The media have obligations to society, and media ownership is a public trust.

2. The news media should be truthful, accurate, fair, objective and relevant.

3. The media should be free but self-regulated.

4. The media should follow agreed codes of ethics and professional conduct.

5. Under some circumstances, government may need to intervene to safeguard the public interest.

Although this paper believes that media messages, acting alone, cannot be blamed for the replication of international conflicts in northern Nigeria, the media still need to be reminded of their social responsibility. Today, as a result of globalization and rapid advances in science and technology, the social responsibility of the media is no longer to their immediate societies alone. This is because the contents of media messages in any corner of the globe can now have spiraling consequences in other far-flung parts of the world, just as demonstrated by the global reactions to the Muhammed cartoons in *Jyllands' Posten* a Danish newspaper. Perhaps, if the Danish newspaper had not published the Muhammed cartoons, the Muslim leaders in northern Nigeria would not have instigated actions which culminated in the killing of hundreds of people. But this is not to say that the media should become so timid because of social reactions that they will abdicate their freedom of expression as well as their social responsibility. The point is that in exercising freedom, they should bear in mind the likely consequences for millions of other people in different parts of the world.

Conclusion

The media play a very important social role in any society where they exist. Today, the global media have the whole world as their constituency, thanks to globalization. Therefore, irrespective of where the media operate from, they should see the whole world as their "immediate environment" and take steps to address the problems of poverty, inequality, injustice and underdevelopment which, over the years, have tended to set some parts of the world against others. When a part of a whole is festering, it is not wise to consider the whole as being whole.

References

Bauder, D. (2006, February 26). Port security puts CNN's Dobbs on attack. (Available online). *http://www.mercury news.com.*

Carnegie Council on Ethics and International Affairs. (2002). Behind the scenes with Al Jazeera: A conversation with Mohammed el Nawawy and Adel Iskander Farag. (available online). *http://www.carnegiecouncil.org.*

CNN.com chat transcript "Peter Arnette: A look Back at Operation Desert Storm." (Available online). *http://www.cnn.com/chat/transcripts/2001/01/16/Arnett*

Duffy, D. (2006). Gulf War II opened the eyes of Americans to the UN and the Media. (Available online) *http://www.backwoodshome.com/articles 2/duffy82.html*

Enemaku, O.S. (2003). Foreign media coverage of Nigerian affairs. In Ndimele, O. (Ed), *Four Decades in the Study of Languages and Linguistics in Nigeria: A Festschrift for Kay Williamson (pp. 50-73.* Aba: National Institute for Nigerian Languages

Fleischer, (2001). 24 hours bias:-CNN's East slant. *The Review,* Australia/Israel and Jewish Council. (Available online). *http//:www.aijac.org*

Folarin, B. (2000). *Foundation of broadcasting.* Ibadan: Atlantis Books

_____ (1998). *Theories of mass communication: An introductory text.* Ibadan: Stirling-Horden Publishers.

Goujon, E and Abubakar, A. (2006, February 24). Nigeria's 'Taliban' plot comeback from hideouts. Mail and Guardian online (Available online).http:www.mailandguardian.org/reports

Hibbard, A. & Keenleyside, T. (1995). The press and the Persian Gulf crisis: The Canadian angle. Canadian *Journal of Communication, [Online] Vol 20(2), 1-10*

IRINnews.org. UN Office for the Coordination of Humanitarian Affairs (Available online). http://www.irinnews.org/S_report.asp

Lewis, P.M. (2002). Islam, protest and conflict in Nigeria. In *Africa Notes, (*Centre for Strategic and International Studies, Washington, DC), p10.

MacBride, S. (1980*). Many voices, one world.* Paris: The UNESCO Press.

McQuail, D. (2005). *Mass communication theory.* London: Sage Publications

Stech, F.J. (1994). Winning CNN wars. *Parameters* (U.S. Army War College quarterly), autumn, p. 37.

Sundar, S.S. (1999). Presentation before the Subcommittee on Justice, Drug Policy and Resources, United States' House of Representatives. (Available online). *http://www.psu.edu/dept/medialab/research/statement.*

Tinubu cautions protesting youths. (2006, February 20). (Available online). *http:wwwindependentng.com*

Uche, L.U. (Ed). (1996). *North-South information culture: Trends in global communication and research paradigms.* Lagos: Longman Nigeria Plc.

UNFPA (2005) *State of Nigerian Population 2005.* Lagos: UNFPA

Chapter 19

Conflict and Ferment in International Communication

Ephraim A. Okoro, Ph.D.
Howard University, USA

Introduction

International communication has attracted a lot of attention over the years as a major source of global conflicts. This chapter attempts to refocus on some of the unresolved issues that continue to fuel debates over aspects of contemporary global communication infrastructure. Central to the ferment are certain controversial and enduring issues that have caused agitation and provoked strong ideological sentiments. Many of the issues of concern emerged right from the beginning–the discernible origin–of international communication, e.g. control of information flow, ownership, and imbalance of information traffic around the world. Others have been the products of the shifts and transformations in the global community. For instance, the issues of globalization and cultural imperialism gained international prominence in the wake of political independence of many of the so-called Third World countries as they sought to assert their sovereignties as nation-states in a changing world.

Communication and Society

Over the years, a plethora of theories have been developed to enhance understanding of the processes of international communication. But like the field of international communication itself, these theories are imbued with controversies and driven by various ideological and philosophical orientations. Some of the theories are pro-West, such as *free flow of information* and *modernization;* others are anti-West such as *dependency* and *structural imperialism.*

As the debates focusing on the structural and functional dimensions of communication continue, it has become apparent also that issues of communication are in fact at the heart of global conflicts. Furthermore, certain enduring issues pertaining to the global communication infrastructure continue to provoke strong sentiments among people of the South–the developing nations. Issues of control, information flow, globalization, ownership, nature of media messages, and now the digital divide as an outcome of innovations in telecommunications, have further complicated the debates.

The resource rich countries of the North, it appears, now own, control and operate over 80 percent of the global communication infrastructure, including the old and new media. The North, collectively or individually, can speak to the rest of the world on a daily basis in real time through its arsenal of sophisticated communication systems. The South still cannot do so because it either lacks the means or because the prevailing communication traffic pattern is still largely one-way. As already noted, this phenomenon, despite the inbuilt disparities, has great potential for promoting global peace and harmony, and to some extent it does. However, because of the non-integrative nature of the system whereby it is mostly the North talking to the South, or the North's interpretations of global events, it perpetuates perceptions of inequities and makes international communication activities counter productive. Constant reminders of tattered penury and deprivations of the South and, indeed, the hopelessness of the human condition in the developing world juxtaposed against the affluence of the North is bound to have some psychological implications for the way people perceive and interact with each other as members of the global community.

Basic Historical Context

During the late 19th century, European nations developed a notion suggesting that global communication was essential for the development, control and domination of capital formation not only in their own countries but particularly around the world. Hence, in 1825, Charles Havas established the Havas News Bureau; in 1848, Bernard Wolff established Wolf News Agency, and in 1851, Julius Reuter established the Reuter news agency. Meanwhile, in the United States, a number of New York newspapers pooled their resources to establish the Associated Press (Cassata and Asante, 1979).

Much later, as its colonial interests expanded, the British laid a network of submarine cables to connect its colonies with the metropolis. The invention of the telephone, radio, television, communication satellite, computers, the Internet, the World Wide Web, etc., all of which are truly forms of communication and information revolutions, can be placed within the context of the European and

American vision of the inevitable connectedness of control of communication and control of the global market economy and dominance of global politics.

Western nations have dominated and continue to dominate these structural and functional processes of communication while the developing nations have been at the extreme end of a continuum based on a trickle-down system in communication innovations. This disparity cannot be dismissed easily because it is part of the core of the political and other social struggles for change around the world today. Hence, global peace and harmony may remain farfetched without a rethinking of the non-integrative nature of global communication toward a redistribution of innovations in communication to enhance human interactions and mutual understandings among people in the world.

Terrorism, Communication and Personal Freedoms

Since 9/11, everyone in the world today has become a potential terrorist, and those who may find this hard to believe only need to attempt to travel by air locally or internationally. Even well-known United States public figures such as former Vice President Al Gore and Senator Edward Kennedy have not been immune to this new attitude about terrorism. Both men have been stopped once on separate occasions at American airports for extra security screening. In many ways, those who commit terrorist acts have succeeded in defining or redefining the psyche and ethos of whole communities of people both in terms of our personal freedoms–the right to free expression of ideas without fear of reprisal, the right to associate with others, and the right to choose our religion. Even our natural identities of race and ethnicity can now be perilous. It was recently announced, for example, that data about passengers flying between European Union countries and the United States will now be gathered and shared among these countries as part of the new global security dispensation. According the to the Washington Post:

> The United States and the European Union have agreed to expand a security program that shares personal data about millions of U.S.-bound airline passengers a year, potentially including information about a person's race, ethnicity, religion and health." (p. A1).

Data about people's racial or ethnic origin, political opinions, religious or philosophical beliefs, trade union membership, health, traveling partners and sexual orientation (p. A1), have come under this new regulation. Contemporary society is thus left with the precarious dilemma that to successfully combat global terrorism, curtailment of our personal freedoms is part of the price we must pay.

Poverty, Communication and Global Conflict

Communication is an invaluable catalyst in almost every aspect of human development. For our basic survival as well as for our well-being, communication is inevitable. It is invaluable for our safety and security and for the peaceful co-existence with our neighbors. Fortunately, every communication tool necessary for the elimination of misery, poverty, and causes of mutual distrust and suspicion in contemporary societies are now at the disposal of this generation. Unfortunately, that the human condition remains as deplorable as ever before across the globe suggests our collective failure and lack of meaningful commitment to improving the lives of people through knowledge generation, knowledge distribution, and through education. In other words, we are yet to utilize communication fully to improve the human condition. As long as human misery remains at its present levels, global harmony also will remain illusive. Brainard and Chollet (2007), drawing from ongoing research and conversations about these issues have not only confirmed the connection between global poverty, conflict, and security, but have suggested that some people may now be "too poor for peace," and this should be of concern to everyone:

> The effort to end poverty is about much more than extending a helping hand to those in need. In a world where boundaries and borders have blurred, and where seemingly distant threats can metastasize into immediate problems, the fight against global poverty has become a fight of necessity–not simply because personal morality demands it, but because global security demands it (Brainard and Chollet, and LaFleur, 2007, p. 1).

Given the unbridled growth in communications technology, the amazing ingenuity and creativity in the application of communication resources in other areas, it is difficult to understand why we have not fully applied these same resources to improve the human condition. That these problems remain unresolved are indication of the failure of humanity, and not necessarily the failure of the victims of these problems. There is absolutely no justifiable reason for poverty in contemporary society, if the available political, social, cultural and economic resources are applied toward alleviating human misery.

Media Messages

The nature of the messages disseminated through the media systems are reflective of the problems outlined in the preceding discussion. Media sociologists have identified a multitude of factors that influence media content. These include the prevailing political processes within nations and around the world, the global news infrastructure, and the people who work within these systems.

the global news infrastructure, and the people who work within these systems. Different social and political structures encourage different types of media systems – whether in terms of the way the media are operated or in terms of ownership and control. In some countries the media are owned and operated by the government, others encourage private ownership, or a combination of both to varying degrees; corollary to the social and political systems are the laws of libel and slander, and other laws pertaining to the media which also vary from society to society. All of these are factors that define media content within national or international contexts.

At the international level, of all the news infrastructures influencing media content, American Cable News Network (CNN) has become the primary *mirror* of the world because of its 24-hour news service. But the reflections in the *mirror* are considered by many as distorted images of reality. Take for instance, CNN report on the beleaguered Niger Delta region of Nigeria that was aired on February 10, 2007 with correspondent Jeff Koinange reporting.

Koinanage and his camera crew went to the region on the invitation of "Jomo", alleged leader of the group Movement for the Emancipation of the Niger Delta (MEND). Upon arrival he shot unique footages of the group with a dozen or so captive oil workers held by the group as hostages. The program was repeatedly aired on CNN and beamed across the world. Quite naturally, Nigerian officials who claimed that the program was one-sided were infuriated and responded angrily with a barrage of condemnation of CNN and its alleged sinister plans to make Nigeria look bad.

Initially, the reaction of Nigerian officials was not surprising as that was the way government officials react to bad publicity. However, upon closer analysis, many questions were raised by some people who watched the program, and Jeff Kionange, the CNN reporter also admitted that the facts emerging after the program was aired were confusing. For instance, the alleged leader of MEND, Jomo, was no where to be found during Koinange's visit to the region. Secondly, MEND members openly dissociated themselves from the group of trigger-happy people in the program who also claimed to be members of MEND.

Months earlier, the same Jeff Koinange carried a special CNN report on Zimbabwe. The aim of the report was to demonstrate how desolate the people of Zimbabwe had become as a result of President Robert Mugabe's mismanagement of the Zimbabwean economy. Pictures of destitute Zimbabweans feeding on rodents were shown to make the point.

That there are serious problems in Zimbabwe is not a question for debate. But the cumulative effect of such portrayals on the image of Africa as a whole has been of serious concern to many people both inside and outside of Africa.

Britain and other Western nations imposed economic sanctions against Zimbabwe over how Mugabe had handled the land redistribution problem in the country, and the sanctions were so effective that inflation skyrocketed into four figures. Then the same Western nations turned around and use the 4,500% inflation figure as evidence of Mugabe's misrule, bad governance and mismanagement of the country's economy.

Is there a hidden agenda in Western media coverage of Africa? May be not. But the cumulative effective on the image of the continent has not been flattering, and the issue has remained contentious in diplomatic circles as well as among academics and ordinary Africans.

News as Commodity

The international media system is as an economic structure in which the news production process is like the production process of a manufacturing industry. In this analogy, the news story represents a commodity, and the factors influencing its production are: (1) the allocation of resources, (2) economic pressures on the production process, and (3) the necessity to produce a saleable commodity (Harris, 1976).

In manufacturing, the allocation of resources is one of the factors that define the amount of production which may take place and the location such production. Similarly, through the allocation of resources, the international news media define the extent of coverage of different areas and the extent to which different events are covered (Harris, 1996).

There are also cultural factors which combined with the economic reality define the nature of media messages. As one researcher noted:

news ... is a daily negotiation among various actors occupying different niches in the information ecosystem: political actors seeking to control news content, journalists who operate simultaneously within a profession dedicated to informing citizens and a business that sells a product to audiences, and those citizens and audiences who are also members of a culture for whom the news must ring true with what they believe about themselves as a people (W. Lance Benet, 1997, p. 108).

Conclusion

In the global community, a myriad of complex social, political, and economic factors are the sources of the ferment in international communication. It is quite interesting to note that conflict among people within nations and in the global community as a whole is always imminent; but the prospects for peace and harmony through the creative use of contemporary global communication infrastructure are much greater today than ever before. For this to happen it will require an agenda for a broader distribution of communication resources as a way of encouraging participation and exchange among all.

References

Brainard, L., Chollet, D. and LaFleur, V. (2007). The tangled web: The poverty-insecurity nexus. In L. Brainard and D. Chollet, *Too poor for peace: Global poverty, conflict, and security in the 21st century*, pp. 1-30. Washington, DC: Brookings Institution.

Brainard, L. and Chollet, D. (eds.). *Too poor for peace: Global poverty, conflict, and security in the 21st century.* Washington, DC: Brookings Institution.

Cassata, M. and Asante, M. (1979). *Mass communication: Principles and practices.* New York: Macmillan.

Davidson, W. P. (1976). *Mass media: Systems and effects.* NY: Holt, Rinehart and Winston.

Harris, J., Leiter, K. and Johnson, S. (1992). The complete reporter: Fundamentals of news gathering, writing and editing. NY: Macmillan.

Washington Post. (2007, Friday, July 27). Travelers face greater use of personal data, p. A1, A7.

Chapter 20

Multinational Corporations, Community Relations and the Niger Delta Conflict

Abigail O. Ogwezzy, Ph.D.
University of Lagos, Nigeria

Introduction

Quarrel, dispute, opposition, and disagreement are composite expressions of the word "conflict". Conflict cannot but occur in the private, social and official dealings and could rightly be said to have become a permanent feature in the Niger Delta region of Nigeria. The conflict in that region, blamed on exploitation and neglect by both the Nigerian state and the multinationals, has led to loss of lives and properties.

Over the years, several agencies were set up to forestall escalation of the conflict and to address the concerns of the Niger Delta people (Alamieyesigha, 2005). These agencies included:

1961: Niger Delta Development Board (NDDB)

1976: Niger Delta Basin Development Authority (NDBDA)

1992: Oil Mineral Producing Areas Development Commission (OMPADEC)

2000: Niger Delta Development Commission (NDDC).

Multinational corporations operating in the area adopted somewhat different strategies by embarking upon a number of community relations projects.

However, during the last violent conflict between rival ethnic groups in the Niger Delta region, many community relations projects provided by Chevron Nigeria Limited (CNL), operator of NNPC/CNL Joint venture, were attacked and destroyed. Years after they had been turned over to the beneficiaries, school buildings and water taps were still referred to as "Chevron projects". Young, unemployed community men were being paid salaries as "ghost workers" for doing nothing at all, except that some were often found to be involved in threats, extortion and disruption of operations. In addition, the system of designating some communities as "host communities" left those not so designated feeling alienated, inadvertently leading to or adding to conflicts among the communities (*Thisday*, 2005). So, ultimately, the huge amount of community relations expenditures have not resulted in a thriving, self-sustaining environment devoid of conflict and conducive to business growth. Instead, the Niger Delta remains to be an unhealthy and conflict-prone and divisive environment. Hence, violence and incessant conflicts have left many community relations projects funded by the multinationals in shambles.

This chapter examines the community relations strategies of an oil multinational–Chevron Nigeria Limited (CNL) against the backdrop of a development strategy–the participatory approach. The aim is to identify the gaps (weaknesses and threats), which could be revisited by the multinationals for future community relations engagements in the quest to deescalate the conflict in the Niger Delta region and to make the environment more conducive for business activities.

The Problem

Conflict in the Niger Delta region of Nigeria has been protracted despite various community relations efforts by both the multinational corporations and the government. In carrying out community relations projects, the absence of a participatory approach, coupled with a system that is outside driven, leads to an environment that thrives on rumors and attributions of blame that escalate existing conflict. More than anything else, it creates a culture of dependency rather than encourage sustainable development, capacity building and ownership of projects designed to benefit the people. Thus, rather than satisfying the stakeholders in the region, the seemingly good intentions of multinational corporations have merely contributed to the prolongation of the conflict. A number of communities are not happy with such projects, as they consider multinationals' investment in them as inadequate, expensive, divisive, and outside driven (Haastrup, 2004). These point to the fact that there are gaps in the community relations approaches adopted by the multinationals.

Using Schramm's communication model and the participatory approach to development, this chapter seeks to determine the effectiveness of the strategies adopted by multinationals operating in the Niger Delta region of Nigeria.

Significance of the Study

Research into community relations interventions of the oil companies operating in the Niger Delta region of Nigeria is still at the embryonic stage, especially against the backdrop of the present cutting edge method in development–participatory approach. So, this study is significant because it would serve as an important attempt to evaluate the community relations dimension to the conflict in the Niger Delta region of Nigeria. The chapter underscores the strengths and weaknesses of the various community relations strategies and, thus, contributes to our understanding of the efforts to resolve or de-escalate the conflict in the Niger Delta Region of Nigeria.

Literature Review

Community relations programs in the Niger Delta region of Nigeria consist of a series of programs and projects designed and executed by oil producing companies for their host communities with the aim of meeting certain basic needs of such communities and thereby projecting the companies to their hosts and government as being socially responsible. Such efforts are designed also to reduce the feeling of marginalization which has been the basis for restiveness in the oil rich Niger Delta region. Some of the projects include the building of schools, hospitals and other public utilities; providing scholarships for students from the affected communities to enable them to pursue courses of study at secondary or tertiary levels, and others as conceived by the companies (Enemaku, 1998).

However, a number of such projects have been conceived, planned and executed by the oil companies with little or no participation of large segments of the community. So, the projects which are aimed at endearing the oil companies to their host communities to create an enabling environment for the conduct of the business of prospecting for and producing of oil, have been greeted with much antagonism. This has led to a series of conflicts between local groups and the oil companies. This might not be unconnected with the fact that the oil companies still see the communities as non-participants in the process of development and therefore conceive, plan, and execute projects for the host communities without their active involvement, i.e. the community relations projects of the oil companies are based on the old top-down model (Ojo, 2004).

Participatory approaches "attach importance to enabling people determine their own concerns and form their opinions, rather than rushing in with an outside agenda" (Cornwall and Welbourn, 2000, p. 16). Participatory methodologies are attracting global interest. Cornwall and Welbourn (2000) posited that "over the last few years, there has been explosion of interest in participatory methodologies [which] has been supported by the realization that involving people more actively in setting priorities and determining needs can make a difference" (p. 16), highlighting the weaknesses/threats of top down strategies and the strengths/opportunities of participatory approach.

According to Welbourn (1991), participatory approach means the equal inclusion of all sections of a typical, stratified community, women, men, older, younger, better-off and worse-off, in development. While Chambers (1997) said that it is meant to enable target audiences to play an active role in their development. From a communication perspective, target audiences should identify their problems and be party to the choices and packaging of community development projects. This approach would render multinational corporations non-prescriptive. The participatory method is currently being used among the *Dalit* women in India (Periyapatna, 2000).

Thus the whole idea of participatory development is to form a *'coalition'* (emphasis mine) between target communities and multinationals. It is for the target community to decide on what should be done and if necessary voluntarily seek information from the multinational corporations. This might account for why in the contemporary field of community relations, scholars and development experts are advocating for the use of participatory approach, an approach this study believes would enhance outcomes in community relations.

Listening to community voices can facilitate improved outcomes in the area of the feeling of neglect that has been causing conflict in the Niger Delta. According to Shah, *et al.* (1999), community relations projects should consider how to tap the energy of community members and build on their talents.

Theoretical Framework

In his communication model (Figure 1), Schramm proposed that "only what is shared in the field of experience of both the source and the destination is actually communicated, because only that portion of the signal is held in common by both source and destination" (Severin & Tankard, 1992, p. 47). The Schramm's model of communication is the theory on which this study relied. It was revised to explain the need for the source of a message and the receiver to have a common experience for communication in other to be effective (see figure 1a).

Figure 1a suggested that source, encoder, decoder and destination should be made up of the target audience, while the field of experience should involve both the target and the facilitator. What this meant was that no matter the volume of community relations project executed by the source (multinationals and government) to the destination (oil producing communities in the Niger Delta) only the ones held in common by both parties are actually appreciated. Community relations projects should take cognizance of the peculiarities of various communities and be such that could ginger positive attitudinal change towards the feeling of neglect that has been the main cause of conflict in the Niger Delta region. To achieve this, it is important to enable people to determine their needs, which is the thrust of the participatory approach.

The Old versus the New Model of Community Relations Strategies

The new model takes a critical look at the existing policies, listens to stakeholders' concerns and finds mutually beneficial answers to the troubling questions of doing business and promoting development in the challenging environment of the Niger Delta. Essentially, innovative ideas are driving new directions in community engagement at Chevron Nigeria Limited. These ideas are the bases for the 2005 Global Memorandum of Understanding (GMOU) concept that is guiding the company's new community relations strategies. The 2005 GMOU defines and guide the relationships between the stakeholders. The expectation is that the expected changes will help to build capacity, reduce conflict (emphasis mine) and promote the spirit of self-help, community ownership and sustainable development (Anonymous, 2005).

The new model supports the views of Welbourn (1991), Chambers (1997), and Cornwall and Welbourn (2000) who argued that participatory approach which enables target audiences to play active role in their development and thus enhance community ownership and project sustainability.

Despite the best intentions and genuine efforts, the previous policies and practices on community relations did not satisfy many of the stakeholders. A number of communities were not happy because the system tagged some communities as host communities and left those not so designated feeling alienated and under privileged, inadvertently leading to or adding to the causes of conflicts in the region; the system was not open to target communities which did not encourage ownership and sustainability of development projects (Anonymous, 2005). These led to the evolution of a new way that addresses many of the shortcomings of the old ways.

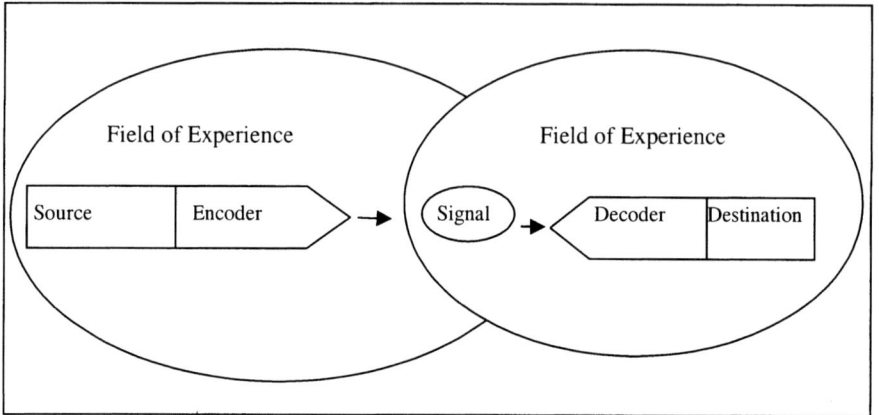

Figure 1: Schramm's Model of Communication. Source: J.W. Severin and J.W. Tankard, Jr. (1992). Communication Theories: Origins, Methods, and uses in the Mass Media, p. 47. New York: Hastings House.

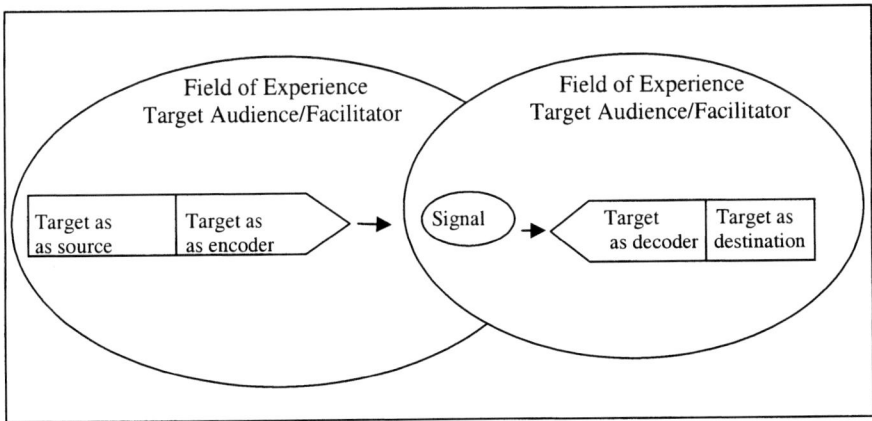

Figure 1a: Revised Schramm's Model of Communication. Framework for Participatory Approach to Communication. Source: J.W. Severin and J.W. Tankard, Jr. (1992). Communication Theories: Origins, Methods, and uses in the Mass Media, p. 47. New York: Hastings House.

Insights from Chevron Nigeria Limited New Model

The new community engagement model is intended to address short-comings of the previous approach, improve transparency and accountability, build community capacity to plan, implement and own the development process, ensure sustainability of development projects, reduce or eliminate conflicts (emphasis mine), and improve company relationship with communities (Anonymous, 2005).

These innovative ideas are driving the new directions in community relations. As these ideas evolve, new concepts and phrases are gaining currency and usage. They include Regional Development, Participatory Partnership, Capacity Building, Community Empowerment, Transparency and Accountability, Conflict Mediations, and Security and the Rule of Law (*Thisday, 2005*).

Regional Development

The concept of regional development directly addresses the conflict-prone issues of designating some communities as 'hosts' and others as 'non-host' as well as accusations of favoring one ethnic group or the other. It seeks to cluster homogenous communities in a contiguous location to form Regional Development Councils (RDC). This way development is not limited and exclusive to only those communities previously designated as hosts but spread within a region and inclusive of all communities in the cluster. More importantly, decisions on development – such as what is needed, where projects should be located, will now be made by the RDC in consultations with the stakeholders and the various communities and aligned with the Master Development Plan for the Niger Delta approved by the Niger Delta Development Commission (NDDC). The RDCs will be taking these decisions, while a joint body of stakeholders will help the councils to resource development, while developing their capacity to own and sustain the projects. This joint stakeholder body of participating partners will ensure transparency and accountability and mediate conflict through a new governance model (Anonymous, 2005).

Participatory Partnership

Participatory partnership is the central concept of the new community engagement model. While the old model focused on a bilateral relationship between the oil companies and the leadership of designated "host" communities and excluded other participants for the most part, the participatory approach to community relations seeks to be more inclusive of other stakeholders in the development of the Niger Delta region. Government and non-governmental organizations (NGOs), donor agencies, development agents (Niger Delta Development Commission [NDDC]) and the regional development councils will work collaboratively to build community capacity, mediate conflict, promote peaceful co-existence and sustainable development. This relationship is defined in the new GMOU governance model as part of the 2005 document. By enlarging the table and brining in other partners, the communities access to other funds for development in the Niger Delta would also be improved. With NDDC and other development agents as participating partners, these regional councils stand a better chance of accessing development funding beyond the limits of CNL Joint Venture's annual budget (Anonymous, 2005). Again, this finding supports the views of Welbourn (1991), Chambers (1997), and Cornwall and Welbourn (2000) who argued that participatory approach which enables target audiences to play an active role in their development and thus enhance community ownership and project sustainability.

This shows that community relations will not be the *midas* touch in conflict prevention and resolution. Strategies used are germane and underpin the synergy achieved in terms of outcomes. This might account for why community relations attempts in the past by multinationals remain half-hearted and piecemeal or else founder in the face of age-old inequalities.

Capacity Building and Community Empowerment

For the most part the old community engagement model tried to provide much needed development for the community. CNL built school blocks and hospitals, trained many young men and women in new skills, funded fish farms and poultry projects, built boat-landing jetties and post offices and provided scholarships and much more. In the old community engagement model, funding, design, planning and contracting implementation of projects resided exclusively with the company. The result was that communities did not take part in most of the processes and would not take ownership of the resulting projects. Most projects bore the name of company and they were seen as owned by the company long after they have been turned over to the beneficiaries.

In fact the maintenance of the projects was seen as the sole responsibility of the company (Anonymous, 2005). This finding buttresses the position of Ojo (2004) who argued that the fact that the oil companies still see the communities as non-participants in the process of development and therefore conceive, plan and execute projects for the host communities without their active involvement, i.e. the community relations projects of the oil companies are based on the old model of top down and that the new approach is now being executed through participatory approach.

In the new model the regional development councils, representing the constituent communities, will lead discussions and decisions on community development. The participating partners will help build the capacity of the councils and empower the communities to plan, design, implement and take ownership of their own development. Rather than focusing on mostly infrastructure projects, the new community engagement model allows stakeholders to give greater attention to some revenue generating projects that can employ community people. Through a transparent process, the councils will be funded, audited, restructured and empowered to take full ownership of their own development.

Transparency and Accountability

This is another key plank of the community engagement model. The previous situation of dealing with a few "leaders and representatives" of individual communities did not promote transparency and accountability. This only led to unfounded rumors about how much was spent on what, and unsubstantiated allegations about improper use of funds meant for community development.

The new governance model for the GMOU will ensure that the regional development councils and the participating partners operate an open and accountable system. This will guarantee that all constituent members of communities know what the leaders are doing, how much a project is costing and how contracts are awarded. It is expected that such a process will reduce conflicts arising from unsubstantiated allegations against leaders and company alike. In addition, donor agencies are only able to fund projects where they are able to deliver value to the general public and at the same time see a demonstrable tradition of transparency and accountability. If we therefore grant to enlarge the pot of funding for development in the communities of the Niger Delta, we have to be willing to build the capacity for transparency and accountability (Anonymous, 2005).

Security and the Rule of law

We believe that a successful and sustainable partnership among all stakeholders rests on an enabling environment characterized by the presence of security and adherence to the rule of law. This has not been the case in many of the areas of the Niger Delta where CNL operates. Experience has shown CNL the difficulty of pursuing development in an environment devoid of the security and the rule of law. The ruins of a hospital built twice, and destroyed twice is a constant reminder to CNL of the waste occasioned by violence and insecurity. The NNPC/CNL Joint Venture has lost huge amounts of money to the destruction caused by incessant violent ethnic conflicts between different groups. Employees and many families in the communities have lost their dear ones to the violence. Whole communities have been completely destroyed and several persons remained displaced and living outside their traditional communities as refugees. A secure environment is both a product of sustainable development and a precursor to it. While government has the primary responsibility to provide security for all citizens, all stakeholders must complement the effort of government in this regard. This issue was also addressed in the new GMOU (Anonymous, 2005).

Conclusion

The study concludes that despite various community engagement programs by the oil companies and various attempts by government to address the twin issues of poverty and under-development, the Niger Delta remains largely poor and under-developed and, hence, prone to incessant conflicts and crises. A possible explanation for the situation is the top-down approach to community relations by the oil companies. So, hearing the experiences of target communities, rethinking assumptions and re-evaluating the supposed needs of the communities in conjunction with target communities would move community relations forward and reduce dissatisfaction and a feeling of neglect which has been causing conflict in the Niger Delta region, as outside driven community relations projects are insufficient to bring about de-escalation of conflict in the Niger Delta.

Although the search for solutions to the Niger Delta conflict has been long and continuous, which at best has yielded temporary peace or uneasy calm, it is hoped that the new direction in community engagements that promotes working together with various stakeholders and the active participation of all the stakeholders would contribute to the long-term search for solutions to the Niger Delta and hopefully de-escalate the conflict.

So, it is hoped that working together with the various stakeholders could bring significant benefits and contribute to the long-term development of communities in the areas of CNL operations.

Reference

Alamieyesigha, D. (2005, March 29). The Niger Delta crises: Yesterday, today and tomorrow. *Daily Independent,* p. C6.

Anonymous (2005). A media relations staff of ChevronTexaco Nigeria. Interview by author, 25 August, Lagos, Nigeria.

Chambers, R. (1997). *Whose reality counts? Putting the first last.* London: Intermediate Technology Publications.

Cornwall, A. and Wellborn, A. (2000). From reproduction to rights: Participatory approaches to sexual and reproductive health. In *PLA Notes 37* London: International Institute for Environment and Development February.

Enemaku, O.S. (1998, August). Preventing, managing and resolving conflicts between oil companies and host communities through increased community involvement in community relations programs. A Seminar Paper Presented in the Department of Communication and Language Arts, University Of Ibadan-Nigeria.

Hastrup, D. (2004). Developing the Niger Delta: The unique challenges of a land of promise. *Corporate Social Responsibility.* vol.1, no. 3. Lagos: Chevron Texaco Nigeria.

Jackson, C. (1993). Doing what comes naturally? Women and environment in development. In *World Development,* vol. 21 (12). London: Pergamon Press Ltd.

Ojo, I. (2004). Jakpa Speaks on CNL's sustainable development policy. *Corporate Social Responsibility*, vol.1, no. 3. Lagos: ChevronTexaco Nigeria.

Periyapatna, S. (2000, May 4th). Media: An issue of local control. A Seminar Paper presented at IDS, University of Sussex, United Kingdom.

Severin, W. J. and Tankard J. W. (Jnr.) (1992). *Communication theories: Origins, methods, and uses In The Mass Media* 3rd ed. New York: Hastings House.

Shah, M. K., Zambezi, R. & Simasik, M. (1999, June). Listening to young voices: Facilitating participatory appraisal on reproductive health with adolescent. *Focus Tool Series* Focus on Young Adults. Zambia: CARE International.

ThisDay (2005, May 4). Listening, learning and evolving new directions in community engagement and sustainable development. pp. 32 and 33.

Chapter 21

Poverty, Professionalism and the Challenges of Democratization among Conflicted Print Media Journalists in Nigeria

Nosa Owens-Ibie, Ph.D.
University of Lagos, NIGERIA

Global projects like the Millennium Development Goals (MDG) derive their primacy from seeking to address key human development issues. Central to these issues is poverty which eradication is not only the first of the goals, but of special significance to transitional economies like that of Nigeria, considering its prevalence. While doubts exist on the feasibility of achieving this goal (Global Monitoring, 2005), other initiatives like the New Partnership for African Development (NEPAD) and the National Economic Empowerment and Development Strategy (NEEDS) in Nigeria, exist as attempts to address trends in national underdevelopment, under a reform agenda, local in coloring, but global in orientation and specifics.

At both the national and personal levels, these programs represent for NEPAD, an attempt at a restructuring process translating into dividends of democracy, greater participation, and economic empowerment (Esan, 2004, p.42), and for NEEDS a strategy for comprehensive reform (Harneit-Sievers, 2004, p.xi). Central to these is the mass media which under the Fundamental Objectives and Directive Principles of State Policy is saddled with the responsibility of holding the government accountable to its mandate (Constitution of Nigeria, 1999). In the process of moderating good governance (Idowu, 2001, p. 23), the media face peculiar challenges as the soul of society. There are expectations which often do not take the context of operation into consideration. The media, bound by professional codes, while trying to navigate the terrain of democratization, also have to contend with issues of their working conditions and corruption.

This study seeks to link these many variables impacting the performance of journalists in Nigeria, with a view to assessing their consequences for journalistic performance in a democratic dispensation. It also seeks to answer questions on the perceptions of journalists on the implications of this context of operation for the sustenance of the momentum in democratization. The focus is on the print media which has been at the vanguard of the evolution of the Nigerian state, with contributions bestriding the pre-colony, colony and the post-colony.

Statement of the Problem

There is a symbiosis between underdevelopment and conflict. Although the logic of social relations presupposes the inevitability of conflict (Owens-Ibie, 2002, p. 30), such conflict manifest in different ways. Conflict, defined as observable products of a breakdown in communication between two interacting parties, often masks the context which defines them. Folger, Poole & Stuttman (1997, p. 69) highlight the influence of such environmental factors in conflicts. Since people are the anchors of their development (Asante, 1991, p. 206), the material condition of not just the generality, but journalists who are expected to catalyze the democratic process to promote such development, becomes important. This study attempts a holistic approach to understanding the prospects for the optimization of the contributions of journalists to democratization in Nigeria, by exploring reality from the perspective of the economic conditions under which journalists in some print media where salaries have not been regular, operate.

The idea is to better situate the role of the press as the fourth estate of the realm, even when professional specifications tend to understate some environmental constraints. This is especially significant given the problem of endemic corruption which Diamond (2001) explains as the cog in the wheel of democracy and the efficiency of states. State structures weakened by globalization, especially in Africa, need the prop of a vibrant and professionalized core of journalists to remain focused and ensure the utilization of lean resources on people-centered development. Ultimately, this study of conflicted journalists seeks a clearer understanding of the desirability of dynamic approaches to ensuring a more professional press in the service of development. If the problem faced by the economically besieged yields a new charter which goes beyond the rhetoric, then this study would have contributed to assisting the needed structural overhaul of thinking and processes which would enable the Nigerian press to remain a part of the democratic space. The study therefore seeks to answer the following research questions, using print media with national circulation:

1. What is the profile of journalists in print media in arrears of staff sala-ries?
2. How do these journalists cope when salaries are not paid
3. Has working conditions affected the enthusiasm of journalists for their job?
4. Have journalists had conflict of interest as a result of such financial conditions?
5. Do journalists see the mass media in Nigeria effectively playing their role in entrenching democracy, if such working conditions persist?

Significance of the Study

Nigeria presents the paradox of a resource rich country gripped by the scourge of poverty. Although the reform agenda of the administration of President Olusegun Obasanjo has through NEEDS targeted poverty eradication, his nationwide broadcast on June 30, 2005, on the cancellation of 60% of the country's debt to the Paris Club, was at least, a celebration of the strides against the scourge. However, poverty remains a key problem, just like the conditions which give rise to and has sustained it. Its eradication by 2015 is the most important global and national priority (Millennium Development, 2004, p.7). While there are those who insist that deepening poverty has its foundation in structures dating back to the colony (Causes of Poverty, 2005, p. 27), its stunting of the potential of individuals and institutions, require its scrutiny for institutional reforms, including of the media which are stakeholders in the struggle for the democratization of the Nigeria space.

This study not only attempts a view of the potential of the print media from the inside – the perspective of journalists who are daily participants in the process of defining a direction for national development, but seeks a better understanding of the relationship between working conditions and professionalism, corruption and the democratic enterprise. Since sections of the print media are credited with helping to shape events through the countries tortuous route to a civilian dispensation, it is expected that the same media would be crucial in the entrenchment of democracy. This study is designed to assist this process.

Limitation

The focus of the study was national newspapers and magazines bases in Lagos, Nigeria. This selection was based on the number and variety of print media in this city which is the media headquarters of Nigeria. Some of the selected media were also active in ushering in civilian rule through their combative and investigative journalism. This means that other national print media outside of Lagos were excluded, just like the electronic media, some of which also owe their staff salaries. This restriction could affect the conclusions of this study. However, and given the antecedents of the print media whose journalists were sampled, the study's findings are expected to be sufficiently representative of the perceptions of journalists in Nigeria on the research questions.

The Selected Media

Five newspapers and two national general interest magazines were selected for the study. The newspapers are *Champion, Comet, New Age, This Day* and *Vanguard,* while the magazines are *Newswatch* and *The News.*

Newswatch was launched on January 25, 1985 under the military by a quartet of tested journalists led by the late Dele Giwa, and including Ray Ekpu, Dan Agbese and Yakubu Mohammed. It was the flagship in that genre of publishing and gave investigative journalism a new face. It has continued to be relevant years after losing their founding editor-in-chief to a parcel bomb, but is now in experiencing difficulties, managing somehow to publish weekly.

The News started February 1, 1993 by a team led by Bayo Onanuga as a fallout of the principled stand of some editors in the *African Concord* who reportedly refused to apologize over a story. The magazine and its stable mates like the rested *Tempo,* epitomized guerrilla journalism in the heat of military rule, while its stories contributed to the resignation of the first speaker of the House of Representatives after the return to civilian rule in 1999.

Vanguard, owned by the veteran Sam Amuka-Pemu, commenced publication in 1984; *Champion* was launched on October 1, 1988 by Chief Emmanuel Iwuanyanwu; *ThisDay* owned by Nduka Obaigbena, started publication on January 22, 1995; and the Comet came on board in June 1999, shortly after the restoration of civilian rule. The most recent of the publications is *New Age* which hit the stands on February 11, 2003 and attracted many young but experienced journalists.

One uniting factor is that all the publications are privately owned and founded by journalists, except *Champion* whose proprietor is a known businessman. Each of the papers is a recognizable brand in the increasingly competitive market with over 40 titles in the magazine segment and over 90 titles in the newspaper segment (Nigerian Media Facts, 2004, p.16). The publications and their journalists feature yearly on the list of winners in media awards, including the Diamond Awards for Media Excellence (DAME) and the Nigerian Media Merit Award (NNMA).

Literature Review and Theoretical Framework

Poverty

Various explanations of the concept of poverty associate it with lack, inadequacy, insufficiency, neglect (Igbuzor, 2004, p. 45; Nnamani, 2005, p. 59). It is a structural problem, the evidence of underdevelopment, and deeply political (Ibeanu, 2004, p. 8). It is also endemic (Thomas (2002, p.2). In Nigeria, it accounts for worsening disparities in income, social inequality and plays a role in social deviation and marginalization (Social Development, 1988, pp. 10-12; Lockwood, 1997, p. 96).

In an analysis of how poverty occurs in Nigeria, the National Policy on Poverty Eradication and t Commonwealth Human Rights Initiative, quoted by Igbuzor (2004) respectively, state that its causes:

> include macro-economic distortions characterized by dependence on oil revenue, …problems of unstable interest and exchange rates, high interest rates, inappropriate policies, structural adjustment program, effects of globalization, bad governance, corruption, debt burden, low productivity , unemployment, high population growth, and human resources development…Poverty is created…born out of consistent and unchecked theft and waste of community resources, corruption and misappropriation of public and private wealth…poverty is caused by largely unaccountable systems (pp. 46-48).

The statistics captured by the UNDP annual Human Development Report, described as showing globalization bereft of a human face (Nuscheler, 2003, p. 383), has consistently ranked Nigeria as one of the poorest countries in the world. According to Nnamani, by 1996, 87% of the population were living in poverty.

This grave scenario point to shortcomings in the management of the country's resources since independence. It suggests a drift in governance irrespective of regime type and poor levels of control. The media have occasional jolt the political leadership which have also sought ways to curtail and compromise the press, sometimes arm twisting journalists to relent. Where the media have succumbed, the development process and the Nigerian people have been the loser.

Professionalism

The media are watchdogs in the service of good governance, but like every guard dog, there are a number of possibilities which could affect or infect performance. The professional media are standard bearers able to promote freedom and the pluralism which hallmark a democratic regime (Chan, 2002, p. 6). Professional considerations constitute the core of codes of ethics which tends to assume a generic character across nations (Owens-Ibie, 2003, pp. 388-407). However, Chambers (1999, pp. 228-229), distinguishes between normal professionalism stressing dominant and acceptable values, methods, ideas and behavior, and the new professionalism which is clear and not hidden behind the cloak of assumptions of what constitutes objectivity. No matter the perspective, there is a general understanding of what in the case of the media, is professional.

Media prejudice engenders conflict (Dembowski, 2004, p.267) and it is not only a source of alienation, but deepens the class divide, further disempowering the poor and constricting the process of democratization. Within the Nigerian space, concerns have been expressed about the commercialization of access through charging of fees for the coverage of politics (Adaba, 1998, p.28), and partisanship in media coverage, including sponsored publications against opponents, for a fee.

Democracy, Democratization, Corruption and the Media in Nigeria

Since Aristotle, democracy which he defined as a government of the people (Rummel, 2005), has developed into a global model of good governance, enabling the people to enjoy political power and freedom (Ayedun-Aluma, 1996, p.50). Deriving its strength from popular consent in an organized setting (Obasanjo, 1992, p.7), understood as a process involving the decentralization of power for it to consolidate (Babawale, 2003, p. 226), and hinged on a virile civil society as catalyst. Its locus is the principle of accountability and the distribution of economic benefits for the greater good (Mittelman, 1997, p. 8).

Bratton & Mattes (2001) show in their study of six African countries, including Nigeria, that democracy is the preferred form of government, but this system of government is still evolving, and characterized by elitism, while fundamental problems persist (Erdmann, 2003, p.378). Subsisting poverty constrain participation (Cheru, 1997, p. 153).

These problems have influenced extreme positions like that of Maduagwu (1996, p.13) who characterized Nigeria as typical of a failed democracy. There are problems of concentration of power at the centre and ethnic polarization (Durotoye, 2000, p.26). Abati-1 (2005) regards what is being practiced as a democracy where the people are spectators and one which is celebrated at the level boreholes and other peripherals, with politicians more interested in their political future than the needs of the governed. This is in spite of the fact that popular support is a key factor in the country's politics (Joseph, 1991, p. 10).

Democratization therefore is a route to the reordering of the structure of power (Chan, 2002, p.6), with emphasis on social justice (Awa, 1993, p.66). It is a complex process (Walle, 2000,) admitting local and international factors, actors and forces. There is consequently the need to develop institutions and processes which are in tune with the needs of society (Brown, 2004, p. 6). This would mean that dissenting voices are accommodated, while the strangle-hood of the elites on the political process is better moderated (see Dauderstudt, 2005, p. 144-145).

It is within this context, that the relationship between the media and democratization can be better analyzed. That the press can promote democracy is fact (Rummel, 2005). Societies need credible media to be efficient, as media role is foundational (Owens-Ibie, Noma, 2002, p.233), although the institution is faced with the choice of whether to be relevant to the needs of the people or not (Idowu, 2001; Chan, 2002). This decision flows from the power structure and requires good judgment conditioned by the working conditions of journalists (Dembowski, 2004), since they have to contend with forces of destabilization (Ogundimu, 1997, p. 8) and in view of the mainstream fixation with fostering the charter of globalization and promoting statistics on economic growth (Thomas, 2002, p.9). The consolidation of elite hold on the media in Nigeria, in itself, raises questions on whether a media constricted by the logic of ownership, is able to break free to promote the greater good of the greater number.

The combination of environmental determinants and corruption, highlight the fundamentals necessary for a clearer understanding of the true potential of the media. While Khan (1996, p. 12, 20) defines corruption as deviance leading to conduct which seek to benefit privately, someone in a position of authority, Olivier de Sardan (1999, pp. 27-45) broadens the concept to a more appropriate "corruption complex", admitting acts like abuse of power and public office, influence peddling, nepotism, misappropriation of resources and embezzlement.

Corruption has become such a problem in Nigeria that it was described, along with the military, as the obstacles to democratic stability in the country (Maduagwu, 1996). Its impact on the poverty index and the development process has manifested in economically unproductive projects (Frisch, 1994, pp. 59-60). The perversion of social values fuelled by corruption, account for the desperation with which political office is sought. Such perversion explains the thinking among some that corruption is an antidote to poverty (Soleye, 1994, p. 63).

Despite the pervading role of corruption, there is an acknowledgement that the media are critical in any meaningful anti-corruption movement (Abati-2, 2005). In Nigeria, this role has been compromised by the material condition of journalists and led to the observation of Karl Maier (see Olukotun, 2004, p.11) that the payment of journalists is a tradition. This may explain accusations that journalists in Nigeria are part of the problem since they "promote the wrong people, defend rogues and celebrate mediocrity" (Abati-3, 2005).

This scenario has spawned the paradox of a more professionally prepared media, operating under an environment not conducive to the fight against corruption (Fatoyinbo, 1994, p.161).

Working Conditions of Journalists

Economic conditions have taken their toll on the media as an industry in Nigeria known to have been the voice of a cowed civil society during the trying days of military rule. But even this role under post military rule is steeped in a basic contradiction, with the media insisting on accountability by the political class, while being themselves implicated in "the abuses they had tried to expose." (Olukotun, 2004, p.3). The accounts of the umbrella Nigerian Union of Journalists (NUJ) was, according to its president, Smart Adeyemi (see Olalere, 2004, p. 24), for instance, not audited between 1993 and 1999.

Within the industry, working conditions have not been empowering. Salaries of "most private media houses" are not paid, noted Adeyemi. In *Newswatch* magazine, the NUJ had to reach an agreement with the management to settle arrears of unpaid salaries of over a year (see Biobaku, 2004, p. 8). At the relatively stable *The Guardian* newspaper, styled the flagship of the Nigerian press, workers went on strike twice in 11 months to press for better working conditions, a claim the paper's management disputed (Are Journalists, 2001, pp. 14-15).

Statistics on the remuneration of journalists in four national newspapers – *Punch, ThisDay, Vanguard* and *Daily Times,* show that as at 2001, editors in the first two papers with 7-10 years experience, earned a minimum of N750, 000 annually. This was the best case scenario of the four publications, and contrasted with the pay of graduate and line reporters. Although such pay was relatively small, compared to those of other professionals in banks and the oil industry, it was remarkable that many of the journalists interviewed were not willing to change jobs. However, such poor pay has been linked to unethical practices by journalists. There is the inherent paralysis of meaningful professional initiative in the process, as resources are not available for investigative work (Kujenya, 2004).

Theoretical Considerations

The Poverty Reduction Strategy Paper (PRSP) offers a viable platform and theoretical framework for examining the relationship between poverty and the capacity of key stakeholders in the democratic enterprise–like the media in Nigeria, to actualize their potential. Ibeanu (2004, pp. 1-20) attempts to dissect Nigeria's PRSP, flawing its fundamental assumptions. PRSP, he states, is ideological and requires an ideological perspective, being a development-related policy attempting to address the subsisting crisis of capitalist development in the South. It is to him, a refurbished version of the Structural Adjustment Program (SAP) of the 1980s which failed to alter the status quo of underdevelopment in the periphery.

The PRSP's neo-liberal orientation locates it within the capitalist development paradigm classified into the economic, social and political phases. This paradigm implicitly recognizes a Western model of the ideal which to a large extent discountenances the African social formation, while also emphasizing minimum government. This contrasts with the Marxist development paradigm which is people-centered and functions on integrated approach stressing the "character of the division of labor". It does not have faith in market forces and general works on the premise that "poverty is an expression of underdevelopment, not its cause." The analysis discusses the four myths of PRSP, including its assumptions on the "immediacy of poverty", that the reduction of poverty is the route to development, that of "learning from the poor", and that poverty can be separated from politics.

Schneider's conclusion (2003, pp. 415-417) is that the PRSP process hardly admits the contributions of representative democratic structures and is in fact in crisis because of the gulf between plans and the enabling environment, including finances for effective implementation. This crisis, for transitional societies like Nigeria, represents a hurdle with clear implications for the democratic project. This study takes a cue from this dilemma.

Methodology

The study sought to investigate the perceptions of journalists in seven print media organizations in Nigeria on issues relating to their working conditions and how this impacts on their professional performance within the democratic space. An 18-item questionnaire was designed and administered on 101 randomly selected journalists covering various beats in the print media which have not been paying salaries regularly. These included rewrite men who are pat of the news structure. The questionnaires were administered between September and November 2005. There were delays in obtaining the completed instruments.

Universe/Population and Sample

The universe included of all mass media and journalists in Nigeria. The sample consisted journalists in selected print media where salaries have not been regular at the time of the survey. The criterion for selection was that the respondent was a journalist working in the particular media long enough to qualify to be paid a salary.

Results and discussion

The findings are discussed in the order of the research questions.

Profile of Journalists.

Two thirds of respondents are male with 57% of them married. Out of the 25% that are female, 42.9% of them are married. The monthly income of a third of them is less than N19, 999, while the majority (63.2%) earn between N20, 000 and N49, 000. Only 3.4% get between N50, 000 and N100, 000. A total of 30.2% have spent less than a year on their current jobs, 46.5% have stayed between 1-5 years, 18.6% have been on the job for 6-10 years, while 4.7% have been there for over 10 years. Most of the respondents (76.8%) had not been paid for between 0-6 months, and 23.2% for 7-12 months. Over 71% of them said that their employers offered explanations for the non-payment of their salaries, with over half saying they have only had the experience of not being paid once, 34.3% have experienced it 2-5 times, while 29% have not been paid salaries on more than different five occasions.

This scenario presupposes pressure on these journalists to take care of dependants. With economic conditions necessitating contributions of wives and sisters to family upkeep, the females, married or unmarried, are likely to face pressures to support members of their nuclear or extended family. Inability to discharge this responsibility could easily become sources of confliction and personality and social problems. The response to such challenges may be the compromise of ethical standards and insinuations about their activities of journalists (see Abati, 2005-3).

In spite of the nature of the question, a little over half of them claimed to depend on friends/relations to survive when salaries are not paid, while a fifth said they moonlight. That four respondents admitted depending on gratifications exclusively, while over a tenth of respondents combine assistance from relations/friends/doing other jobs, with relying on gratifications, is important. Some additional responses included "I trust in God", "divine intervention" and "advert commission", paid to those who are able to source for adverts. A related question seeking to know if journalists get voluntary support from news sources show 48 or 77.4% agreeing that they do, four or 6.5% admitted requesting for such support, while 10 or 16.1% agree to both being voluntarily supported and requesting for such support. These provide some justification for the assertion that there exist a tradition of paying journalists in Nigeria (see Olukotun, 2004), although such conclusions negate the fact of the presence of principled journalists with a record of recognition and awards internationally, including the CNN African Journalist of the Year and a Pulitzer Prize.

Coping strategy when salaries are not paid.

Table 1: Coping Strategy

Publica-tion	Relations/ Friends	Do other Jobs	Gratifi-cations	Relations/ Friends/O ther Jobs	Relations/ Friends/ Other Jobs/Gratifications
Cham-pion	6	4	1	1	2
Comet	8	1			1
New Age	8	2	2	2	
ThisDay	3	2			
Vanguard	3	2	1	1	4
News-watch	1	1			
The News	1				
Total	N = 30 52.6%	N = 12 21.1%	N = 4 7.02%	N = 4 7.02%	N = 7 12.3%

Effect of working conditions on enthusiasm for the job.

Table 2: Has Working Condition Affected Job Enthusiasm?

Publication	Yes	No
Champion	8	6
Comet	8	5
New Age	12	3
ThisDay	10	2
Vanguard	9	8
Newswatch	6	4
The News	7	8
Total	N = 60 62.5%	N = 36 37.5%

More than half of the journalists admit that their working condition has affected their enthusiasm for the job. Only more than a third of them claim not to be affected. This finding is in itself a problem, with implications for commitment to duty and professionalism. When asked if they were willing to remain on the same job if job conditions are okay, an overwhelming 79 (86.8%) of 99 respondents said "yes", but when asked if they would remain on the job if offered another job, a lesser number–54 or 58.1% said "yes", while 39 or 41.9% said "no". When the "yes" group was further asked what the attraction is of being a journalist, 51 or 83.6% mentioned "natural interest", five or 8.2% said it was because journalism "makes me known", while five or 8.2% mentioned various other reasons, ranging from "it places me where I can influence change", "it is a step to what I want to achieve", "it opens a world of opportunities and education", and "love for the profession and time". These support views of proponents of the media who believe that the challenge is to build on the strengths by exploring a way to retain the commitment of journalists who are determined to negotiate their "way to a better future in the profession.

Sanctions for non-performance of duties when salaries are not paid.

Table 3: Any Sanctions Not Meeting Job Expectations Since Non-Payment of Salary?

Publication	Yes		No
Champion	11		3
Comet	2		7
New Age	9		4
ThisDay	5		7
Vanguard	7		7
Newswatch	1		10
The News	3		6
Total	N = 38	46.3%	N = 44 53.7%

Although the rules of engagement prescribes minimum expectations and high professional standards as enshrined in codes of ethics (Owens-Ibie, 2003), it is remarkable that less than half of the respondents said they were sanctioned for failing to meet job expectations during periods of non-payment of salaries. That over half of them are not sanctioned may either mean that they discharge their responsibilities and meet deadlines, or that management is not persuaded to wield the stick, since the organizations too failed to meet their part of the bargain. A related finding that close to 66 or 72.5%, claim that workers, which would include themselves, have not protested the non-payment of their salaries, could mean that the new status quo may have offered other opportunities which were not stated. It could also mean that given the scarcity of jobs and high unemployment figures, working without salaries which are likely to be paid at a later date, was better than unemployment. The 25 or 27.5% who said that there have been protests could have been expressing reactions at individual levels. If there were major incidents like the strike of staff of The Guardian in 2001, they could have been reported. These may be indications of what Olukotun (2002, p.103) refers to as the "weak capacity profile of the media". They negate the requirements for an efficient media in an equally conflicted state structure.

Conflict of interest as a result of working conditions.

Table 4: Conflict of Interest Due to Financial Condition

Publication	Yes	No
Champion	4	10
Comet	2	13
New Age	6	9
ThisDay	3	9
Vanguard	4	10
Newswatch	1	10
The News	10	5
Total	N = 30 31.3%	N = 66 68.75%

That a third of journalists agree that they experience conflict of interest in the course of their assignments due to their economic disempowerment is remarkable. Even if working conditions are normal, a variety of factors could moderate the focus or level of neutrality of journalists in the course of duty. These could relate to religious, political, cultural or economic interests and influences which affect what to accord priority, whom or what to focus on, the subject of the next investigative piece, the scope of coverage, who is the potential advertiser and how to secure his patronage, security concerns and other considerations which translate to self-censorship.

Prospects for media effectiveness in entrenching democracy given current conditions.

Table 5: Can Media Assist in Entrenching Democracy Under Current Working Conditions.

Publication	Yes	No	Only Partially
Champion	2	9	4
Comet	4	4	5
New Age		9	6
ThisDay			12
Vanguard	4	3	7
Newswatch			7
The News	1	4	8
Total	N=11 12.5%	n=29 32.6%	n=49 55.1%

The perceptions of respondents on the capacity of the media to assist current efforts to democratize if the situation of non-payment of journalists persist, is important. A combination of those who say the media cannot assist the process, given such conditions, and those who say media can "only partially" be relevant if poor working conditions continue is 87.7%. This suggests that journalists are aware of how much poor working conditions can hinder the effectiveness of the fourth estate of the realm. As Dembowski (2004) has noted, where working conditions are not right, journalists cannot be effective catalysts of the democratic process.

Summary, Conclusion and Recommendations

This study sought answers to five research questions in order to better understand the perceptions of journalists about how working conditions affect their performance and potential contributions to the democratization process in Nigeria. The findings presented using five tables but with other related answers, included those on the profile of the respondents, how they coped during periods of non-payment of salaries, whether they were sanctioned for not meeting job expectations when not paid, whether they experienced conflict of interest due to such financial constraints, and whether they see the media being effective in assisting the process of democratization, if such working conditions persist.

The findings show that most of the journalists are male, married, on monthly incomes of between N20,000 and N49,999, spent between less than one and five years on the job, and have not received their salaries for between zero to 12 months. While over 73..7% rely on relations/friends/ and do other jobs to cope during periods of non-payment of salaries, some others admitted relying on gratifications, in some cases using it to supplement assistance from family, friends and the proceeds from moonlighting. Close to eight of every 10 agree that news sources voluntarily support them, while some others said they request for support from such sources. Almost one in six of them both request for and get voluntary support. A majority of journalists agree that working conditions have affected their enthusiasm for the job with a little over half expressing a willingness to change jobs if they got an offer. Although a little over half of them said they are not sanctioned if they fail to meet job expectations during periods of non-payment of salary, a higher percentage said workers have never protested over their conditions. While only a third admits conflict of interest due to their material condition, an overwhelming majority believe that the media would not be able to assist the democratization process or can only partially assist the process, if such economic conditions persist.

Conclusion

The implications of the findings of this study are serious for the Nigerian print media and mass media in general, given their antecedents in being catalyst during various phases in the countries development. The media and journalists are apparent victims of the poverty they are supposed to hold government accountable for its eradication. Given the history of previous mismanagement and a reform agenda, symbolized by NEEDS, which is being promoted as a local strategy targeting poverty eradication (Amadi-1, 2004, p.10), it is obvious that an empowered mass media is a necessity.

Recommendations

The structural and institutional reform needed to consolidate the country's democracy, must therefore start with the mass media. Stakeholders in the democracy project would need to explore strategic options to extricate the mass media (especially the print media) from a terminal condition. The democracy dream may well be an illusion without this. In spite of the liberalization of the economic space, based on the logic of globalization which is further entrenching Nigerian media into a mainstream (Owens-Ibie, 2000, p.42), the circumstances giving rise to the emasculation of a privatizing media, needs be examined. As Amadi-2 (2004, p.42) has noted, by its character, privatization as a political tool does sometimes work against the practice of democracy. It is in striking a balance between restoring the virility of a professional mass media in Nigeria without a recourse to the debilitating constriction of the highly bureaucratized media of hopefully blessed memory, that there would emerge a print and mass media with enabling working conditions and able to discharge its constitutional mandate. Market forces operating solely may be poor arbiters of such a strategic imperative.

References

Abati, R. (2005)-1. How not to celebrate democracy. *The Guardian.* Retrieved from the Web May 27, 2005. http://www.ngrguardiannews.com.
_____ (2005)-2. Obasanjo and the media. *The Guardian,* Retrieved from the Web April 15. http://www.ngrguardiannews.com.
_____ (2005)-3. A parable for Nigeria. *The Guardian,* Retrieved from the Web June 17, 2005. http://www.ngrguardiannews.com.
Adaba, T. (1997, December/1998, January). Selling news on the air. *Media Review.*
Amadi, S. (2004) -1. Contextualizing NEEDS: Politics and economic development. In S. Amadi & F. Ogwo (Eds.) *Contextualizing NEEDS: Economic/political reform in Nigeria.* Lagos: The Human Rights Law Service & Center for Public Policy. Retrieved from the Web June 21, 2005. http://www.boelnigeria.org/index.html.
_____ (2004). Privatizing without reforming: The case of Nigeria, In S.
Amadi & F. Ogwo (Eds.) *Contextualizing NEEDS: Economic/political reform in Nigeria.* Lagos: The Human Rights Law Service & Center for Public Policy. Retrieved from the Web June 21, 2005. http://www.boelnigeria.org/index.html.
Are journalists really poorly paid? (2004). *Media Review,* July/August
Asante, S.K.B. (1991). *African Development: Adebayo Adedeji's alternative strategies.* Ibadan: Spectrum Books Limited.
Awa, E. (1993). Strategies for achieving democratization in Africa. In A. Aderinwale, (Ed.) *Conclusions and Papers presented at conferences of the Africa Leadership Forum on sustenance of democratization and good governance in Africa, Cotonou, Benin Republic 5-6 October 1992 and challenges of leadership in democracy and good governance in Africa, Nairobi, Kenya 10-12 March 1993.* Abeokuta: Africa Leadership Forum.
Ayedun-Aluma, V.S. (1996). The role of the press in promoting democracy. In I. Ibrahim & T. Akanni (Eds.) *The mass media and democracy.* Lagos: Civil Liberties Organization.
Babawale, T. (2003). The 2003 elections and democratic consolidation in Nigeria. In R. Anifowoshe & T. Babawale (Eds.) *2003 general elections and democratic consolidation in Nigeria.* Lagos: Friedrich Ebert Stiftung.
Biobaku, S. (2004). *Newswatch directors are govt. contractors – NUJ. Sunday Sun,* November 7.
Bratton, M. & Mattes, R. (2001). Democratic and market reforms in Africa: What "what the people say". Retrieved from the Web June 22, 2005. http://democracy.stanford.edu.
Causes of poverty in Africa, by Summa Guaranty boss (2005). *ThisDay,* 11: 3718, June 27.
Brown, M. M. (2004). Governing for the 21st century. *Choices,* March.
Chambers, R. (1999). *Whose reality counts: Putting the first last.* London: Intermediate Technology Publications.

Chan, J.M. (2002). Media, democracy and globalization: A comparative perspective. *Media Development*, 1. Retrieved from the Web June 5, 2002. http://www.wacc.org.uk/publications/md/md2002-1/chan.html.

Cheru, F. (1997). New social movements: Democratic struggles and human rights in Africa. In J. Mittelman, *Globalization: Critical reflections*. London: Lynne Rienner Publishers Inc.

Dauderstudt, M. (2005). Lost in transition, *D & C*, 32:4.

Dembowski, H. (2004). The Fourth Estate. *D + C*, 31.

Diamond, L. (2001). Developing democracy in Africa: African and international imperatives. Retrieved from the Web June 22, 2005. http://www.democracy.stanford.edu.

Durotoye, A. (2000). The bumpy road towards sustaining democracy. *D & C*, 4, July/August.

Erdmann, G. (2003). Twelve years of hope for democracy: An interim assessment. *D & C*, 30, October.

Fatoyinbo, A. (1994). The mass media and the campaign against corruption. In A. Aderinwale (Ed.) *Corruption, democracy and human rights in West Africa (Summary report of a seminar organized by Africa Leadership Forum in Cotonou, September 1994*. Ibadan: Africa Leadership Forum.

Frisch, P. (1994). Effects of corruption on development. In A. Aderinwale, *Corruption, democracy and human rights in West Africa (summary report of a seminar organized by Africa Leadership Forum in Cotonou, September 1994*. Ibadan: Africa Leadership Forum.

Global Monitoring Report (2005) *Millennium Development Goals: From Consensus to momentum*. Retrieved from the Web November 26, 2005.http://www.worldbank.org

Esan, O. (2004). African Media and the new partnership for African development (NEPAD), *Africa Media Review* - in press, 12:2, 41-57.

Folger, J.P., Poole, M.S., & Stuttman, R.K. (1997). *Working through conflict*. New York: Addison-Wesley Educational Publishers Inc.

Harneit-Sievers, A. (2004). Reforming the state: Some thoughts on NEEDS. In S. Amadi & F. Ogwo (Eds.) (2004) Contextualizing NEEDS: Economic/political reform in Nigeria. Lagos: The Human Rights Law Service & Center for Public Policy & Research. Retrieved from the Web June 21, 2005. http://www.boelnigeria.org/index.html

Ibeanu, O., (2004). Alternative poverty eradication strategy: introductory issues. In Centre for Democracy & Development (Ed.), *Alternative poverty reduction strategy for Nigeria*. Lagos: Centre for Democracy & Development.

Idowu, L. (2001). The media, democracy and good governance. *Media Review*, July/August.

Igbuzor, O. (2004). Poverty eradication and public policy in Nigeria. In Centre for Democracy & Development (Ed.), *Alternative poverty reduction strategy for Nigeria*. Lagos: Centre for Democracy & development.

Joseph, R. (1991). *Democracy and prebendal politics in Nigeria: The rise and fall of the Second Republic*. Ibadan: Spectrum Books Limited.

Khan, M.H. (1996). A typology of corrupt transactions in developing countries. *IDS Bulletin*, 27:2.

Kujenya, J. (2004). Lack of money impedes investigative journalism in Nigeria. Retrieved from the Web June 22, 2005. http:// IJNet: International Journalists Network.

Lockwood, M. (1997). Reproduction and poverty in sub-Saharan Africa, *IDS Bulletin,* 28:3.

Maduagwu, M.O. (1996). Nigeria in search of political culture: The political class, corruption and democratization. In A. Gboyega (Ed.) *Corruption and democratization in Nigeria.* Ibadan: Lagos: Friedrich Ebert Foundation.

Millennium Development Goals Report 2004 – Nigeria

Mittelman, J.H. (1997). The dynamics of globalization. In J.H. Mittelman (Ed.). *Globalization: critical reflections.* London: Lynne Rienner Publishers Inc.

Nigerian Media Facts 2004. Retrieved from the Web on *September 9,* 2005. http://www.mediareachomd.com.

Nnamani, C. (2005). Poverty in Surplus. *The News,* August 15.

Nuscheler, F. (2003). Globalization – opportunity or obstacle for development. *D + C,* 30, October.

Obasanjo, O. (1993). Welcome address. In A. Aderinwale (Ed.) *Conclusions and papers presented at conferences of the Africa Leadership Forum on sustenance of democratization and good governance in Africa, Cotonou, Benin Republic 5-6 October 1992 and challenges of leadership in democracy and good governance in Africa, Nairobi, Kenya 10-12 March 1993.* Abeokuta: Africa Leadership Forum.

Ogundimu, F.F. (1997). Mass media and democratization in sub-Saharan Africa – introduction. *African Rural and Urban Studies,* 4:1

Olalere, A. (2004) "Journalists'll have to take their destiny in own hands – Adeyemi". *Sunday Sun,* November 4.

Olivier de Sardan, J.P. (1999). A moral economy of corruption in Africa? *The Journal of Modern African Studies.* 37:1, March.

Olutkotun, A. (2002). The media and national development: Opportunities and constraints, In L. Oso (Ed.) *Communication and development: A reader.* Abeokuta: Jedidiah Publishers.

_____ (2004). Media accountability and democracy in Nigeria, 1999-2003, *African Studies Review,* December. Retrieved from the Web June 24, 2005. http://www.furl.net/index.jsp.

Owens-Ibie, Noma (2002). Mass media and the construction of political ideals : A discussion on the United States and Nigeria. In S.O. Amali, Noma Owens-Ibie, F. Ogunleye, C. Uji, O. Adesina (Eds.) *Consolidation and sustenance of democracy: The United States of America and Nigeria.* Ibadan: American Studies Association of Nigeria.

Owens-Ibie, Nosa (2000). Globalization and the mass media in Nigeria, *Unilag Sociological Review,* 1, July.

_____ (2002). Socio-cultural considerations in conflict reporting in Nigeria. In U. Pate (Ed.) *Introduction to conflict reporting in Nigeria.* Lagos: Friedrich Ebert Stiftung.

_____ (2003). Towards the democratization process: Ethical dimensions in reporting political affairs in Nigeria. In B. Olasupo (Ed.), *Electoral violence in Nigeria: Issues and perspectives.* Lagos: Friedrich Ebert Stiftung.

Rummel, R.J. (2005). Democratization. Retrieved from the Web June 22, 2005. http://www.hawaii.edu/powerkills/DEMOC.

Rummel, R.J. (2005). Freedom of the press: A way to global peace. Retrieved from the Web June 22, 2005. http://www.hawaii.edu/powerkills/DEMOC.

Schneider, A.K. (2003). Between poverty reduction and macroeconomic stability: PRS-structural adjustment under a new name, *D & C*, 30, November.

Social Development Department, (NISER) (1988). Social impact of structural adjustment program. *NISER Monograph Series.* Ibadan: Nigerian Institute of Social and Economic Research.

Soleye, O. ((1994). Effects of corruption on development. In A. Aderinwale, *Corruption, democracy and human rights in West Africa (Summary report of a seminar organized by Africa Leadership Forum in Cotonou, September 1994).* Ibadan: Africa Leadership Forum.

The Constitution of the Federal Republic of Nigeria (1999)

Thomas, P. (2002). Beyond the pale: Poverty in an era of cutting-edge communications; A view from India. *Media Development,* 2. Retrieved from the Web May 23, 2002. http://www.wacc.org.uk/uk/publications/md/md2002-2/thomas_poverty.html.

Walle, N. v d, (2000). The impact of multi-party politics on sub-Saharan Africa. Retrieved from the Web June 22, 2005. http://democracy.stanford.edu.

Chapter 22

Language of Conflict and the Coverage of Global Terrorism in Kenyan Mass Media 1998-2005

Benson Oduor Ojwang'
Maseno University, KENYA

Introduction

Improved communication systems and globalization have given rise to increased concerns over new conflict dimensions such as transnational terrorism and the proliferation of nuclear arms and other weapons of mass destruction. How prepared is the world to counter this trend? Developing countries like Kenya are the most vulnerable and ill equipped to deal with eventualities like bomb attacks and the attendant death and destruction.

In this chapter, the Kenyan experience is presented to exemplify how global conflicts give rise to a host of other problems. Newspapers have the advantage of being permanent records and are only second to radio in terms of reach in Kenya. Therefore, it is through the eyes of the news writers that we shall examine the causes, management and interpretations of conflict situations arising from terrorist attacks. As Wolfsfeld (1997) observes, 'the news media have become the central arena for political conflicts today' (p.3).

Kenya, hitherto a relatively peaceful nation, has suffered terrorist attacks twice in a space of only four years. First was the bombing of the U.S. Embassy in Nairobi in 1998, which killed 224 people and wounded well over 5,000 others. Secondly, in November 2002, Paradise hotel near Mombasa was bombed, killing 20 and leaving the hotel shattered. On this occasion, there was also an unsuccessful missile attack on an Israeli airliner that was just taking off from Mombasa airport with several Israeli tourists on board. The two incidents awakened the Kenya government and her ring of friendly nations to the reality of international terrorism, proving that Kenya was no longer a safe haven or the world famous trouble-free destination that thousands of tourists from Europe and many parts of the world had always known.

The reaction of the U.S government, a key political and economic ally of Kenya, was immediate and decisive. Forensic experts were flown in and humanitarian assistance facilitated. Israel sent rescue teams as well, complete with sniffer dogs and world attention turned to Kenya. The Kenyan mass media was also squarely on the spotlight. However, despite the international concern and empathy showered on Kenyan victims, many Kenyans including the then President Arap Moi saw the attack as a foreign war replayed in Kenyan territory.

The two attacks marked a turning point in Kenya's intelligence strategies, disaster preparedness, foreign policy, communication network and both internal and cross-border security systems and operations. The need to comprehend terrorism as a major conflict situation with significant consequences became urgent because there is an interconnectedness of peace, conflict and development. It should also be borne in mind that peace does not only mean the absence of war. It must also include the absence of the threat of war. Moreover, it is now a reality that global security can impact greatly on regional security and vice versa. Kenya's numerous appeals to the United States government in the wake of the 1998 bombing of Nairobi demonstrate the fact that most African nations depend on the co-operation or assistance of other nations or on international organizations to meet the challenges of peace and security. Unfortunately, it is instructive that there still are problems of pending compensation claims by the 1998 bomb victims.

In the next section, some theoretical perspectives are presented to help explain the recurrence of terrorism within the wider context of social, political and religious conflict.

Theoretical Framework

This chapter adopts the sociological theory of terrorism to approach the conflict situation caused by terrorism in Kenya and Africa in general. Modern sociological perspectives on terrorism are primarily concerned with the social construction of fear and panic, and how institutions and processes, especially the media, primary and secondary groups, maintain that expression of fear (O'Connor, 2000, Gibbs, 1989). However, the social constructionist viewpoint is all about consequences [of terrorism], not its causes.

The sociological framework provides the criteria to chart the way terrorism impacts on the evolution of a whole society by affecting core values of achievement, competition, and individualism. It is argued that some societies become softer targets after experiencing terrorism, and other societies become stronger afterwards. The framework predicts that how a society comes out of a terror attack depends not only upon interaction patterns, but also stabilities and interpenetrations among the structural subsystems (economy, politics, religion, and law) of that society.

Illustrations in our discussion show how terrorism can be constructed by the media both as a cause and an outcome of conflict. It will also become apparent that terrorism entails a number of subcultures and personality factors as well as competition for world political supremacy. We shall adopt the definition by the U.S Department of State that describes terrorism as a 'premeditated, politically motivated violence perpetrated against noncombatant targets by sub-national groups or clandestine agents, usually intended to influence an audience' (Essner, 2003 p.6).

The Genesis of the Terrorism Conflict in Kenya and its Aftermath

After the 1998 bombing of the U.S. Embassy in Nairobi, investigations began both locally and internationally. However, Kenyan police faired amateurishly, arresting and releasing suspects and sometimes failing to identify them even after the CIA released their pictures. This laxity later emerged in 2004 in New York during the trial of some bomb suspects. According to evidence from the trial in New York of four men charged with conspiracy in the bombing of the U.S. Embassy, suspected terror mastermind Osama Bin Laden reportedly sent some of his men to Kenya in 1993 to scout out bombing targets, including not only the American embassy but also unspecified Israeli interests. Evidence introduced in the trial also indicated that Al Qaeda had operated in the Kenyan capital since 1993 and in Mombasa since 1994. All this time, Kenyan state security agents never detected their activities.

A series of conflicts ensued. Firstly, an announcement of an evacuation program for Americans living in Kenya was released. This abrupt order would only serve to heighten fear and panic not only among the Americans but also the affected Kenyans. Various news agencies reported that Americans in both Kenya and Tanzania were urged to depart if they deemed it appropriate. Such advice led to the abandonment of a lot of unfinished business.

The second conflict that arose from the bombing was a travel advisory discouraging incoming tourists against choosing Kenya as a destination. The cancelled travel and hotel bookings caused massive loss of business. This is significant considering that 'in Kenya, tourism accounts for over 500 million U.S dollars in annual revenue, 500,000 jobs and a significant portion of foreign exchange earnings' (Essner, 2003, p.7).

The U.S. State department officials expressly warned Americans against traveling to Kenya and Tanzania. The tensions from this action would later become protracted leading to strained relations between Kenya and the U.S. The global web of loyalties to the U.S. led other countries including the U.K. to follow suit later, thereby causing more losses to Kenya's struggling economy. In fact, the 1998 bombing was so crippling that Kenya's foreign currency and stock markets closed business prematurely on that day as dealers fled the trading hall.

Thirdly, Kenya's sovereignty further faced an affront as the bombing suspects were ferried to the U.S. to stand trial. This was a conflict of power and a demonstration of America's military might. This was in line with a U.S law that provides criminal penalties for terrorist attacks on Americans abroad. It should, however, be noted that initially, officials in the U.S, Kenya and Tanzania refused to speculate on who was responsible for the killer explosions in Nairobi and Dar-es-Salaam only to be convinced later that the key suspect was Osama bin Laden.

The fourth conflict came in the form of bomb victims who all looked up to the American government to compensate them for their injuries and deaths of their relatives. Seven years down the line (at the time of writing this chapter), not all victims have been compensated and hundreds including blind and lame still go on hunger strikes periodically at the August Bomb Memorial Park in Nairobi. They were rendered physically challenged and are increasingly being seen by the media as the social scar that is a living reminder of international terror. The conflict of compensation arises because they believe that Kenyans suffered because of the local presence of Americans or their proximity to the then American Embassy building, which was clearly the target of the bombers. The embassy has since been relocated to the outskirts of Nairobi city.

The fifth conflict has come in the form of the demand by the U.S. for the enactment of anti-terrorism legislation. Many Kenyans believe the U.S is pushing this requirement down their throats. Such a law is seen as potentially dangerous since it will infringe on the citizens' fundamental rights and freedoms as well as polarize Kenyan Christians and Muslims. This proposal is suspiciously viewed as one donor conditionality since the U.S. is Kenya's political ally and a key development partner. If enacted, it may provide a legal framework for charging and punishing of terrorists but total eradication of their activities may prove an uphill task. It would also appear to alienate Kenya's minority Muslim community who share a religious faith with the terror suspects.

The sixth conflict pits Kenya against her East African neighboring states, namely Somalia, Ethiopia, Djibouti, Eritrea and Sudan all of which are seen by the U.S. as fertile grounds for terrorist activities. Intelligence reports have indicated that the core leadership of the Kenyan terrorist cell consisted primarily of citizens of the Gulf States, Somalia, Pakistan and the Comoro Islands who had assimilated into local cultures along the Indian Ocean. Kenya's porous borders and the less restricted movement among the East African community member states only serve to aggravate the problem.

The Bombing of Paradise Hotel (November 2002)

The reaction of Kenyan authorities to this second attack also exposed the lack of rapid response despite the lessons learnt in the 1998 incident. The slow response to terrorist threats grew from a denial based on the perception that Kenya is a victim, rather than a source of international terrorism. This denial was also tied to the inability to acknowledge the wider context that led to the growth of terrorism locally: the erosion of governance structures, notably weak law enforcement and lack of strong gate keeping institutions such as the immigration department.

In the Paradise Hotel incident, 13 Kenyans and 3 Israelis were killed. However, with investigations localized unlike in the 1998 case, Kenyan police admitted that they had found no evidence to link around 20 people they had arrested with the attack. Police also said they had been unable to trace the histories of two vehicles used by the terrorists. A Spaniard and an American suspect were freed by the police unconditionally while six Pakistanis and four Somalis, arrested for entering Kenya illegally, were held for further questioning. Five minutes before the hotel attack, a missile was fired at an aircraft full of Israeli tourists as it took off from Mombasa airport. This time, Israelis, a key ally of the U.S and antagonists in the Middle East war, were clearly targeted. However, unlike in 1998, Kenyan authorities refused to heed Israeli demands to turn over some evidence on the attacks saying it would conduct the probe alone.

Kenya Government's Action Plan

The Paradise hotel attack of 2002 coupled with the September 11 attack of the World Trade Centre and the Pentagon in the U.S. have pushed the government of Kenya to take some concrete security and policy measures against terrorism. Although the *Suppression of Terrorism Bill* was finally drafted, it has met with stiff opposition from various stakeholders and its enactment has been postponed to allow for public input and further amendments. By actually drafting the Bill, the new government of President Mwai Kibaki demonstrated commitment towards establishing mechanisms to meet the growing threat of terrorism in Kenya. In February 2003, the government formed an anti-terrorism Police unit composed of officers trained in anti-terrorism. Legislation on detection and punishing suspected terrorists was also initiated, and a task force on anti-money laundering and combating the financing of terrorism was set up. These measures point to a more proactive policy on terrorism, but their long-term viability hinge on fundamental reforms in the security services, immigration and effective policing of the seafront.

What role has the Kenyan media played in interpreting and presenting this conflict situation to consumers of information in Kenya and globally?

The Role of the Media

This section examines the reporting frames adopted by Kenyan media as well as the language and the various angles they have chosen when communicating terrorism related news. According to Wolfsfeld (2004), 'conflict can be considered the *sine qua non* of news, but peace and news make for awkward bedfellows and the media have an obsessive interest in threats and violence' (p.2). Whether this is true of the coverage of terrorism related news in Kenya is the subject of this section.

The content analysis adopted here is qualitative and is based on purposively selected news reports. Four leading newspapers published in Kenya are used. These are: *The East African Standard, The Daily Nation* and their sister weekend editions *Sunday Standard* and *Sunday Nation*. These newspapers enjoy wide circulation and are staffed largely by Kenyan journalists. The selected news reports from the Kenyan press are apparently characterized by images of vulnerability, asymmetry, foreign policy contradictions, and propaganda by the aggressors, sovereignty, other secondary conflicts and guilt by association. The writers' choice of words determines both the direct and implied meaning that the reader may attach to the news stories and editorials.

The underlying principle in the analysis is that media can be used effectively to inform, persuade, focus attention, shape attitudes and set trends and agenda for public debate and discussion. However, the ways in which these roles are accomplished may turn out to be constructive or destructive in a particular cause but 'journalists should refrain from practices that raise the level of hate, distrust, and violence between communities' (Wolfsfeld, 2004, p.5). We now turn to the news stories along the various themes that they seem to emphasize.

Images of Vulnerability

Since 1981 when a radical Palestinian group was implicated in the bombing of the Norfolk Hotel in Nairobi, Kenya has been seen as a soft target by international terrorism experts (U.S. Institute of Peace, 2004 p.6). The trial in New York of the four bombing suspects of the US embassies in East Africa in 1998 also revealed a terror network that had flourished in Kenya since 1993, taking advantage of lax immigration and security laws. The Kenyan press has perpetuated this image in the post '98 period.

Firstly, it is reported that after the 1998 bombing, 'President Moi said Kenya was not at war with any country and wondered why the country should be destroyed by outsiders' (Othello, 1998, p.2). However, the illusion of relative peace and innocence expressed above is watered down by the laxity of Kenyan security as seen in the report by the same writer that 'police were holding three people believed to be the same ones who filmed the US embassy a few days before the blast' (p.2). This implies that no threat had been detected in the filming incident, which was a precursor to the bombing. The ill- preparedness and lack of technical know-how to aid prevention is also seen through a news item headlined 'Firms not capable of combating terrorism' where it is reported that:

> Private security firms have admitted their lack of capability to thwart terrorism attacks on installations in Kenya... the PSIA chairman said guards manning most of the country's sensitive installations are not trained to detect explosives and subversive activities and called for training (Wabala, 2005, p.4).

However, a Kenyan columnist, referring to the London underground railway bombings of July 2005, captures a reverse of the image of Kenya's helplessness viz:

> Striking only two days after Ambassador Bellamy's criticism of Kenya and its anti terrorism efforts, the London explosions could not have come at a more significant time...they have sparked off the realization that terrorism is alive and well even to the most seemingly secure (Mwinzi, 2005, p.9).

The media has also sought to link Kenya's vulnerability to the poor economic status of most citizens. As one report says soon after the Paradise Hotel bombing in 2002, 'porous borders and poverty make Kenya a target [of terrorism] and due to prevalent poverty, people come from all over-Yemen, Somalia, the Middle East. They bring weapons. They bring whatever they want if they pay a bribe' (Mwakio, 2002, p.11) Furthermore, after the Paradise Hotel bombing, it was reported that Kenyan police were not making any significant steps in their investigations. The report says that there was complicity by locals such that:

> A Kenyan woman owned the Pajero which was used by 'suicide bombers in the attack on Mombasa's Paradise Hotel... but sources in the Police force confided that investigators had lost track of the other Pajero that was used by those who attempted to bring down the Israeli plane at the Moi international airport with missiles. The sources added that Police had been closing in on the vehicle before it suddenly disappeared (Mwakio, 2002, p.11).

The above report portrays the Kenya police as either uncoordinated in their efforts or lacking in equipment and expertise of effective car tracking. The choice of phrases like 'closing in', 'lost track', and 'suddenly disappeared,' which amplify the susceptibility of Kenyan police to making mistakes, do not augur well because 'in a terrorism situation, the government leaders often want the media to boost the image of government agencies' (Perl, 1997, p.3). Therefore, a report that ridicules the police and exposes their inadequacies would not be welcome by the authorities. It would also result in lack of cooperation between the latter and the media.

Claims of possible complicity by local residents and failure to suspect the motives of potential terrorist threats are also reported among citizens in far-flung but high risk areas in Kenya. For example, the Paradise Hotel bombing mastermind Abdul Karim became a celebrity in Siyu Village on Lamu Island and married into one of the wealthiest families. He was tolerated due to his over-generosity such that no one suspected anything even when he set up two football teams named Al Qaeda and Kandahar. Note that both of these names are associated with terrorist activities but the villagers did not suspect anything peculiar in them.

While commenting on the dangers of such insensitivities, a reporter noted aptly that the Paradise [Hotel] bombing highlighted the potential for instability posed by the neglect of these desolate lands (e.g. Siyu Island) that are on the frontline of Kenya's efforts to contain terrorism. In this case, Abdul Karim alias Fazul capitalized on the people's poverty and used the goodwill to assemble bombs on the island. The article is headlined 'Sleepy village that welcomed terror mastermind.'

A related report later appeared in the *Daily Nation* to the effect that 'Lamu is safe'. It was attributed to Islamic leaders who asked 'security agents fighting terrorism to mount their searches elsewhere adding that Islamic dressing and lifestyle should not be linked to terrorist activities' (Beja, 2005, p.14). The Kenyan press has also propounded the stance that Kenya is made vulnerable merely by its geographical location. In an article titled 'The terrorist next door', it is reported that:

A report by the Crisis Group Africa of July 11 indicates that some operatives with links to the world's most deadly terror cells have been to Kenya from their bases in Somalia. For example, Fazul Mohamed, a Comoros born Somalia, is widely suspected to have been the mastermind of both the Nairobi and Dar-es-Salaam U.S embassy bombings and that of Hotel Paradise (Kamau, 2005, p.25).

Moreover, in setting up the U.S. Combined Joint Task Force-Horn of Africa (CJTF- HOA) in Djibouti that seeks to check terrorism, it was noted with concern that:

Somalia has played a role in Islamist terrorism, albeit a specialized one. It has served primarily as a short –term transit point for movement of men and material through the porous and corrupt border between Somalia into Kenya, which has been a preferred site of terrorist attacks (U.S Institute of Peace, 2004, p.4).

Such a strong case against Somalia puts it on a collision course with Kenya setting the stage for a potentially explosive regional conflict. It is instructive that Kenya has now stationed two army battalions to patrol the common border with Somalia. It was also reported, after Al Qaeda suspects were arrested in Somaliland, that: 'UN security council analysts say Somalia was used as a transit point for those who carried out the 1998 attacks on the US embassies in Kenya and Tanzania and the 2002 suicide bombing of an Israeli-owned hotel near Mombasa.

Still in reference to the potential danger from Somali, Mutiga and Babo (2005) noted that 'the global terrorist network Al Qaeda, has established a foot hold on Kenya's doorstep from where it can operate unhindered almost in the same fashion as it did in Afghanistan in the 1990s' (p.15)

Such a report is more likely to heighten tension in a situation rather than help to diffuse it. The terrorists' ability to assimilate quickly and lead ordinary lives within Kenyan territory unfettered is also reported. The pattern of attack used in the 1998 US Embassy and Paradise Hotel in 2002 was similar. According to Mutiga and Babo (2005), 'Sadeek Odeh, (from Palestine), the man at the centre of the 1998 bombing, settled down in Mombasa and worked as a fisherman for over three years in preparation for the attack…and similarly, Fazul (the suspect bomber of Paradise Hotel) came to the coastal village of Siyu where he took a new identity as Abdul Karim and married a local girl as he prepared his bombs' (p.16)

The net effect of these images of Kenya's vulnerability appears to be counter-productive because they would boost the terrorist's confidence. As Perl (1997) says, 'from the terrorist perspective, media coverage is an important measure of the success of a terrorist act or campaign' (p.6). By and large, the terrorists are presented as having had a series of successes against Kenya, rendering it a soft target in the eyes of the U.S. and other affected parties.

A War of Asymmetry

The second theme that tends to dominate the Kenyan media is that which illustrates the imbalance of power between various actors in the context of the terrorist attacks on Kenya. The war on terror has exposed the reality that Kenya is the underdog in the conflict. Other key players are always deemed to be several steps ahead in terms of strategies and pace of official reaction. Whereas the U.S. government and its allies like Israel have the financial, technical and bureaucratic finesse to counter terrorism, Kenya is portrayed as lacking the specialized personnel and appropriate legislation to do the same.

In addition, the suspected perpetrators of terrorism have the advantage of using advanced communication gadgets that elude the Kenyan security and intelligence networks. This imbalance of resources is reflected in the news reports surrounding the 1998 Nairobi bombing. To begin with, the media reported that 'local rescue operations had been boosted by international military teams from Israel and the U.S. ...and what Kenya needs now is assistance in terms of technical advice and material needs to complete ongoing rescue operations' ("Kenya needs help", 1998, p.12).

The economic cost of the 1998 bombing was placed at 30 billion Kenya shillings and an editorial piece underlined the fact that 'it had taken Kenyans and other foreigners painstaking periods to build this,' the editorial went on to say that it was therefore 'unfair for any nation, which truly considers Kenya as a meaningful international partner to abandon it because of Friday's unfortunate incident [since] blacklisting Kenya as an unsafe country will be adding insult to injury' (Karumba, 1998 p.4).

The editor implies that there ought to be a symbiotic North-South relationship characterized by tolerance instead of untimely withdrawal of the economic support by one party. In a situation where America and other development partners abandon their allies when the latter fall victim to terror, it is the terrorists who benefit. In the words of Perl (1997), 'terrorists seek media coverage that causes damage to their enemy's reputation. If Kenyans eventually hate the Americans for abandoning them at the hour of need, then the terrorists will have succeeded in creating a general hate for America (p.7).This image is reinforced by reports of the plight of those who got no help from the U.S. government after the 1998 bomb attack. As one victim complained through *The Standard* recently:

> Does it make sense that the Americans who were affected by the blast got so much, including life-long medical care and cash compensation, while Kenyan victims received treatment for raw injuries and were later abandoned? (Muringu, 2005, p.8).

Since the region already had security problems and arms proliferation from the great lakes region in addition to the South Sudan war and the Somalia and Eritrea conflicts, it was felt by the Pope that: 'the terrible attacks on Kenya and Tanzania have helped make the security of the African continent even more precarious' (Kilonzo, 1998, p.6). Kenya and by extension, Africa, was going to have more than its fair share of aggression with the new dimension of terrorist attacks which would further strain the meager security resources available.

After the 1998 bombing, the imbalance of military power was demonstrated in an editorial in *The East African Standard* that described U.S. reaction as exaggerated and an act akin to locking the stable when the horse had bolted. The article said that in Parklands where the American nerve centre had transferred, there were: 'roadblocks, car searches, marines in Desert storm gear bristling with weapons and the obligatory sniffer dogs' ("The ugly side", 1998, p.6). This description would make the ill-equipped Kenyan security forces feel intimidated and look like minnows unable to have any impact on the anti-terrorism war. In contrast, the American soldiers are portrayed as invincible through words like bristling and obligatory. This news item would also widen the gap between the local and foreign forces thereby hampering future joint security operations.

The 1998 Nairobi and Dar-es-Salaam bombs are reported to have gone off within minutes of each other. This enabled the bombers to get maximum world attention and to prove their technological prowess. It is reported that the bombers had very powerful communication gadgets to coordinate the attacks. The *modus operandi* of the Al Qaeda operatives is also portrayed as too fast paced for investigators in Kenya. This is exemplified by the report that 'in July 2002, Kenyan police arrested Fazul in connection with an armed robbery in Mombasa but they did not realize he was a wanted terrorist with a $25 million bounty on his head, and he escaped the following day' (Kamotho, 2005, p.18).

Foreign Policy Conflicts

Security cooperation has long been an important aspect of Kenya-U.S relations. This is underscored by the presence of a U.S. airbase, free port access and unrestricted over-flight agreements since the Cold War. Despite occasional political disagreements [on Kenya's slow democratization pace] between the U.S. and the Moi government in the 1990s, the security components of the relationship have endured.

Since 1998, the U.S. has spent nearly $ 3.1 million on anti-terrorism assistance, including training more than 500 Kenyan security personnel in the U.S. Despite the above arrangements, the U.S. was quick to issue anti-Kenya travel advisories in the wake of the two recent terrorist attacks. This caused doubts as to the level of commitment of the U.S. as a development partner. After the 1998 bombing, it was reported that the US State Department had warned all Americans not to travel to Kenya due to the perceived level of insecurity. This is confirmed by the news report by Knight (1998) to the effect that 'an official in Washington told the East African Standard that there is no functioning U.S. Embassy in Nairobi as a result of the bomb and we don't want our people going there without back up' (p.5). In comparison, the U.K government's reaction was more restrained. It said that:

...the British foreign and commonwealth offices said the risk of a repeat incident seems low and there is no need for travelers to alter their plans... and British Airways and Lufthansa reported that all their Nairobi bound flights from Europe were running normally. (Knight, 1998, p.5)

The conduct of American forces at the scene of the bomb in 1998 was roundly condemned in the local press. Claims of their aloofness and partisan statements by Ambassador Prudence Bushnel who described rescuers as potential looters drew the wrath of many Kenyan observers and belied the purported cordial relations between Kenya and the U.S. The situation is summed up by this news report:

American soldiers have not assisted with the operations. They are not giving any help while their embassy was the target of an international terrorist attack. The damaged U.S embassy has been under tight security with soldiers unwilling to talk even to journalists especially local ones. ("U.S. soldiers accused", 1998, p.4)

In terms of commitment to the rescue process, the media widely reported that many Kenyans instead praised the Israeli and French teams for their sterling work at the rescue site. The political class joined the fray of condemnation and a Kenyan Minister also took issue with the U.S. embassy for flying out American citizens hurt in the blast for specialized treatment in Germany while ignoring the plight of the Kenyan employees at the embassy who were also injured.

That the U.S. State department withdrew their earlier travel warning a few days later was an indication that they were avoiding frosty relations with Kenya at a time when every Kenyan believed that they had been attacked because of the presence of American interests in their midst. However, the tinge of caution remained despite the change of policy on U.S. citizens' travel abroad as seen in the report that 'the U.S. state department withdrew a warning it had issued to its citizens about traveling to Kenya...but called on Americans to be cautious when in the country' (Karumba, 1998, p.4).

The Kenya Tourism Board welcomed the lifting of the warning issued by the U.S. government saying that the revision of the advisory removed a major threat to Kenyan tourism, noting that by 1998, U.S. tourists to Kenya ranked sixth accounting for up to 5% of bed nights compared to 23% from Germany and 20%, the U.K.

It also came as a big relief when U.S. President Bill Clinton is reported as saying: 'we now must work to rebuild our embassies ... and... to support our friends in Kenya and Tanzania as they rebuild and he vowed not to retreat from the anti-terrorism war' ("We will rebuild", 1998 p.2). Clinton's words were reassuring but Kenyans, feeling greatly aggrieved, expected what an editorial summed up by indicating that 'Kenyans will want to see more American involvement in helping the injured and in reconstruction of damaged property and infrastructure' (Karumaba, 1998, p.4).

These same hopes were kept alive as seen in another editorial which read, in part, that 'those who suffered and others with an interest in US-Kenya relations are expecting Mrs. Albright will carry a specific offer of assistance but Kenyans are aware that any assistance given will be subject to very stringent accounting procedures' (Njau, 1998, p. 2)

The above report alludes to the reality of donor conditionality through which the aid dependent nations are not given a free hand to determine the course of their own development agenda and control their budgets despite their common interests with the donors in the war against global conflicts. In order to correct the bad image of American soldiers earlier created by the Kenyan press, when Albright did come to Kenya it was reported that she: 'recognized that the U.S. soldiers, harshly criticized by the Kenyan press, had not acted perfectly after the U. S. embassy bombing" (Njau, 1998, p.2).The U.K government is also reported as attempting to set the agenda in their foreign policy arrangements with Kenya. The tone of their statement sounded overbearing when the U.K Deputy High Commissioner Ray Kyles commented:

> Our position since the Kibaki Administration came to power has been that Kenya faces a real terrorist threat. That threat has not gone away. We have made it clear to the Kenya government our wish to work with them in the war against terrorism. We want to see this as a priority in our bilateral relations with this government. (Kwamboka, 2005, p.2).

Despite this categorical statement, Kenya's commitment to the anti-terrorism war has been questioned by most of her international partners. For example, it is reported that: 'the U.N is unhappy because the Kibaki Administration officials, including ministers recently snubbed a special envoy sent to Kenya by the UN secretary General Kofi Annan who had expressed interest in supporting the country's anti-terrorism strategy" (Kwamboka, 2005, p.3).

The fact that all is not well between Kenya and Britain is also evident in the recent tussle over the extension of the agreement for British soldiers to train on Kenyan grounds. Kenyan authorities have been reluctant to renew the agreement amid allegations of corruption in government by High Commissioner Sir Edward Clay. The Muslim community in Kenya is also up in arms against the UK's foreign policy on terror, which they consider as condoning indiscriminate acts of punishment on blameless communities. To this effect, the media reported that:

> Muslim leaders have asked the UK to change its foreign policy on the fight against terrorism. The council of Imams and Preachers of Kenya, said Muslims were not happy with the force used in the pursuit of terrorism suspects and it

was not fair for the British security forces to bomb places they suspect harbor terrorists without considering the safety of the innocent ("Muslims petition", 2005, p.2).

The lack of motivation by Kenya government bureaucrats and political elite to enact the Suppression of Terrorism Bill (2003), which had been shelved, is now attributed to the apprehension of the ruling class that two clauses dealing with money laundering and forfeiture of suspected terrorist property may target their assets. The said Bill is reportedly being used as a bargaining chip by the ruling class i.e.:

> Some [Kenya] government insiders are of the view that some influential Ministers were using the Suppression of Terrorism Bill as a blackmail tool against the US, UK and its EU partners who have been demanding the sacking of corrupt Ministers (Namwaya, 2005, p.15).

It is also instructive that this reported obstinacy on the part of senior government officials has led to the collapse of the Joint Counter Terrorism Task Force that had been formed with the help of the U.S. government in 2004. However, the word 'blackmail' is a choice by the media to heighten this particular conflict and compel the donors to react. The use of the word 'against' in this report clearly indicates competition for political supremacy. Through this initiative, the US government had begun to train officers to bring the work of investigation, prosecution, intelligence and other arms like immigration, customs and airport security under one umbrella. Twenty-eight such officers graduated in March and the US policy was that they would remain in their current stations for five years. But, in contravention of the US condition, all the officers who were trained were later sent on leave and transferred thereafter.

Perhaps to drive the point home to the US on Kenya's policy shift on terrorism, 'the Minister of internal security John Michuki commented at a meeting that fighting terrorism was not Kenya's priority. He said the government's priority was to fight insecurity' (Namwaya, 2005, p.17).

Such reports have clearly put Kenya, the U.S. and U.K. in conflict and increased the degree of mistrust as far as foreign policy on terrorism is concerned. In the next section we shall see how some of the measures taken in an attempt to stamp out terrorism might impinge upon Kenya's sovereignty thereby aggravating the conflict situation.

Kenya's Sovereignty at Stake

Various news reports have portrayed certain acts of foreign involvement in Kenya's internal affairs as a threat to the nation's sovereignty. In some cases, international protocol has been overlooked in the rush to provide a quick solution to the often-urgent problem of terrorism. However, the Kenya government and citizens have hit back at such moves. Attempts to overshadow Kenyan state security apparatus came to the fore through reports such as the controversy that surrounded where exactly bombing suspects would be charged. For example, after the 1998 bombing suspects were arrested, both FBI and Kenya's Criminal Investigation Department (CID) agents declined to comment on whether the suspects would be charged and tried in Kenya or the U.S.

Another report said that Pakistani authorities handed over an Arab man (suspect Mohamed Sadik Howaida) to the Kenya government for grilling and reportedly turned away FBI agents who had wanted to handle the suspect right from Pakistan. Two days later, the FBI, led by Howaida, raided the hotel where the Nairobi bomb was made, again outdoing Kenyan security who played a minor role there.

As anxiety built over the right place of trial, an editorial in *The Daily Nation* of August 20, 1998 posed the question 'who has right to try bomb suspects?' It went on to explain that: 'the terrorist act was perpetrated on Kenyan soil, Kenyan laws were broken with impunity, most of those who died were Kenyan and there is in Kenya a working legal system which can deal with any juridical matters...' (Muiruri, 1998, p.6).

The use of repetition here for emphasis implies that Kenya had all the rights to try the suspects. However, after putting such a strong case in support of Kenya's independence and sovereign rights, the same editorial had a warning which came as a contradiction and showed a conflicting standpoint by observing that 'Kenya would be setting itself up as a potential terrorist target in future if it insists on trying to sentence the suspects here.'

The above prediction came to pass when the Nairobi bombing suspects were charged in the U.S. a week later. However, despite the U.S taking the risk of extraditing the suspects and relieving Kenya of the threat of further strikes, the animosity against Kenya was to persist as Kenya suffered another terror bombing four years later in Mombasa.

Key witnesses and the Kenyan detectives were flown to the U.S. at the expense of the U.S. government when the trial began and only ten minor suspects would be tried in Kenya. Although top police officers in Kenya were torn between having the bomb suspects tried in Kenya or the U.S., they eventually conceded that it was likely to end up being a political rather than a purely legal decision. They were also of the opinion that the terrorists should be extradited to the U.S. lest Kenya should expose itself to renewed attacks. It was observed that Kenya had an extradition treaty allowing the exchange of criminals.

In 2002, after the Paradise Hotel bombing, Kenya came out in defense of its sovereignty and denied Israel access to evidence. Unlike in 1998 where Kenya acceded to most of the demands by the U.S, this time Kenya told Israeli authorities that they would conduct the probe alone. There was a clear conflict in the offing. In this event, the Israeli Defense Minister was quoted as saying that 'the dispute threatened to delay the investigation into the suicide bombing of an Israeli-owned hotel which killed fifteen people, and the failed downing of an Israeli charter jet moments earlier' (Associated Press, 2004, p.12). The fact that the hotel was owned by an Israeli national and the jet had 270 Israeli tourists aboard made the Israeli government deem it as their right to get involved in the investigations but this time round, Kenyan bureaucrats were not willing to be pushed, despite the international press concern that Kenyan police reported few leads by merely calling on the public to report any suspicious behavior.

The international community also believed that 'the record of recent years suggests the difficulties Kenyan police may have in cracking the case' (Lacey and Weiser, 2002, p.3). Further conflict on sovereignty issues arose after the failed bomb attack on a London bus and the underground rail network on July 21, 2005.It was soon reported that the UK bombing suspects had Kenyan passports. Consequently, anti-terrorism police in London said they believed there was an active Al Qaeda cell in Kenya and wanted to question people who were believed to have a connection with it. This claim led to another diplomatic row with Kenya's government spokesman emphasizing that:

> Kenya would not allow the British agencies to interrogate Kenyans. Instead Kenyans would conduct the interrogations and relay the results to the British counterparts [but the fact that] the suspects had names similar to those found in East Africa does not mean that they were Kenyans (since) the region is wider than Kenya (Otieno, 2005, p.2).

In the above report, Kenyan authorities came out strongly to directly defend their turf and the country's image, not wanting the country to be seen as a source of terror or worse still, an unsuspecting accomplice. This was an act of damage control. The policy conflicts also came to the fore when modalities of undertaking a joint project led to disagreements. It was then reported that international pressure was mounting on President Kibaki of Kenya to appoint a cabinet that was devoid of corrupt Ministers who were suspected of sabotaging the anti-terrorism war. For example, earlier:

> ...the US government declined to give money to the Kenya government directly [for building the JTTF head office] insisting on paying contractors directly, something that some think may have disappointed some government officials, who had hoped to misappropriate the money (Namwaya, 2005, p.16).

The reportage on terrorism after the year 2002 shows an increasing desire for self-determination by Kenya. The images of vulnerability that had been reinforced by reports discussed earlier in this chapter tended to diminish as Kenyan authorities became more eager to set their own internal agenda unfettered by external pressure.

Secondary Conflicts

Since acts of terrorism are a major jolt to any political system, 'political leaders, activists and journalists all abandon their normal routines and move into a crisis mode of operation' (Wolfsfeld, 1997 p.12). In the crises that followed the bomb attacks on Kenya, the Kenyan security system was slow to get into a crisis mode and this is perhaps what generated conflicts between them, the foreign rescuers and Kenyan journalists.

Therefore, the international efforts against terrorism have caused many other indirect conflicts on the Kenyan scene. Direct confrontations took place at the rescue scene after the 1998 Nairobi bombing which appeared as a superiority contest. For example '...the refusal of the American Marines to allow rescue workers to use part of their compound to evacuate the injured portrayed them as inhuman' ("U.S. soldiers accused", 1998, p.4). Another headline story accused U.S. soldiers of hampering rescue work. The same feeling was captured in an editorial, which read in part: 'like it or not, there is discontent among ordinary people and their perception of the American attitudes towards the local population and this tragedy ("Kenyan press hits", 1998, p.5).

The then American envoy to Kenya, Prudence Bushnell, had to go on record to deny that American troops were only busy rescuing their own people and guarding the embassy instead of joining the rescue efforts. It was also explained later that the Americans had allowed the Israelis to go on with rescue work in order to avoid a conflict since the latter had arrived at the scene first. Another conflict came in the form of harassment of journalists at the bomb rescue scene. It was reported that:

> Local and international journalists protested to the government against harassment by Kenyan security personnel. They said they were being molested and manhandled by security personnel at the scene and despite being allocated a press center; police were denying them access ("Journalists cry foul", 1998, p.3).

The local Kenyan media people were the major targets of harassment. Kenyan police accused the journalists of portraying them as inexperienced and irrelevant in the wake of the bombing such that 'they (local security) claimed the local media was biased in reporting, adding that they are not spanner boys as alleged by the local media. Kenyan journalists [in turn] accused the security personnel of bias in favor of foreign journalists" ("Journalists cry foul", 1998, p. 3).

Conflicts were also witnessed between local and foreign soldiers. For example, an Israeli soldier stopped Kenya Army personnel from snatching a camera from a Kenya News Agency reporter saying that 'the press had a right and a role to let the world know what Israeli, American and French troops were doing at the scene' (Ngesa, 1998 p.6). The Kenyan soldier referred to here could just have been overzealous because, with the advent of multiparty politics in Kenya in 1991 and subsequent democratization, press freedom in Kenya had tremendously improved.

Another major conflict arising from the anti-terrorism war in Kenya comes in the form of the defense of Islam as a religion. Opondo (1998) notes that 'Muslims accused sections of the media of associating their faith with the terrorist bombing in Nairobi. The negative portrayal, they said was a deliberate move by the enemies of Islam to demonize and vilify the faith' (p.3.). It was generally felt by the Muslims that since terrorism was a worldwide bane, it should not be attributed to the followers of any single religious faith. The Muslims hold that their faith has always preached peace and understanding among people of different color, creed, race and religion and they asked the media to let the investigators get the perpetrators of the blast. The Supreme Council of Kenya Muslims was therefore surprised that:

> Even before the identities of the terrorists and their motives are determined by local and international investigators, there have been concerted efforts by some sections of the mass media to make it look as if Islam was to blame for the unfortunate event (Opondo, 1998, p.3).

In this instance, the press was clearly in a crisis mode. The attempt to seek a ready explanation based on prejudice and public opinion could cause panic among the populace and jeopardize police investigations. The 'Islamic extremism' angle adopted by some media reports would antagonize Muslims, the media, the Kenya government, the U.S and security forces for a long time to come. Nganga (2005) later commented in *The Standard* of August 3, 2005 that 'terrorism has nothing to do with Islam and Christianity too has enough lessons to show it is not innocent' (p.13).

Moreover, in rejecting the Suppression of Terrorism Bill, which coincided with hundreds of Muslim protestors taking to the streets, the Kenyan Parliamentary committee on the Administration of Justice and legal Affairs committee observed that '...the proposed Bill threatens to tear apart the very fabric of one nation and could offer fertile ground for inter-religious animosity and suspicion" (BBC, 2003, p.4). However, the Justice and Constitutional Affairs Minister assured Kenyans that the Bill is supposed to meet certain concerns of national security and that there is no clause that targets the Muslim community. Legal experts and human rights groups in Kenya have also dismissed the Bill as an absurd imitation of the US Patriot Act 2001, the South African Terrorism Bill 2002 and Britain's Anti- terrorism, Crime and Security Act 2001.Also joining the chorus of condemnation was Amnesty International, which released a memorandum to the Kenya government complaining that they were '...seriously concerned that Kenya's Suppression of Terrorism Bill 2003 contains measures that violate Kenyan law, human rights, treaties to which Kenya is a party, and may result in human rights violations" (Amnesty International, 2005, p.2).

Guilt by Association

The last image created by the Kenyan press that we review in this chapter concerns the notion that Kenyans are suffering because of their association with America and other Western allies. This is seen in reports like the one that expressed speculation on the culprits in the 1998 bombing by saying that 'it was not immediately clear who launched the attacks, but as recently as this week, Egypt's banned Jihad group warned it would retaliate against what it said was Washington's role in extraditing Islamists to Cairo from Albania' (Opondo, 1998, p.3).

The comradeship of the allies in the fight against terrorism is seen in the words of an Israeli Rabbi Tsadok Shallom who told the *East African Standard* in the 1998 incident that 'what had happened was due to diabolic hate, Kenya had done nothing to deserve this terrorism... like Kenyans, Israelis are peaceful and have nothing against others but some people hate them' (Ngesa, 1998, p.7). The statement portrays Kenya's innocence in the larger war, which they least have a stake in. It was also reported that days prior to the bombing, suspected mastermind Osama bin Laden had vowed a 'holy war' on Americans and that:

He (Osama Bin Laden) has vowed to wage Jihad (holy war) against US forces in the Kingdom of Saudi Arabia and elsewhere in the world because of American support of Israel and US occupation of the land of Islam's two most sacred shrines in the holy cities of Mecca and Medina (Reuters, 1998, p.5).

As one story summed it up, 'although the fanatics know their enemy, they prefer the wrong targets to generate general hate for their enemies. This trend is inspired by the pro- Jewish tendencies of the U.S.' (Okech, 1998, p.6). Finally, in delinking themselves from suspicions of terrorism, Muslim leaders in Lamu said the district does not harbor any Al-Qaeda suspects, noting that the Islamic dressing and lifestyle in Lamu should not be linked to terrorist activities.

Conclusion

The news reports discussed in this chapter, taken singly and collectively, are a reflection of the complex web of conflicts and counter-conflicts that global terrorism has created among Kenyans, between Kenya and her regional neighbors and between Kenya and her international development partners in the West. The reports have the potential to antagonize various stakeholders thereby sabotaging or delaying the strategies that are being put in place in an attempt to contain the menace that is terrorism.

Currently, there are unstable efforts aimed at forging a strong US-Kenya partnership on terrorism. The success of such efforts apparently hinges on whether Kenya is primarily considered a soft target or a source of terrorism. The news reports that we have considered indicate that the West feels that Kenya is both a soft target and a source of terrorism. However, the policies that have shaped security collaboration since 1998 are geared towards meeting the challenges of strategic security collaboration with a soft target like Kenya. Such policies are largely protective, and are aimed at denying terrorists a chance to exploit current vulnerabilities of the Kenyan system.

From the media reports analyzed in this chapter, it emerges that without the commitment of enormous resources, it may take a long time for Kenya to rebuild local institutions and address the host of cross-border, refugee and immigration issues that are central to an effective anti-terrorism policy. The Kenyan newspapers seem to advocate home made solutions for terrorism in Kenya, with editorials and opinion columns coming out strongly against Western jingoism and donor conditionalities. A Eurocentric approach is largely seen as overbearing and entailing interference with Kenya's internal security, legislative and political agenda.

References

Amnesty International (2004) Kenya: Draft anti-terrorism legislation may undermine Kenyan constitution and international law .Press release. Retrieved August 12, 2005 from http://news.amnesty.org/index

Associated Press (2002) Kenya denies Israel access to evidence. *Daily Nation,* p.12

British Broadcasting Corporation. (2003) Kenya's terror bill rejected. Retrieved October, 30, 2005 from http://www.news.bbc.co.uk/2/hi/africa

Beja, P. (2005, December 7). Lamu safe. *The Standard,* p.14

Essner, J. (2003). Terrorism's impact on tourism: What the industry may learn from Egypt's struggle with al-Gama'a al Islamiya. Unpublished project paper.

Gibbs, J. (1989). Conceptualization of terrorism. *American Sociological Review,* 53(4) 329

Journalists cry foul. (1998, August 10). *East African Standard,* p. 3

Kaman, N. (2005, July 31). The terrorist next door. *Sunday Standard,* p.25

Kamotho, K. (2005, December 4). Why terrorists elude Kenyan authorities. *Sunday Standard*, p.18

Karumba, T. (1998, August 15). U.S withdraws travel warning. *East African Standard*, p.4

Kenya needs help, not condemnation. (1998, August 10). *East African Standard*, p.12

Kenyan press hits at U.S rescue bias. (1998, August 13). *East African Standard*, p.5

Kilonzo K. (1998, August 10). Pope condemns attack. *East African Standard*, p.6

Knight, J. (1998, August 10). Travelers cautioned. *East African Standard*, p.5

Kwamboka, O. (2005, December 4). Cabinet: International pressure mounting on Kibaki. *Sunday Standard*, pp.2-3

Lacey, M. and Weiser, B. (2002, December 1). After blast, Kenya reviews Al Qaeda trail in   East Africa. Retrieved October2, 2005. http://www.nytimes.com/africa/KEN.html

Muiruri, P. (1998, August 23). Politics key to bombers' trial. *Daily Nation*, pp.1-2

____ (1998, August 20). Who has right to try bomb suspects? *Daily Nation*, p.6

Muringu, E. (2005, December, 12). How explosion destroyed woman's bright dream. *East African Standard*, p.8

Muslims petition U.K government. (2005, December 4). *Sunday Standard*, p.2

Mutiga, M. and Babo, A. (2005, December 4). Al Qaeda comes calling on Kenya's doorstep. *Sunday Standard*, pp.15-16

Mwinzi, M. (2005, July 10). War on terror requires new approach. *Sunday Nation*, p.9

Mwakio, P. (2002, Dec 12). Police close in on owner of Pajero. *East African Standard*, p.11

Namwaya, O. (2005, December 4). Government's commitment to war on terror questioned. *Sunday Standard*, pp.15-17

Nganga, J. (2005, August 3). Terrorism has nothing to do with Islam. *The Standard*, p.13

Ngesa, M. (1998, August 10) Israelis express their fury. *East African Standard*, p.7

Njau, M. (1998, August 18) New twist in bomb. *Daily Nation*, pp.1-2

O'Connor, T. (1994). A *Neo-functional Model of Crime and Crime Control*. Cambridge: C.U.P

Okech, K. (1998). Terrorists took advantage of the lull to win attention. *East African Standard*, p.6

Okwemba, J. (1998, August 10). More Americans arrive. *East African Standard*, pp.4-5

Opondo, O. (1998, August 19). Reports irk Muslims. *Daily Nation*, p.3

Othello, G. (1998, August 14). Five arrested over blast. *East African Standard*, pp.1-2

Otieno, D. (2005, July 27). U.K bombing suspects had Kenya passports. *Daily Nation*, p.2

Perl, F.R. (1997). Terrorism, the Media and the government: Perspectives, Trends, and Options for policy-makers .Congressional Research Service. Retrieved November 10, 2004 From www.au.af.mil/au/awc/awcgate/state/crs-terror-media.htm

Reuters. (1998, August 10). Bombing suspects vowed holy war on Americans. *East African Standard*, p.5

The ugly side of terrorism (1998, August 12*).East African Standard*, p.6

U.S. soldiers accused of hampering rescue bid. (1998, August 12). *East African Standard*, p.4

U.S. Institute of Peace. (2004). Terrorism in the Horn of Africa. Report No.113.Retrieved November, 20, 2005 from http://www.usip.org/pubs/specialreports/sr113.html
Wabala, D. (2005, July 10) Firms not capable of combating terrorism. *Sunday Nation,* p.4
We will rebuild, says Clinton. (1998, August 16). *East African Standard,* p.2
Wolfsfeld, G. (1997). *Media and political conflict. News from the Middle East.* Cambridge : CUP
Wolfsfeld, G. (2004). *Media and the path to peace* .Cambridge:C.U.P.

Chapter 23

Managing Conflict in Nigeria through Television

Olufemi Onabajo, Ph.D.
University of Lagos, NIGERIA

Introduction

Human beings all over the world have interests which often conflict with one another. The developed world to a large extent has been able to manage these conflicts because of the nature, scope, philosophy and the sophistry of their mass media. In multicultural Nigeria which is still religion sensitive and whose citizens are significantly illiterates, mundane issues often spark up violence amongst ethnic groupings and different religious adherents because of poor conflict management by our mass media, which churn out news without taking cognizance of the repercussions of such news dissemination.

Television is a veritable tool of mass communication, which brings news actions in vivid colors to their numerous audiences at homes or in their offices. This paper attempts to examine the truth and objectivity doctrines of mass communication vis-à-vis the social responsibility theory and suggests how television news gatekeepers can harmonize these doctrines in effectively managing conflicts in the Nigerian Society.

Conflict

Conflict can be described as any situation, which may result in controversy, struggle, strife or contention and in consequence, bring about an uncertainty within self or bring about a state of incompatibility between human beings in a society.

According to Wilson (1997, p. 163), conflict can be psychological and cultural and could be inter-group or institutional. It is a built-in device within human society and could work for good or evil. A stable democracy requires relatively moderate tension while a lot of conflicts are embedded in nascent democracies and as Lipset (1970, p. 44) puts it, political moderation can only be facilitated by the system's capacity to resolve key dividing issues before new ones arise. Since conflict can only be manifested through some communication behavior, then it follows that communication may be the channel to manage any emerging conflict.

No society can completely avoid conflict since such society is made up of human beings. This view is also echoed by Debrendorf's (1959, p. 161) conflict theory which submits that every society displays at every point dissent and conflict because every element in a society renders a contribution to its disintegration and change, since every society is based on the coercion of some of its members by others.

Conflict can arise as a result of environmental, cultural as well as religious factors. Conflict can result from frustration, denial of success and lack of effective communication or no communication at all. Since television is a very credible medium of communication, it can be used in effective conflict management if its properties are well harnessed.

The Media and Conflict Management

When considering the role the media play in the management of a conflict, what readily comes to mind is the extent and nature of such coverage and whether or not the coverage was executed professionally. According to Unah (1995, p. 29) the following have to be taken into consideration in determining how well a conflict situation was managed by the media.

1. Did the media coverage over-sensationalize the events mirrored?
2. Were the events politicized, trivialized or badly distorted?
3. Were there glaring cases of unethical reporting or the peddling of outright falsehood?
4. Did the unethical practice serve to fuel such crisis?

It is worthy of note that the potentials of the media to act as a facilitating agent in moments of crisis is not in doubt. The media depending on its orientation can either act as a diffusing agent, dousing the flame of conflict and helping bring warring factions to the negotiating table or it can overblow the magnitude of an issue or event, creating more confusion in the process (Sobowale 1995, p.

37).

In the various theatres of conflicts, the media can lead in the crusade for diplomatic solutions, although sometimes they have been instrumental in escalating tensions. The media can provide guidance and assurance in periods of critical events and can arouse our awareness of crises of various descriptions just as they can foster integration among diverse groups.

In a multiethnic country such as Nigeria, the media had often in the past fanned the embers of sectionalism.

According to Sobowale (1995, p. 43), in major crises situation, the Nigerian media had always performed along the North-South divide. In the annulled June 12 presidential elections in which Chief Moshood Abiola from South West of the country was believed to have emerged victorious, the media from the North were clearly in support of the annulment while the media in the South West decried the annulment, while a few other media whose interests were considered more paramount, than political or regional allegiance charted a middle of the road course.

Egbon (1995, p. 57) opines that the Nigerian media have often demonstrated over-zealousness and sanctimonious behaviour that is deep-rooted in freedom of expression. They have failed to properly align new responsibility with new power of modern technological advancement in the propagation of information, hence they have unwittingly yielded to trends and tendencies that now hurt rather than help the course of a well informed citizenry.

The Objectivity Question

Objectivity subsumes all the mass communication virtues. It covers the individual journalist and the institution that employs him. It is a kind of operational guideline for professional competence. It is a way of trying to understand reality based on the collection of observable, verifiable facts. According to Onabajo (2002, p.54), objectivity is an essential correspondence between knowledge of a thing and the thing itself. Objectivity is problematic in public affairs journalism because elements and practices are taken for granted and perpetuated by journalists, when they should be critically examined. The reporter, reader, viewer, the conventions, the forms and processes of communications institutions, language, the investigative and interpretive functions of the reporter, affect the objectivity of mass communication.

Objectivity is a truthful, comprehensive and intelligent account of the day's event in a context, which gives it meaning. It requires that in reporting news, a reporter should not inject his emotions and personal opinions into the news stories. When media professionals claim they are objective, they mean some or all of the following:

1.   They gather and present materials without prejudice or partisanship.
2.   They act as impartial witnesses to events.
3.   Their work is not affected by their preconceived notions and ideas.
4.   Their work is not influenced by emotion.
5.   They keep personal opinions and judgments out of their messages.
6.   They are neutral and do not pass judgment in the information they present.
7.   Their messages are the sum of independently verifiable facts.

Objectivity can lead to good conflict management; however there are factors which may hinder a journalist and these include the following:

1.   The Reporter: He or she is often a product of his or her personal history and experience and these are brought to play in the selection of news sources, the questions that will be asked and the interpretation given to such responses.

2.   Journalistic Conventions: - These were established to meet historical conditions and they can be modified or even discarded, when those historical conditions no longer exist, or the objectives are no longer useful in the interest of objective reporting. Sometimes context is discarded because of journalistic assumption, which believes that only the bizarre, conflict, novelty and recent happenings can make news.

3.   Time and space: - The time and space allotted for reporting can significantly affect the objectivity of the journalist's work. The daily rhythm and tempo of mass communication correspond to the rhythm and tempo of human life. Objectivity is affected by the often-lazy assumption by some journalists that breathless journalism is adequate to the communication of public affairs and can also be affected by the indiscriminate application of speed and the forcing of all public affairs into the mold of instant journalism.

4.   Language: this demands the ultimate in craftsmanship, moral sensitivity and intelligence. The use of language therefore is crucial to the possibility of objective journalism. Language and meaning depend on past experiences of men and different words can mean different things to different men. Language alone is an imperfect medium, for the expression of truth. Words can be inexact, when precision is needed; ambiguous when univocal meaning is required; connotative when definition and denotation are demanded; allusive when identity is sought.

5.   Employers: It is possible for mass media reporters to be objective while institutions that employ them remain largely unobjective. The objectivity of a journalist is dependent on the following:

    a.   The use to which employers put their reporters.

b.   The working conditions established for them.
c.   The news policies of the employers.
d.   The extent to which the commercial and profit interests influence the institution's communication performance.

The Truth Concept

Truth exists, as a human need in the sense that human beings do not wish to loose their relations to tangible reality and also that human beings feel that communication between them is worthy of respect, only if the criterion of truth is given its proper place. Therefore, truth can be spoken as a three fold need of human beings:

1.   In relation to reality
2.   To oneself
3.   To other people

From these perspectives, truth becomes a good act that is morally worth striving for and it is also a moral obligation. The essence of truth distinguishes between a variety of perspectives, which include faithfulness to reality, consensus, coherence, contextuality, and narration. Man's ability to perceive something effectively, cognitively and practically constitute part of a performative understanding that enables the truth in its different facets to be incorporated into practical living through the very fact of perceiving or taking something to be true. Faithfulness to the truth in communication is more strongly felt as an externally infringing obligation that exists in humanity's claims on an individual, and the credibility of journalists in reporting conflicts is further enhanced if they abide by the truth doctrine.

Truthfulness means commitment to the truth on the part of the individual, to the truth between individuals and the truth in relation to reality. Truth can be spoken by knowing what roles apply to this realization of truth in terms of criterion of responsibility.

There are five major impediments against the obligatory nature of truth. They are:

1.   Concealment of truth when there are legitimate claims to learn it.
2.   Falsification where knowledge of the facts exists.
3.   Assertion of facts in spite of ignorance or partial knowledge of these facts.
4.   Unreasonable expectations when someone adopts a defensive position.
5.   Exaggeration in communicating the truth.

The Media and Social Responsibility

The social responsibility theory has generated considerable discussion about who should see to it that the media act in a socially responsible manner and how decisions should be made as to what is or is not a significant opinion worthy of media space or time (Severin & Tanlard, 1997:350). The theory holds that everyone who has something of significance to say should be allowed a forum and that if the media do not assume their obligation, somebody must see to it that they do. Under this theory, the media are controlled by community opinion, consumer action, and professional ethics and in case of broadcasting, government regulatory agencies. According to Siebert et al (1956,p74), the media should be allowed to report news unhindered but this kind of freedom should portray commitment and obligations, which should make the media to be responsible to the society for carrying out essential functions of mass communication in contemporary society. However, considering the enormous power the media wield, such priviledge according to Egbon (1995, p.65) deserves to be matched or counterbalanced with equally sense of responsibility.

The media have often been accused of disinformation and over-sensationalism in reporting conflicts and have often allowed the shield of press freedom to lure them into sensational headlines, which throw the doctrines of fairness and balance to the dogs. Sometimes, the media are not to blame because politicians may foul up political order with such impunity as to create chaos. When this happens, the question that readily comes to mind is: - Should the media report the true situation or refuse to report in the hope that the crisis created will soon subside? If the media is to effectively manage conflicts then their rights to free expression should be balanced not only against the private rights of others but also against vital social interests.

The Power of Television

Television as a means of mass communication is becoming increasingly popular and as rural electrification is being embarked upon by many states in the federation, the urge to acquire television sets is also likely to increase. Onabajo (1995) had discovered that the possession of television sets was a status symbol in the rural areas of Badagry and these sets were run by motorcycle batteries and disused car batteries. The poverty level of Nigerians notwithstanding, television has caught the fancy of both urbanites and ruralites alike and affluent children have often bought and sent television sets to their parents in the villages. O'Neil (1989, p.8), submits that although there is increasing awareness of television in recent years, the tendency however is to revel in the power and wield if freely rather than accept any corresponding increase in responsibility. It has been discovered that television reporters have become overzealous in reporting conflicts and have failed to properly utilize the power of television to advance the propagation of information. Instead they have yielded to trends and tendencies that now hurt rather than help the cause of the Nigerian citizenry. There is the fear that if a balance is not maintained in the influence of television in reporting crises through inciting close-up shots, the capacity for effective democratic governance will be seriously and dangerously weakened.

According to Akpan (1988, p. 37), television is the greatest communications mechanism ever designed and operated by man. It pumps into our brains an unending stream of information, opinion, moral and communal values and does influence greatly our perception of politics, religion, governance and culture. Television is not just a mere transmission device but it is a medium, which brings its massive audience into a direct relationship with particular sets of values and attitudes (Onabajo 1999, p. 32). It is also believed that the era of private ownership of television have compounded the problem of conflict management by our television stations, since different owners have motives for establishing television stations, some of them being to foster sinister intentions. Television is now being touted as having been held hostage by the ruling elites for economic interests and political power-play. There is therefore the need for television news reporters and producers to acquire the proper techniques and skills in the management of crises news.

The Way Forward

Since television journalists must be socially responsive, there is the need for news re-orientation which will promote more of developmental news than news of crises occasioned by conflicts.

Editorial boards of news departments should be invigorated and expanded to include media experts from the ivory tower. This will make deliberations more meaningful and the board will serve as the gatekeeper for what to disseminate and how to disseminate such information. There is the need for training and re-training of television news staff to appreciate and understand what instructions to give to news cameramen, on what to film on assignment points when covering news about conflicts within a society.

Video Tape Recorders editors should be taught what shots to assemble and how to assemble them while editing for television news.

Television journalists should remain neutral when reporting conflicts whether religious or ethnic and should not use their reports to incite one group against another. They should bear in mind that the unity of the nation is paramount. In other to effectively manage conflicts, television journalists must purge themselves of the erroneous belief that it is the negative that makes news. There is the need for proper investigation before ascribing the cause of a conflict to a particular ethnic or religious group and should not forget that news stories must be perceived to be fair and balanced at all times.

News about conflicts that may tear Nigeria apart should be downplayed while appeal for calm is disseminated to all concerned parties. The fragile nature of unity in the Nigerian nation has made the question of national unity an obsession since independence and journalists must take cognizance of this in the dissemination of conflict information, since collective national interest should always override sectional, ethnic and religious affiliations.

Conclusion

While press freedom is desirable and the truth and objectivity doctrines are not in doubt, it must be noted that such freedom should be judiciously exercised where national peace and security are threatened. The press should not constitute itself as the adversary of government and society since such attitude creates barriers to clear observation and analysis necessary for objectivity. In order to provide a balanced coverage of national crises, journalists should learn to curtail their negative tendencies and must learn to take the good with the bad by highlighting both the positive and negative. If the press must improve on its performance in effectively managing conflicts, it should understand that free expression cannot be selfishly claimed without taking into consideration its publics on one hand and the government on the other. Television journalists must understand that freedom of coverage and reporting of events should be exercised responsively and responsibly. One's right to free expression and unrestricted news coverage should be balanced not only against the private rights of others, but also against vital social interests.

References

Akpan, E. D. (1988). Television and national security. In Akinfeleye R. A. (ed). *Contemporary issues in mass media for development and national security*. Lagos: Unimedia Publications Ltd.

Dabrendorf, R. (1959). *Class and class conflict in an industrial society*. London: Routledge and Kegan Paul.

Edeani, O. O. (1993). Objectivity and responsibility in the press. In C. S. Okunna et al, *Theory and Practice of Mass Communication*, Enugu: ABC Publishers.

Egbon M. (1995). Social responsibility and the Nigerian mass media: Strategies and tactics for balanced media coverage of crises. In NPC Publication, *Nigerian mass media and national crises*. Lagos: Nigeria Press council.

Lipset, S. M. (1970). Social conflict, legitimacy and democracy. In Olsen E. M. (ed.). *Power in societies*. London: Collier – Macmillan.

Onabajo, O. (1995). Impact of radio and television rural development programs on the rural people of Badagry local government area of Lagos State. Unilag: Ph.D Thesis.

Onabajo, O. (1999). *Essentials of broadcast writing and production*. Lagos: Gabi Concept.

Onabajo, O. (2002). *Essentials of media law and ethics.* Lagos: Gabi Concept.

O'Neil, M. J. (1989). The Power of the Press. In P. Agee et al (eds.), *Main Currents in Mass Communication,* New York: Harper Collins Publishers.

Severin, W. J. & Tankard, J. W. (1997). *Communication theories: Origins, methods and uses in the mass media.* New York: Longman.

Siebert F. S. et al (1973). *Four Theories of the Press,* Urbana: University of Illinois Press.

Sobowale, I (1995). Nigerian press coverage of national issues. In NPC Publication, *Nigerian Mass Media and National Crises.* Lagos: NPC.

Unah, J. (1995). Nigerian press coverage of National crises. In NPC Publication, *Nigerian mass media and national crises.* Lagos: NPC.

Wilson, D. (1997). *Communication and social action.* Port Harcourt: Footstep Publications.

Index

About the Contributors

Ritchard T. M'Bayo, Ph.D., editor
rmbayo@aaun.edu.ng or rmbayo@aol.com

Dr. Ritchard T. M'Bayo is Professor of Communication and Multimedia Studies at the American University of Nigeria (AUN). He was previously at Bowie State University (BSU), Bowie, Maryland, USA; in 2005/2006 a Fulbright Scholar at the University of Lagos (UNILAG), Nigeria, where he also served as Head of Department–Mass Communication. While in Nigeria he conducted research on *Media and Conflict in Africa,* gave press briefings to journalists at the U.S. consulate, and delivered public lectures on free press issues, African Politics and the democratic culture. In 1996, he served as UN media consultant to Sierra Leone. With over 20 years of teaching experience at graduate and undergraduate programs at universities in the United Sates and Africa, Professor M'Bayo has received awards from the Poynter Institute of Media Studies, American Society of Newspaper Editors, and the American Press Institute. He is the founding editor of the *Journal of African Communication*, and currently edits the *Journal of African Social Sciences and Humanities Studies*. Professor M'Bayo received his PhD from Howard University, Washington, DC.

Chuka Onwumechili, Ph.D., editor
conwumechili@bowiestate.edu

Dr. Chuka Onwumechili is Professor of Communication at Bowie State University in Bowie, Maryland, USA. Dr. Onwumechili received a BA in Mass Communications from the University of Nigeria in Nsukka, Nigeria; MSA (Advertising) from Northwestern University in Evanston, Illinois and a Ph.D. from Howard University in Washington, DC. His published books include *Reform, Organizational Players, and Technological Developments in African Telecommunications: An Update* (2003); *Press and Politics in Africa* (2000), *African Democratization and Military Coups* (1998), and *Communication and the Transformation of Society: A Developing Region's Perspective* (1995). His works have also appeared in several peer-reviewed journals. Dr. Onwumechili also worked with a group of renowned international scholars and United States ambassadors in a funded study on Islam and obstacles to democracy and modernization under the auspices of the Center for Strategic and International Studies (CSIS).

Bala A. Musa, Ph.D., editor
bmusa@apu.edu

Dr. Bala A. Musa is Associate Professor of Communication Studies at Azusa Pacific University, Azusa, California. He received his PhD in Mass Communication from Regent University, Virginia Beach, Virginia. A communication studies generalist, Musa has taught a variety of graduate and undergraduate communication studies courses. He was formerly chair of Communication Studies Department at Northwestern College, Orange City, Iowa. His research interests include mass media ethics, media and conflict, development communication, political communication, media and popular culture. Musa has published several journal articles and book chapters. He is author of *Framing Genocide: Media, Diplomacy, and Conflict Transformation* and co-editor of *Emerging Issues in Contemporary Journalism.* He is a fellow of the Applied Media Ethics Colloquium and an editorial board member of the *American Communication Journal* and the *Journal of African Social Science and Humanities Research.*

Ifeoma Theresa Amobi
teribabe57@yahoo.com

Ifeoma Amobi (nee Ebuzeme) is a versatile Mass Communicator, with over 15 years of cognate experience. She holds a B. A. in Mass Communication from the University of Nigeria, Nsukka, Nigeria, an M.A. in Public Administration and an M. Sc. in Mass Communication, both from the University of Lagos, Nigeria. This work is the author's first attempt at collaborating with colleagues to write a book chapter aimed at contributing significantly to the use of communication as a tool for resolving societal problems.

Nicholls K. Boas, Ph.D.
nkboas@comcast.net

Dr. Nicholls K. Boas is an Assistant Professor of Communication Studies at Morgan State University, Baltimore, Maryland, USA, where he teaches both undergraduate and graduate courses and coordinates the Communication Theory and Research programs in the Department. A graduate of Columbia University, New York, and Howard University, Washington, DC, where he received his

Ph.D. in Mass Communication in 1995, Dr. Boas' research interests are in exploring communication in development, politics, and social issues.

Ogu Sunny Enemaku, Ph.D.
ogusen@yahoo.com

Dr. Ogu Sunny Enemaku holds a Ph.D. in Communication and Language Arts from the University of Ibadan, Nigeria. He has taught Communication for Development among other courses at the Department of Mass Communication, University of Lagos, Nigeria since October 2000. His areas of interest include communication and conflict, cultural studies and public relations. From February to May 2006, Dr. Enemaku was a guest researcher at the Nordic Africa Institute, Uppsala, Sweden, working on the theme of Communication and post-conflict Transition. He was also a participant at the 2006 Cultural Studies workshop on 'The Governance of Cultures', organized in Bhubaneswar, India, by the International Institute for Social History (Sephis Program) Cruquisweg, the Netherlands, and the Centre for Advanced Studies in the Social Sciences, Calcutta, India. He has attended academic conferences and workshops in South Africa, India, Sweden, Denmark and Norway. His works have also been published both locally and internationally. He is currently with UNICEF in Abuja, Nigeria, implementing a national avian influenza preparedness and response plan.

Sola Isola
sola_isola@yahoo.com

Sola Isola is currently lecturer at Redeemer's University, in Lagos, Nigeria. He is a doctoral candidate at the University of Ibadan, with research interest in media and conflict. He has years of experience as a journalist and was until recently Executive Director, College of Journalism, Independent Journalism Center, Ikeja, Lagos. He has contributed articles to academic journals and publications.

Kehbuma Langmia, Ph.D.
klangmia@bowiestate.edu

Dr. Kehbuma Langmia teaches courses in Mass Communications, Broadcast Journalism and Media Studies at Bowie State University. With previous degrees in Fine arts, Television and Film, Dr. Langmia was awarded the Ph.D. in Mass Communication and Media Studies by the Department of Journalism, Howard University; his dissertation was on the Internet as the construction of the immigrant public sphere. He has had significant publications in the area of new media, mass communication and interpersonal communication. A graduate from

Television Academy, Munich, Germany, Dr. Langmia continues to produce and direct independent productions. He also serves as executive producer for students' Television projects at Bowie State University.

Ali A. Mazrui, Ph.D.
Amazrui@binghamton.edu

Professor Ali A. Mazrui is one of the most renowned scholars in the world today. He currently serves as Director, Institute of Global Cultural Studies and Albert Schweitzer Professor in the Humanities at the State University of New York at Binghamton, New York, USA. He presently holds several other appointments concurrently, including Albert Luthuli Professor-at-Large, University of Jos, Jos, Nigeria; Andrew D. White Professor-at-Large Emeritus and Senior Scholar in Africana Studies, Cornell University, Ithaca, New York, USA, and Chancellor of the Jomo Kenyatta University of Agriculture and Technology, Nairobi, Kenya.

Eronini R. Megwa, Ph.D.
emegwa@csub.edu

Dr. Eronini R. Megwa, (Ph.D., University of Missouri-Columbia) is associate professor in the Department of Communications at California State University, Bakersfield. He coordinates the Department's programs at the Antelope Valley Campus in Lancaster, California. Formerly chair of the Department of Journalism at Cape Peninsula University of Technology (formerly Peninsula Technikon) Cape Town, South Africa from 1993-2003. Dr. Megwa has taught at Howard University, University of Maryland, College Park and University of Swaziland. He has worked as a television news editor at the Nigerian Television Authority (NTA) Channel 6, Aba. He has served as media consultant to international organizations such as UNESCO, Ford Foundation, the Netherlands Institute for Southern Africa (NIZA), and regional governments in Africa. He has authored and co-authored book chapters and published numerous articles in peer-reviewed journals including *Journalism Studies*, *Journal of Radio Studies*, *Howard Journal of Communications*, and *Africa Media Review.* He serves on the editorial boards of *Journalism Practice*, *Ecquid Novi*, *Fifth-Estate-onLine*, and *Journal of African Communication.*

Matt Mogekwu, Ph.D.
mogekwu@yhaoo.com

Dr. Matt Mogekwu is a graduate of the Indiana University School of Journalism in Bloomington, Indiana, where he earned his Ph.D. in Mass Communication. He has a Masters degree in Communication from Michigan State University and a BA (Journalism) degree from the University of Wisconsin-Whitewater. He has taught journalism and mass communication for over twenty years in universities in Africa and the USA and has published articles in the areas of journalism education, media and development, media and peace building as well as communication and conflict. He is a member of several professional organizations. Dr Mogekwu was, until recently, a professor of communication at the North-West University in South Africa. He has moved back to the USA where he teaches at Bowie State University in Bowie, Maryland.

Mohammed Musa, Ph.D.
Muhammed.musa@cantebury.ac.nz

Dr Mohammed Musa is Senior lecturer and Director of Program, Mass Communication at University of Canterbury, New Zealand. His research interest and more recent publications are in the areas of globalization, media and migration and new media.

Abigail O. Ogwezzy, Ph.D.
abigaily2k@yahoo.com

Dr. Abigail O. Ogwezzy teaches Mass Communication at the University of Lagos, Nigeria with emphasis on advertising, public relations, popular culture and communication for development. She has degrees in Linguistics and Communication, Mass Communication, Gender and Development, and Communication Arts. She started her career in the news and current affairs department of a media house from where she proceeded to an advertising agency and served in the client service division. Later on she joined the corporate affairs department of a leading financial institution from where she got the prestigious British Chevening Scholarship to study in the UK. She is a fellow of African Association of Political Science (AAPS)/Harry Frank Guggenheim (HFG) Foundation; was the best Graduating Student in the Department of Linguistics and Communication, University of Port-Harcourt, Nigeria in 1991 (University Convocation Merit Award) and also won ELF Petroleum Coy Ltd (Secondary School Scholarship) from 1978-1980. She consults for local and international development organizations\management consulting firms; has attended several local and international conferences; and has published articles in local and international journals and books.

Benson Oduor Ojwang'
kojwa@yahoo.com

Born in Kabondo, Kenya, **Benson Oduor Ojwang'** earlier attended Koru Primary and Onjiko Secondary Schools. In 1990, he joined the University of Nairobi from where he graduated with a First Class Honors B.Ed degree in Linguistics and Literature in 1995. He taught for the Teachers' Service Commission in two secondary schools and later won a Kenya Government Scholarship to pursue a Master of Arts degree in Linguistics which he successfully completed in 1998. From 1999 to date, he has taught Linguistics, English and Communication at Maseno University, Kenya. His main research interests are in language and media, description of Dholuo and applied linguistics. He has published three journal articles and there are several other articles and chapters forthcoming in his name. He is currently a PhD candidate at Maseno University where he is conducting research on the dynamics of communication in nurse-client interaction in Kenya's public hospitals.

Emeka Okoli, Ph.D.
raybourne.dean@yahoo.com

Professor Emeka Okoli received his Ph.D. in Organizational and Intercultural Communication from Howard University, Washington, DC (1994); Master of Arts in Television Programming and Photojournalism from Regent University, Virginia Beach, VA (1990); Postdoctoral professional development and training include a Master of Arts degree in International Law and Diplomacy, University of Jos, Nigeria(2006), certificate courses, seminars and workshops on global education, workplace conflict resolution, and diversity management. Prof. Okoli served as Professor in the Department of Mass Communications and Journalism, Norfolk State University, Norfolk, Virginia (2003-2007). He spent two academic years at the University of Abuja, Nigeria (2004-2006) as a Fulbright Senior Fellow. He is also a Fellow of the Salzburg Seminars. Prof. Okoli currently lives in Nigeria and consults for government and the private sector in organizational and intercultural communication dynamics. He is the Managing Partner /CEO, Raybourne & Dean Consulting Ltd, Abuja, Nigeria.

Ephraim A. Okoro, Ph.D.
eaokoro@howard.edu

Dr. Ephraim Okoro is an assistant professor at Howard University, School of Business in the Department of Marketing. He is a researcher, academic administrator, and organizational development specialist. An educator with over fifteen years experience in higher education, Dr. Okoro has the multifaceted ability to manage a range of teaching and administrative priorities simultaneously. He is adept at resolving conflicts and promoting harmonious relationships among students and faculty. In addition, he has worded extensively with traditional students, working professionals, and adult learners from different backgrounds. Dr. Okoro's earned degrees are interdisciplinary within the fields of business management, marketing, public administration, and communication. He holds a PhD in Communications from Howard University, an MBA in Business Management, an MBA in Marketing, and an MPA in Government Management from Southeastern University. He also earned the Higher National Diploma (HND) from Yaba College of Technology in Lagos, Nigeria.

Christine Ombaka, Ph.D.
Ombakac@hotmail.com

Dr. Christine Oduor-Ombaka is senior lecturer in the department of Communication and Media Technology at Maseno University, (Kenya) where she teaches Culture and Communication, and Media and Gender. She was Head of the department for eight years. She holds a PhD in Linguistics from the Irish International University (UK), M.A from Lancaster University (UK) and Bachelor of Education (Hons) from University of Nairobi (Kenya), Dr. Ombaka has published widely in the areas of Culture, Gender and Sexuality especially on HIV/AIDS. Her other publications include War and Environment (1998) in *Literature of Nature*, Indiana: Deaden Press, My war Dirge (1996) in *The Space Between*, National Library of Poets, Owing Mills Watermark Press and Born To Die (1993) in *The Coming of Dawn*, National Library of Poets, Owing Mills Watermark Press and Nyamgodho son of Ombare (1998) in (eds FEMART) *Holding The Centre*. Kisumu: FEM-ART- KENYA. Currently, she is researching on Culture, Gender and Sexuality. She is also a poet, creative writer and film-producer.

Olufemi Onabajo, Ph.D.
olufemionabajo@yahoo.com

Dr. Olufemi Onabajo is a veteran mass communicator whose professional experience span over 20 years. He worked in the Nigerian Television Authority between 1981 and 1991 where he rose to the position of Controller News and Current Affairs. He was also Group corporate affairs and Advertising manager with an advertising outfit in Lagos between 1992 and 1996 before exiting to join Africa Independent Television where he became Manager, News and Current Affairs before joining the University of Lagos as a Lecturer in 1998. He is at present a Senior Lecturer with the Department of Mass Communication University of Lagos, Nigeria. He has authored 10 mass communication books and edited two others. He is a priest of the Anglican Communion in Nigeria and he is married with children.

Nosa Owens-Ibie, Ph.D.
nosaowens@yahoo.com

Dr. Nosa Owens-Ibie, a former senior lecturer at the Department of Mass Communication, University of Lagos, Nigeria, specializes in mass media and society, communication for development and political communication. He has published on globalization, popular culture and other areas of mass communication in local and international journals and books in the United Kingdom, the USA, Malaysia, Zimbabwe, South Africa and Nigeria, the latest being an article on "Communication and Development in Nigeria: A Discussion," in the *African Journal of Political Science*. He is a communications specialist and researcher, with stints in professional public relations practice, and has consulted for international development organizations, served as media ombudsman, columnist, media awards panelist and written for various radio and television stations and print media in Nigeria. He is a fellow of the Salzburg Seminar, Austria and the International Institute of Journalism in Germany.

Abiodun Salawu, Ph.D.
salawuabodun@yahoo.com

Dr. Abiodun Salawu, a former practicing journalist, has been teaching mass communication for more than a decade. He taught the discipline at The Polytechnic, Ibadan and the University of Lagos, Nigeria. He currently teaches at Ajayi Crowther University, Oyo, Nigeria where he is Head of Communication and Media Studies. Media and Conflict is one of his areas of research focus. He has published amongst others 'Identity Politics and the Indigenous Language Press: A case study of Alaroye Publications'. He also has, for the Conference of

RC21 of International Sociological Association, a paper entitled, 'Media Narrative of Ethno-religious Conflicts in Nigeria'. He has to his credit several journal articles and book chapters. He also edited an anthology, *Indigenous Language Media in Africa.* Dr. Salawu is a grantee of the University of Oxford's Centre for Research on Inequality, Human Security and Ethnicity. The title of the study that won the grant for him is "Impact of State Policy on the Non existence of Minority Language Newspapers in Nigeria."

Oloruntola Sunday
Sonyto1@yahoo.com

Oloruntola Sunday holds a B.Sc. and an M.Sc. in Mass Communication from the University of Lagos, Nigeria. He did his National Youth Service Corps (NYSC) with the News Agency of Nigeria. He has worked for several newspapers and magazines in Nigeria, as Feature Writer, Business Correspondent and Senior Production Sub-editor. He is presently a lecturer at the Department of Mass Communication, University of Lagos and pursuing his doctoral studies at the University of Agriculture, Abeokuta, Nigeria.

Gani Yoroms, Ph.D.
ganiyoroms@yahoo.com

Dr. Gani Yoroms is the Director of Defense and Security Studies at the African Center for Strategic Research and Training at the National War College, Abuja, Nigeria. He holds a PhD in Political Science (International Relations) with special interest in regional security, Conflict and Development in Africa. He has been very active in working with the West African regional Office of Fredrich Albert Stiftung (FES) for the formation of the West African Network on Security and Democratic Governance (WANSED). He is also instrumental in working with the Institute of Security Studies, South Africa in the formation of African Research Network on Terrorism and Counter Terrorism (ARTACT).